# VILLAS
## AT TABLE

Books by James Villas

*American Taste*
*James Villas' The Town & Country Cookbook*
*James Villas' Country Cooking*
*Villas at Table*

# VILLAS AT TABLE

## A PASSION FOR FOOD AND DRINK

## JAMES VILLAS

HARPER & ROW, PUBLISHERS, New York
Cambridge, Philadelphia, San Francisco
1817  London, Mexico City, São Paulo, Singapore, Sydney

FIRST EDITION

Copyeditor: *Margaret Cheney*
Designer: *Mary Beth Killkelly/Levavi & Levavi*

Library of Congress Cataloging-in-Publication Data

Villas, James.
  Villas at table.

  Includes index.
  1. Gastronomy.    I. Title.
TX631.V48   1988     641'.01'3     88-45068
ISBN 0-06-015995-2

88  89  90  91  92  DT/RRD  10  9  8  7  6  5  4  3  2  1

*In memory of*
*Harold J. Villas*
*the noblest Greek of them all*

*We may live without poetry, music and art;*
*We may live without conscience and live without heart;*
*We may live without friends; we may live without books;*
*But civilized man can not live without cooks.*

*He may live without books,—what is knowledge but grieving?*
*He may live without hope,—what is hope but deceiving?*
*He may live without love,—what is passion but pining?*
*But where is the man that can live without dining?*

—*Owen Meredith*

# CONTENTS

# FOREWORD

James Villas is not your ordinary, run-of-the-mill, low-calorie food writer. He is admittedly our best American culinary journalist (give or take one or two of the older hands at the game), a reputation developed over the past sixteen years as food and wine editor for *Town & Country* magazine. As a writer, Jim wears his heart upon his kitchen apron. He is passionate about food and writes passionately about it. Unlike many of his peers, he is admirably objective, except when he is confronted with one of the more outlandish mannerist bizarreries of nouvelle cuisine. Then he is apt to lose his Apollonian cool and throw a Dionysian tansy. Nouvelle he is not. For him, style without substance has no nutritional value—on platter or page.

Villas is an artist at his craft, a perfectionist who employs language with the scholar's discipline he learned in acquiring a Ph.D in Romance Languages and Comparative Literature. He eschews the gaucheries that commonly mar gastronomy's belle lettres. He would never, never, for instance, stoop so low as to describe a room, a setting, a dish, a wine or even a sauce as "brilliant," though that word is the garlic of the food writer's lexicon and is constantly misused to spice up a limp sentence or an underdone phrase. Like any writer worth his salt, Villas knows that adjectives are seasonings, to be used with epicurean delicacy.

For *Town & Country*, Villas has produced 600,000 words of copy, some 255 articles in all. The quality of his work throughout this output has remained impressive, for it is wrought with Flaubertian attention to structure, detail and color. The range of topics and depth of coverage is no less extraordinary. Villas is a first-rate reporter and goes to the source of his material. Like his larder, his briefcase contains nothing stale. He "walks the facts" in the tradition of the late, great travel writer Karl Baedeker, who included the pyramids in his pioneer guide to Egypt not on hearsay, but only after he saw with his own eyes their vast triangular bulk lifting from the desert floor.

On his alimentary voyages, Jim Villas has drunk the waters of near and far places, tracking down the mystery of crème brûlée to its English source and sampling the succulences of sardines from the world's seven seas. It is from this bountiful granary—reported in prose that is at once engaging, vigorous, informative and forthright—that the present viaticum of vintage Villas vittles has been concocted. And what a zestful reading experience it is! The flavors of the older pieces have grown richer with time, like a good brandied fruitcake; his newer ebullitions have not lost their freshness in replication.

If this book were a restaurant, Michelin would give it three stars. As for me, I think it's brilliant.

—Frank Zachary
Editor-in-Chief
*Town & Country*

# INTRODUCTION

There are times, I must confess, when I actually suffer a sense of guilt over my obsession with food and drink. I ask myself, for instance, if it's normal and mentally healthy to awaken each and every morning of my life eagerly anticipating a full, hearty breakfast, contemplating what to prepare for lunch, and wondering which restaurant I might try for dinner. Sometimes it disturbs me that I fail completely to comprehend those pitiful souls who begin their day with no more than an insipid sweet pastry washed down with floods of weak coffee; that I reel in horror when I see a friend or colleague dismiss lunch with an anemic confusion of designer lettuce, bean sprouts, raw veggies, and cottage cheese; and that my temper flares when, while making plans to dine out in New York or Cannes or Jamaica, my companions express little interest in when or where or what we eat. There was a youthful time when travel was undertaken nobly to see new sights, attend the theater, visit museums and other places of cultural interest, and generally expand my horizons. But, as the vicissitudes of middle age take greater hold and my jaded quest for fine food and drink only intensifies, I try not to admit that the only sane justification for now leaving the nest is to experience the next meal, savor new dishes, and perhaps learn a bit more about man's hunger and how he can nurture himself sensibly.

Fortunately, this type of instinctive self-analysis and questioning of motives is usually short-lived, since the demands of my palate and stomach almost always have a way of winning over those of the brain. Even before I decided to make a serious vocation of writing about food and drink, there seems never to have been a familial, social, or professional activity that wasn't somehow connected with gratifying the appetite. Having been raised in a multi-ethnic home, I was exposed virtually at birth to the culinary traditions of Greece, Sweden, the British Isles, and my native South, and, by the time I was in my teens, I was already familiar with numerous other cuisines as a result of my epicurean parents' dragging me along on the great ocean liners and steering me through many of the world's finest restaurants. When I was lucky enough to receive a Fulbright student grant to study in France, I must admit I spent many more hours in bistros and brasseries than in libraries, and, as a young, rather confused college professor of language and literature in various universities around the United States, I spent almost as much time researching regional styles of cooking and restaurants as the literary subjects I was teaching. Little wonder, therefore, that when a certain moment arrived in life that demanded making a career choice, I opted for Lucullus over Flaubert, never losing that strong teaching instinct but determined to devote myself to what I was and still am convinced is an altogether worthy form of art.

What this collection of essays represents perhaps more than anything else is the gradual gustatory, spiritual, and aesthetic development of a gastronome over a period of fifteen years. It begins with an evocation of home and the basic forces that continue to inspire my passion, moves through my many years of exposure to both the most sophisticated and humblest aspects of gastronomy, and ultimately attempts to portray a well-seasoned, mature, combative gourmand with a very definite and trenchant gustatory philosophy to relate. In many respects, the book is the story of one who has "seen the elephant," survived to tell the tale, and wants to open up new paths of adventure that will prove exciting and challenging to thousands of American amateurs and professionals caught up in this country's gastronomic frenzy.

Just five years ago, I would not have been so sure that the majority of Americans, so involved in learning how to cook properly and choose a bottle of wine, were yet quite ready actually to read lots *about* food, wines and spirits, the workings of great restaurants and chefs, and the multiple problems involved in developing oneself into a true epicure. Today, however, as people become increasingly interested in and sophisticated about food, drink, and entertaining, I am convinced they want to know more about the fine differences among caviars, exciting ways to give new dimension to such beloved classics as boiled beef, baked beans, and strawberry shortcake, which cheeses and dessert wines to serve at the end of a meal, and how to assure a perfect meal in a restaurant. This compact volume attempts to answer these and many more such questions—and on a level that speaks to both the expert and novice.

I believe that over the years in my writing I've maintained a pretty sane head, acknowledging and often promoting sensible eating and drinking trends while never abandoning the basics, refusing to tolerate pretension and phoniness, and believing firmly that my traditional, no-nonsense, sometimes stubborn approach to food and drink would eventually prove to be what the public really wants—and today this certainly seems to be the case. It's no secret to anyone, for example, that I've always championed French classic and country cooking over the ill-fated nouvelle cuisine, that I'd prefer any day a luscious cassoulet or platter of beautifully fried chicken to the silly conceits of the so-called New American style of cooking, and that the individuals I admire most in the restaurant world are hardly the young superstars who come and go like thunderstorms but real professionals like the ones profiled in this book. For years, I've stuck by my guns in my essays, proclaiming the eternal virtues of old-fashioned home cooking; seeking to upgrade the social status of such hitherto neglected personal favorites as the spud, the onion, elegant dessert wines, and the Manhattan cocktail; introducing readers to the venerable bistros and brasseries of Paris, the malt distilleries in the highlands of Scotland, and the truffle hunters of Périgord. I've tried to inspire people to really *think* about numerous aspects of gastronomy, reflect, get angry, laugh, develop opinions and prejudices, and gradually become part of my fascinating world.

Since, over the years, my editorial responsibilities at *Town & Country* have required that I produce at least eight food and beverage features per year, most of the material included here was originally published in that magazine, the remainder either having appeared first in the pages of *Travel & Leisure, Cuisine, Food & Wine, Esquire,* and other such reputable imprints or being published here for the first time. The topics covered are totally eclectic in nature, ranging from the innocent exclamations of a youngster intrigued by French onion soup, Greek pastries, and strong spirits, to a man's romance with elegant foie gras, gutsy risotto, and noble wines, to the seasoned epicure bursting with all sorts of controversial convictions and declamations. Here you read about the heroes who helped fashion my taste; the highly personal places, events, and pleasures that have contributed so much to my evolution; the important role that France and the French have played in my never-ending search for culinary perfection; the multitude of restaurants around the world where the daily drama unfolds; and the many dishes and styles of cooking that I either champion or curse. The tone may be frivolous, snobbish, or dead serious, but, throughout it all, I'd like to think there emerges the figure of a man embarked on a mission to better understand himself and humanity by analyzing how and why we break bread and quench our thirst together.

# PART I
# THE FLAVORS
# OF HOME

As I state elsewhere in this book, we all, for better or worse, carry the baggage of our past with us into the present, and for no one has this maxim been so true as for myself. My southern childhood and adolescence (the people, the food, the great traditions, just the inflated idea of "being southern") have always had tremendous impact on the ways I approach food and drink, entertain, and form quick opinions, and although my cultural and gastronomic horizons are now extended to the ends of the earth, I've never forgotten my basic roots, how I was taught initially to eat and cook correctly, and what it's like to share a table where honest sustenance, zestful conversation, and lots of family love make most other facets of life seem almost negligible.

# BÖCKLING, BAKLAVA,
# AND BISCUITS

1986

Quite often when confronted with still another restaurant menu that includes the likes of an elaborate seafood terrine with a delicate sauce, a sautéed fresh duck foie gras, and a couple of pristine veal medallions perfumed with exotic wild mushrooms, my thoughts drift to crisp southern fried chicken, short ribs of beef falling off the bone, baked cheese grits, Greek-style lamb stew with lots of garlic and briny black olives, and Swedish meatballs redolent of fresh dill. I gaze at the inocuous, dried-out fancy roll on a china plate and dream of oven-warm puffy biscuits or crusty country yeast bread. I try to negotiate the perfectly sculptured, undercooked, tasteless vegetables while entertaining visions of unctuous, flavor-packed Kentucky Wonder green beans that have simmered for hours with pork fat. And when the waiter reels on about the mango tart, the crème brûlée with ginger, and the passion-fruit sorbet, I yearn for a wedge of gutsy baklava dripping with honey, a bowl of fresh strawberry-peach cobbler topped with vanilla ice cream, or a hunk of homemade chocolate pound cake with a pale undercooked "sad streak" floating through its center.

Don't get me wrong. There's nobody on earth who appreciates fresh caviar, paper-thin *carpaccio* sprinkled with grated Parmesan and virgin olive oil, or truffled roast chicken more than I do. I eat Chinese sea slugs, stuffed gooseneck, tiny fragile game birds you pop in your mouth, eyeballs and all, and, when forced, I'll even consent to an occasional nouvelle dish of French or American persuasion. But the food I respect, the food that sustains me, the food I truly love on a regular basis is the honest, wonderful, home-cooked fare I knew as a child in a household that was at once southern, Greek, and Swedish.

Today when I entertain in my own home (which is often), I might well serve anything from snails stuffed in puff pastry to *blanquette de veau* to a copious duck paella with olives and almonds. But as my closest friends know, what you find on my table more often than not is shrimp pilau, meaty barbecued pork spareribs, spicy okra and tomatoes, slabs of salty country-cured ham with red-eye gravy, the spicy Greek lamb stew known as *arni kapama*, buttermilk biscuits, Bourbon spoonbread, all types of home-made pickles and chutneys, and Swedish sugar cookies. These were the dishes prepared at home some four decades ago by my southern mother and Greek and Swedish grandparents, and these are the same dishes my gifted mother continues to cook with love and care on an almost day-to-day basis.

When I reflect on the monumental role that food played in my youth, it becomes easily understandable to me why, after years of professional training and experience in the academic world, I eventually decided that my palate and stomach were more important than my brain. Times were not easy for anyone during those very lean war and postwar years, but nothing prevented my family from making sure that fresh, wholesome, home-cooked meals would be not only on the table but in the lunch boxes as well. Never in the deepest recesses of memory do I recall going down a cafeteria line at school, not when I had a colorful tin box packed full of fried chicken, country-ham biscuits, a chunk of feta cheese, small jelly cookies, and a Thermos of mellow buttermilk. Nor do I remember ever seeing in my mother's kitchen packages of processed meats and cheeses, canned vegetables, or, heaven forbid, store-bought cakes and cookies.

Although we were citified folks living in a major North Carolina metropolitan center, we ate farm-fresh chickens whose necks my grandmother taught me how to wring at an early age (the very thought terrifies me today), and for well over half the year, most of the vegetables (pole beans, butter beans, tomatoes, spinach, collards, okra) that graced our table were harvested from my grandfather's huge garden out back. During the summer months, it was always something of a ritual for the entire family to climb periodically into the old Ford, drive over the border to South Carolina, and collect that state's Elberta peaches, Silver Queen corn, thick-rind watermelons, and fat blackberries Mother needed for canning and pickling. And after the first frost, there was nothing I looked forward to more on cool Saturday mornings than driving to a county market for real country sausage or making the half-day trip to a farm in the mountains to spend a couple of hours choosing just the right country ham. It seemed, in fact, we were always dashing somewhere for food—back and forth to Mother's faithful butcher, attending one church barbecue after another, going out to pick strawberries or gather pecans, and forever searching for the goat cheese and black olives that my father and grandfather could eat morning, noon, and night.

From the time I was fed my first spoonful of buttery grits till the year I left for college, everything at home revolved around the meals we shared three, four, often five times in any given twenty-four-hour period. The fact that to this day I must consume a full breakfast every morning is most surely due to my mother's insistence that no sane, intelligent creature should ever awaken to anything less than freshly squeezed orange juice, melon, eggs, fried country ham or sausage, grits, sliced ripe tomatoes, biscuits, homemade preserves, lots of chicory coffee, and possibly a Swedish pastry or two.

Our other meals took the form of midmorning breaks with cheese, Swedish limpa bread, fruit, and coffee (like all Swedes, my grandmother always kept a pot of coffee on the stove); lunches featuring steaming bowls of vegetable soup, thick meat sandwiches, and puffy omelets oozing with Greek cheese; midafternoon nut pastries and coffee; and dinner (or, more correctly, supper) that included classics such as *böckling* (smoked herring), chicken pot pie, seafood and sausage gumbo, *spanakopita*, and moussaka, at least three different vegetables, bowls of various pickles, plenty of fresh bread, rich desserts, and either wine or iced tea.

On any given evening (depending on which other family members or friends may have been invited), I listened as *avgolemono* soup was discussed in half-Greek, half-English, as the different ways of making limpa bread were argued in Swedish, and as the southerners in the family went on and on about what constitutes proper crab cakes or authentic Brunswick stew, or how to keep biscuits and spoonbread light, or why you simply cannot make decent bread-and-butter pickles unless the cucumbers and onions are first allowed to stand under crushed ice at least three hours. To say it was a somewhat unorthodox scene and that my initial exposure to gastronomy involved a certain eclectic element would be a triumph of understatement. But I learned, I absorbed, and years later I would realize the full impact all those rare, wonderful, crazy family meals and conversations had on a youngster who would one day make food his career.

Although my early gastronomic education was given an edge of sophistication on the many trips I took with my parents to New York and throughout Europe (trips always undertaken with the goal of eating well), no doubt the most influential of our forays were those made in the coastal areas of my native South. If food at home represented a fundamental passion that one and all simply took for granted, cooking and eating became nothing less than an obsession when we moved every summer to our beach cottage on the Carolina coast for a month. That is where I really learned to cook, from

Mother, and that is where I was first exposed to such local specialties as she-crab soup, shrimp pilau, the meat custard known as hobotee, daube glacé, and Huguenot torte.

Not a day passed that we didn't roam the vegetable and fish markets for ingredients with which to prepare any number of dishes indigenous to the region, and at least every other night we ended up in still another new fried-seafood house, barbecue joint, or serious restaurant, forever in search of the best shrimp-and-corn chowder, the finest lump crabmeat au gratin, the spiciest coleslaw, and the perfect hush puppy (the quest for the last item continues to this day). Of course, the highlight of any stay in the Low Country was dinner in Charleston at Henry's, in those days a veritable bastion of southern good taste and great food, where we devoured Bull Bay oysters by the dozen, spiked our bowls of thick she-crab soup with extra Sherry, ordered second helpings of delicate soft-shell crabs, and raved about the shrimp omelet and baked stuffed Spanish mackerel topped with olives and smoky bacon.

Creole and Cajun food are currently the rage of the entire nation, as if these age-old styles of American cookery were just recently invented by a couple of superstar chefs and food journalists. Well, the cuisine of New Orleans and the Louisiana bayou country was as familiar to me as a youngster as the fried chicken back home, and rarely did we return from one of our pilgrimages to the delta without Mother's having obtained a pocketbookful of recipes for still other gumbos, étouffées, rémoulade sauces, rice cakes, beignets, and stuffed mirlitons. At an early date my father learned the trick of avoiding the lines at Antoine's in New Orleans by booking a table through a certain waiter (Sammy Leblanc), and to this day I know that the only way to savor the inimitable oysters Rockefeller, eggs Sardou, trout Marguéry, and oysters en brochette at Galatoire's without standing outside for an hour is to spend time first knocking off a few dozen fat Gulf oysters a block away at the Acme Oyster House before showing up at the restaurant about 1:45 for lunch. It was in New Orleans that I tasted my first turtle soup (at Commander's Palace), my first red beans and andouille sausage (at Chez Hélène), my first crawfish étouffée (at the Bon-Ton), and my first po 'boy sandwich (at Mother's). And it was in Breaux Bridge in Cajun country that I developed my love for crawfish pie, Louisiana crab boil, and redfish prepared in many more succulent ways than the overrated "blackened" version that's so ubiquitous and fashionable today.

I left home to broaden my horizons, live in Europe, and eventually teach at a number of universities. But no matter how far I went, no matter what and whom I was exposed to, no matter how worldly my habits might have become, I no more lost track of the flavors of my childhood than I did the syrupy southern accent that's as thick today as thirty years ago. While studying in France, not a month passed that I didn't find a large parcel from home bulging with spicy cheese biscuits, jars of carefully packed pickles and preserves, bags of fresh pecans, a slab or two of moldy cured country ham, and all sorts of homemade cookies that I relished even when they were no more than crumbs.

Over the years, my parents and I traveled on the world's great luxury liners and dined at many of the world's great temples of gastronomy; we hobnobbed with the likes of the late Henri Soulé of Le Pavillon in New York, Paul Bocuse, and New Orleans's Ella Brennan; and we familiarized ourselves enough with various ethnic cuisines and cooking techniques so that Mother and I both could turn out as tasty a *navarin d'agneau, risotto milanese,* and *Gulaschsuppe* as the next amateur cook. But for me there still remained nothing like those visits back home to North Carolina, the bountiful breakfasts, the overflowing pork-barbecue sandwiches with peppery vinegar sauce, the black-eyed peas and collard greens glistening with their simmering streak-o'-lean, the overcooked Greek lamb knuckles with rice and tomatoes, and, at Christmas, the tins and tins of Mother's homemade fruitcakes, cookies, and candies kept on the side porch. Still today, when I call to say I'm coming home, everyone automatically takes it for granted that for the first dinner there will be a mess of spicy boiled Carolina shrimp, short ribs of beef baked with potatoes and tomatoes, squash soufflé, corn bread or buttermilk biscuits (enough made so that there are also plenty to be split, buttered, and toasted for breakfast the next morning), a Greek salad, and sticky fruit cobbler topped with ice cream.

That I have little respect or use for many pretentious dishes now associated with this trendy movement called the New American Cuisine stems mainly from my conviction that the food is simply not and never will be American—in concept, execution, or flavor. The fare I knew as a child— albeit southern, Greek, or Swedish—had a solid cultural foundation based on certain well-defined cooking techniques and unalterable taste factors, and the very idea of trying to add novelty to that venerable foundation by formulating strange new ingredient combinations and radically different cooking methods is about as foreign to my gastronomic senses as producing a rouxless gumbo.

Yes, today I often modify my moussaka by substituting zucchini for eggplant, or I'll give dimension to my short ribs by adding green olives, or I'll blend shrimp with corn and peas and pork cracklings to make a tasty salad. But never do I veer too far from the basic indelibles with which I was impressed while growing up. Like my mother, I still knead bread properly with my hands, dice onions to the exact size with a heavy knife, and produce a satiny-smooth purée with a food mill. Like my father, I would never corrupt a Greek salad by including sun-dried tomatoes, cilantro, and any goat cheese other than feta. And like my Swedish grandmother, I could hardly imagine serving *gravlax* or herring with crème fraîche instead of thick, old-fashioned sour cream.

While others, when traveling about the country, break their necks to snag reservations in the snazziest new restaurants serving still another exotic fish grilled over mesquite, designer pizza, and contrived pasta salad, I go out of my way whenever possible to eat the sort of food that may not offer earth-shaking surprises but that I know will taste great and make me feel wonderful inside. In San Francisco, I still dash to Tadich Grill for hangtown fry, crisp corned-beef hash and fish croquettes, and succulent rex sole simply broiled, as well as to my beloved Jack's for the same juicy mutton chop and baked apple I enjoyed so often with my parents in the past. I couldn't imagine a visit to Boston without dropping into the venerable Locke-Ober's for thick oyster stew, delicately fried scallops, and Indian pudding, and I think I'd almost cancel a trip to Houston if I learned there would be no time to go to Otto's for genuine barbecued brisket. In New Orleans, it's the inimitable shrimp rémoulade, crabmeat imperial, and fresh trout with roasted pecans I knew years ago at Commander's Palace; in Detroit, it's grilled whitefish and thick fried onion rings at the London Chop House; and in Miami, it's those remarkable stone crabs at Joe's. In New York, my profession demands that I stay abreast of virtually every new major restaurant that opens, but when the tensions of life become oppressive and I crave the dishes that work that special magic, I sneak off to The Coach House for piping-hot corn sticks, Greek tripe soup, crab cakes, and pecan pie, to Gage & Tollner's in Brooklyn for tender clam bellies, fried chicken Maryland, and the world's best hashed browns, and to the Gloucester House if only to get my fill of homemade biscuits. If this fare sounds outdated to some, that's their problem. I love it.

Experimenting with food and creating new dishes can be fun and is indeed necessary if any given cuisine is to be allowed to evolve, but if I learned nothing else from my family, I learned that the dishes we loved as adolescents not only are the most representative of our rich (yes, rich!) gastronomic heritage but also are what sustain the body and soul throughout life. The foods of which we should be proud and which should serve as a departure point for exploration of regional cuisines by chefs and restaurateurs are simply the very dishes we knew and loved at home. For me, these dishes happen to be of southern, Greek, and Swedish origins. But for others it could mean a smoky pumpkin soup served at a German-American farmhouse in the Midwest, a codfish stew in the house of a Massachusetts family with strong Portuguese ties, a steaming brisket of beef or stuffed cabbage prepared for Jewish holidays in a New York apartment, an exotic California composed salad, or a long Texas table groaning with sliced barbecued beef and links, spicy chili, jalapeño corn bread, and pecan tassies.

These and hundreds of other homespun dishes that testify to our diverse regional and ethnic backgrounds are what American cookery should be all about. They are dishes you don't tamper with, and they are dishes that add tremendous meaning to our lives no matter how long we live and how sophisticated our tastes become.

# CHRISTMAS: THE BREAKFAST

*1975*

E xcept maybe for the British, no people on earth enjoy (and demand) a good wholesome breakfast like the inhabitants of America's Southland, and when it comes to the generations-old southern tradition of Christmas breakfast, nothing can equal the culinary extravaganzas that grace tables from Virginia to Tennessee to Arkansas. Of course everyone in the South has his or her own interpretation of this very special meal. For some it's the moment to cut into the savory country ham that's been aging in the attic; for others it's the time to share a luscious oyster stew dipped from a treasured family tureen kept stored high up in the cabinet; but for me it's the occasion for the same elaborate buffet that my mother in North Carolina has been serving guests for as long as I can remember and that I still travel many miles each year to experience.

At home, as in many areas of the South, it has always been customary to begin the celebration of Christmas Day by attending the early-morning church service, a worthy obligation that does wonders for the soul but plays havoc on the nervous system. While in younger days my thoughts would stray innocently from religion to all the gifts waiting to be opened under the tree, today I'm afraid my vision in church is of a more gustatory nature, focusing on all the food and beverages to be consumed later in the morning.

After the service, the first ritual of the day is the mixing of the milk punch, a sinfully Bourbonated libation that originated in New Orleans and that perks up spirits during the opening of the presents. By midmorning, everyone in the family is busy helping in the kitchen—cracking eggs, frying ham and sausage, peeling fruit, preparing the dough for biscuits, opening jars of homemade preserves, and generally making ready to satisfy the appetites of about a dozen hungry friends and relatives.

At 10:30 guests begin at arrive, and by 11 everyone's cupping a glass of milk punch, telling of gifts received, and, to be sure, waiting anxiously to see the buffet Mother is laying out on the long mahogany side table covered with a handmade festive cloth. Christmas breakfast is an occasion that warrants the finest linens, crystal, china, and silver, and few southern hostesses consider the meal anything less than a formal affair. Normally this breakfast lasts for hours, everyone eating at a leisurely pace while indulging in lively conversation, and, in good native style, nobody thinking twice about returning to the buffet at least two or three times—if only for another hot baking-powder biscuit.

No doubt the array of food included on this buffet would cause outsiders to stagger in disbelief, but for us it's all quite normal. From year to year Mother might add or subtract an item, but generally the menu is predictable and composed of traditional favorites served in the family for decades. First, there's always a large crystal bowl of fresh fruit compote flavored with kirsch or light white wine. Next is a tureen of oyster stew, a sublime preparation that always inspires discussion of the superiority of Carolina oysters over those harvested along the Gulf states. Then a silver chafing dish full of the same cheese-and-eggs I recall watching my grandfather concoct on Christmas mornings and which I understand was passed down to him by his mother in Georgia.

Meat is an essential staple of any southern breakfast, and for the buffet nothing will do but three different varieties. Never absent is cured country ham, a mouth-watering regional specialty, which is ordered months in advance from a mountain farmer, hung in a dry area to age, sliced thick, fried, and served with red-eye gravy (made by deglazing the frying pan with water or coffee), and a mess of baked grits. There are also fat patties of country sausage, slab bacon, and a creamy chicken hash that someone back in the family learned to cook while visiting the South Carolina Low Country.

For a ceremonial breakfast we also insist on a nice selection of breads representing different flavors and textures. Of course some guests would almost take it as an insult if Mother by chance forgot to produce her inimitable biscuits, while others would suspect mental disorder if she denied them her hot orange muffins or apricot nut bread. And as for the luscious strawberry, peach, and damson-plum preserves that she puts up during the previous summer—well, without those to spread on hot biscuits, the Christmas breakfast would undoubtedly be a dismal failure.

Add to all this pots of strong, steaming chicory coffee and a few bottles of icy rosé wine and the result is not only a unique adventure in great regional eating but also a means whereby the joys of Christmas morning can be extended well into the otherwise depleted afternoon. After such a gastronomic marathon, no one really thinks much more about food—not, that is, till the early evening, when it's time to begin mixing Sazeracs and getting down to the equally serious business of Christmas dinner!

Although Mother, like so many southern cooks, prepares dishes more according to instinct than to books, the following recipes are detailed enough to ensure at least reasonable success. I must confess, however, that after baking biscuits for as long as I can remember, I've yet to turn out one that can equal Mother's fluffy wonders. Don't ask me why, please.

# Milk Punch

9 *ounces Bourbon*
1 *pint whole milk*
4 *teaspoons confectioners' sugar*
4 *drops vanilla*
 *Cracked ice*
 *Nutmeg*

In a tall cocktail shaker, combine the Bourbon, milk, sugar, vanilla, and plenty of ice, and shake till icy cold. Pour the punch through a strainer into six Old-Fashioned glasses and sprinkle each drink lightly with nutmeg.

Yield: 6 drinks

# Paw Paw's Cheese-and-Eggs

8 *tablespoons (1 stick) butter*
8 *slices white bread, trimmed and cubed*
2 *cups milk*
2 *pounds extra-sharp Cheddar cheese, grated coarse*
10 *eggs, beaten*
 *Salt and freshly ground pepper*

In a large, heavy skillet or sauté pan, heat the butter over moderate heat, add the bread and milk, and mash thoroughly with a fork till the mixture has the consistency of a soft roux. Add the cheese and continue mashing and stirring till the cheese is well incorporated and the mixture is smooth. *(continued)*

Add the eggs and salt and pepper to taste and stir slowly and
constantly with a large spoon (do not rush!) till the eggs are set and
the mixture is creamy, reducing the heat if the mixture seems to be
sticking to the bottom of the skillet.
Serve hot in a chafing dish or large heated bowl.

Serves 8


# Baked Grits

4 cups water
1 cup quick grits
2 teaspoons salt
3 cups milk
4 eggs, beaten
1 teaspoon Worcestershire
8 tablespoons (1 stick) butter, cut into pieces
  Freshly ground pepper

Preheat the oven to 350° F.
In a large saucepan, bring the water to a brisk boil, add the grits
and salt, and stir. Reduce the heat slightly and cook the grits for 5
minutes, or till thick, stirring often. Add 2 cups of the milk, return
the mixture to a boil, stir, reduce heat, and continue cooking the grits
for 5 minutes or till thickened.
Add the remaining milk, mix thoroughly with a wooden spoon, add
the remaining ingredients, and stir till the butter has melted. Pour
the mixture into a buttered 2-quart baking dish and bake for 1 hour.

Serves 6 to 8


# Southern Biscuits

2 cups flour
1 teaspoon salt
1 tablespoon baking powder
¼ cup vegetable shortening
¾ cup milk

Preheat the oven to 450° F.
Sift the flour, salt, and baking powder together into a large mixing
bowl, add the shortening, and work it quickly into the flour with the

fingertips till the particles of shortening are about the size of oatmeal flakes. Add the milk and stir quickly with a fork or just long enough to dampen the flour.

Transfer the dough to a lightly floured surface, knead for about 10 seconds, and roll it out to ½-inch thickness. Cut into rounds with a biscuit cutter or a small juice glass, place the rounds on a baking sheet, and bake for 12 minutes, or till golden on top.

Yield: 12 to 15 biscuits

# THE GOOSE

C hristmas Eve dinner has always been one of the most festive occasions of the year in our home, a time when family and close friends gather in the big white house, exchange stories about all that's gone on during the past year, sip eggnog, and, to be sure, indulge fully in the lavish meal that Mother has spent so long organizing. It's a joyful moment for young and old alike, and even though I must travel a long distance to get home, I can't imagine not being there for this particular event. Normally I arrive a week in advance, aware already of what the menu will be and eager to get into the large kitchen, strap on an apron, and begin helping out with the more complicated, time-consuming preparations. Unlike most people, we complete our shopping and decorating days in advance, for it's always taken for granted that the culinary extravaganza on Christmas Eve will require working—on and off—the better part of a week. And we love every second.

Some might consider it a bit extravagant to begin planning a holiday meal two or three months in advance, but when it comes to the dramatic feast for ten that takes place every Christmas Eve in my mother's home, there never seems to be enough time for adequate preparations. A cured ham might have to be purchased and hung in the attic for additional aging; arrangements must be made with the right contacts to acquire certain fowl and regional seafood; the last of the season's fresh fruit and vegetables must be preserved or canned and stored in the cellar; a large homemade fruitcake must be drenched with Bourbon and left to mellow; and, of course, there are always any number of cookies and candies to be carefully stacked between wax paper and sealed in decorative tins.

Mother has coordinated some mouth-watering spectacles over the years: huge turkeys bursting with fresh oysters; a haunch of venison basted with currant jelly and consommé, served with hominy and puréed chestnuts; braces of quail larded with pork and roasted in grape leaves; not to mention the elaborate arrays of stews, vegetables, and desserts. All were memorable, but for some reason none seemed to come off quite so perfectly as the goose dinner we prepared one year.

As usual, we'd begun planning the meal a few months ahead, which meant I was able to lug to North Carolina a luscious fresh goose from a certain farm on Long Island. By the time I got home, the ingredients for most of the dishes had already been assembled, so that no sooner had I walked through the back door and sniffed the familiar aromas of Christmas cooking than we were able to get started on serious business. For days we worked casually: Making pâtés that would be weighted down, chilled, and left to mature till the last possible minute. Chopping and slicing the ingredients for items to be molded. Changing marinades. And baking a few extra goodies we decided it might be nice to include. After other members of the family arrived, the house became more and more filled with the old-fashioned spirit of Christmas: excited children racing through the kitchen and asking to taste; Yuletide music playing on the stereo; the fragrance of miniature pine cones being tied with bright ribbon atop small fruitcakes to be given as gifts; and above all the inimitable smell of food emanating from every corner. Any spiritual malaise I might have been suffering before my arrival was totally dispelled, for I was home.

By early Christmas Eve, everything was ready for our guests. The lights on the big spruce tree in the living room flickered, causing the multicolored glass balls and ornaments to reflect almost surrealistically the same images they'd mirrored for so many years past. In the fireplace, the flames leaped over giant pine logs, releasing the same stimulating aroma I recalled as a child. On the mantel, holly partially concealed the small needlepoint elves Mother had once created, and on the sideboard in the dining room was draped an elegant net skirt on which she'd sewn sequined white reindeer, red Santa Clauses, and other such colorful characters. For this special occasion, our finest china, flatware, crystal, and linen had been brought out, and amid tall candles on the table were placed oversized Swiss goblets in which floated small poinsettia blossoms.

The guests showed up around seven, at which time eggnog and Bourbon punch were served with the liver-and-veal pâté, galantine of duck, and shrimp mousse I'd laid out on a buffet in the living room. After the children had studied every present under the tree, they were taken to the den to eat turkey, rice, and cranberry sauce and later to amuse themselves while the grownups dined. At eight the dinner began, and once the guests noticed in front of their plates the miniature goose figurines Mother had found somewhere, it was no longer a secret what main dish we were featuring.

The first course was she-crab soup, a luscious combination of milk, fresh crabmeat with the roe, onion juice, Worcestershire sauce, and mace, all christened with the same dry Sherry, served in special crystal glasses that I'd once found in Spain. To go with the soup were freshly baked corn sticks, and for those who wished to do a little extra dunking, there was plenty of soup left in the tureen.

The large goose, stuffed with apples, prunes, and walnuts, was prepared according to a recipe I'd learned from Pearl Byrd Foster, for years the highly gifted owner and chef at Mr. & Mrs. Foster's Place in New York. Surrounded on the silver platter by blanched plums, cherry tomatoes, and watercress, the golden bird appeared nestled in holiday colors, and the effect was heightened even more when Port gravy was ladled over each portion. The accompanying vegetables included glazed turnips and tiny Brussels sprouts with sautéed peanuts, and in place of a salad was a mold of cranberry-and-orange relish. Because of the constant pricking and basting during the roasting, the skin of the fowl was impeccably crisp, yet the meat was correctly moist and full of natural flavor. To wash everything down, my father chose from his fine collection of California wines two noble bottles of '68 Heitz Cabernet Sauvignon. Spirits began to soar as we virtually devoured the goose, and when Mother carried the pitiful carcass back to the kitchen, everyone broke out in a round of applause.

For dessert we served a hot lemon soufflé pudding topped with lemon zest cream, a remarkably light creation that provided just the right tartness needed after the rather robust main course. Mother's homemade cookies were passed, and, to consummate the occasion, I popped the cork of a '74 Schramsberg Blanc de Blancs—tingly, festive, and eminently satisfying. After this we poured hot chicory coffee, filled snifters half full with a delectable old Cognac, and eventually drifted back to the living room to relax, talk, and simply enjoy together the spirit of the Yuletide.

# She-Crab Soup

4 tablespoons (½ stick) butter
2 small onions, minced
3 tablespoons flour
2 cups milk
2 cups heavy cream
1 teaspoon mace
1 teaspoon white pepper
2 teaspoons salt
2 ounces Worcestershire sauce
2 tablespoons cornstarch
1 pound fresh crabmeat, picked over carefully
½ cup crab roe (available in specialty food shops)
   Dry Sherry

In the top of a large double boiler, heat the butter over low direct stove heat, add the onions, and sauté over low heat till just soft. Add the flour gradually and stir over low heat till the mixture thickens.

Place the pan over the bottom of the double boiler half-filled with boiling water, and slowly add 1½ cups of the milk, stirring. When the milk is hot, add the cream, mace, pepper, salt, and Worcestershire sauce, and cook for 5 minutes. Dissolve the cornstarch in the remaining ½ cup milk, remove the pan from the boiling water, and stir in the cornstarch mixture.

Return the pan to the double boiler and cook the mixture for 5 minutes longer or till hot. When ready to serve, add the crabmeat and roe, heat the soup thoroughly over boiling water, and lace with Sherry to taste. Serve the soup with additional Sherry on the side.

Serves 6

## Roast Goose with Apple, Prune, and Walnut Stuffing

*The Stuffing:*

½ pound extra-large pitted prunes, washed and drained
½ cup seedless raisins, washed and drained
1 cup Port wine
1 lemon, sliced thin and seeded
1 onion, chopped and sautéed till soft in 1 tablespoon butter
1 large sour apple, peeled and chopped coarse
1 cup coarse-chopped walnuts
½ teaspoon mace
  Salt and freshly ground pepper to taste
2 tablespoons lemon juice, strained
½ cup minced celery, tops included
2 cups bread crumbs


*The Goose:*

  One 12- to 14-pound goose
  Salt and freshly ground pepper
1 tablespoon dried sage
8 slices thick bacon
1 tablespoon flour, or more


To make the stuffing, soak the prunes and raisins in the wine and refrigerate overnight.

In a large saucepan, combine the soaked prunes and raisins, wine, and lemon, bring to a boil, reduce the heat, simmer 30 minutes or till tender, and drain thoroughly. Chop the prunes, raisins, and lemon, place them in a mixing bowl, add all other ingredients but the celery and bread crumbs, and toss. Correct the seasoning. Add the celery and bread crumbs, cover the stuffing with plastic wrap, and let it stand while preparing the goose.

To prepare the goose, remove the giblets, place in a saucepan with enough water to cover, and simmer 30 minutes.

Meanwhile, rinse the goose well inside and out, dry with paper towels, salt and pepper the cavity and exterior (to taste), and rub the sage thoroughly throughout the cavity.

Preheat the oven to 325° F.

Spoon the stuffing into the cavity of the goose, either truss or skewer the bird, and bard the breast with the bacon slices. Place the goose in a roasting pan, breast side up, and roast approximately 2 hours, pricking the skin with a fork about every 30 minutes. Remove the bacon, increase the heat to 450°, and continue roasting about 20 minutes, or till the goose is golden brown. Transfer it to a heated platter.

Skim the fat from the pan juices, add 1 tablespoon flour, and stir till smooth, adding a little more flour if necessary. Add about 1 cup of the giblet stock slowly, stirring constantly. Bring the sauce to a boil, reduce the heat, and stir till the desired consistency is attained.

Serve the goose with stuffing and sauce on the side.

Serves at least 6

## Pearl Byrd Foster's Hot Lemon Soufflé Pudding

The Pudding:

6 tablespoons unsalted butter
2 cups sugar
1 cup fresh lemon juice, strained
3 tablespoons grated lemon rind
4 eggs, separated
7 tablespoons flour
2¾ cups milk
¼ teaspoon salt

The Lemon Zest Cream:

6 lemons
1½ cups sugar
1½ cups hot water
1½ cups heavy cream

Preheat the oven to 325° F.

To make the pudding, place the butter and sugar in a mixing bowl and cream with an electric mixer. Add the lemon juice, lemon rind, and egg yolks and beat till well blended. Fold in the flour and milk alternately till well blended. In another bowl, beat the egg whites with the salt till stiff but not dry and fold into the butter mixture. Pour the mixture into a low, well-buttered 1½-quart casserole, set in a pan of hot water, and bake 25 minutes or till firm.

Meanwhile, prepare the Lemon Zest Cream by carefully cutting the rind from the lemons, avoiding the bitter pith. Dissolve the sugar in the hot water in a saucepan, stirring, for 5 minutes. Remove syrup from the heat and let cool. Place syrup in a blender, add the rind,

(continued)

and blend (rind should not be too fine). In a bowl, whip the cream, add the lemon syrup, and fold till well mixed.

Serve pudding from the casserole and top each serving with the zest cream.

Serves 6 to 8

# THE CAKE

*1979*

N ever does my Greek-Swedish-southern background come into clearer
focus than when I recall all the ethnically diverse and wonderful
baked goods that filled the Christmas kitchen at home when I was a child.
Naturally, there were literally a dozen varieties of buttery Scandinavian
cookies and fruited cakes prepared by Grandmother Sigrid and her friends,
goodies intended to be consumed almost round the clock (usually with
coffee) before, during, and after the holidays. From the Greek relatives
came large yeast loaves (*vasilopeta*) redolent of cinnamon, nutmeg, and
grated orange peel; rich cakes oozing with honey; and delicate cookies filled
with nuts, sesame seeds, and anise. And how could I forget the array of
confections turned out by my Georgia grandmother and mother?—nutty
fingers dusted with powdered sugar, colorful jelly cookies, benne wafers,
lemon squares, date bars, heavy pound cakes with undercooked "sad
streaks" in the center, pecan rolls, and dark fruitcakes wrapped in Bour-
bon-soaked cheesecloth. Everyone had a favorite dessert, and I loved none
more than the big luscious cakes, all of which had been made well in
advance and many of which had been aging in their tins since early fall.

Over the years, my fondness for Christmas cakes has dwindled no more
than my waistline, most likely because there's scarcely a time during the
entire year that I'm without some remnant of my mother's Christmas baking (rum cake seems to keep forever, and fruitcake doused periodically with

Bourbon just gets better and better). To say that I would endorse those store-bought cakes packaged in cellophane would be almost as ridiculous as to suggest that my mother might even have one in her home. It's been years since I've had the opportunity actually to watch her go about making the same large and small fruitcakes, chocolate pound cakes, rum cakes, whiskey-pecan cakes, orange-date-nut cakes, coconut cakes, and lemon cheesecakes she's been serving the family and giving away to friends for as long as I can remember. But I know that after the first frost out come the battery of pots and pans, the grinder, the extra-large chopping knife, the bottles of spirits, the mounds of crystallized fruit and nuts, and heaven knows what else, all required to produce her mouth-watering creations. It's a labor of love that continues week after week, but never am I so filled with the Christmas spirit as when I return home each year from far away, hurry to the cold side porch, and view with amazement the stacks of cake tins just waiting to be opened.

Unfortunately, holiday cake making in most American homes is hardly the same art today that it was in an era when packaged baked goods didn't exist and exaggerated fears of cholesterol and calories were unknown. I can at least try to understand why, given the pace and tension of present-day existence, home cooks wouldn't exactly relish baking their own cakes year-round when what I suppose are palatable commercial products are so conveniently available in any supermarket. On the other hand, why not, I ask, really go all out for once and produce one or two delicious homemade cakes that you can be genuinely proud to serve? Sure, it takes time and effort, but think how gratifying it will be to start your baking early, work at your own pace, store your confections away in attractive tins, and eventually offer family and friends very special cakes that will be the highlight of any festive meal.

## Mother's Dark Fruitcake

½ pound crystallized citron, chopped
¼ pound crystallized orange peel, chopped
¼ pound crystallized lemon peel, chopped
1 pound crystallized pineapple, chopped
2 pounds seedless raisins
1 pound dates, chopped
1 pound figs, chopped
1 pound whole crystallized cherries, cut in half
2 pounds whole pecan meats
4 cups flour, sifted
1 pound butter
2 cups sugar
10 eggs, beaten
1 teaspoon ground cinnamon
½ teaspoon finely ground cloves
½ teaspoon ground nutmeg
1 teaspoon salt
1 cup Bourbon

In a large mixing bowl, combine the crystallized citron, orange peel, lemon peel, pineapple, raisins, dates, figs, and all but 12 each of the cherries and pecans. Add 2 cups of the flour and mix well.

In another large mixing bowl, cream the butter and sugar with an electric mixer, add the eggs, spices, salt, and remaining flour, and mix till well blended. Add the contents of the first bowl to the second, add ¾ cup of the Bourbon, and mix thoroughly with your hands.

Preheat the oven to 300° F.

Grease and line three 8-by-3-inch-long loaf pans with heavy brown paper, allowing the paper to extend over the sides by 1 inch. Pack the batter firmly in equal amounts into the three pans, decorate the tops with equal numbers of the reserved cherries and pecans, and cover snugly with wax paper. Place the pans in one or two large roasting pans with 1 inch of water, place in the oven, and bake 2 to 2½ hours, or till a straw inserted in the centers comes out clean. Remove the wax paper during the last 15 minutes of baking. Remove the pans from the oven, douse the cakes with the remaining Bourbon, and allow to cool. Remove the cakes from the pans, remove the brown paper, wrap the cakes securely in cheesecloth soaked in Bourbon, and store in tightly closed tins at least 3 weeks before serving.

Yield: three fruitcakes, about 1 pound each

## Lemon Buttermilk Cake

*The Cake:*

4 *eggs*
2 *cups sugar*
1 *cup vegetable shortening, room temperature*
1 *cup buttermilk*
3 *cups flour, sifted*
2 *tablespoons lemon extract*
½ *teaspoon baking powder*
½ *teaspoon baking soda*
½ *teaspoon salt*

*The Icing:*

5 *tablespoons orange juice*
5 *tablespoons lemon juice*
2½ *cups confectioners' sugar*
½ *teaspoon salt*

Preheat the oven to 325° F.

In a large mixing bowl, combine the eggs, sugar, shortening, and buttermilk, and beat with an electric mixer till frothy. Add the flour 1 cup at a time, beating constantly. Add the lemon extract, baking powder, baking soda, and salt, and continue beating till well blended. Scrape the mixture into a lightly greased and floured 10-by-5-inch tube pan, and bake for 1 hour or till golden brown.

Meanwhile, combine the ingredients for the icing in another mixing bowl and beat with the electric mixer till well blended and smooth. Loosen the edges of the hot cake, spread the icing over the top, and return the cake to the oven for 3 minutes. Let cool and transfer to a large plate to serve.

Serves 8 to 10

# Chocolate Pound Cake

### The Cake:

½ pound (2 sticks) butter, softened
½ cup shortening
3 cups sugar
5 eggs
3 cups flour
½ teaspoon baking powder
½ teaspoon salt
¼ cup cocoa
1 cup milk
1 teaspoon vanilla

### The Icing:

6 ounces German chocolate
1 tablespoon shortening
¼ cup water
1 cup powdered sugar
  Salt

Preheat the oven to 325° F.

In a mixing bowl, cream the butter and shortening with an electric mixer, add the sugar, and beat till well blended. Add the eggs one at a time, beating well after each addition. In another bowl, sift together the flour, baking powder, salt, and cocoa, and add to the batter alternately with the milk, beating. Add the vanilla and beat till the batter is smooth.

Turn the batter into a greased Bundt pan and bake 1 hour and 20 minutes. Remove cake from the oven, let cool, and transfer to a cake plate.

To make the glaze, combine the chocolate, shortening, and water in a saucepan and melt the chocolate over low heat, stirring. In a bowl, combine the sugar and salt, add the chocolate mixture, stir till well blended, and drizzle the glaze evenly over the entire surface of the cake. Let cool.

Serves 12

# HEROIC HAMS

*1984*

E very Sunday morning I take a carefully wrapped slab of ham out of
the refrigerator, cut off a piece about two inches wide, slash the edges
of fat, and fry it gently on both sides. I then pour a little water into the
cast-iron skillet used for this ritual, scrape up the bits and pieces on the
bottom, and pour the rich, aromatic red-eye gravy over the meat. Eaten
with fried eggs and biscuits, the dark, salty, earthy ham is sheer gustatory
ecstasy, a treat as compelling and rare to me as three ounces of fresh beluga
caviar.

Of course I'm not talking about ordinary ham. One thing that makes my
ham so special is that to get it I travel twice a year to a small farm in the
mountains of North Carolina. This is country ham, slowly dry-cured with
nothing but coarse salt (as opposed to hams quickly cured in or injected
with brine and preservatives), smoked for days over a hickory fire, sacked,
and aged at least nine months in the air. The resulting flavor is pungent
and smoky, with an assertive, nutty savor that distinguishes it from the
flavorless hams mass-produced for the supermarkets of America. Its texture
is firmer, drier, and chewier, and such is the effect of the cure that this
ham will last almost indefinitely in the freezer. Some people prefer to eat
this type of ham soaked, simmered, baked, and sliced very thin. I still like
mine the way I've eaten it my entire life—salty, thick-sliced, and fried.

Similar slow-cured country hams are made in Virginia, Georgia, Kentucky, Missouri, Pennsylvania, and Vermont, but, like my North Carolina ham, these too are produced on such a small scale that only the most impassioned gastronomes ever have occasion to enjoy them. Even the better-known Smithfield hams of Virginia can be obtained only in the most sophisticated food shops or through the mail. No matter where you find a well-aged twelve- to fifteen-pound ham of this caliber, rest assured that the price will rarely be less than fifty dollars—and usually considerably more. As to whether these specialty hams are really worth all the trouble and expense, let me simply say that, once you've become accustomed to great country ham, consuming one of those bland products found in supermarkets is not unlike consuming a mildly seasoned marshmallow.

The ancient Greeks, as well as the Etruscans, were experts at salting, smoking, and aging hams, and by 200 B.C. ham of this type was held in such esteem by the nobility in Rome that even Cato went to great lengths to describe the exact curing and smoking method (virtually identical, curiously enough, to the one still used worldwide by reputable producers). Gauls in the vicinities of what are today Bordeaux and the Beaujolais region of France turned out beautiful hams that were regularly sent to Rome for special occasions, and during the Middle Ages no prince organized a Crusade that didn't include among the rations at least thirty or forty aged hams. Nothing was prized more on the tables of Elizabethan England than a regal York or Suffolk ham stuffed with fruits or forcemeats, and such was the reputation of French Bayonne ham by the seventeenth century that when Louis XIV and Maria Theresa of Spain were married at St.-Jean-de-Luz in 1660, literally dozens of the succulent joints were among the presents showered on both the young couple and the Queen Mother, Anne of Austria. Country hams have been cured in the American South ever since the original Jamestown settlement, and so fond was Queen Victoria of our Smithfield ham that regular shipments were made from Virginia to Buckingham Palace during much of her reign.

Although few foreign specialty hams find their way to the American market (so far, U.S. government regulations strictly prohibit the importation of uncooked or air-dried hams because of the rather exaggerated risk of trichinosis), experienced travelers know that hardly a major country exists that cannot boast at least one distinctive ham. In the British Isles, we seek out the delectable York and Bradeham hams from Yorkshire, the sweet Suffolks, and the peat-smoked Irish Limericks, ideally made from the hogs' left hind legs only. (And why the left? For the simple reason, so they say, that swine scratch with their right legs, and this toughens the meat!) In Spain, we look for the mild, delicate *jamón de Asturias* and *jamón Serrano*, while in Portugal, what could be a greater treat than a *feijão-branco* stew chock-full of dried white beans and aromatic Presunto ham from Chaves? There are those who insist that the beechwood-smoked Prazska Sunka (Prague ham) of Czechoslovakia is the world's finest; others believe that Germany's Westphalians, produced from hogs fed on sugar-beet mash, have no equal; and still others rave about Belgium's *jambon d'Ardennes*, Italy's rare San Daniele, Poland's Szynka, and Yugoslavia's Prsut. In France, there's hardly a province that doesn't turn out its own superb dry-cured ham, the result being such memorable regional dishes as *jambon persillé* (parsleyed ham in aspic) from Burgundy, *jambon en saupiquet* (ham slices in vinegar-cream sauce) from the Nivernais, and, from the Ardèche, festive *jambonnettes* (ham knuckle ends) stuffed with fresh pork and herbs. So important is ham to the French, in fact, that ever since the Middle Ages there's been an annual ham fair held during the fall on the Boulevard Richard-Lenoir in Paris, where epicures can sample savory joints from all over the country.

Surely the most famous specialty ham is the Italian *prosciutto di Parma*, a raw, slightly salty, exquisite ham that has been produced for centuries in the province of Parma (particularly at Langhirano). Made from the hind legs of special hogs fed partially on chestnuts and cheese, genuine Parma ham is first packed in salt from thirty to sixty days (depending on size), turned every week, then washed and hung in warm air one week. After the cure has "equalized" the ham (or permeated it entirely), the ham is cooled one month at a temperature of exactly 68 degrees Fahrenheit, then dried another month at 59 degrees, and, finally, aged in circulating air for three to six months. The procedure is complicated, time-consuming, and costly, but, as with other great country hams, there can be no shortcuts.

Equally complex is the age-old production of *jambon de Bayonne*, the luscious ham from the French Basque country and region around Béarn. (The ham is named Bayonne only because that town was once the chief point from which the hams were exported.) A symbol of great wealth during the Renaissance, Bayonne ham must, to earn the legal appellation *Véritable Jambon de Bayonne*, be made only from pigs bred and fattened in one of three prescribed geographical departments. It must also be cured with not one but two highly special varieties of local salt, *saliés-de-Béarn* and the gray *sel de Bayonne*, both of which are subjected to periodic chemical analysis. Today there is a *syndicat* of no more than ten recognized producers, each of whom is given an identification number, which, when he dies, cannot be assigned to his successor. The curing and drying of Bayonne hams (which are not smoked) are tedious, almost painful operations that require as much human instinct as technological knowledge. But once you've sniffed the ham's enticing aroma, studied its firm ivory fat, and experienced its mellow, almost sweet flavor, you not only know automatically why the hams are in such demand but also regret even more that the genuine article, with its *marque déposée*, cannot be shipped to the United States.

The famous Smithfield hams of Virginia, produced in the same manner since the days of the Jamestown settlement, have been loved and respected over the centuries by everyone from Sarah Bernhardt to Woodrow Wilson to present-day restaurateurs throughout the nation. Determined to protect their product from commercial exploitation, the state's General Assembly issued in 1968 the following statute: "Genuine Smithfield hams are cut from carcasses of peanut-fed hogs, raised in the peanut belt of the State of Virginia or the State of North Carolina, and cured, treated, smoked, and processed in the town of Smithfield in the State of Virginia." Presently, there are only four legitimate producers of Smithfield ham: Gwaltney (with their "Williamsburg" brand), Smithfield Packing Company ("Luter's"), Joyner ("Red Eye"), and Smithfield Ham and Products Company ("Amber"). Each brand has its loyal following, but so traditional is the three-hundred-year-old method of curing that only the most disciplined palate can detect the subtle variations in taste and texture. Smithfields, which derive their translucent fat, deep amber color, and slightly oily flavor from the hogs' peanut diet, are dry-cured at least a month, covered with pepper to keep away flies and their destructive larvae, smoked five days over hickory, red oak, or applewood, and then air-dried a minimum of six months and as long as two years. Like all well-cured country hams, Smithfields keep almost indefinitely (aficionados know that a coating of mold actually sharpens the distinctive flavor of the ham), and it's not unusual in the South for families to sack and hang an "heirloom Smithfield" intended for a newborn child to cut only when she's married!

No doubt the Smithfield is our most celebrated ham, but, unbeknown to most of the public, there are also other American specialty hams (cooked or uncooked) of equally fine quality that can be obtained by mail directly from the producers and that make for some very elegant dining. It's sadly true that modern food technology and commercialism have had a devastating effect on the small-scale production of genuine dry-cured hams, and that even in the state of North Carolina (the nation's country-ham capital) the number of producers has dwindled from four hundred in 1955 to fewer than a hundred today. Nevertheless, great hams are still available. Not a Christmas passes that I don't receive a year-old Kentucky beauty from Critchfield Meats in Lexington, Kentucky—simmered, coated with brown sugar and ground cloves, and expertly baked by Stanley Demos at his redoubtable Coach House restaurant (where they also serve a hefty slab of fried ham with red-eye gravy). I've had memorable corncob-smoked hams from Vermont, tangy pepper-coated hams from Fulton Provisions in Portland, Oregon, and the same delectable Booneville County ham I used to drive miles to savor while living in central Missouri. A very credible Bayonne-style ham, now being produced by a French family in San Francisco, is available under the brand Fabrique Délice at San Francisco International Cheese Imports, while domestic prosciutto made by Citero in Pennsylvania, Carando in Massachusetts, and John Volpi in St. Louis can be found at most specialty food shops and in supermarkets that cater to the carriage trade. Some of the best country hams anywhere are cured in Georgia, and real ham lovers know that one of the easiest ways to latch onto one is by stopping in at the Callaway Gardens store while passing through the Atlanta airport.

While many European country hams (Parma, Bayonne, Westphalian, Prsut, and others) are simply sliced thin and eaten raw, most American hams, even though they've been fully cured and often smoked, should be cooked before serving. The eternally debated question of whether or not to soak a great ham to release salt before simmering or frying depends strictly on personal taste. Those like me who were raised on country hams swear that much of the meat's distinctive character is lost by long soaking; yet others insist a ham is virtually inedible unless left overnight in a large pot of water. One point, however, on which all ham lovers agree is that a fine specialty ham must never be overcooked (no more than 15 minutes per pound) and, to prevent toughness, should be simmered (not boiled) very slowly and gently. Purists simmer their hams in nothing but fresh water, but I must say I've tasted delicious hams that were cooked with apples, vinegar, molasses, bay leaves, peppercorns, and even blackberry jam. Of course, a very nice final touch to any noble ham is to trim it well after simmering, score the fat, rub it well all over with brown sugar and ground cloves, and bake it until the exterior is beautifully glazed. Positioned on a handsome rack and carved in delicate, paper-thin slices, this type of ham not only makes for a wonderful change in festive entertainment but also honors a culinary tradition that spans many centuries and many continents.

## Basic Country Ham Preparation

1   12- to 15-pound dry-cured ham
1   cup dark brown sugar
10   to 12 cloves, ground

Scrub the ham thoroughly with a stiff brush under running water and place it in a large oval roasting pan. Add cool water to cover and let the ham soak 12 hours, changing the water twice. Rinse the pan thoroughly, scrub the ham again with a stiff brush under running water to remove all traces of mold and pepper, and return it to the roasting pan. Add fresh water to cover, bring the water very gradually to a gentle simmer, cover the pan, and simmer the ham very gently for 15 minutes per pound, adding more water if necessary to keep the ham covered.

Preheat the oven to 425° F.

Remove the skin from the ham and all but about ¼ inch of the fat. Score the fat in diamonds, cover with brown sugar and ground cloves, and rub the seasonings well into the ham with the fingers. Place the ham in the roasting pan, fat side up, and bake 15 minutes, or till the exterior is nicely glazed.

Carve the ham into paper-thin slices with an electric or serrated knife.

Serves at least 12

# THE COMFORT OF HOT SOUP

*1979*

H aving dropped off a couple of large copper pots to be relined at Dehil-
lerin, my friend, an expatriate bon vivant, and I ventured back out to
the snow-covered rue Coquillière. Never could I recall a colder day in
Paris, and never did I crave a steaming hot bowl of French onion soup more
—particularly the one I'd loved so many years ago at Au Pied de Cochon.

"But Au Pied de Cochon is just down the street," my companion re-
marked, struggling to light up a Gauloise with fingers that were already
slightly blue.

"You've got to be kidding," I exclaimed. "You mean that restaurant still
exists?"

"Of course it exists," he mumbled. *"Viens,* I could use a good bowl of
soup myself."

Climbing the stairs to the familiar second floor of the venerable restaurant and noticing the inimitable aroma of onions and cooked cheese that
permeated the air, I was suddenly overcome by nostalgia as my thoughts
wandered back to the fifties and early sixties when this area of Paris was
still Les Halles, the city's legendary food market. Fresh in my memory were
the many brisk nights when, first as a student in Paris, then as a tourist, I
would leave the theater or opera with friends, stop for a few snifters of
Cognac and good conversation at a café that has long since disappeared,
and end up "doing Les Halles" in the wee hours of the morning—a unique

ritual that, sadly, generations after mine would never have the opportunity to experience. Like hundreds of other adventurers, my friends and I would arrive in the district about 1:00 A.M., fully garbed in evening dress—a striking contrast with the wholesale greengrocers and butchers clad in their light-gray or blood-stained *blouses*. For hours we would roam from one gigantic iron-columned trading pavilion to the next, engaging the food merchants in small talk, admiring the exquisite displays of meats, fish, fruits, and vegetables set out for the discerning restaurateurs and shopkeepers, and, from time to time, snipping a few sprigs from enormous wreaths of watercress or, with Madame nodding her approval from behind the stall, sampling a fragile peach cosseted in cotton batting.

Chilled to the bone and fairly exhausted, we would eventually make our way to Au Pied de Cochon, for decades one of the more popular late-night spots in Les Halles and for us the one and only place to end the evening over large individual tureens of *soupe à l'oignon gratinée,* a crisp salad, freshly baked bread, and a bottle or two of Burgundy. Although over the years I heard it said that the restaurant actually did offer a full menu that most surely included grilled pigs' feet, I never once saw any main course served on the second floor of Au Pied de Cochon but that incredible onion soup—piping hot, thick, full-flavored, and so encrusted with Gruyère that the tureen itself was barely visible. After a few gooey spoonfuls, all the gloom of winter was dispelled, a calm warmth returned to the body, the spirit soared, and we were young and in Paris. Eventually, of course, the wreckers came to lay open "the belly of Paris," most of the famous old shops and restaurants were forced to close down, something glitzy called the Beaubourg was developed, and an era ended. It was a joy, therefore, to discover that my beloved onion soup was still available twenty-four hours a day, seven days a week, and to this day I've still never tasted a *soupe à l'oignon* quite like it.

Say what you will about other restorative foods, when that time of winter approaches when the temperature never seems to rise above freezing, I still insist there's nothing better than a steaming homemade soup containing chunks of solid food. Served with a simple salad, good bread, perhaps a little cheese or dessert, and an appropriate beverage, this type of hearty fare is not only gustatorily sound during the cold months but also wonderfully satisfying to prepare for both family and guests. With the multiple advantages of today's blenders and food processors, most ingredients can be ready for the pot in a matter of minutes, and while I personally find nothing more sensuous than a thick Brunswick stew or aromatic gumbo simmering for hours on the back of the stove, many delectable main-course soups (oyster stew, chowders, onion soup, minestrone, even cioppino) can be either started in the late morning and served for lunch at noon or prepared on the spur of the moment for an early dinner. Whichever soup you make, do give serious thought to preparing as much as you can handle and freezing quantities for future needs. If you set out to produce a really first-rate homemade potage you might want to serve on still another occasion, it's really a shame not to double or even triple the recipe, depending, of course, on space in your freezer.

In *How to Cook a Wolf*, the ever-intuitive M. F. K. Fisher writes: "Probably the most satisfying soup in the world for people who are hungry, as well as for those who are tired or worried or cross or in debt or in a moderate amount of pain or in love or in robust health or in any kind of business hugger-muggery, is minestrone." The fact that Mrs. Fisher doesn't also prescribe her Italian favorite for those who are bone-cold would suggest that she has another soup in mind for that human condition. I think my choice would still have to be onion soup fully cloaked in strong, crusted cheese, but on the other hand, if the snow is deep enough and the icy wind sufficiently debilitating, I'd most surely attack with gusto any well-made concoction placed in front of me.

## Old-Fashioned French Onion Soup

 4  tablespoons (½ stick) butter
 1  tablespoon vegetable oil
 4  cups thin-sliced onions, loosely packed
    Pinch of sugar
 1  teaspoon salt
 2  tablespoons flour
1½  quarts beef stock or bouillon, boiling
 ⅓  cup dry red wine
    Freshly ground pepper
    Rounds of crisp-toasted rye bread
1½  cups mixed grated Gruyère and Parmesan cheese
 3  tablespoons melted butter

In a large, heavy casserole, heat the butter and oil, add the onions, stir, cover, and cook about 15 minutes. Remove the lid, add the sugar and salt, and continue cooking over moderate heat about 30 minutes or till the onions turn a deep golden brown. Add the flour, stir in thoroughly, add the stock, wine, and pepper to taste, and simmer 30 minutes longer. Taste for salt and pepper.

When ready to serve, preheat the oven to 325° F., bring the soup almost to a boil, and pour it into individual ovenproof pots. Float rounds of toasted bread on top. Sprinkle with the grated cheese, then with the melted butter. Place the pots on a heavy baking sheet and place it in the oven. Bake 20 to 30 minutes, or till the tops are nicely crusted and golden brown.

Serves 4 to 6

# PART II
# PEOPLE ALONG
# THE WAY

Whereas most people stand in awe of certain statesmen, athletes, and entertainment stars, my heroes are all involved in the art of gastronomy. Distinguished restaurateurs, truly gifted chefs, expert food writers, perceptive restaurant critics—these are the individuals who interest me, the ones who share my passion for gratifying the palate and stomach, those who have taught and guided me so much along the way.

What links the personalities profiled in this chapter is not only a keen sense of professionalism but also a humanistic element that has had tremendous impact on my approach to writing about food and drink. Witnessing, for instance, the way Pearl Foster would discuss with any and every customer the origins and historical evolution of her dishes, or Jovan Trboyevic's method of instilling pride and loyalty in every chef or waiter under his command were experiences I could never forget. To this day, I read M. F. K. Fisher and James Beard much more for what they have to say about the bonds between human emotions and what we ingest than for such-and-such a dish. And I'm convinced there's still no one more capable of articulating a recipe or defining the various subtleties involved in great dining than Craig Claiborne. That today there seem to be fewer and fewer professionals of this caliber and insight coming along is a lamentable possibility I choose not to contemplate.

# THE INIMITABLE MRS. FOSTER

1978

You arrive at the front door of Mr. & Mrs. Foster's Place in proper attire, having been informed while making a reservation on the phone that it's jacket and tie for the gentlemen. You've also been told politely by that soft Virginia voice not to be late and not to have much for lunch. You knock just as you would at a private home, the locked door opens, and there stands the elegant Pearl Byrd Foster swathed in dark Ultrasuede and hardly the image of one who's been cooking since noon. The place is minuscule; the décor would be described as austere were it not for the exquisite flower arrangements. No menu, no fancy china or flatware, a limited but intelligent wine list, no nonsense. You're here to see Mrs. Foster and taste her American food, and, like the others waiting to be served, you know this is serious business.

To suggest that Mr. & Mrs. Foster's Place has become an institution in New York City is not hyperbole, and to insinuate that Pearl Byrd Foster is a veritable anachronism in this graceless age of submediocrity is a triumph of understatement. Professional gastronomes and journalists show up repeatedly on East 81st Street in hopes of discovering the secrets of Pearl's duck pâté, hot lemon soup, and snow cream. Such luminaries as Robert Redford, Walter Cronkite, Ethel Merman, and Malcolm Forbes consider the restaurant a haven where great food can be enjoyed in much the same manner as at home. As for myself, I've come to cherish this place as a sort of culinary shrine, just as I've come to cherish my close friendship with Pearl more than that with anyone else in the profession. The truth is that, whether the subject be the Biblical origins of carob, the gustatory merits of mutton, the medicinal qualities of garlic, the intricate seasoning of pâtés, or the boning of a gigantic goose, she is an encyclopedia of knowledge. Most food enthusiasts flock to their vast culinary libraries when in need of inspiration and information; I pick up the phone and call Pearl Byrd Foster.

"Exactly who is Mrs. Foster and what is she really like?" are the questions asked most by those who visit the restaurant, watch her ring the small silver bell that preludes the description of her famous soups and desserts, and listen to her informal table discourses on food and wine punctuated throughout by her very southern "Honey" this and "Darling" that. Well, I suppose I could go into biographical detail about how, as a child, she crossed the Oklahoma prairie in a covered wagon, foraged for wild persimmons and Jerusalem artichokes (which she crunched raw), cultivated her own quarter-acre of tomatoes, and, by the age of twelve, was creating and preparing dishes for the family meals; or how she played the New York stage before meeting her late husband; or why she turned over the opportunity to be the first passenger to fly the Atlantic to a girl named Amelia Earhart ("I was frightened, let's face it, and she was brave"); or why she used to meet her celebrated cousin, Admiral Richard E. Byrd, under the clock at the Biltmore ("Don't forget, honey, I'm a Byrd on both sides of the family"). Over the years her pink cloche hats and smart white turbans contributed much to the orchidaceous July transatlantic sailings of the *France* and *QE 2*, and Pearl still boards the magnificent Cunarder each year bearing such staples as almonds, carob powder, and raw sugar as precautions against the possibility that she might be asked by Chef Bainbridge or somebody in England or France to prepare her carob almond torte. Summers in Europe find her rambling about the kitchen of some Scottish castle, talking food with Waverley Root in Paris, learning to skin eels in Brussels, grilling *loup au fenouil* at an apartment in southern France, observing the subtleties of pasta making at the Gritti Palace in Venice, or savoring the glories of Alsatian cuisine at her beloved Auberge de l'Ill in Illhaeusern. When there's something new to learn about food, no place is too distant for Pearl.

"Oh, darling, why must you go on about those aspects of my life?" she's forever chiding. And indeed the only topic that really sustains Pearl's interest at any given time is the dish or the formal dinner on which she currently happens to be working. Most customers are content enough just to hear her discuss the luscious creations served on a regular basis as part of the six-course, fixed-price dinner: tiny chicken livers in Madeira; a wedge of feathery quiche (the recipe for which even I have never managed to obtain); a choice of homemade soups (Virginia peanut, hot lemon, mushroom consommé, cold apple) with fresh corn sticks "for dunking"; such main courses (ordered in advance on the phone) as Crustacean Broil, Bourbon Beef and Oyster Pot, and Boned Duck with Apple and Wild Rice; and, for dessert, Pecan Pie, Carob Cheesecake, Snow Cream, or Frosty Lime Pie.

But Pearl's inventive mind is eternally in search of new flavors, different textures, and new combinations that might contribute to her lifelong campaign to elevate the spirit of American cookery from the banal to the sublime. When someone sent her a case of California walnuts, she set out to create both a new pâté that had crunch and a plantation molasses-and-walnut pie; when a twelve-pound country ham arrived from an admirer in Kentucky, she first tested it in her jambalaya, found the cured flavor too assertive, then incorporated it successfully into Texas wheat puffs; and no sooner had she received a freshly killed goose from Long Island than she devised an apple, prune, and walnut stuffing for the goose (see page 18), which was served with Port gravy. Yogurt pie enriched with pure clover honey, Brussels sprouts sautéed with peanuts, squash soup spiked with apple, shrimp-and-corn chowder, boned roast chicken with curried chutney glaze, potato salad with hot Creole mustard, lemon soufflé pudding— Pearl's creations go on and on, year after year, and after begging so long for recipes, friends and customers of Pearl wait patiently for her forthcoming cookbook.

No one who knows Pearl can be unaware of her short temper in the face of phoniness and pretension, and nothing incurs her wrath faster than any suggestion that Paul Bocuse, Michel Guérard, and other famous French chefs have brought about a radical change in the food world by insisting that the freshest ingredients be prepared in the simplest manner possible. "Baloney!" she retorts. "I've personally done the Lyon markets with Bocuse —at a date, that is, when he actually shopped himself—and what I saw him doing was no different from what I've been doing for decades. No doubt Paul is a very fine chef during those increasingly rare moments he's actually in the kitchen, but as for creating a new approach to food and cooking, well, it's just not so. Darling, if you want to see a couple of truly serious cooks in France who share many of my own views, either make your way into Paul Haeberlin's kitchen at the Auberge de l'Ill or visit Richard Olney at his villa near Toulon."

Unlike the many other chefs of whom she doesn't exactly approve, Pearl *does* do her rounds of the markets every single working day of the week, and she *does* stay in her kitchen from exactly twelve noon till the last order is served late in the evening. Having picked up a few kiwi fruit (and Pearl was using "New Zealand gooseberries" years before other eastern chefs even heard of the fruit), salad greens and fresh vegetables, dairy products from a health-food store, perhaps an especially handsome chicken or slab of calf's liver, and heaven knows what other items intended for heaven knows what dishes to be either tested or served that evening, she prepares herself for deliveries of meat and seafood in much the same way Henri

Soulé used to await his caviar merchants at Le Pavillon. "Honey, those lobsters had better be kicking!" I once heard her say to a terrified delivery boy, "and if there's one shiff of odor to that lump crabmeat, you'll be making a trip back here within the hour." "You see, honey," she continued, turning to me while grabbing for a tin of crabmeat, "the question you must always ask is 'How fresh is fresh?' Sure, they'll tell you that the shrimp and pompano are fresh, but what I want to know is how long did it take that shrimp to arrive in New York from the Carolinas, and how long did it sit there on ice before reaching my front door? You just never know, not till you smell it and check the texture."

Although a lady of a certain age (a subject one would be well advised not to pursue in her presence), Pearl is generally viewed as a cyclone of energy, determination, and self-confidence, the type of dynamic individual who has tremendous faith in her own instincts and abilities and little respect for those who don't strive to realize their full potential. If some might accuse her of *amour-propre* when it comes to the way she enjoys talking about her food, it's only because they don't quite understand her overall sense of mission and her profound devotion to the art of cooking and eating well. "My taste buds are alive and I have a lot of energy," she once wrote me from France. "My vitality seems endless, and my desire to learn is so deep it burns inside me. Change my style of American food at the Place? No, no, a thousand times no! But I must learn more about French foods—the uses of butter and fats, the fascinating ways of preparing vegetables, the different cuts of meat, the sauces." People who mistake this almost childlike enthusiasm and dedication for egoism had best, indeed, stay clear of Pearl Byrd Foster.

Over the years I must have exchanged with Pearl hundreds of notes, letters, and spur-of-the-moment memos resulting from our mutual obsession with the gustatory experience (as well as our mutual loathing of the telephone), but I treasure none of her astute communications more than the one she was once forced to write during a typical night of insomnia. Scrawled, as always, on sheets of personalized Tiffany stationery, the rambling missive not only sums up much of her gastronomic philosophy but also identifies her, like M. F. K. Fisher, as a female Brillat-Savarin of the twentieth century. I doubt that Pearl will mind my sharing a few timeless random examples:

—"Purity and simplicity: the keys to great cooking."

—"Food must be beautiful in the cooking pan, on the serving platter, and on the dinner plate. This is a big order, but an important one."

—"Nature's own earthy ingredients are mouth-watering, and the flavors must be maintained by not overcooking."

—"Clear consommé should be a must at any great dinner."

—"Plates should be spare—never overloaded."

—"Fullness and richness of flavor must not be lost in a blanket of sauce."

—"When invited to a dinner, punctuality is the loftiest virtue."

—"With food there must always be a rhythm of design. Color effects a delight to the eye. Harmony is the key."

—"Like life, food must not become routine. There are many things to do just ahead in a full life. So with food—many new experiences of taste. So one must work with great zest coupled with the desire for achievement. And there must be a bit of glory about it all."

## POSTSCRIPT

Pearl Foster always said that when her time came to leave this earth she prayed she'd "drop" while working in her kitchen. Her wish was not granted in full, but sure enough, the afternoon she was stricken with her first stroke and I rushed over to "the Place," where she and her small staff had been preparing for the evening meal, I noticed that she had been boning a duck. Although she was unable to continue cooking and the famous little restaurant on East 81st Street was thus forced to close, Pearl, with typical fight and determination, lived just long enough to complete her remarkable cookbook, *Classic American Cooking*, published in 1983. She was eighty-three when she died—I think.

Quite often, people get perturbed at the way I severely criticize many of today's young American superstar chefs: their lack of training and experience, their arrogance, their much-too-frequent absence from the working kitchen, their claims to be "revolutionizing" American food. Well, believe me, Pearl Byrd Foster, along with other legends like James Beard, was demonstrating true culinary innovation twenty years before most of these kids were even born; all would be wise to study her legacy. Pearl had it all: a strong sense of discipline and responsibility to her public, a devotion to basics, an insatiable craving for greater knowledge, and, God knows, a distinct style not only in the dishes she created but in everything she did.

# THE OPERATIC BEARD

*Unpublished*

"**H**i, kiddo," he had addressed me rather frantically one morning on the phone. "I really think these doctors are trying to kill me with this miserable diet, and I'm craving just a small juicy steak, and do you think the two of us could hop out this evening and talk a little opera?"

Shortly after 7:00 P.M., Jim Beard and I were perched around a table at the Post House in New York, Beard's looming presence, as always, creating the atmosphere of a papal audience for staff and customers alike. In his genteel style, he listened patiently while the owner of the restaurant volunteered what he was trying to accomplish at his new place; he sat quietly while the waiter described each and every item on the menu and wine list in minute detail; and he even tolerated an abrupt interruption by a total stranger eager to explain how *she* prepared fried chicken. After about twenty minutes of all this, Jim was noticeably nervous.

"God," he whispered while buttering the first of many rolls, "I'm definitely not allowed to drink any wine, but would you please get me a double malt whisky on the rocks? And now, let's see, what should we eat? To begin, I think I'll have the lobster cocktail followed by a little clam chowder. Then, why don't you take the steak so I can have double lamb chops, and don't you agree we should at least try the hashed browns and fried onion rings and creamed spinach, and . . . umm . . . maybe a portion of

Caesar salad? For dessert, there's cheesecake, apple Betty, blueberry tart —hell, let's order all three just to sample."

That was going to be Jim's simple little steak dinner, and while I did feel a bit guilty for not protesting his illicit overindulgence, I wasn't about to dilute the joy of this man who, even in his final years, relished good food and drink like nobody I'd ever known. Instead, I simply agreed to the vast array of dishes he wanted to order, sipped my Manhattan, and proceeded to tell him about the performance of Wagner's *Parsifal* I'd attended the night before.

Of course what most of the world never knew about James Beard was that his true love was not really gastronomy but opera, and what people still find so ironic is that, just as the last topic Craig Claiborne and I discuss at table is food, virtually every meal I ever had with Jim (a frustrated tenor if there ever was one) was spent extolling the genius of Puccini or criticizing the upper range of Callas or analyzing the leitmotives in The Ring. On this particular memorable evening, one subject at hand was the Good Friday spell in the third act of *Parsifal,* one of the greatest moments in all opera, demanding the ultimate in interpretive ability from both the tenor and bass.

"Now, how did Hans Sotin phrase *'Das ist Charfreitags Zauber, Herr!?'"* asked Beard, cutting into the first pink lamb chop and washing down the bite with a slug of his second Scotch.

"Not much pause after *'Zauber,' "* I related while pouring Cabernet into my glass.

"Ah, that's wrong, so wrong," he reacted, taking a few fingerfuls of fried onions and buttering another hot roll. "Too bad you weren't old enough to hear Otto Edelmann's Gurnemanz. Here's how he handled that phrase." With which Jim, in his best basso attempt, leaned back in his seat, cleared his throat with whisky, and sounded forth the line, emphasizing a long pause before *"Herr"* and causing a few heads close by to turn. "I remember it like it was yesterday," he added, stabbing at the platter of potatoes, "and . . . umm, good potatoes . . . what a shame you never heard Melchior's Parsifal. You know when Kundry kisses Parsifal and he recoils with that incredible response *'Amfortas!—die Wunde!'?* Well, I can hear Melchior now at this dramatic moment of revelation, extending the second syllable in the name Amfortas so long you could almost feel the man's pain." Jim sat straight up, head very erect, holding a piece of meat up with his fork the way Parsifal holds up a sword. *"Amforrrrrtas!"* he vocalized with trembling fervor, provoking a momentary hush throughout the restaurant to which he now seemed oblivious. *"Amforrrrrrtas!—die Wuuuuunde!"* he repeated, raising the lamb high into the air.

And so it went for close to three hours, the two of us recalling and singing phrases and motives from maybe a dozen operas, picking casually at delicious charred meat, crisp onions, and rich desserts, getting progressively smashed on booze, wine, and fine Cognac, and once again savoring a very private and meaningful world that Jim could share with so few people. No doubt we were utterly outrageous that evening, but today, I never sink teeth into a thick sirloin or spoon creamed spinach on my plate that I don't still envision that wonderful great man of gastronomy grabbing his walking stick and my arm, humming ecstatically the final notes of some aria or another, and, with doggie bag in hand, making his way happily out of the restaurant like a gratified Wotan being escorted from the sacred halls of Valhalla.

# A SIMPLE COUNTRY LUNCH
# WITH M. F. K. FISHER

*1978*

S he is now in her seventies and a strikingly beautiful woman, with knowing blue eyes, impeccable skin, and silver hair drawn back sleekly over the ears. Her voice is soft and she speaks slowly, but as one might suspect, every word is weighed and every thought carefully composed. She is polite, often tender, but when confronted with examples of human mediocrity, pretension, and hypocrisy she can be brutally critical. In another age she would have been stamped a libertine; today she is respected as one of the world's finest food writers and, in the eyes of many, the grande dame of gastronomy.

None other than W. H. Auden once said of M. F. K. Fisher, "I do not know of anyone in the United States who writes better prose." That some people in the present generation either have never heard of this distinguished lady or, if so, believe her to be a man, is most probably due to the lamentable fact that until recently, when five of her books were republished under a single title, *The Art of Eating*, most of her work has remained out of print. "Back in 1936," she recalls, "my first publisher was stunned when he eventually discovered I was female, and I still get letters that begin 'Dear Mr. Fisher.' " But for those of use who've been lucky enough over the last three decades to happen upon her volumes, M. F. K. Fisher has remained our guiding light, the source of infinite gastronomic and philosophic wisdom, the model of what a truly refined food writer should strive for.

Often considered a rebel and eccentric, she didn't write cookbooks or publish restaurant reviews or dwell on endless numbers of uninteresting recipes. Rather, she has always devoted her exceptional talents to explaining and illustrating a very simple principle that is as valid today as fifty years ago: Since we must eat to live, let's learn to do it intelligently and gracefully, and let's try to understand its relationship with the other hungers of the world.

With the maxim fixed in our brains, we followed Mrs. Fisher across oceans and continents, we admired her wit, intelligence, and fierce independence, and no doubt we discovered through her experience that "there is a communion of much more than our bodies when bread is broken and wine drunk." In her first book, *Serve It Forth*, we read about the art of dining alone, we were challenged to eat bananas with Limburger, and we studied carefully the components of the ideal kitchen. In *Consider the Oyster*, we tested a recipe for oyster catsup, while in *How to Cook a Wolf*, we learned how to prepare tasty dishes even under the shadow of war rationing and poverty.

We laughed at Mrs. Fisher while she strove to get her fill of caviar in *The Gastronomical Me*, but we shared her pain and heartbreak when she and the dying man she loved sipped champagne and talked slowly on the final voyage of the *Normandie*. *An Alphabet for Gourmets* taught us how to train a child's palate correctly, why salad should indeed be eaten before the main course, what the perfect meal should involve, how to drink Martinis, and so much more.

We admired her brilliant translation of Brillat-Savarin's *La Physiologie du Goût*, and how proud we all felt in the late sixties when this great American lady was chosen to write *The Cooking of Provincial France* for the Time-Life food series.

Today M. F. K. Fisher lives alone on a ranch in Sonoma County, California, one of the greatest wine-producing areas of the world. Having been invited to lunch, I ignored the sign warning that trespassers would be prosecuted, proceeded to drive through lush green countryside redolent of eucalyptus, and eventually arrived at exactly the type of unconventional but stylish home in which you would expect to find Mary Frances Kennedy Fisher.

Outside is a small porch filled with wine bottles, baskets of fruit ripening, pots of flowers, boxes of books and papers, and various bric-a-brac awaiting delivery to neighbors. Inside is a large bathroom with paintings and mementos covering the walls, a larger second room that doubles as bedroom and study, and a magnificent redwood-beamed third room that serves as kitchen, dining room, library, workroom, or simply an area where one could sit for hours in undisturbed tranquillity before an open fire and gaze out at the pastoral setting. There is no television set, only a 1940s-vintage record player perched atop a well-stocked liquor cabinet, and a slim cat named Charlie whose beckonings always draw Mrs. Fisher's undivided attention.

The kitchen is practical, but nowhere in sight is there a food processor or wok or any other fashionable equipment now considered essential to an up-to-date kitchen. What you see instead on the counters are a few time-proved cooking vessels and utensils, bowls of ripe fruit, fresh vegetables, a bin of homemade cookies, loaves of fresh Sonoma sourdough bread, and a few bottles of wine. The house is livable and comfortable, and above all, it seems right.

After preparing a gin and tonic for me and a white vermouth for herself, Mrs. Fisher sank down in the corner of a deep old sofa, took Charlie into her lap, and, looking every bit the sensuous individual she is, began discussing her fascinating life and her views on food. From time to time she'd move over to the kitchen to work on lunch, and at one point she stopped to answer the phone and give a neighbor a little heated advice on what to do with kumquats. Her attitude was generous and her interest clearly genuine.

And the lunch? Oh, nothing really fancy: a few large Mexican prawns marinated in oyster sauce, baked quickly and served on a bed of duxelles; sliced plum tomatoes and zucchini topped with mild chilies; fresh sourdough bread with individual crocks of the sweetest butter; baked pears with fresh cream; and a carafe of Chablis from a local winery. No, nothing fancy, just one of the best-prepared and most-memorable meals of my life.

Since M. F. K. Fisher's life and career have always involved radical and complex changes, it's not that easy to draw out of her definitive responses to subjects that today might require a totally different approach than they would have thirty or forty years ago. Throughout our conversation, I was constantly reminded that her present opinions on certain topics might be totally contradictory to what she once said or believed or wrote, but, she emphasized, "that's what learning is all about, and I've never stopped learning." I suppose what is so interesting is that, although many of the questions I asked were inspired by what I'd read in Mrs. Fisher's books, never once was I able to anticipate a certain answer, and at times I was completely surprised by what she had to say.


J. V.: When did you develop such an intense interest in food?
M. F. K. F.: I'd guess I first became interested in the relationship between digestion and emotions in about 1914—when I was five or six years old. As a child I was always exposed to and aware of good food in the family. We

never ate anything but homemade breads, the freshest vegetables, and real butter. Of course my grandmother was totally dedicated to gastric interests, and although she always considered things like French sauces immoral, she had a great influence on me.

[As the author talked, I couldn't help recalling from *The Gastronomical Me* how her grandmother would discourse at table on the virtues of "plain good food," then proceed to belch voluptuously in reaction to Ora's (the cook's) inventive dishes. What she said of her childhood also reminded me of something else important she'd once written: "I was very young, but I can remember observing, privately of course, that meat hashed with a knife is better than meat mauled in a food chopper; that freshly minced herbs make almost any good things better; that chopped celery tastes different from celery in the stalk, just as carrots in thin curls and toast in crescents are infinitely more appetizing than in thick chunks and squares."]

J. V.: How did you begin to write about food?

M. F. K. F.: It all came very naturally since, after all, I really didn't have anything else to write about. But, specifically, I suppose it happened one day in Los Angeles when, while awaiting my first husband, Al Fisher, to finish his teaching day, I went to the public library and was fascinated by the smell of an old book of Elizabethan recipes a man was reading. Well, when he left the book on the table, I began to absorb every page. Later I wrote about those recipes simply to amuse my husband and our friends, just as to this day I write books for myself. Actually I've never written with the idea of publishing. I produce a book simply because I want to.

[And, indeed, there is almost no cuisine, be it Elizabethan, Byzantine, or Ancient Roman, that M. F. K. Fisher has not investigated with the same keen interest that others express only in something like French cooking. Who, for example, but this extraordinary lady would not only have written with honest curiosity about an unsavory Roman seasoning called *garum* but actually produced a recipe: "Place in a vessel all the insides of fish, both large fish and small. Salt them well. Expose them to the air until they are completely putrid. In a short time a liquid is produced. Drain this off." Unappetizing? Perhaps so, but Fisher always has her reasons: "Romans used *garum* not as a condiment in itself but combined with a startling variety of spices. . . . Almost every known savour except parsley, which they wore in garlands on their heads, made the simplest banquet dish a mess of inextricable flavours."]

J. V.: How do you feel about being referred to as the grande dame of gastronomy?

M. F. K. F.: I haven't the faintest idea why anyone would call me that. I haven't said anything about food that hasn't been said a dozen times before. I guess since I didn't split infinitives people thought I just wrote better than others.

J. V.: You have said you don't write cookbooks, only books about food. Yet certainly you know food and cook it well, and readers cook from your recipes. How exactly do you make that distinction?

M. F. K. F.: For me there's always been so much more to food and cooking than just recipes or specific ways of preparing certain dishes. No doubt a good cookbook has its place in any kitchen, but I feel that if what I cook and eat doesn't relate somehow to my emotional and intellectual life, then something's wrong. When I compose a recipe, there's always some reason why, some personal inspiration that causes me to want to pass along a dish I enjoyed. If others care to try it, fine.

J. V.: What do you consider five basic cookbooks?

M. F. K. F.: Certainly *Fannie Farmer* and Mrs. Rombauer's *Joy of Cooking* —which I still consider my bible. Then I'd have to say Julia Child, the *Larousse Gastronomique,* and always Escoffier.

[Quickly I glanced over at a small book shelf in the kitchen. Mrs. Fisher must have hundreds and hundreds of cookbooks amidst the large library that covers much of the wall space in both rooms, but sure enough, within easy reaching distance in the kitchen are the titles she mentioned, plus, of course, a handsome leather-bound edition of *The Art of Eating.*]

J. V.: You once wrote that "Gastronomical precepts are perhaps among the most delicate ones in the modern arts. They must, in the main, be followed before they can be broken." Can you expand on that statement?

M. F. K. F.: It's very simple: We must respect the work of those innovators who spent their lives analyzing and interpreting the subtleties of preparing food. Sure, it's fine to experiment and create, but there are certain basics which must always serve as a foundation for new methods and ideas. Take, for example, the *nouvelle cuisine française.* The entire trend toward lightness and simplicity is no more than an extension of a few basic principles established by Escoffier more than a half-century ago.

J. V.: Your book *A Considerable Town* revolves around Marseille. Where in the world would you most like to be living now? Is it here in Sonoma?

M. F. K. F.: No. If I were able I'd like to live in Aix-en-Provence, which is near Marseille. I first went there in 1929 and have loved it ever since, most likely because it is so close to that dirty, mysterious port town. I wrote the book on Marseille in an attempt to explain to myself this inordinate attraction I've always had to the place.

[Suddenly M. F. K. Fisher's blue eyes became fixed on the flames quietly lapping the small logs in the fireplace, and I tried to imagine to just what point in the far distant past my question had forced her to retreat momentarily. Perhaps she was thinking about the time she, Al, and her sister Norah (who now lives down the road and is still one of her closest companions) sat in a small restaurant overlooking the Old Port in Marseille, played an accordion, and shared a steaming bouillabaisse. Or maybe the vision went back further, to the whorehouse in Marseille where she and Al innocently booked a room and spent the evening eating fresh cherries. Or, who knows, she could have been remembering the old butcher, César, whom every woman in town thought to be the devil himself but who once prepared the best steak she'd ever eaten.]

J. V.: How is your health?

M. F. K. F.: Pretty good, I suppose. Of course I have a horrible liver, but I really can't help that and have no intention of doing anything about it.

J. V.: Do you diet?

M. F. K. F.: No, never. I eat and drink exactly what I like.

J. V.: What do you prepare at home for breakfast, and how do you feel about breakfast?

M. F. K. F.: I don't eat breakfast, never have ever since as a child I was forced to eat my grandmother's boiled oatmeal every single morning. But even though I personally don't like this meal, I can't help but feel it's good for most people.

J. V.: How do you feel about drinking cocktails before a fine meal? Would you frown upon a good Martini or Manhattan?

M. F. K. F.: Of course not. Who's to tell anybody he or she shouldn't take a drink? I love a good Martini or Gibson before a meal, though I should say that I personally never mix gin and red wine. But if a well-prepared cocktail makes you feel good and stimulates the appetite, well, why not?

[When my hostess asked if I'd like my gin and tonic freshened, I was almost tempted to say that what I'd really like is a Martini prepared by this sybarite, who once wrote that "a well-made dry Martini or Gibson, correctly chilled and nicely served, has been more often my true friend than any two-legged creature." But I held back since it was the middle of the day, once again chuckling to myself when I thought what today's mineral-water-apéritif purists might say to Mrs. Fisher's very sensible reasons for loving and respecting this sinful libation: "It is as warming as a hearthfire in December, as stimulating as a good review by my favorite critic of a book I have published into a seeming void, as exciting as a thorough buss I have yearned for from a man I didn't even suspect *suspected* me."]

J. V.: What do you drink with your meals?

M. F. K. F.: Generally wine. I love beer with food, but the wine here in the valley is now so superb I'm in the habit of drinking it most of the time. As for the fashionable vogue of drinking mineral water with meals, it's not for me. Before or after a meal, but not during.

J. V.: Have you ever had your fill of caviar?

M. F. K. F.: Never!

J. V.: Do you enjoy a good hamburger as much as a well-made steak tartare?

M. F. K. F.: I certainly do. And a good hamburger is hard to find these days.

[M. F. K. Fisher's recipe? Here it is with her typical concern for detail and, believe me, the burger's great—the very antithesis of those concoctions called "Rite-Spot Specials" she ate as a child and which now "make me gag":

>1½ to 2 pounds best sirloin, trimmed of fat and coarsely chopped
>1 cup red table wine
>3 or 4 tablespoons butter
>1 cup mixed chopped onion, parsley, green pepper, herbs, each according to taste
>¼ cup oyster sauce

Shape the meat firmly into four round patties at least 1½ inches thick. Have the skillet very hot. Sear the meat (very smoky procedure) on both sides and remove at once to a hot buttered platter, where the meat will continue to heat through. (Extend the searing time if rare meat is not wanted.) Remove the skillet from the fire. When it is slightly cooled, put the wine and butter in and swirl, to collect what Brillat-Savarin would have called the "osmazone." Return to the heat and toss in the chopped ingredients, and cover closely. Turn off the heat as soon as these begin to hiss. Remove from the stove, take off the cover, add oyster sauce, swirl once more, and pour over the hot meat. Serve at once, since the heat contained in the sauce and the patties continues the cooking process.]

J. V.: Do you follow the seasons when planning your menus?

M. F. K. F.: Yes, I try, but I must say that "following the seasons" doesn't mean today what it once meant. Now so much is picked green, put into controlled rooms with all these mirrors and lights, injected with chemicals and colorings, and sprayed with God knows what-all. It's horrible. And I don't see much hope for improvement. But those willing to make the effort can still find naturally grown vegetables and fruits, picked in the morning, purchased at noon, and eaten in the evening.

J. V.: Have you ever needed to use canned or frozen foods?

M. F. K. F.: Sure, and my freezer and "emergency shelf" are full of them. Some of the frozen products are quite good. As for the canned, I use them only when forced by necessity, and, of course, I'd never serve something like canned peas to guests.

J. V.: What are your favorite time-saving machines in the kitchen?

M. F. K. F.: I have two machines in this house: a blender and a toaster that doesn't work. People are always surprised that I don't own a food processor. Well, I don't and have no desire to get one. Don't get me wrong. We live in a machine age, and if a food processor can serve to inspire people to cook, fine. But I personally don't want to have to push another button; I love cooking too much.

J. V.: What is the biggest cooking emergency you ever had, and how did you solve it?

M. F. K. F.: Probably when the electricity here went off for eight straight days and nights. But I had my "emergency shelf" full of canned goods and homemade pickles and preserves, and I wouldn't be caught dead without a chafing dish in the house.

J. V.: Is there any food that you hate?

M. F. K. F.: No, though there are some I don't like particularly: parsnips, turnips, even broccoli.

[I didn't have the nerve to ask Mrs. Fisher if, as she suggested in *An Alphabet for Gourmets,* she still had the desire to taste elephant meat, crocodile, white termites, and roasted locusts basted in camel butter. Knowing her, however, she probably sampled each and every one of those delicacies somewhere along the way and savored them with the same curiosity she had when she ate her first oyster and fillet of wild boar. "I have always believed," she wrote, "that I would like to taste everything once, never from such hunger as made friends of mine in France in 1942 eat guinea-pig ragout, but from pure gourmandism."]

J. V.: Can anyone learn to cook? Where does a novice begin?

M. F. K. F.: I hate to say this, but some people will simply never learn even how to put a pat of butter in a skillet, no matter how hard they try. Cooking involves an instinct based on some complex communication between the brain and the body, and as with any fine art it's not something you can master automatically. Just recently, for instance, I was talking with Jim Beard, who told me that out of a class of thirty students, he had exactly one who showed great promise.

J. V.: You have publicly aired your disdain for the trend toward posh cooking courses. What should a student looking for a cooking class use as a criterion for selection?

M. F. K. F.: Generally I don't have much faith in cooking classes. I never took any myself. Essentially, if you really want to cook, just get a good cookbook like *Joy of Cooking* and start.

J. V.: How do you feel about women professional chefs? Do you think they are progressing?

M. F. K. F.: Yes, indeed they are. And with encouragement from societies like the Dames d'Escoffier in New York, things will get better and better. The idea that no woman can stand the heat and weight on her feet is absurd. If she can't, she'll drop out, just as a man would in those circumstances.

J. V.: What do you think of restaurant cooking in the U.S.? Of restaurants in general, as opposed to those in, say, France?

M. F. K. F.: I take a pretty dim view, for the overall situation seems to be deteriorating. First, there seems to be more and more precooked food being served, even in the finest restaurants. Second, neither chefs nor waiters have much training now, much less pride in their work. Very few have the faintest conception of what their counterparts in Europe go through. It's really two different worlds.

J. V.: Is there much hope for improvement in this country?

M. F. K. F.: Not in the sense you're referring to. We have regional cooking —often superb. We do not, and perhaps cannot, have "American" cuisine because of the country's size. We are just too big, too vast and stretched-out, to enable a cuisine such as the one in France to develop. A chef in New Mexico, for example, who tries to satisfy the demands of a man from Minnesota is up against a real challenge. And how do you think the manners and dress of someone from Texas are going to go over in a posh Manhattan restaurant? These things create terrible emotional friction among human beings, and this all has some bearing on the development of our cookery and eating habits. Within the various regions of the U.S., however, there is tremendous room for improvement, and I definitely think there are exciting things happening with our regional cuisines.

[Never letting up for air while giving me examples of what all she felt could be accomplished in the way of regional American cookery, M. F. K. Fisher moved into the kitchen and signaled me to join her. "Lovely, aren't they?" she said with a smile, lifting a large prawn from its bath of oyster sauce. She then gingerly spread out a layer of duxelles on the bottom of a baking dish, artistically arranged the prawns on top, and placed the already seasoned dish in the oven. "If they overcook," she said, "it's your fault since you've got me talking so!"]

J. V.: Who are the most influential food persons in the world today?

M. F. K. F.: Bocuse, Guérard, and the whole school of la nouvelle cuisine française are of course having a tremendous impact on food and cooking everywhere, and I'm all for what they're trying to accomplish. In this country, though, I'd have to say Julia Child and James Beard, mainly because they've created such a widespread interest in food and shown people how to deal with the subject intelligently. As for most food writers I read in magazines, they don't seem to have too much of importance to say.

J. V.: Do you see anything redeeming in today's fast foods?

M. F. K. F.: Nothing, absolutely nothing.

J. V.: Recently I heard a prediction that by the year 2000 there would be no home cooking. Do you think home cooking could disappear?

M. F. K. F.: No doubt with the power of Big Mac and Colonel Sanders and Roy Rogers the odds are pretty rough, but I refuse to believe the situation is hopeless. Out there in America there are mothers who still care and youngsters who are eating properly. Here in the Sonoma Valley I see young people growing their own food and making their own bread. And, of course, the American people seem to be demanding so much more and, with exposure, choosing more wisely what they put in their stomachs. No, I refuse to despair.

J. V.: When all is said and done, how important is fine food in the great scheme of life? What does a preoccupation with food contribute to the creative experience?

M. F. K. F.: I can only repeat what I've said for many years: Since we're forced to nourish ourselves, why not do it with all possible skill, delicacy, and ever-increasing enjoyment? I just can't help but feel that a sensible approach to how we satisfy the hunger of the stomach has a direct connection with those other two important needs: security and love. The three are so related we can't think of one without the others, and not until we acknowledge this fact can we possibly begin to understand something about what can be accomplished in this life.

Driving back to San Francisco, I had a strong feeling that M. F. K. Fisher is indeed a person who has managed, through her generosity, truthfulness, and hard work, not only to satisfy many hungers but also to accomplish a good deal more than most of us can ever hope for. Just as I was leaving the small ranch house, she informed me that after attending a dinner in New York given in her honor by the Dames d'Escoffier, she and her sister Norah would continue straight on to Aix-en-Provence. No doubt the first evening these two headed for Marseille—most certainly to find an unpretentious restaurant overlooking the Old Port, and order a steaming bouillabaisse like the one they shared with Al back in '32. I'd like to think they toasted their survival with glasses of fresh local wine.

## POSTSCRIPT

I'm very proud of this profile, not only because I consider M. F. K. Fisher the most important and relevant American food writer of this century but also because this was the first interview she had granted for many years. Although now well into her twilight years, Mary Frances is still as astute, original, and trenchant as ever, a true professional whose ideas and refined style of expression represent standards every food journalist would do well to emulate. After disgracefully being out of print for so long, most of her classic works are now once again available, providing intelligent and refreshing counterpoint to the embarrassing number of shoddy cookbooks and illiterate food articles that plague today's market. James Beard is gone, and when M. F. K. Fisher follows to join her old friend at that celestial banquet table, a void will exist in the food world that we can only pray may one day be filled.

# CRAIG CLAIBORNE:
# SOPHISTICATE IN
# SHIRT SLEEVES

*Unpublished*

I remember first meeting Craig Claiborne back in the early seventies at a very fancy reception in the Riviera Lounge aboard the S.S. *France* while the ship was docked in New York. He didn't know me from Adam, but already he was the most influential food writer and restaurant critic in America, and I was determined to introduce myself as a fellow southerner who shared his passion for all things gastronomic. As we tried to chat—mainly about our rebel backgrounds, mutual acquaintances in North Carolina and Mississippi, and reasons for abandoning our native regions—people kept interrupting: newspaper columnists who wanted a statement from Craig about the ship (he had just recently proclaimed the first-class dining saloon on the *France* the greatest restaurant in the world), photographers asking him to pose, waiters insisting he sample still another delicacy they were passing, fans eager to compliment him on so-and-so article or book or restaurant review. Suddenly, Craig turned to me. "Good God," he whispered, "I just can't take this anymore. What would you say to slipping out of here and going somewhere for a good Martini and club sandwich?" Which we did.

Suffice it to say that, since that initial episode almost twenty years ago, Craig and I have slipped away for many a Martini, club sandwich, and just about every other type of libation and dish imaginable. Together, we've closed many a bar and restaurant, judged great and mediocre food at numerous March of Dimes Gourmet Galas around the country, and, since our houses in East Hampton on Long Island are only one mile apart, entertained multitudes of friends and colleagues. What we have *never* done, however—and what really stuns others when I relate the fact—is "discuss" food the way food writers are supposed to do. Yes, from time to time while researching an article, I might call Craig to ask if I can use his incredible library, or he might call me to verify some fact or another, or one may call the other for a certain recipe. But the idea of analyzing every dish in a restaurant (for Craig, a dish is simply good or bad), discoursing on the merits and failures of a chef, or describing orally what he and his celebrated colleague, Pierre Franey, are creating in the East Hampton test kitchen for columns in the *New York Times* is about as foreign and distasteful to Craig's nature as undertaking a press trip with a bunch of other food journalists. Some might consider Craig a snob, others find him merely timid, but I've always known and understood him as a very complex gentleman who prefers as much privacy in his work as in his life, who refuses to wear his lofty reputation on his sleeve, and who maintains a sense of mission that is virtually unknown to most others in his field.

"All I've ever done is try to take the hocus-pocus out of cooking" is about the only comment I've ever heard Craig Claiborne make to define his career. And, needless to say, that is far too simple an explanation for a body of work that began basically when a young boy in Sunflower, Mississippi, was first shown at his mother's boardinghouse how to make biscuits. Now we take it as a matter of fact that the entire nation is consumed by an interest in gastronomy, but back in the fifties Craig was a true pioneer in the movement that has made cooking—indeed, the whole subject of food —a social phenomenon in this country. From the moment he invaded the "Women's Page" of the *Times,* food journalism assumed new meaning as suddenly his readership, male and female alike, found themselves in aprons, cooking their way around the world with Craig. The dishes he presented were glorious, the recipes were outlined in simple steps, the directions were clear and to the point, the measurements were precise. His following knew that he could be trusted to guide them well, so they diced and blended, sautéed and clarified their way to successful dishes that changed the look of the American table forever.

At the *Times,* Craig also set a standard for the restaurant critic that remains as valid today as a quarter century ago. During an era when fine restaurants were relatively few in number and when, for the average American, they were a "special occasion" treat, he encouraged people to go out regularly for meals. He portrayed the dining experience in depth; he sketched the guidelines with clarity; and he demanded that we learn to develop our own critical senses. Moreover, he did not damn restaurants out of any inflated investment of power, and, in fact, it was the weight of that very power that he ultimately found so unbearable that he relinquished the responsibility. When an establishment missed the mark, Craig (an accomplished chef in his own right) knew and explained *why,* illustrating a point of view that could only come from a man with the technical skill, ability, and taste to do the job correctly. A sauce was not criticized simply because he didn't like the flavor but because the flavor and possibly the texture were wrong. And indeed Craig would have been able to go into the kitchen and prepare the perfect sauce himself.

Craig has always taken his responsibility to the public very seriously, and anyone who is witness to the creative process in the kitchen (Craig at the typewriter, Pierre Franey at the range) senses immediately that these are men hard on the job. In spite of the country music or Verdi that might be blaring in the background, there is no nonsense, no idle chatter, for all the energy in the room is focused intensely on producing a dish that is correct, a recipe that works, a food concept made comprehensible and exciting. Once, when I arrived and stupidly burst through the door to show Craig an exceptional country ham I'd just received, he glanced up from the typewriter, smiled politely, and said, "Please, not now, we're having problems with a leek measurement, and if I lose my concentration, the recipe could turn out a mess." I never interrupted the two again.

Craig approaches all his life and work with a rare combination of enthusiasm and precision, throwing himself headlong into a project but never allowing a single detail to escape his eye. Whether shaping a succinct phrase or laying an impeccable table, his method is at once spontaneous and orderly. He is, in other words, a southerner to the core, one who always entertains a new idea with a bit of skepticism, one whose excitement is never without a hint of doubt, one who dreams in the delta gloom. For good or ill, we all carry the baggage of our past along with us into the present, and no one typifies this truth like Craig. At a point in his life when he is held in highest esteem by the world, he is not content to isolate himself, contrary to what some might think. Yes, Craig is a very private person, but he's also forever an old-fashioned, homespun son of the South endowed with a natural graciousness that extends to friends and public alike. An acquaintance with a problem will find understanding with Craig; an aspiring talent will find a mentor and champion; and even a sincere stranger, a fan, might be received in the East Hampton kitchen and given advice on the placement of a range or chopping block. But approach Craig with the slightest suggestion of sham or deceit, present him with sloppy work or with a disregard for the precision he values so highly, and you will be met with a severity and harshness that are belied by his usual cheerful, almost impish demeanor.

For all the great fame that Craig has achieved through his many articles and cookbooks, he's never taken that success for granted. Harshly schooled in the Protestant work ethic, he is an industrious professional whose job is his life, and to quit, to coast, to cut corners would be unthinkable. To the world, Craig Claiborne would seem the ultimate sophisticate, yet he has somehow preserved in himself an innocence that allows him to look on the universe with an ever-renewed sense of wonder, with the eye of the inquisitive, restless child poking about in every corner of the globe for a new taste experience, picking, nibbling, savoring, studying. He astounds and outrages by the lengths to which he'll go in his exhaustive research. Once, in Brazil, he traveled a thousand miles out of the way just to sample one dish; another time, he and Pierre Franey evoked the wrath of not only thousands of *Times* readers but also the Vatican itself by spending $4,000 for a single dinner in Paris that they had won through a TV auction; and, on still another occasion, Craig thought nothing of journeying through the war zone of Vietnam to learn about the country's cuisine. He leads us on an adventurous culinary trek; he chronicles the life of man through the food he consumes; he reports our gastronomic history; and, indeed, his is a scholarly and fascinating work.

I suppose what I admire most about Craig is that, despite his exalted position in the food world, he remains, quite simply, a man in shirt sleeves, one who tells us what we need to know in a comfortable, easy manner, a dear friend who can still find as much virtue in a Martini and a club sandwich as in a vintage Champagne and his beloved *coulibiac* of salmon. If James Beard and Pearl Byrd Foster encouraged me to champion our wonderful American cookery, and Julia Child showed me how to play at being a French chef, then it is Craig who, along with M. F. K. Fisher, has taught me that there's a great deal more to nurturing the body and palate than picking up a knife and fork.

# JOVAN THE OMNIPOTENT

1982

A t Les Nomades on a sunny afternoon in Chicago, Jovan Trboyevic
stands at military attention in the center of his private dining club's
small first-floor salon, surrounded by only a few friends, dignitaries, and
members of the press. As they fall silent, the consul general of France steps
forward, withdraws from his pocket a gold medal attached to a colorful
ribbon, and delivers his succinct, formal address to the stout Yugoslav:
"Jovan Trboyevic, over the years you have brought a mood of friendship to
Chicago and the United States, a spirit of joy, good taste, and deep generosity. Above all, you have stood as a representative of the highest quality in
your profession. Therefore, in the name of the French government, I have
the honor of making you a Chevalier of the Mérite Agricole." As the consul
pins the medal on the recipient's left lapel, discreet applause breaks out
and Jovan cracks a quick smile. He is obviously proud and, at least for a
moment, happy.

The following day, Chicago's gastronomic arbiter—and the most important restaurateur in the United States since Henri Soulé—is more typically
on the verge of still another rage. At Le Perroquet, the more famous
restaurant that he created in the early seventies and sold to his maître
d'hôtel in the early eighties, and where he still lunches with some regular-
ity, Jovan arranges his massive bulk on a red velvet banquette, fixes his
wrists firmly against the edge of the table, and prepares to share with me

two luscious *paupiettes* of sole stuffed with salmon and periwinkles, along with a rare bottle of Meursault '28 that we both know cannot be in very good condition. I know that forbidding look: pallid skin, arched half-eyebrows, distended veins, Serbian eyes black as truffles, and an overall facial tension that betrays frustration and too little sleep. The tranquil, elegant room is still full of well-heeled, knowledgeable, relaxed customers, the same stylish breed I served some years ago as an undercover captain in order to experience life behind the scenes in a great French restaurant. There's no tinkle of glass and china here, no clanging of silver, no noticeable conversation among the polite and talented black-tied waiters and captains, who fastidiously whisk things off tables and help one another prepare the extraordinary dishes at various serving stations. The room still functions just as it did when Jovan was in control—like clockwork.

"You know, this is still a great restaurant, but I'm really glad I'm no longer running the place," whispers Jovan in familiar fashion, thrusting his chin downward just far enough to cause the neck flesh to fold in duplicate and compulsively grabbing one of the lapels of his handsome, dark-blue suit. "I mean, look, just look at that waiter working the floor, nose already to the ceiling as if he owned half the place. And did you see that character I was bawling out when you came in? Well, he used to pester me for months to buy his lesser Bordeaux, then would say he couldn't deliver on a steady basis. Then, these strangers would try to push over on me some shark, saying it was swordfish. Shark for swordfish! Can you imagine? Parvenus! I'm still confronted constantly by parvenus and amateurs who have no conception of what I'm trying to accomplish or maintain. Then you food journalists come in and try to find fault. Always these minute irritations. Yes, I'm glad I sold out, and maybe I should sell Nomades, too. I'm bored. Now tell me, how was the flight? You didn't eat *that* food?"

Of course I've heard all this from him many times before: how the press (especially in Chicago) doesn't understand Jovan and is out to destroy him; how others are always trying to steal his chefs and imitate his dishes; how difficult it is to get the very finest ingredients; and how he should just give it all up, leave Chicago, and spend his golden years wandering the globe. Fortunately, not one of the Perroquet customers tucking away crayfish mousse with lobster sauce, preserved duck leg, and veal fricassee with sorrel would so much as suspect the eruptive tensions gnawing away at this gracious, respected host, whom most still know simply as Jovan and who jumps up periodically to say hello to old friends and customers he's likely to greet that evening at Les Nomades. I, on the other hand, having had occasion to associate with the man in Chicago as well as other locales about the globe, am totally accustomed to his forthrightness and these cushioned tirades. A perfectionist who has always refused to bow to any form of mediocrity or to compromise his principles, Jovan's harmless outbursts are characteristic of his restless, complex nature. Yes, I suppose you could say I know Jovan, though it's certain I'll never really know him. No one will. For many friends and enemies alike—all aware of the publicity about his international honors and awards, his reputation for booting undesirable customers out of Le Perroquet, and his decision a few years back to open Les Nomades as a private bistro where only he and the people he likes can eat, drink, and be happy together—Jovan remains an enigma.

For years I've been asked to take a stand on what I consider to be the finest French restaurant in the United States, and for years I've hesitated, haunted by delicious evenings at La Caravelle and Le Cirque in New York, Ernie's in San Francisco, Jean-Pierre in Washington, D.C., and Le Bec-Fin in Philadelphia. But now I'm convinced thoroughly not only that Les Nomades is in a class by itself but that Jovan Trboyevic is the legitimate heir to the standard of excellence and integrity established years ago at Le Pavillon in New York by Henri Soulé. Needless to say, any highly respected restaurant is the reflection of its owner's incorruptible values, tastes, and convictions. This maxim, proven by Soulé in the fifties and sixties, was later affirmed by such rare individuals as Robert Meyzen and Leon Lianides at La Caravelle and The Coach House respectively in New York, Ella Brennan at Commander's Palace in New Orleans, the Gotti brothers at Ernie's in San Francisco, and Tony Vallone at Tony's in Houston. But, to attain true legendary status, a restaurateur must stand as the greatest innovator of his time and must also fuse his own personal conception of quality so intimately with the restaurant itself that the two assume the same identity. Le Pavillon was Soulé, and when he died in 1966, there was no way his citadel could survive for long. By the same token, if Jovan Trboyevic was ever to stop battling his demons, still another sacred philosophy of fine dining would be no more than a memory for those who truly love and respect distinguished restaurants.

Jovan is over sixty, and his fascinating life story could easily provide the makings of a full-length adventure novel or film. He was the son of a prosperous Yugoslav lawyer and landowner. His youth was cut short by World War II. He became a member of a naval crew that took over a submarine for the purpose of joining the British fleet; he parachuted back into his occupied country and managed to escape the Germans; he served as a French spy for British and American intelligence; he journeyed from Crete to Egypt to northern Italy; and eventually, because of political developments, he abandoned all hope of ever returning home. "At the end of the war," he once told me with his deep sense of melancholy, "I was completely on my own in Paris, lost, without family or a country or any credible idea of what the past meant or the future held. Like so many others of that generation, I was forced to learn early about life and survive by my wits."

The nomadic Jovan drifted between odd jobs, studied political science and economics in Geneva, and found himself increasingly in the upper social circles of Europe. In Vevey, Switzerland, he met a wealthy, aristocratic English lady, who not only invited him to her fashionable salons and teas but also arranged for the intelligent, multilingual young man to enroll at the famous hotel school in Lausanne. "I hated the place," says Jovan with his slight, indefinable accent, "but I respected the discipline, and they taught me basics." Afterward, his credentials opened the way to India, Ceylon, France, Germany, and the great luxury liners of the sea. "All I really had to offer was my linguistic ability and my knowledge of food and restaurants, but those served as my passport till I was thirty-five years old."

Still a man of strong political awareness in 1955 ("Today I guess you could just call me a political libertarian"), Jovan arrived in Washington, D.C., to work for the CIA. Soon disillusioned with government, however, and forever restless, he accepted an offer to serve as maître d'hôtel at the well-known Jacques's French restaurant in Chicago. Then it was back to New York, first with Restaurant Associates in Manhattan ("I just couldn't take the bureaucracy"), next as a captain at Sardi's ("where they insisted on calling me Ivan"), and "21," and finally as the owner of his first restaurant, in the town of Larchmont ("Not a bad place, but I got fed up with all the boozy weekenders from Manhattan"). The next two years were spent at sea amid the dining splendor of the *Constitution, Independence,* and *Excalibur,* followed by stints at other restaurants in Los Angeles, New York, and Washington. Plans to open a restaurant in the early sixties for the Gaslight Club back in Chicago fell through, but the peripatetic Serb, now a little weary, decided to stay and open a small, elegant restaurant called Jovan's. "The whole concept was new to Chicago restaurant-goers: no regular menu, fixed-price dinners that changed daily, and innovative French food at reasonable cost. The place was so successful that after ten years I got bored, sold out, and moved on to develop Le Perroquet—so named, by the way, for the simple reason that I've always been fascinated by parrots."

Jovan knew from the very start exactly what he wanted to accomplish at Le Perroquet. With the help of an extraordinary, attractive artist named Maggie Abbott, who originally decorated the restaurant and later became his wife ("and only stability"), he transformed the third floor of a small office building off Michigan Avenue into "a luxurious but discreet operation without gimmicks." Little has changed there since 1972, even under the new ownership of Jean-Pierre Nespoux and his brother Gérard: the almost invisible name plaque at street level; the controversial off-duty cop who checks your name on a reservation list before sending you up in a miniature elevator; the soft lighting, ecru draperies, colorful murals, velvet banquettes, and small silk-shaded lamps on each of the twenty-four tables; the crystal animals that serve as sugar bowls, millefiore glass vases filled with nosegays, unopened bottles of mineral water; and, of course, the magnificent frosted-glass room dividers and Lalique vases overflowing with fresh flowers. Le Perroquet, much like the dining room of a great luxury liner, was conceived to be very proper without being stuffy, a tailored, comfortable restaurant that would mirror the impeccable taste, dignity, and absolute civility of the owner and his wife.

To analyze the cuisine Jovan supervised in the kitchen at Perroquet would be to attempt to relate what balanced food textures, taste harmonies, true precision in cooking, and, indeed, inspired imagination are all about. At other restaurants, the captain will stand there with pad in hand, jot down whatever you order, and walk away; at Perroquet he was trained from the start to discuss, suggest, discourage, and explain. A cauliflower mousse with sea scallops in lobster sauce should not be followed by medallions of swordfish with periwinkles in still another cream-based sauce. A preserved goose leg with sliced breast after an equally rich suckling-pig pâté? Never. But an elusive terrine of crayfish with a feathery, uncomplicated cucumber sauce before a bold veal chop stuffed with vegetables, sweetbreads, brains, pistachios, and herbs, and sauced with reduced apple-lemon veal stock, both consumed with a fine white French burgundy or California chardonnay? Perfect. Textures were weighed, colors were balanced, flavors were measured. Jovan understood the chemistry of eating.

By and large, the food was (and still is) very light, even those items that, by nature, could come off heavy as lead: *confit d'oie,* roast duck with green peppercorn sauce, fricassee of veal with sorrel on noodles. But in contrast to all the pseudo-nouvelle haunts about the country, there was never any such thing as a *menu de dégustation,* whereby you're served six or seven different miniature courses just to taste. "That's what I call *dim sum* dining," says the irritated Serb, "and I was running a serious French restaurant." On and on the dishes were created, changed, modified, refined. One night a homemade ravioli was stuffed with cream cheese and smoked salmon, the next with sea urchins or wild mushrooms, the next with spinach or salmon caviar. There were delicate mousses made with every vegetable and seafood imaginable, airy main-course soufflés containing mussels, mushrooms, and goat cheese, and every flavor of sorbet from hazelnut to rhubarb to boysenberry. Even the brand of mineral water varied from time to time. "We didn't like boring ourselves or our regular customers," says Jovan. "A restaurant that can't surprise, one that can't provide dishes you wouldn't prepare at home, would do just as well to use a good caterer."

To provide what Jovan refers to obsessively as "customer protection," he would risk constant harassment, loss of clients and friends, and even nasty lawsuits. At Le Perroquet he demanded not only reservations but also confirmations; he tolerated no man without a necktie, no babies, no large groups, no table hopping, no cigar smoking, no special food requests, no boisterous behavior—nothing, in fact, that might have interfered with the smooth operation of the restaurant or affected the comfort and dignity of his guests. One day a customer who had openly insulted the veteran maître d'hôtel, Jean-Pierre, refused to leave the restaurant when told he wouldn't be served. Jovan coolly called the police and, unbeknown to other guests, handled the matter in the back office. On another occasion, a couple brought their eleven-month-old baby in for a birthday party, only to have the owner turn them back toward the elevator ("Can you believe the guy brought suit, claiming the incident had caused the child 'mental duress'!"). When a party of architects once spread a set of blueprints across their table and commenced to get drunk on Martinis, I witnessed Jovan quietly but sternly inform them there would be no check but that they'd have to leave. Pity any fool who ever failed to show up without canceling the reservation ("white-collar vandalism" in Jovan's terminology) and called again later to book a table. "You know, it's not so much food as people that can destroy a dining occasion," I've heard him say more than once, "and I'm simply trying to minimize that possibility for the vast majority of guests who respect what we stand for. Look, the food at a restaurant can be beyond reproach, but if you have to wait at the bar or listen to a lot of noise or stare at a bunch of poorly dressed people—well, there's no way that evening is going to turn out well. Sure, they say I'm tough, cold, belligerent, but I couldn't care less. What matters are my guests and my own self-respect."

Some believe that Jovan opened Les Nomades because he was tiring of Le Perroquet, but I'm convinced he made the move simply because he needed an entirely different format in which he could expand his horizons even further. Virtually hidden among other nicely restored town houses on East Ontario Street between Michigan Avenue and Lake Michigan, and identified by no more than a small brass plaque reading "Private Club," the bistro is intentionally just the opposite of Le Perroquet. There are no carpets on the unpolished wooden floors, no velvet banquettes, no fancy wall murals, and no fixed-price menu. There are handsome wooden tables, comfortable chairs with needlepoint fabric, and aproned waiters and waitresses. There are also working fireplaces, priceless old ocean-liner posters, and some exquisite hand-painted wall tiles Maggie designed and had painted in Portugal. For a while the front room was highlighted by a spectacular zinc bar Jovan had made in Paris, but when members showed no interest in occasionally having their grilled rib steak and glass of wine while seated at the bar, he had it removed and put in storage. ("I just couldn't make the idea catch on with Americans.") By the same stroke, when the upstairs Salon de Thé failed to catch on as a room for after-dinner coffee, dessert, and Cognac, a disillusioned Jovan turned it into a romantic dining room and increased his seating capacity to sixty-five. "Either I'm a hopeless dreamer or I didn't plan this place well," he moans. "But it is fun experimenting."

At first all the gossip about candidacy for membership at Nomades was held to a local pitch, but as soon as word about the private restaurant had spread round the country, the first thing any gastronome or socialite heading for Chicago wanted to know was how to get a one-dollar membership: that is, become a friend of Jovan Trboyevic. Numerous luminaries have been refused, but there's at least one taxicab driver who drops by when he craves good food and companionship. Food and wine societies, the majority of French chefs in America, and most professional restaurant critics ("who seek out and *enjoy* imperfection just like plumbing inspectors") are frowned upon, while such figures as Saul Bellow, Rex Harrison, Julia Child, George Shearing, ex-mayor Jane Byrne, and Malcolm Forbes remain in good standing. If a friend of a member wants to join, the member either brings along the friend as a guest to be introduced or writes a letter of recommendation. He may be accepted; he may not. Jovan has his reasons. If a member doesn't show for a reservation, or table-hops, or lights up a cigar, he'll most probably receive notice that his annual membership will not be renewed. While all this just adds to Jovan's share of bad publicity, he remains unmoved. "I guess I'm just getting too old to worry about who likes me and who doesn't. People have to understand that this restaurant is for friends who think like I think, and that we get frustrated by those who don't consider eating the most important aspect of dining out. I detest the notion that Nomades is snob and élitist. Different, yes, but certainly not . . . forbidding. The club is right for some people and wrong for others. It's that simple."

Although Jovan insists that the cuisine at Nomades is uncomplicated, those lucky enough to have sampled a few dishes realize almost immediately to what extent Jovan is upholding his reputation as a radical innovator. A quick glance at one of the mimeographed ever-changing à la carte menus does indeed evoke traditional bistro fare: duckling pâté, cassoulet, *navarin* of lamb, roast venison, charcoal-grilled fish, chocolate mousse. Then you study closely, ask questions, and make every effort not to devour every crumb of the yeasty, rustic, incredible homemade bread and sweet slab butter. You discover that the silky salmon is cured on the premises, that Jovan smokes his own haddock and ages his own goat cheese in herbed vinegar, and that the white bar wine served by the glass is vintage pinot chardonnay.

By some culinary miracle, the lean, fatless cassoulet is packed with flavor. A smooth asparagus sauce gives character to a zesty flan of fresh herbs, and ordinary sautéed duck livers take on new definition when served tepid in a champagne vinaigrette with red cabbage salad. Who could imagine that an appetizer of string beans, shrimp, and duck cracklings would work as it does, and who but Jovan would serve a sautéed pork fillet with green olives and old-fashioned mashed potatoes topped with fried onion strips? There are sweetbread fritters with a mustard-ginger sauce, a moussaka made with pigeon, fresh Maryland crabmeat in cabbage leaves with a buttery white-wine sauce, a fricassee of veal and cucumbers, steamed mussels and scallops with sea-urchin butter on caramelized onions, and rich chocolate ice cream with whole coffee beans. On occasion Jovan tips his hat to the more earthy sides of Fredy Girardet and Michel Guérard (both of whom he admires greatly), but unlike so many others in the business who are satisfied simply to imitate, the Chicago rebel modifies, elaborates, and transforms till the dish takes on not only an identity all its own but actually a different nationality. At Le Perroquet Jovan added a dimension to classic French cuisine that astounded even the three-star chefs of France and confounded most American critics. And at Les Nomades he is illustrating better than anyone else that the application of certain culinary principles to our vast store of native ingredients can eventually evolve into a very lofty style of American cookery.

Exactly how, you ask, does Jovan come up with his conceptions, and what makes his gastronomic philosophy so radically different from that of his peers? "I don't sleep very well," he explains, "especially when I've been out drinking till three in the morning to wind down. So I guess most of my ideas develop while I'm lying there waiting to telephone my fish man in Boston at the crack of dawn. On the other hand, I might see some vegetable in the market and remember a certain cut of meat we have coming in. Something clicks, I get excited, so I buy it and take it back to the kitchen, where a chef and I begin testing. I can also get inspired by what I eat in other restaurants, or even in a plain roadside diner. I love things like that, you know. Good diner food. I guess the world would be shocked if it knew how many of those so-called fancy dishes in Nomades are the refined results of something I've been served in a French brasserie or Swiss beer hall or American diner. It's honest food, and, yes, honesty—that's what I find missing in so many deluxe restaurants. Just look, nobody today wants to eat meat or fish on the bone, or take the trouble to prepare succulent stews, or serve a simple mound of braised cabbage. They think all this is crude, fattening, and unhealthy. Well, I think we're proving at Nomades that, when this sort of honest fare is prepared with competence and imagination, it certainly makes for more interesting and delicious eating than a couple of puny, overcooked fillets of this or that drenched in some heavy sauce."

Jovan is perhaps most forthright and controversial when he expounds on nouvelle cuisine, the very style of cooking he embraced and virtually introduced to America years ago but which he is now the first to criticize severely. "The initial revolt was really against all those dreadful, heavy, hotel-type preparations that had come to dominate the French repertory," he contends, "and in the beginning the principles were sound, the potential very exciting. Then, as always, came the exploitations, the abuses, the stupidities, all in the hands of amateurs who simply didn't comprehend what Guérard, Bocuse, the Troisgros brothers, and Jacques Manière had in mind. Nouvelle cuisine, you see, should be a patrician cuisine, but most of what you see in this country is a farce, a real mockery of what nouvelle represents at its best. A chef who comes up with no more than a poor imitation of a tired cliché is praised by an uninformed public as being creative. A guy who previously sold insurance now spends a few weeks visiting restaurants in France, opens his little restaurant, places a few weird combinations in a sauté pan, and soaks them in *beurre blanc*. He then charges outrageous prices and is heralded as a culinary genius. And take stocks, the foundation of any sophisticated sauce. It's absolute nonsense that youngsters with little or no experience can deal with stocks. It takes years to learn to produce clean, perfect stocks, to *understand* stocks. Yet today a kid comes into a professional kitchen looking for a job and guess where he's put to work first? It's depressing."

Eager as Jovan is to please everyone who frequents his restaurant, he's as ready to air his opinions of the dining public as of the culinary excesses in other restaurants. "The curious problem is that the people who are so indiscriminate about what they eat and how they're treated are the same ones who love and demand what I call dining-room gimmickry. By that I mean a couple will come into a luxury restaurant, tolerate mediocre food, indifferent service, and astronomical prices, yet be perfectly content so long as they have a certain table, can wave at their friends, and receive so-called special attention from the owner. Well, I'm not running an arena for masochists. In my restaurant, the little guy gets the exact same treatment as all the celebrities we serve. As far as I'm concerned, anyone who comes for the food and is nice is a big shot. But you see I'm a very nervous, frustrated man, which I suppose accounts for the reason I don't get along so well with the back-slapping, country-club, après-ski crowd. I guess I simply don't understand people who are content and self-satisfied and always happy. Sure, I treat them well, but the ones I really go out of my way to please are those who appear tense, restless, and melancholy. I have something in common with these people; we make up a weird little species that is almost extinct."

Of course, to portray Jovan Trboyevic as a forever suspicious, demanding, and brooding cynic hopelessly devoted to professional perfection is to reveal only one important facet of his complex personality. Yes, he is fully capable of manifesting the darker side of human nature, but, as those few who are close to him know, he is also a charming, extremely generous, old-fashioned gentleman with a refreshing wit and remarkable zest for living. Although keenly intelligent, reflective, and articulate, Jovan can produce tears of laughter in the eyes of those about him as well as luster in the eyes of a lady whose hand he kisses. On those rare occasions when he leaves his restaurant in the trustworthy hands of Maggie and flees to pursue his favorite hobby, he thinks nothing of grabbing a jet to Paris, Geneva, or

Rome, meeting up with food-loving cronies from somewhere in his past, and checking out five or six new restaurants in a matter of a few days. "It's really horrifying," he admits openly, popping another Rolaid into his mouth. "When these crazy guys and I are not eating, we're discussing where and what we *should* be eating. And my cholesterol count just gets higher and higher." He loves good jazz, gypsy music, imported vodka, and romance ("My only real happiness is sitting quietly alone with Maggie from time to time at a corner table and sharing a little food and wine"), and it's nothing unusual for him to buy a hot dog from a street vendor, talk serious politics with a cabdriver, or palm a hard-working waiter an extra twenty-dollar bill. He refers to his staff as "my pals"; he smiles understandingly when a Chicago bartender greets him as "Joevan" instead of the correct "Yovon"; and he would no doubt risk his life for a cause or person he believed in.

Perhaps the greatest fear of many Chicagoans is that their eminent gastronome will indeed decide one day to abandon the Windy City and, as he's always proposing, move on to test his fate in New York City or . . . wherever. On one trip to Chicago, I resolved to pin Jovan down, hoping a bit nefariously that the Big Apple eventually might lure the one titan in the business who could restore New York dining to its former grandeur. That evening, after still another memorable dinner at Nomades, Jovan suggested that we all pile into his Wagoneer and go out to a remote Yugoslavian restaurant "where they do some serious eating and drinking." He was obviously in a good mood, relaxed, and ready for his nightcap. Raising her eyebrow in warning, Maggie begged off, leaving us in the hands of a man who can be as comfortable in a crowded, red-flocked-walled, smoke-ridden cabaret reminiscent of Paris in the twenties as amid the quiet, tasteful surroundings of his restaurant. The wild gypsy music soared, the Dom Pérignon flowed, strange faces appeared and disappeared at the table, and the language changed from French to Yugoslavian to English to Russian. Jovan remained jovial. Then, when the violinist began to play an old, doleful melody, the infamous Serb of Chicago began to stare dreamily into space as if sobered momentarily by the heavy tyranny of time and memory. Was he perhaps thinking of some past friend, or maybe reliving a desperate youthful moment in the streets of some bleak European capital, or simply trying to remember a beloved country and family lost to him forever? Suddenly, just as I was preparing to bring up the topic of his future, he turned his head back and leaned across the table. "You know," he said, taking a swig of Champagne, "there was definitely something wrong with that duck you had tonight, but I guess that can wait till morning. You want to know something else? I was just sitting here thinking about this ridiculous town I live in, and you know Chicago's really not a bad place at all." With that I knew my question was unimportant, that the nomad had finally found his home.

## POSTSCRIPT

Yes, Jovan Trboyevic is still in Chicago; yes, he still runs Les Nomades as a private dining club with the same iron hand that ruled Le Perroquet for so many years; yes, he still wanders the globe seeking out ghosts from his intriguing past; and yes, I still consider him the greatest restaurateur of our time, a peerless legend that continues to demand the admiration and respect of everyone in the profession. I have learned since doing this profile that the annual membership fee at Les Nomades has been raised to two dollars ("I decided the place was now in the big time," quips Jovan). I have also learned that the creator of some of the world's most refined French dishes has a favorite snack: raw bacon!

# PART III
# PERSONAL PLEASURES

During my career, I've always tried to be open-minded and receptive to most all evolutionary changes and developments connected
with the world of food and drink. I've written with enthusiasm
about the blossoming California wine industry and the new American caviars. I've visited any number of domestic health resorts to
compare them with the Baden-Baden experience described here,
to learn what "spa cuisine" is all about, and to see if there are
further ways my jaded body might be regenerated. I've sipped every
trendy apéritif from Kir Royal to the Bellini, as well as every postprandial from *vin santo* to Chartreuse with soda. I've sampled a few
hundred examples of flourless chocolate torte and cheesecake made
with low-cal ricotta. And I've even flown some twenty thousand
miles for the express purpose of discovering whether there is indeed a single gustatory reward aloft (there's not) that can compare
to the feasts I remember on the great luxury liners. No doubt my
palate and life have been enriched by the exposure to multiple new
experiences, but there are some pleasures that can never be altered, some classic flavors and longings that never change. When
Lucius Beebe, one of the most celebrated grandees of our century,
once crossed transatlantic in the majestic *Aquitania* as a young
college student, he was given a bit of worldly wisdom by a certain
veteran of the sea lanes. "I think," said the older gentleman, "you
will learn more that will be useful to you in life in six days aboard
a Cunard steamship than in a semester at any university in the
world." I know what he meant.

# A FEW CHOICE WORDS ABOUT THE MANHATTAN

*Unpublished*

Not meaning to invoke the wrath of my many highly regarded fellow tipplers, I don't hesitate one second to say that when it comes to real cocktail pedigree in America, the so-called mysterious and ever-popular Martini—not to mention hundreds of other alcoholic concoctions—simply is not and never has been in the same class with the Manhattan. Over the decades, the virtues of the Martini have been extolled by celebrated novelists, songwriters, and veteran boozers around the world, but what tribute has been paid to that wondrous, subtle, classic mixture of whiskey, sweet vermouth, and Angostura bitters that for serious connoisseurs still symbolizes both the ultimate in sophisticated drinking and the very spirit of the great city that shares its name?

I mean, let's face it: After all is said about what does and does not constitute a great Martini, it's still a pretty crass drink that involves little more than straight gin or (heaven forbid) vodka that is *flavored* with dry vermouth, stirred or shaken with any form of ice, and served straight up or on the rocks in almost any glass with an olive, lemon peel, stuffed onion, or who knows what else. By contrast, a properly made Manhattan represents the height of the mixologist's art. The whiskey must be fine Bourbon or blended American, the vermouth must be the best sweet Italian, the bitters must be Angostura, and the proportions must be measured exactly, chilled quickly but thoroughly with large ice cubes to prevent dilution, and poured through a strainer over a stemmed maraschino cherry into a chilled 4- to 6-ounce stemmed cocktail glass. The result is a beautiful amber drink that is at once complex but discreet, potent but mellow, short-lived but eminently satisfying. Contrary to what some might have you believe, devoted Martini fanciers still slug down their silver bullets day and night: at lunch, in the office, after work in bars, throughout a meal, and whenever a situation calls for getting smashed. Urbane Manhattan aficionados, on the other hand, make a veritable ritual of their cocktail, rarely indulging anytime except right before dinner, never exceeding more than two drinks, and generally respecting the object of their bibulous passion as the genteel but powerful aristocrat that it is.

For years enthusiasts have believed that the Manhattan was created in 1874 by a bartender at New York's Manhattan Club especially for a banquet given by Lady Randolph Churchill (mother of Sir Winston) to celebrate the election of Governor Samuel J. Tilden. Well, after having been put in touch with Carol Truax, a prolific octogenarian food writer who states in one of her twenty-seven cookbooks that none other than her father, Supreme Court Judge Charles Henry Truax, came up with the drink when he was president of the Manhattan Club around 1890, I'm now ready to dispute the long-time theory. "It's true that the old Manhattan Club on lower Fifth Avenue was originally the home of Jenny Jerome (Lady Churchill)," said Miss Truax, "but she really had nothing to do with the invention of the cocktail. What really happened was that my father, who was very fat, would stop his carriage at the club every day on his way home from court and drink a few Martinis (two at a time, since they were two for a quarter!). When the doctor told him he absolutely had to cut out the Martinis if he hoped to lose weight, he swiftly dropped by the club, told the bartender they had to come up with a new cocktail, and the Manhattan was born—named after the club. Of course, when he later returned to his physician, heavier than ever, and told about the delicious substitution for Martinis he'd come up with, the doctor roared, "But that's even worse!"

If memory serves, I sipped my first Manhattan cocktail at the ripe age of twelve, the same year I first crossed to Europe in a majestic superliner and the year I was confirmed in the Holy Episcopal Church of America. The location was the now legendary bar at the Hotel Astor in New York, and the occasion was an early-evening rendezvous my father and I had with my sartorial-minded Swedish uncle to determine which items should be included in my wardrobe during a planned shopping spree the next day at Brooks Brothers.

"Two Manhattans," my father directed as the distinguished gray-headed bartender arranged three napkins on the oak, "and a Coke for the boy."

Of course for years back home I'd watched my father go through the ceremony of mixing his colorful drink each evening before dinner, and it had always been a special treat when he would let me pluck the rye-flavored cherry from the glass. But not till that night in New York, not till I had reached adolescence, was I finally allowed to take a sip of the mysterious potion. I'm sure if I had been of age he wouldn't have hesitated a moment to order three Manhattans. Given the antiquated restrictions of our forever overprotective drinking laws, however, he simply pushed my Coke aside, moved his stemmed glass in front of me, and said, "Here, son, see how you like this."

Suffice it that since that epiphanic evening the Manhattan cocktail has remained my steadfast companion through years of grueling education, joy, heartbreak, success, failure, and, needless to say, gustatory hedonism. The ice-cold libation I still share today with my father must, by his orders, be composed of exactly 2½ ounces of blended American whiskey, 1 ounce of Martini & Rossi sweet vermouth, "less than a dash" of Angostura bitters, and a maraschino cherry, and must be strained into a 4-ounce stemmed cocktail glass. An estimated two to three hundred bartenders, maîtres d'hôtel, restaurant captains, waiters, hoteliers, and friends around the globe know automatically when I arrive on the scene that a Bourbon Manhattan is in order—and preferably a single bolt made with 2½ ounces of bonded whiskey, 1½ ounces of Cinzano red, a quick dash of Angostura, and a fat stemmed cherry, and served in a chilled stemmed 6-ounce cocktail glass. Unfortunately, a perfect Manhattan (and by "perfect" I'm by no means referring to the abomination by that name that includes a shot of *dry* vermouth) is as rare in a bar or restaurant these days as 100-proof sipping Bourbon, so much so that the absurd and shoddy practice in some places of not stocking maraschino cherries in order to protect unwary customers from Red Dye No. 2 has even forced me to carry my own cherries at all times in a special pocket vial. While experts like the bartenders at The Four Seasons in New York or a couple of old vets at the Drake hotel in Chicago still care enough to ask not only which brand of whiskey and vermouth you like but also the proportions you prefer, what you run up against more often than not are amateurs who do little more than slosh unmeasured cheap whiskey and domestic vermouth with shaved ice in a shaker, pour the diluted sacrilege into an unchilled glass, and ask the ridiculous question: "A cherry or lemon twist?"

Exactly which proportions of ingredients constitute the perfect Manhattan does depend on personal taste and can only be determined after considerable experimentation. Years ago I insisted on 3 ounces of Bourbon to 1 ounce of vermouth with a full dash of bitters, but today I prefer a more-subdued drink with less whiskey and bitters and can usually tell whether the formula is correct just by looking at the cocktail. The main things to remember, whatever blend you finally decide upon, are to stick with it till age or taste buds or whatever coaxes you to reconsider, and, when ordering a Manhattan in public, demand that the bartender measure the drink according to your exact specifications. Furthermore, if a bartender or restaurant captain informs you that the establishment does not have proper cocktail glasses (why in all French restaurants must they serve cocktails in those impossible sherrry glasses?), Angostura bitters, or maraschino cherries, order a glass of ale or walk out.

In this rather anemic present-day society, when the very trendy but rather silly practice of slugging down glasses of cheap white wine has virtually stifled the civilized art of drinking a well-made cocktail before dinner, I must say I often find it consoling and revealing the way innocents always stare at my Manhattan in wonderment, comment on its beauty, ask what it tastes like, and eventually have to take a sip. Without exception they smile, their eyes light up, and, with an almost evil sense of fulfillment, I am reassured once again that this mellow prince of cocktails will not only survive an era of spurious values but will continue for generations to nourish the souls of those with both style and substance.

## The Original Manhattan Cocktail

This is the original Manhattan formula created around 1890 by Supreme Court Judge Charles Henry Truax when he was president of New York's Manhattan Club.

> 2 ounces rye (blended American) or Bourbon whiskey
> 1 ounce sweet Italian vermouth
> Dash of Angostura bitters
> A stemmed maraschino cherry

Combine the whiskey, vermouth, and bitters in a mixing glass or pitcher, add 2 or 3 ice cubes, stir quickly till well chilled, and strain into a 4-ounce stemmed cocktail glass. Add the cherry.

### POSTSCRIPT

I don't remember when, where, or exactly why I composed this unpublished encomium to my beloved Manhattan cocktail, but I can reconfirm that each statement expressed here remains as alive as ever. There was a very tense and trying period not long ago when, after the doctor insisted I cut out Bourbon Manhattans to help reduce an alarming triglyceride count, I switched to the Negroni as a regular cocktail. The experiment was a dismal failure, and I'm happy to report that once again virtually no major dinner is undertaken without my noble and potent companion as a prelude.

# I'VE NEVER HAD
# ENOUGH CAVIAR

*1973*

O ne of the most dramatic gifts I ever received arrived early one evening
at my New York apartment just as I was finishing up last-minute
details for a special buffet dinner prepared for some very special guests.
There were jellied eggs I prayed were not overcooked, a poached bass I'd
spent hours decorating, a roast goose I had stuffed with sausage and chestnuts, an elaborate array of vegetables, fruit, and a rich torte I'd ordered
from the baker days in advance. Chilling in a cooler were bottles of vintage
Clos Blanc de Vougeot, while breathing quietly on a small table were two
precious magnums of '66 Margaux. Everything seemed right.

Suddenly the doorbell rang. Thinking that someone who had misplaced
the invitation was arriving early, I quickly threw my jacket on and hastened
to open the door, only to find a local delivery boy holding a large sack under
his arm. Inside there was no tissue, no wrapping, no ribbons. Just three
items: a fourteen-ounce tin of fresh Iranian beluga caviar, a chilled bottle
of Dom Pérignon, and a note from a fellow sybarite many miles away: "How
about really starting that party out right!"

For well over a century the delectable mating of caviar and Champagne
or vodka has symbolized throughout the world the ultimate in festivity, joy,
and gustatory luxury. Who can imagine a wedding celebration, golden
anniversary, bon voyage party, or great culinary feast without these delicacies? Caviar: the aristocratic "food of the czars," the "black pearls of

heaven." As one grandee of our century, G. K. Chesterton, described succinctly and nobly the sentiments of more than one dreamy-eyed epicure hopelessly impassioned over the inimitable taste of those shiny grains: "There is more simplicity in the man who eats caviar on impulse than in the man who eats Grapenuts on principle."

I say with unabashed pride that I've never had my fill of fresh caviar (and I'm talking about fresh Iranian or Russian eggs, not the questionable domestic products). Foie gras, truffled fowl, she-crab soup, aged Stilton, yes, but never enough caviar. There is no moment of the day or night when I'd refuse its hedonistic succor. Ecstasy is waking up on a luxury liner to servings of freshly-squeezed orange juice, scrambled eggs, caviar, and a split of Krug. A single spoonful of fresh beluga accompanied by a glass of bubbly at elevenses dispels morning drags and perks up the appetite for more of the same at lunch. A late-afternoon dip into the tin accompanied by slow sips of Champagne does wonders for stimulating interest in a fine dinner (highlighted, of course, by a portion of caviar with iced Russian vodka or Niagaras of you know what); and what better way to coax a good night's sleep than with a little caviar on black bread and two goblets of that liquid miracle? There's always an appropriate time for this princely and incredibly expensive aristocrat and its noble companions.

So, practically speaking, what is so rare about caviar, and what justifies shelling out $350 in a reputable gourmet shop for fourteen ounces of fresh beluga? Nothing demoralizes me more than to watch the uninitiated assault a mound of precious caviar as they would a bowl of peanuts—a gesture nothing less than sacrilege. Caviar is a blessed item, to be consumed and savored with utmost respect and with at least a little knowledge of this extraordinary speciality of nature and the artistic procedures involved in its production. Such awareness, too, helps you understand that more than greed and rarity account for its high price.

Surprisingly, few Americans have tasted fresh Russian or Iranian *malossol* caviar (*malossol* being the Russian word for "little salt"). And there are a number of logical reasons why. First, it's not that easy in most areas of the country to find imported fresh caviar, mainly because so few retail markets and delicacy shops stock it in quantity. Second, fresh caviar is scarce and prohibitively expensive, and even those willing to pay today's high prices in fashionable restaurants think twice before shelling out $50 to $75 for no more than a spoonful of precious black or gray roe. Third (and perhaps most significant), the so-called caviar to which most Americans have been exposed is no more than the pressed, processed, dyed, and extremely salty eggs of cod, whitefish, shad, mullet, and God knows what other inferior imitations packed in jars. As a result, many people with memories of glubby palates simply shy away when given the chance to savor the fresh, clean-tasting genuine article.

True Russian or Iranian whole-grain caviar comes from only four species of sturgeon yielding four types of choice roe that are laboriously removed from the large fish and processed by hand. The most popular variety is beluga, a mammoth creature of the Caspian Sea that can weigh over two thousand pounds and often extends to fourteen feet in length. The roe of beluga are large, black to steel-gray in color, and rather soft. Osetra and sevruga sturgeons yield eggs that are smaller than the beluga but are generally equal in flavor and considerably less expensive. Sterlet caviar comes from a smaller sturgeon (about seven hundred pounds). Its rare grains are tiny and firm and often deemed the finest by certain connoisseurs. Some Russian experts prefer a heavily salted, coarse-grained black caviar known as *pajusnaya*. This caviar, lightly packed and barreled for export at Astrakhan, is produced from any variety of genuine grains that are either premature or have suffered damage in the sieving process. Since *pajusnaya* is not whole-grain caviar, it is much less expensive, though some people (myself included) find its flavor too snapping. The same would hold true for a domestically packed, fresh pressed caviar, a solid mass with a jamlike consistency and a zestful flavor.

As to the differences between Russian and Iranian *malossol,* some professional purveyors seem to feel that the Russian version (which is usually more expensive) is a degree higher in quality. Quite honestly, I can detect no difference whatsoever in the choice grades and suspect that even the specialists too often equate rareness and high cost with superiority.

All epicures will agree that there is no comparison between fresh caviar and that which is processed with a high content of salt. The same epicures also agree that there is considerable difference between fresh caviar treated with borax (a preservative unfortunately forbidden in the United States, but the substance that gives the luscious caviar you find throughout Europe its delicate, mild, almost sweet savor) and that cured exclusively with salt. U.S. regulations require that even fresh caviar contain from 3 to 4 percent salt preservative—enough, in other words, to allow a tin to be kept under proper conditions up to six months but not so much that the caviar tastes like brine. As much as I adore caviar, I simply cannot eat the bitingly saline processed varieties. Some enthusiasts don't mind the strong flavor; I do. Even the taste of non-refrigerated large-grained roe of red salmon is too intense and too oily for my palate, and the only time I find it acceptable is when it's mixed with other ingredients such as raw onion or sour cream. I realize this is all a matter of individual taste, but I'm also firmly convinced that, once you've become accustomed to the quiet delicacy of fresh *malossol,* any lesser grade is always a brutal disappointment.

Untrained bon vivants frequently commit the most serious crimes against the delicate wonders of man and God. I watch people pour alien brandies into a glass of the purest Champagne, see others smear rich foie gras over sweet soda crackers, and observe with despair when fragile raspberries are drowned in a bath of syrupy liqueur. But surely the gravest gastronomic vulgarity is to fracture the unique flavor of fresh caviar by embellishing the noble grains with such incidental whimsies as chopped eggs, sour cream, onions, capers, and—well, why continue? The one and only way a true caviar lover enjoys his luxury is *au naturel*—that is, by spooning and eating it directly from the original ice-packed metal container or spreading it carefully over thin black bread or small fresh blinis and adding no more than a sprinkle of lemon juice. Whatever the case, there should be no tampering with the oily grains, no transferring the roe to elegant crystal or silver serving bowls, nothing to disturb the sublime essence of a delicacy which by itself is perfection.

There are a few gastronomic unions that will forever seem to have been decreed by the gods (foie gras and Sauternes, pasta and fresh white truffles, Stilton and Port), but none is so sensual, so mystical, so unique as the marriage of fresh caviar with fine Russian or Polish vodka or French Champagne. Together they provide a gustatory experience that virtually defies description, and together they will continue for a long time to consummate in a very special way those many joyful and gracious occasions that make life worth living.

## POSTSCRIPT

Okay, the truth is I did eventually get my fill of caviar when once I crossed transatlantic aboard *QE 2* for the express purpose of losing weight painlessly. For those who still don't know, the only place in the world where you can still consume unlimited amounts of fresh Iranian caviar (morning, noon, and night) for no more than the price of a first-class ticket is the *QE 2*. And for those who still don't know that even inordinate amounts of caviar have relatively few calories, let me inform you that I did indeed knock off six ugly pounds in five days by eating little more than Cavaillon melon, cold lobster, truffled pheasant, Lauris asparagus, and heaven knows how many three-ounce crocks of fresh sevruga. After my caviar diet, however, I couldn't so much as look at the delicacy for months. I was wrong to pull that caper, for even today in the *QE 2*'s Princess Grill there are times when I can savor my caviar no more than three days in a row, forced by a sense of contrition to resort to smoked Scotch salmon during the last two nights at sea.

# I TOOK DIE KUR

*1974*

It was on a Friday afternoon in the Oak Bar of the Plaza Hotel in New York that I once again realized I was headed for big trouble. Headache, a touch of vertigo, incredible fatigue, listlessness. All the symptoms that would indicate in most people either a severe illness or total nervous collapse I recognized in myself as simply another attack brought on by gastronomic overindulgence and social stress. Most revealing of all was the pain on the right, below the rib cage, a depressingly dull discomfort that betrayed an all too familiar ailment. This time, however, the pain was more than slight, and when I casually slipped my hand underneath my vest to give the liver a little nudge, what I felt could have best been described as a medium-sized truffle.

Utterly demoralized, I was about to order another glass of Champagne (without doubt the best *temporary* remedy for this type of condition) when a Lucullan colleague and hard-core hedonist arrived. He looked worse than I felt, so we ordered two goblets of bubbly.

"Do you realize," he moaned, "the amount of food and wine we consumed last night at The Forum (of the Twelve Caesars)?"

"Don't remind me!" I said. "It was fabulous. But please, let's discuss something else."

"Like what?"

"Like the fastest and easiest way to get me back on my feet, calm my nerves, and soothe a swollen liver, that's what!"

"Well, I can tell you how," my comrade asserted with what I considered a rather dubious tone of authority. "You need to take the cure."

"Cure! What cure?"

"Just the Cure, simple and clear. In Germany, at Baden-Baden. They have this new Anti-Stress program at the legendary Brenner's Park-Hotel. It helps you calm down, lose weight, dry out, stop smoking, and generally restore your physiological and mental balance. It's what the Germans call an *Entschlackungskur*, which means something about cleaning out a stopped-up grease trap."

"Just one minute," I interrupted. "Is all this about doctors and special diets and all that sort of thing? If you think for one minute I'm traveling thousands of miles just to have some German quack throw me in hot mineral waters and tell me to lay off the goodies—well, the idea goes against every one of my principles."

"Listen," he insisted. "Be reasonable. You're tired, overworked, glutted from all the eating and drinking, a victim of big-city and social pressures, and you refuse to change. I think it would be fun to try this type of therapy. After all, it won't last forever, and apparently it can be taken with a bit of style."

Still I hesitated, finding it a little hard to believe that in the short period of a week the most fashionable of Germany's 153 spas could virtually rejuvenate the body and perk up the soul. On the other hand, my friend usually knew about these things, and I figured I really didn't have that much to lose—except about ten pounds of undesirable adipose tissue I'd been richly nourishing over the past couple of years. Besides, if such a mission was planned very carefully—and taken gradually to avoid metabolic shock—it just might turn out to be a marvelous vacation, with or without the added attraction of a possibly successful cure. A few weeks later I was on my way.

Since, of course, Paris happens to be between New York and Baden-Baden, I took advantage of the opportunity, checked into the Ritz, and was shown to my favorite room overlooking the garden. Appointments were impeccable as usual, and on the mantel above the marble fireplace were a large Murano vase holding twenty fresh red tulips, a tiny tin of Russian beluga sunk in ice, a chilled bottle of the hotel's reserve Champagne, and a single greeting card: "Charles C. Ritz." Just as I spooned the first bit of caviar and started to open the bubbly, the phone rang.

"*Mon cher ami*, how was the trip?" began M. Ritz in his inimitable style of alternating French and idiomatic English. "Now what's this I hear about your taking a cure in Germany? *Absurde, mon cher, absurde* that you should let yourself get in that condition. But while you're here there are a few things you must taste, like the new sausage I recently found! And wait till you see how we're preparing our *saumon à la Champagne*. And the new

Italian asparagus. Best they've ever sent me. Why not come down now to taste them?"

Knowing that you never argue with the son of César, I consumed a few more delectable grains of beluga, a few more sips of wine, and hastened to the first of many such epicurean tastings, none of which exactly enhanced my already jaded system. When I wasn't sampling or sipping at the Ritz the next few days, I was sampling the *ris de veau* at Aux Lyonnais, the stuffed goose neck at Le Pizou, the *soupe de poissons* at Marius et Janette, and the *soufflé à la liqueur de framboise* at Taillevent.

After four sublime days of gourmandism in Paris, I headed by train to Strasbourg, spending most of the first hour of the trip readjusting the rear belt of my vest. Waiting at the station was the Brenner's Park's Herr Axmacher, the hotel's assistant manager and one of those rare Germans who are visibly undernourished. "And now, off we go to Baden-Baden, where you'll feel like new in just a few days."

"Uh, Herr Axmacher," I stuttered, "apparently someone forgot to tell you, and I know it sounds a little strange, but I'd hoped we could stop on our way for a little lunch at this Alsatian restaurant. Just a small out-of-the-way place I'm sure you'd enjoy."

"But I thought you'd come to take the cure."

"Oh, make no mistake, Herr Axmacher, I have. But it is lunchtime and we're so close to this charming little place."

About forty minutes later our Mercedes pulled up in front of France's most remotely located (and possibly finest) temple of gastronomy. Waiting to greet us inside the spacious, colorful, and rustic dining room was Jean-Pierre Haeberlin, one of the two brothers who own and operate the Auberge de l'Ill. Herr Axmacher appeared a bit stunned, but after a few glasses of chilled Muscat d'Alsace, we got down to serious business, indulging ourselves shamelessly in the ritual of *la haute cuisine*. I had advised Jean-Pierre that as much as possible had to be tasted, especially the specialties of the region. The drama began. Frogs'-leg soup, *brioche de foie gras*, and one giant hot truffle wrapped in foie gras, baked in puff pastry, and served with a Madeira sauce. We were off to a good start and fully ready to sample a salmon soufflé and a bottle of Hügel's vintage Riesling.

Hopes and spirits and appetites remained strong, and although my German host-become-guest still surveyed the scene with a look of incredulity, he managed to help do justice to a truffled guinea hen, as well as a bottle of local pinot noir. After dipping our silver into luscious chocolate profiteroles, we retired to the flower-lined terrace for coffee, flutes of '64 Taittinger Blanc de Blancs, and a few puffs of Montecristos. The "little lunch" had lasted four hours.

An hour later, we had crossed the Rhine and were deep in the majestic Black Forest. By the time we approached the Oos Valley into which Baden-Baden is tucked, I was in a postprandial daze, quite convinced that my liver would explode any moment. Then I caught my first glimpse of noble Baden-Baden. It is a domain of dignity and grace, a refuge from the commonplace, a leafy world of tranquillity. Passing through the small town, I admired all the elegant shops, the old Memorial Church, the dazzling casino designed a century ago by Parisian architects, the sylvan promenades on the banks of the River Oos, the veritable multitude of signs with doctors' names, and the imposing Friedrichsbad and Augustabad, considered by many to be the best-equipped and most-fashionable thermal baths in the world. By the time we pulled up at the hotel, there was no doubt in my mind that Baden-Baden was, indeed, the queen of German spas.

Entering my room at the Brenner's Park was like moving into another age—or, to be more precise, into the setting of a Thomas Mann novel. Fresh flowers and fruit, period furniture, a decades-old crystal chandelier, heavy lush draperies and Persian carpets, a small mahogany boot stand, a tall eight-prong clothes tree—and no detestable television set. It all evoked a spacious comfort and way of life that elsewhere today is hardly more than a dream. By contrast, the gray-marble bathroom was equipped with all modern conveniences: six-foot tub with bath thermometer, magnifying mirror, and, of course, a scale. My private terrace overlooked the quiet forest called the Lichtentaler Allee, and when I stepped out to view the well-dressed curists taking a late-afternoon promenade at the edge of the small river, I understood why so many for so long have chosen this hidden corner of the world to unwind, forget, and reacquire a sense of well-being.

The first night I had a typically restless sleep, only to be awakened early the next morning (and each succeeding morning) by the hotel's seventy-year-old veteran masseur, whose hands have remained supple and strong from kneading the muscles of such ailing guests of the past as Henry Ford, Mary Pickford, Lillian Gish, and Neville Chamberlain.

"*Guten Morgen,*" he greeted me. "Now you will have your first massage, before you get up, before you have breakfast, before you have the chance to start your day with unnecessary worries or concerns. It's all a question of good circulation." And with that dictum Herr Meier thrust open the terrace doors to let in fresh air, then began pushing, pulling, stretching, and pounding every joint, muscle, connecting tissue, and blood vessel in my body.

"Breathe deep," he instructed.

I tried and gasped.

The workout continued a good thirty minutes, after which Herr Meier directed me to get up, go on the terrace for more deep breathing, then drink one of the bottles of mineral water that had been placed next to the bowl of fruit. The taste could best be described as a slick salty water, but it contained *no* salt.

"You must drink our water all during the day," he said sternly. "Everywhere, anywhere. Here in your room, over at the Trinkhalle and Kurhaus, in the bathhouses, anywhere you find it. The water heals, soothes, purges, and stimulates the circulation. The cure is worthless without the water. And you must walk—everywhere, anywhere. *Auf Wiedersehen.*"

Herr Meier left as abruptly as he'd entered, leaving me in what I was sure was a state of total collapse. After, however, a recuperative half hour on the chaise longue, I regained my strength, ordered breakfast, and breathed a little more ozone.

My breakfast came: fresh orange juice made from blood oranges, a split of the house Champagne, fat little German sausages scattered around a mound of scrambled eggs, and a tray of breads and jams. Delightful. Little did I know that this was the last real breakfast I'd see for a week, for within a couple of hours I had received one official *Kurkarte;* one anti-stress booklet entitling me to consultations with a doctor and to social events at the Kurhaus, theater, and casino; one map of the town; and one slip of paper on which was written the name and address of Dr. Werner Hess.

Since I was told I should walk everywhere, I began making my way through the charming streets to keep my first medical appointment, noticing once again on every block the incredible number of druggists, physicians' offices, and young people carrying the same batch of cure material I had. (Everything in Baden-Baden is *Kur* something or something *Kur.*) Arriving at Dr. Hess's office, I informed the doctor of my basic problems, only to be asked in perfect English why I indulged to excess.

"Because I enjoy it," I explained. "And, besides, it's part of my chosen profession to eat and drink."

"So you're not here to learn how to curtail forever your social and gastronomic habits?" he continued.

"Sir, I don't think that would be possible even if I had the volition. I know it sounds bad, but no, that's out of the question. What I'm really looking for is what you call an *Entschlackungskur,* which, if I'm not mistaken, has something to do with what we call a complete overhaul."

Dr. Hess declared me a peculiar case, but after giving me a semi-complete physical (which did, indeed, reveal a swollen liver and eleven pounds of overweight), he sat me down and came forth with a lecture that I both respect and will never forget.

"Listen, young man, I can sympathize fully with your predicament, but your defensive attitude is all wrong. Here no one is going to force you to do anything; we only suggest and hope you'll care enough to force yourself. To respect the type of highly specialized therapy that's been developed here over the past two thousand years, you must first respect your own mind and body. I can, of course, prescribe certain treatments and waters, but unless you acquire the right mental attitude you're simply wasting your time and mine. Less than five percent of all who come here are Americans, and most of them have your same defenses at first. They eye spa therapy with suspicion and contempt, but after they've completed a program and seen what can be accomplished in as little time as a week, most return year after year."

Dr. Hess talked for forty-five minutes, and by the time I left his office I couldn't have been any more dead serious about anything than I was about *Die Kur*. The man was honest and highly intelligent, but, above all, I had the impression that he, unlike most doctors in the United States, cared about something more than how many patients he could shuffle in and out within the period of an hour. I received no boring moral recriminations regarding my smoking, eating, drinking, and lack of exercise. But somehow Dr. Hess convinced me that while I was at Baden-Baden I should change my thinking considerably, go the way of the other curists, curb—but not discontinue!—my natural inclinations, and really make an effort to follow his suggestions.

And for one solid, blessed week that's the way I lived. Each morning there was a massage, followed by a light breakfast on my sunny terrace, deep breathings, and as much water as I could drink—and I did drink gallons of that water! Later I would ascend the grand staircase of the Friedrichsbad and, following the sign language of attendants, find my locker, strip, and join the other ailing and non-ailing curists moving from one balneotherapeutic phase to the next in the Grand Communal Bath. (Germans, young and old alike, take balneotherapy for preventive as well as corrective purposes.)

First I sat in a dry-heat room and gazed up at colorful tiled tableaux of swans and butterflies. After ten minutes I was led to bake in a much hotter room, this one tiled with figures of cattle and fowl resting amiably under palm trees. Curious indeed, but so comforting and civilized. Dripping with perspiration, I was next directed to spend a specified amount of time (huge wall clocks were omnipresent) in three separate bathing pools, the first scalding hot, the second ice cold, the third warm. This was followed by fifteen minutes of lying flat on a marble slab and breathing moist thermal air heated to a demonic temperature by a steaming natural fountain.

So weak I could hardly walk, I was stretched out on a wooden table, lathered with soap made from beef fat, scrubbed from head to toe with a floor brush to remove dead skin cells, and rinsed with bucketfuls of warm water. My body was delightfully numb—or so I thought until an attendant steered me under a frigid shower before draping me in a floor-length towel and leading me to the "rest saloon." There, in a dark, carpeted room with a domelike ceiling, I was shown to a bed and wrapped like a mummy in a sheet and a wool blanket. I slept soundly for an hour, dressed, stopped at one of the cone-shaped thermal fountains for a few glasses of hot mineral water from the Nürtinger Heinrichsquelle spring (good for the liver, bile, stomach, and intestines), and walked back to the hotel without a worry in the world.

Strangely enough, after the first day I scarcely thought about lunch, and, even more strangely, I hadn't the slightest thirst for Champagne or any other alcoholic beverage. If I had hunger pangs, I simply dropped into the Schwarzwald Grill at the hotel for a little fruit or cheese, but in a couple of days I skipped lunch altogether, took excursions through the Black Forest and vineyards, and discussed in detail my thermal treatments with others over glasses of water at the Trinkhalle (a fashionable classic temple where everyone gathers to socialize over water instead of cocktails).

Midafternoons were spent at the Augustabad, an ultramodern bathhouse where it's not uncommon to see two or three chauffeured Rolls-Royces parked in front waiting for curists. There I was packed in mud, given underwater jet massage, bubbled in pine baths, scrubbed with more soap, walked through alternating hot and cold water in troughs with rock beds, and, most remarkable of all, hosed down while I held on to a bar for dear life. It was all fascinating. After these treatments, I was usually so limp I could hardly make it to the water fountains before returning to the hotel for a nap. But what mattered was I felt good, great, fantastic—so much so that I was overly eager to take long late-afternoon walks.

In the evenings, in black tie or a dark suit, I sipped a single highball made with lots of mineral water and learned the cure-saving trick of never studying the hotel's menu. After a light dinner, there was coffee in the lounge and more cure conversation with newly acquired friends from France, Scandinavia, England, and, of course, Switzerland and Germany, but by 10 P.M. we were out for a final walk, breathing deeply on terraces, or making ready for bed. It was all quite that simple, uninvolved, and delightful.

By the end of that almost mythical week, I was rested and "unstressed." My liver was proclaimed normal in size by Dr. Hess, and I'd knocked off exactly nine pounds. Now, I'm still not sure just how, when, or why it all happened. But it did happen. I enjoyed every minute, and I highly recommend the place to those of high moral caliber. For I'm unhappy to report that today I'm the same wreck I was before leaving for Baden-Baden. What brought on the decline? Well, I suppose it all began the moment the Mercedes left that land of the Rhine Maidens, and I was feeling a bit peckish, and there was this little restaurant.

## POSTSCRIPT

I'm gripped with such nostalgia when I reread this early, youthful essay: New York's glorious Forum of the Twelve Caesars (now gone), where I virtually cut my gastronomic wisdom teeth; Mr. Charles Ritz, that wonderful old gentleman who once slapped my hands for taking knife and fork to asparagus ("Your fingers, young man, only with the fingers!"); Thomas Axmacher, who eventually graduated from the Brenner's Park to become a prominent hotel manager in Texas; and the consumption of all that bubbly, which I still adore but which can now play havoc with the digestion.

And yes, I still return periodically to the Brenner's Park, not only for the traditional *Kur* but also for skin revitalization and cell therapy; I still consult Dr. Hess; and alas, I still resume my wanton gastronomic ways the second I leave Baden-Baden.

# FARE THEE WELL
# ON THE S.S. FRANCE

*1973*

L ike anyone obsessed with great food, I allow nothing to stand in the way of a new and exciting gastronomic experience. Although my sensual excursions in the realm of fine eating always have wavered between the ridiculous and the sublime, I don't suppose I ever took such drastic measures to savor exceptional cuisine as when, on a moment's notice, I recently flew to Cannes for the sole purpose of joining the last leg of the return trip to New York of the S.S. *France* on her thirty-three-day *Fantastique Voyage.*

An inveterate steamship buff whose steadfast love affair with this luxurious liner began nearly ten years ago, I was by no means unfamiliar with the culinary miracles produced by head chef Henri Le Huédé and his brigade of 180 experts. Until now, however, my exposure to this extraordinary cuisine had been limited to short transatlantic crossings. And, although I knew that neither my liver, my waistline, nor my wallet would allow me thirty-three days of unabashed hedonism, I felt compelled to experience firsthand for at least a week the civilized elegances and extravagances that more than 1,200 well-heeled, courageous connoisseurs had been enjoying day after day halfway round the world. After all, this particular voyage was supposed to be *fantastique,* and I was determined to discover whether the term was justified.

To sail on this mighty 66,000-ton vessel (one of the few remaining fortresses of old-world gracious living in the nostalgic world of passenger liners) is to move back to a time when travel implied comfort, insouciant relaxation, personalized service, all-out grandeur, and exciting cuisine. Passengers on the *France* clearly know where the snows of yesteryear are. Most modern-day ships have lost that indefinable atmosphere, that magic, that *je ne sais quoi* that once characterized the great liners. But not the *France*. When I boarded at Cannes, that familiar fragrance of polished wood, the quiet rumble of giant turbines under my feet, and the spit-and-polish look of the neatly dressed crew immediately transported me into a timeless realm of existence. Escorted to my spacious stateroom by veteran steward Yves, I noticed that nothing had faltered in the tradition of Transat (our informal abbreviation of the Compagnie Générale Transatlantique). A rainbow of fresh flowers adorned the bureau, two huge pillows decorated the head of the bed, soft white towels billowed across long steam-warmed rods in the bathroom (the retractable clothesline had already been drawn across the tub), and the glorious sounds of Bach, emanating from a speaker beneath the dressing table, filled the room. I could have been on no other ship but the *France*.

It would be an understatement to suggest that those who sail with Transat make up an exceptional breed. Although I was surprised (and impressed) to find a remarkable number of young people on board, the passengers generally were perhaps the most experienced travelers on earth: those who have seen everything and been everywhere and who would not be caught dead on one of those cramped miniature vessels that shuttle back and forth between the States and the Caribbean. Transat regulars have often been referred to as the silent rich, and anyone who witnessed the glamorous sartorial display each evening or caught a glimpse of the palatial suites (the two finest were booked to the tune of $23,460, and the Île de France suite houses a giant bed that was designed especially for the epic frame of former French President Charles de Gaulle) would agree that the feeling of affluence that permeates the atmosphere is not unlike that some of us recall aboard the old *Queen Mary* and majestic *Île de France*.

Isolated and insulated from the "real" world, everyone is dressed to the hilt. Fine crystal is outsparkled by even finer jewelry. Where else but on this emporium of luxury would you read such "Lost and Found" notices as those posted on the *France*:

"A round, large mobe pearl (from the top of an earring) has been lost. If found, please contact . . ."

"An oval Sapphire earring, surrounded by brilliant antique diamonds, has been lost. Please contact . . ."

"Valuable emerald-and-diamond brooch shaped like a crucifix with fine emeralds lost between 8:00 and 10:30 P.M., perhaps on Boat Deck, perhaps on the First-Class dance floor. Five hundred dollar reward. Please contact . . ."

While there can be no doubt that physically and socially the *France* stands in a class by herself, it is the exceptional cuisine that really sets the ship apart from all others. Typically, a certain few passengers in both the Versailles and Chambord dining saloons could usually find something to complain about with regard to décor or service, but whenever the subject of food came up, only the most pretentious snob dared risk criticizing the kitchen's extraordinary efforts to satisfy every palate and to pamper even the most discriminating gastronome. A staunch champion of *la cuisine classique*, M. Le Huédé has always prided himself on never duplicating a luncheon or dinner on a cruise or crossing, and for those who might doubt this, I have a full collection of menus as proof. From beginning to end, I marveled not only at the number of imaginative dishes offered each day at no extra cost whatsoever to passengers, but even more at the consistent quality of what we consumed. And *consumed* is not at all too strong a term.

As one who harbors epicurean instincts, I always try to exercise restraint in order to assure a satisfying and harmonious gastronomic experience. Normally I hold strictly to self-imposed, sensible rules of dining, thereby avoiding the possibility of staring down at a beautiful menu and finding that I have no appetite. But on this cruise I became hopelessly lost after a matter of days, my will power totally depleted by the most captivating food I'd seen, smelled, or tasted anywhere. And no one would deny that eating was the major activity on the ship, morning, noon, and night. Dedicated gourmands could easily spend the entire cruise in the dining saloons, and often it appeared that many did just that. In the beginning, I found the idea utterly incredible that these veterans were physically capable of devouring French *haute cuisine* daily for more than a month. But then, through helpless self-indulgence, I simply took things in stride, forgot about my increasing girth, and began to enjoy the eight-day movable feast with total abandon.

Since food is ubiquitous on the *France*, anyone obsessed with weight control or cholesterol counts should never set foot on board. In addition to three copious meals per day, there is bouillon delivered to your deck chair each morning at eleven, tea and sandwiches in the lounge at four, elegant hors d'oeuvres at cocktail parties, and a sumptuous midnight buffet. Further, hot onion soup can be savored in your stateroom anytime day or night, as can smoked salmon, delicate sandwiches, Champagne, and heaven knows what else. Those who have no great desire to discuss and learn about fine cuisine well might become absolutely bored on the *France*. We not only ate a great deal, we spent hours talking about food, inspecting the kitchens, and attending cooking lectures and demonstrations. While eating is a necessary pastime on other ships, on the *France* it's a serious business around which all other events revolve.

Breakfast, like all meals, may be taken either in the dining saloons or in your staterooms. Anyone who thinks the French won't or can't serve a wholesome breakfast clearly has never traveled with Transat. Traditional (and delectable) freshly-made croissants, brioches, and *petits pains* (served with no fewer than nine jams and strong French café au lait) await your order, but brave crusaders eschew the Continental breakfast in favor of something more substantial that will tide them over till bouillon time. Fresh or stewed fruits, melons, a choice of ten cereals, onion soup, broiled kippers or poached haddock, a mere sixteen different egg preparations with ham, bacon, sausages, or lamb chops (perhaps with a few steamed or Lyonnaise potatoes) will be whisked to your table or delivered to your stateroom under polished silver domes.

For an elaborate display of *haute cuisine* the likes of which I have never seen on ship or shore, nothing equals the mouth-watering cold buffet served on the enclosed Promenade Deck. Here your will power will be put to the test merely by the visual presentation of the food, designed to tempt you to taste every sensual item. Bowls of capers, white asparagus, marinated artichoke hearts, multiple varieties of herring, tuna, sardines, shrimp, king crab, lobster tails, eel, salmon, and innumerable jellied fish dishes decorated with truffles, mushrooms, pimentos, and carrots present themselves to choice. Next come dazzling salads, an array of raw vegetables, and baskets of freshly baked breads. Platters of turkey, pheasant, Charolais beef, *pré-salé* lamb, pigeon, chicken, and York ham follow, their appeal enhanced by huge showpiece viands garnished with feathers, paper frills, and pictorial images engraved on outer surfaces. Next come sausages from Lyon, Arles, and Italy, followed by perfectly ripe French cheeses, seven or eight fresh fruits, and finally a galaxy of glorious French pastries designed to destroy the lofty resolutions of calorie counters. The *embarras du choix* makes selection difficult, but everyone somehow manages decisions. At one point, M. Le Huédé informed us that thus far the bons vivants on board had consumed 880 pounds of caviar, 820 pounds of fresh foie gras, 6,600 pounds of cheese, nearly 8,000 pounds of lobster and crayfish, and more than 40,000 bottles of Champagne, wine, and spirits. So join the assemblage, choose your dishes and wine, locate a table overlooking the sea, and settle down to the lunch of a lifetime.

While other passengers spent their afternoons snoozing or swimming or watching movies, I usually put my time to use designing special dinner menus to be sent in advance to M. Le Huédé and discussing with sommelier Jean-Jacques Régolle which wines would best complement the evening meal. Don't get me wrong. I don't want to slight the regular menu or the very palatable *vin ordinaire* placed gratis on every table. I mean, who would not be impressed when confronted night after night with fresh caviar; terrines of hare, pigeon, and duck; smoked eel; slabs of truffled foie gras; braised salmon; and all the preparations of turbot, lobster, and other fresh seafood taken on at various ports. And they're only starters! Hard on their heels come roasted stuffed squab, tenderloins of veal, saddles of lamb, multiple beef dishes, a cold plate composed of half a dozen meats, fresh vegetables dripping with butter, platters of cheeses, fruits, and spun-sugar desserts.

Exciting as it is, however, the regular menu conveys but a fraction of the wonders of which the *France*'s kitchen is capable, a truth I learned on one particular occasion when, curious to test the legend that, given advance notice, M. Le Huédé could and would prepare virtually any meal imaginable, I put in my request. The first course was a velvety *bisque de langoustine* spooned from a small tureen placed dramatically in the center of the table, followed by a sinful *tourte chaude à la morue,* chunks of succulent cod with numerous vegetables encased in delicate puff pastry and served with a light truffled sauce. Then came a *filet de boeuf bressane,* a whole Charolais fillet studded with fresh truffles and roasted just long enough to ensure a rare, juicy interior. Christian, my dining steward, then sautéed a handful of chopped *cèpes* in a chafing dish, poured in seasoned natural juices plus a little red wine, reduced the uncomplicated sauce, and added three center-cut slices of beef. With the help of his young assistant, he arranged the meat on a large dinner plate, ladled a suggestion of sauce on the side, then garnished the edges with braised salsify, tender artichoke hearts, and a few sprigs of watercress. Everything—the preparation at table, the formal presentation, the quality and flavor of the dish—amounted to gastronomic perfection. I reserved some of my '67 Nuits-St.-Georges to accompany a few wedges of runny Brie and to prepare my palate for the feathery strawberry soufflé that terminated the spectacle. After two cups of strong *café filtre,* I made my way up to the smoking lounge and consummated the occasion with a snifter of icy pear brandy and a ceremonial Havana.

And so it went, day after day, with M. Le Huédé and his staff producing a wealth of classic dishes for more than 1,200 demanding passengers. He had honored hundreds of requests for special dishes; he had kept his lockers and pantries stocked with the freshest ingredients; and, above all, he had refused to compromise the solid culinary standards that distinguish a great chef from a mediocre one. When I once asked how he managed to conduct such a complex organization, his answer was quick: "It's quite simple. You care for and respect each individual who works under you, and you treat every passenger on every voyage as if he or she were someone special." In his own realm, M. Le Huédé is indeed one of the last true aristocrats.

## POSTSCRIPT

I knew when I composed this essay that the days of my beloved *France* were numbered. The French Government had made it clear in 1973 that it would not continue losing two million dollars annually to subsidize an extravagant style of travel relished primarily by "rich Americans," and

Transat had absolutely no intentions of compromising its standards or re-structuring the ship to save money on fuel. Thus, this last great French liner was laid up in 1974, and I was aboard during her last two sad voyages.

From 1962 to 1974 I made sixteen transatlantic crossings on the *France,* first in the bowels of tourist class as a poverty-stricken student, and eventually (with a highly sophisticated beagle named Mr. Beauregard) in the first-class luxury of Stateroom T-6 on Boat Deck and the opulent splendor of the Chambord dining saloon. Since the main reason for sailing on the *France* was to eat, my preferred routine was to book a double round-trip, dine regally for ten days in the company of such characters as Salvador Dali, Hermione Gingold, and Sir Stephen Spender, disembark in New York only long enough to check the mail, and resume the feasting for another fortnight. It was all too glorious to believe, a gastronomic spectacle and way of life that had tremendous impact on my early development and that was to influence my approach to food and restaurants for years to come.

For a number of years after the liner's demise, I tried to remain in contact with M. Le Huédé, the chief purser (Paul Ermel), my faithful stateroom steward (Joseph) who delivered me those elaborate breakfasts, and various chefs and waiters with whom I'd often share *boeuf bourguignon* at Café des Sports when the ship was turning around in New York. Then they all faded away like the majestic Atlantic greyhound on which they served with such pride.

The *France* was not broken up in the dignified manner she deserved. Instead, the ship was sold to a Norwegian company, converted pitifully into a gigantic cruise vessel destined to roam the Caribbean, and rechristened the *Norway.* I have never set foot on board.

# CHASING CHEESECAKE

*1982*

T he cheesecake so beloved and respected by New Yorkers is suicidally rich, dense, solid, heavy as lead, delicious. The smooth, silky, moist texture is chewy enough so that part of every bite sticks to the fork and the roof of the mouth, and the flavor is at once sweet and sour with just the right hint of vanilla and citrus. The light-golden crust is a buttery, sugary pastry that is sheer hell to apply evenly to the springform pan in which the cake is correctly baked. Only cheesecake made with cream cheese, eggs, sugar, and heavy cream is true New York cheesecake; any filling containing cottage cheese, pot cheese, ricotta cheese, sour cream, yogurt, fruit, artificial sweetener, or half-and-half is phony and automatically disqualified. The real McCoy does not have a crumb crust, nor is it baked in a loaf pan, mold, or pie plate. It is not light, fluffy, airy, spongy, grainy, or dry, and if the traces of lemon and vanilla are more than barely detectable, the cake is wrong.

Although it has always been permissible to top New York cheesecake with a cherry, blueberry, strawberry, or pineapple glaze, native aficionados eat only the plain version, leaving the others for tourists. The nature of truly great New York cheesecake is such that no matter how weak your appetite or how guilty you feel about consuming some six hundred calories a wedge or how much you fight not to scrape up every messy morsel, you succumb every time.

Now, I must insist that, for some strange culinary or psychological reason, eating New York cheesecake anywhere but in New York is almost as weird an experience as trying to savor a hot corned beef with brown mustard on rye in Topeka. I mean, look, it just doesn't taste right—even when it's imported frozen from New York. Over the years, I've sampled the highly touted cheesecakes at the Beverly Hills Hotel and at Zucky's in Santa Monica, at Pumpernik's in Miami, at Salas in Newport, and at all those other famous places where starved New Yorkers attempt to cure their homesickness. It's never the same. Maybe the water or altitude in these locations has some effect on the cake, or maybe there's something incongruent about eating cheesecake in surroundings that lack the proper noise level, aroma, and degree of human rudeness and indifference that New Yorkers expect in a great deli or steak house. Whatever the reason, I'm convinced resolutely that New York cheesecake, like San Francisco sourdough bread and Texas barbecued brisket, is a food to be sought after and consumed only on its home territory.

Of course, things have never really been the same since the closing of the original Lindy's on Broadway and other legendary cheesecake emporiums, and it gave everybody a big scare when Junior's in Brooklyn burned down a few years back (the place blessedly reopened). But most experts agree that, for absolute authenticity, S & S in the Bronx (which supplies cheesecake to such popular steak houses as the Palm, Christ Cella, and Spark's), Junior's (which distributes in Manhattan at all Food Emporium supermarkets), and Turf are New York's Rolls-Royce cheesecake makers. Some people swear by Baby Watson cheesecake, others by the elegant mounds produced at Pastrami 'n Things, and still others by the old-fashioned beauties served at the Stage Delicatessen and at Ratner's Dairy Restaurant. In recent years, there has been lots of talk about the cheesecakes sold at Miss Grimble and at a fashionable East Side pastry shop called Délices La Côte Basque. Well, I personally have no use for the Sylvia Hirsch (alias Miss Grimble) cake: its flavor isn't rich enough and it doesn't have a real crust. And even to suggest that the feathery, loose, overly sweet, outrageously expensive goo at Délices La Côte Basque is the same cheesecake as that once served at Lindy's (a claim that proved embarrassing to the New York Times after the recipe was published) is downright ludicrous.

As it happens, I am one of the few enthusiasts anywhere who possess the original, genuine, and unalterable Lindy's cheesecake recipe. Since this is and always will be the quintessential New York cheesecake, I can only take great pleasure in sharing with the world the recipe that, many years ago, my father easily obtained for my mother one evening by palming our longtime and trustworthy waiter, Sammy, a crisp ten-spot. Even the most skeptical of cheesecake lovers consider this recipe definitive. Follow the directions to the letter, suffer, and enjoy.

## Lindy's Cheesecake

*Pastry:*

1  cup flour
¼  cup sugar
1  teaspoon grated lemon rind
    Dash of vanilla
1  egg yolk
8  tablespoons (1 stick) butter, softened


*Filling:*

2½  pounds cream cheese, room temperature
1¾  cups sugar
  3  tablespoons flour
1½  teaspoon each grated lemon and orange rind
  ¼  teaspoon vanilla
  5  eggs
  2  egg yolks
  ¼  cup heavy cream


To make the pastry, combine the flour, sugar, lemon rind, and vanilla in a large mixing bowl. Make a well in the center, add the egg yolk and butter, and mix with your hands till well blended, adding a little cold water if necessary to make a workable dough. Wrap the dough in plastic or waxed paper and chill for 1 hour in the refrigerator.

To make the filling, place the cream cheese in another large mixing bowl and cream with an electric mixer. Add the sugar, flour, lemon and orange rinds, and vanilla, and beat well. Add the eggs one at a time, beating lightly but thoroughly after each addition. Add the cream, beat lightly, and set the mixture aside.

Preheat the oven to 400° F.

Butter the base and sides of a 9-inch springform pan and remove top from the pan. On a lightly floured surface, roll out about one-third of the dough ⅛ inch thick, fit it over the bottom of the pan, and trim by running a rolling pin over the edges. Bake 15 minutes or till golden, then let cool.

Increase the heat to 550° F.

Place top of springform over the base. Roll the remaining dough ⅛ inch thick, cut in strips to fit almost to the top of the sides of the pan, and press so that the strips line the sides completely. Fill the pan

(continued)

with the cheese mixture, bake for 10 minutes, reduce the heat to 200°, and continue baking 1 hour.

To serve, loosen the pastry from sides, remove the top of the pan very carefully, and cut the cake into 12 wedges.

Serves 12

# THE ROYAL BLUES

*1985*

E picures, no doubt, will continue debating for centuries whether the title "King of Cheeses" should be applied to Stilton, Blue Cheshire, Roquefort, or Gorgonzola, but the one point on which all serious turophiles agree is that, when it comes to after-dinner cheeses, few are in the same class with the blue-veined monarchs. Don't get me wrong. There are certain occasions where nothing is more appropriate than an unctuous Gruyère or Double Gloucester, a perfectly ripened Brie or Camembert, a tangy Taleggio or a truly well-made, creamy *chèvre* or *triple-crème*. But a great blue . . . ah, a great blue is a cheese that virtually demands to be served only as the ideal coda to a well-orchestrated meal. Blue . . . a cheese that, by its very nature, defies all competition, a cheese that is to be contemplated and revered in much the same way as a magnificent red Burgundy. The fact that the postprandial advantages of the world's distinguished blues are not more appreciated by Americans is sad; that even the most noble of these cheeses often end up in salad dressings or in stuffings for baked potatoes is a disgrace.

It is, therefore, with pleasure that I recount an undeniably spectacular dining experience recently savored in a great English restaurant. After mounds of fresh beluga caviar on plates lined with thin-sliced smoked Scotch salmon, delicate double consommé sprinkled with tiny herbed profiteroles, whole poached Dover sole finished in a light cream sauce, roast venison served with braised salsify, minted green peas, *roesti* potatoes, and Niagaras of vintage Champagne, mellow white Burgundy, and noble claret, I was not about to destroy perfection by ordering even one of the sumptuous desserts.

"Nothing but Stilton and a little Port," I directed the tail-coated maître d'hôtel when he came to take my final order.

Immediately, a young waiter rolled over a handsome trolley highlighting a tall, cylindrical wheel of blue-veined cheese. He removed the crusty half-inch crown that had been sliced away earlier and replaced to keep the surface of the cheese from drying out. Next, he carefully cut away wedges of equal thickness and served the Stilton with trimmed celery stalks and English water biscuits. I tasted. The cheese was firm but not chalky, buttery but not overly moist, saltily piquant but not aggressive. The next morsel, spread on a bland cracker, yielded an altogether different flavor when counterpointed with a sip of sweet vintage Port, and the third, consumed with a bite of celery and the remains of the rich, fruity, complex Château La Tour in my glass, assumed still greater character. No confection on earth could have heightened the glory of this particular meal like that small wedge of blue-mottled cheese. As I savored the last remaining nuggets, I again recalled Clifton Fadiman's poetic declaration that "there's such divinity does hedge a Stilton as aureoles no other cheese. It is magisterial."

Although blue-veined cheese is produced in such countries as Australia, Argentina, Israel, Ireland, and even South Africa, the most celebrated examples come from France, Italy, England, and, to a lesser degree, Scandinavia. Over the years, I've sampled the earthy Cabrales, made in very limited quantities by farmers in the Asturia region of Spain; Austria's creamy, intensely moldy-flavored Edelpilzkäse; Germany's distinctive Bavariablu, produced at Wagingam-See, southeast of Munich; Switzerland's zesty Sarrazin from the district around Lake Leman; Canada's soft and assertive Ermite, made by Benedictine monks in Quebec; and our own luscious Maytag Blue from Iowa, and Nauvoo Blue, developed in caves along the Illinois side of the Mississippi River shortly after World War II. All make definite impressions, but none really has the discreet bite, the elusive elegance, the strange mystery that for centuries have characterized England's Stilton, Blue Cheshire, and Blue Wensleydale, France's Roquefort and Persillé des Aravis, and Italy's Gorgonzola. These refined taste sensations should never be served as throwaway hors d'oeuvres with cocktails or as picnic complements. Such fine blue-veined cheese is special in the same way that genuine prosciutto, fresh foie gras, and beluga *malossol* caviar are special, and, at least as far as I'm concerned, the one and only place for a prime Roquefort, a moist, silky Gorgonzola, and a well-developed, creamy Blue Cheshire is next to an extraordinary wine at the end of an important meal. The well-known eighteenth-century French gastronome Grimod de la Reynière had a penchant for hyperbole, but I heartily sympathize with his conviction that "Roquefort should be eaten on one's knees."

France produces more superb blue-veined cheeses than any other country, and to spend a morning in Paris browsing through such aromatic shops as La Ferme St.-Hubert near Place Madeleine, Tachon on the rue de Richelieu, and Lillo in the 16th arrondissement is to get a good idea of exactly what this variety of cheese has meant to the French since before the Middle Ages. Real enthusiasts, of course, make the pilgrimage to the southwest village of Roquefort to witness the age-old production of Roquefort in the caves of Mount Cambalou (the first reference to the cheese is found in a document dating from Charlemagne's rule). Here they learn how loaves of bread are inoculated with the mold *Penicillium roqueforti,* left in a humid atmosphere for four to six weeks, then ground into a powder bearing the spores. They are shown how the powdery culture is sprinkled in layers over the curds of sheep's milk, how the solidified curds are punched with needles to encourage the interior growth of blue mold, how the cheeses are scraped and brushed and salted, and how, in these unique caves (said to provide unrivaled conditions for the aging of cheese), the six-pound wheels are allowed to sit from three to six months to develop their characteristic blue mold before being wrapped in foil stamped with the familiar red sheep. The process is arduous and time-consuming, but the resulting cheese is so distinctive that an international agreement has been established whereby only cheese produced by one of fourteen commercial companies in the region and bearing the red sheep seal can be marketed as genuine Roquefort.

Today Roquefort is easy enough to come by in the United States if you're willing to pay the price, but finding other exceptional French blues can pose a problem unless you have access to a well-stocked cheese shop or dine frequently in restaurants that take their cheeses seriously. I'll go out of my way, for instance, to savor a Fourme d'Ambert, a luscious cheese much like Roquefort that's made from cows' milk near Clermont-Ferrand, and there's one restaurateur who knows to inform me whenever he lays his hands on a really good Bleu d'Auvergne (often marketed as Bleu de Bassilac, Bleu de Quercy, or Bleu de Figeac and sold with a label bearing a distinctive green band), produced in central France. Also occasionally available are the small rounds known as Bleu de Bresse, an exquisite blue created in 1950 at Servas near Lyon and often distributed under the fine-imitation labels "Pipo-Bleu" and "Pipo Crem'." Aged in Gascon caves, Bleu des Causses is a full-flavored, creamy cheese produced from the rich cows' milk of the southwest. Anyone near the Alpine pastures of Savoy or the Jura Mountains should make the special effort to sample Bleu de Lavaldeus, made from goats' milk, Bleu de Sassenage (my daily staple when I was a student living in Grenoble), Bleu de Tignes, and the powerful, aromatic

Bleu de Gex, which by French law must be produced from the milk of cows that graze at an altitude of at least 2,500 feet!

Legend has it that Gorgonzola got its start during Roman times when cows being herded north from the Lomellina Valley near Milan were halted at the small town of Gorgonzola for milking, thus leaving the villagers with such an abundance of milk that cheese was made and taken to mountain caves for aging. While we may never know how valid this story is, we do know that since the ninth century this rich, moist, suavely pungent blue has been turned out in at least a dozen locales throughout the province of Lombardy. Officially called Stracchino Gorgonzola, the cheese is still produced laboriously by hand and aged in either limestone caves or one of many large curing houses. Unlike Roquefort and Stilton—which Italians tend to check off as second-rate products—Gorgonzola is not sown artificially with *Penicillium* spores but simply penetrated with copper wires and allowed to develop its distinctive blue-green mold naturally throughout the curd. From the blending of fresh cows' milk with partially fermented milk, to the long period of maturation needed to encourage the initial mold, to the fastidious turning of the wheels on racks, the Gorgonzola process is time-consuming and costly. The result is an exquisite soft cheese with a slightly wrinkled, orange-gray crust, a highly developed aroma, a melting quality not unlike that of a ripe Camembert, and a piquant, mellow, "fat" flavor that cannot be duplicated. Imitations like Dolcelatte, Zola, and Castelmagno can provide wonderful after-dinner delight at half the cost, but again, comparing these cheeses to authentic Gorgonzola is like comparing a blue-veined cheese from France's Périgord region to genuine Roquefort.

If the Italians often speak cruelly of Roquefort and Stilton, most British epicures are fully convinced that their Stilton, Blue Cheshire, and Blue Wensleydale are what Roquefort and Gorgonzola could be, if only the French and Italians knew a little more about cheese making. Such comparisons, of course, are really a bit ludicrous since the very nature of the great English blues is altogether different from that of their distinguished counterparts. Stilton, for example, which is inoculated with *Penicillium glaucum* but requires no unique setting like the caves of Roquefort for development, is a semi-hard, almost sweet-smelling cheese that is produced not just from cows' milk but from rich, whole summer milk to which enough extra cream is added to give it about 10 percent more butterfat content than either Roquefort or Gorgonzola. Debate still rages throughout Leicestershire over whether the original formula was perfected by a Mrs. Orton or a Mrs. Paulet over two centuries ago, but enthusiasts do agree that the famous cheese was created by a woman and made its initial reputation when first sold around 1780 at the Bell Inn in the small town of Stilton. The cheese reaches its prime after about six months of aging, and, since it tends to dry out rapidly when exposed to air, even the large wheels should ideally be consumed as soon as possible—within a couple of months, at the latest.

Trying to restore a dry, flaky Stilton by pouring Port or red wine over the top is nothing less than a futile desecration. (As one authority puts it, "When Stilton needs moistening, it needs throwing away.") The same holds for scooping out the cheese with a spoon. Stilton packed in crocks is a respectable enough product for those who have no way of utilizing a whole cylinder, but for the purist about to attack a perfect, evenly veined, velvety seven- or eight-pound specimen, the old British slogan still applies: "Cut high, cut low, cut level," meaning that, after slicing away a half-inch crown from the top, you should remove a whole slice from the round and cut the slice into wedges, remembering always to replace the crown on top to maintain maximum moistness.

In the same league with Stilton are Blue Cheshire, Blue Wensleydale, and Blue Vinny, all of which seem more and more difficult (and often impossible) to acquire as factory production continues to make anachronisms of old-fashioned farmhouse cheeses. Made from milk that is naturally high in acidity, a genuine, buttery, tangy Blue Cheshire is rare indeed, and partisans such as I certainly agree with the gastronome Maurice des Ombiaux's suggestion that the cheese is "fit only for heroes." Blue Wensleydale from Yorkshire can trace its lineage back to medieval times, and although it is somewhat less subtle than Stilton and Blue Cheshire, many consider it superior to the better-known aristocrats. My obsession with Blue Vinny began back in the early seventies when I sampled my first crumbly, earthy slab at a shop in Dorchester called E. Parsons. Characterized by writer John Arlotte as having "essentially a male taste," this blue, made from hand-skimmed milk and exposed to strange microorganisms said to be indigenous to Dorsetshire, seems now to have virtually disappeared. I last tasted Blue Vinny a few years back in Berkshire at Patrick Rance's Wells Stores, a shop in the small village of Streatley that for decades has housed the world's finest collection of English cheeses. Perhaps Major Rance still has a source for his monthly ration, but when I recently stopped by London's most renowned purveyor of fine cheeses, Paxton & Whitfield in Jermyn Street, I was told by a sad-faced clerk: "Ah, Blue Vinny . . . sorry, but we haven't had any in well over a year. A beautiful cheese, yes indeed, but they just don't seem to be making it any longer." My quest continues.

Although there's nothing like the great blue-veined cheeses of France, Italy, and England, some others in the international repertory are certainly worth seeking out in this country and abroad if you're really interested in this type of cheese. Danablu, Denmark's most famous blue and the one most readily available in the United States, can be a little too sharp and cloying when overripe, but at its prime the cheese is delicious with fresh fruit and a sturdy ale. Also keep an eye open for the Danish Blue Castello, the triple-cream Saga, and the recently developed Mycella, which bears some resemblance to Gorgonzola. Norway's best blue is Gammelost, a highly aromatic, piquant cheese made from sour skim milk, while both

Ädelost and Grönmögelost from Sweden (the latter is marketed in the United States simply as "Swedish Blue") can make for the perfect pungent ending to a dinner that highlights lots of spicy dishes.

If you can find it, the Portuguese Castelo Branco is almost as savory and rambunctious as Spain's Cabrales, and if you happen to live in an area with a large Italian community, ask in the food shops about the mellow, bluish-green-veined Verdo Sardo, made in Sardinia from rich sheep's milk. Lymeswold, distributed in small, 150-gram packages, has been the talk of all England ever since it was developed just a couple of years ago. Some people consider it a mediocre blue; I find it delectable, though certainly not in the same class with Stilton and Blue Cheshire. Treasure Cave, Oregon Blue, and Nauvoo Blue are names to remember here at home, and as for Maytag Blue, produced in Newton, Iowa, I must say I've had occasional examples of this magnificent cheese that inspired me to check the wrapping to make sure it wasn't stamped with the red sheep of Roquefort!

One word of advice about purchasing blue-veined cheeses in the United States. Many imports arrive in this country insufficiently aged. Do not, however, automatically refuse a blue that does not appear to have reached its prime, especially if it is well-marbled. Simply unwrap the cheese, cover it with a slightly damp cloth, and let it stand at room temperature about twenty-four hours or till it reaches the desired texture.

As for serving a distinctive blue, it goes without saying that the cheese must be at room temperature and accompanied by both a knife and a fork. I frown upon serving a vinegary salad before or with any dinner cheese, not only because it interferes with the cheese but because the dressing can completely destroy the palate for any fine wine that might be on the table. Both crusty fresh bread and bland water crackers are appropriate with all blue cheese, and, in the case of the English monarchs, a small, trimmed, compatible stalk of celery can produce a remarkable taste sensation. Blue cheese and red wine constitute a marriage made in heaven, so much so that professional wine tasters try to refrain from eating Roquefort or Gorgonzola for fear of distorting their judgment. The more aggressive the cheese, the more sturdy the wine should be. A well-aged claret or premium ale goes very well with English cheeses, but if you've never consumed a morsel of prime Stilton or Blue Cheshire with vintage Port or Amontillado Sherry, you've missed out on one of life's great gustatory moments. I also recommend serving a mellow old Sauternes or sweet German Trockenbeeren-auslese with Roquefort, Bleu de Bresse, Edelpilzkäse or maybe Bavariablu. Some turophiles don't agree. Try it and judge for yourself.

# THE QUIET PLEASURES OF COGNAC AND CIGARS

*1973*

A great meal involves much more than simply devouring one succulent course after another. The serious epicure knows how to prepare himself, how to practice restraint, how to balance flavors and textures, and, above all, how to attain that sublime moment when total physical and mental satisfaction is realized. A truly distinguished dinner is like a well-constructed opera. The overture or prelude is a subtle but stimulating apéritif; the performance demonstrates an intelligent sequence of imaginative dishes, fine wines, and rich coffee that blend into perfect harmony; and the finale is an excellent Cognac accompanied by a good cigar. Remove one element from the spectrum and the overall experience is incomplete.

Dining properly is no facile pastime. It requires study, concentration, and the exploitation of all the senses. Most enthusiasts eventually acquire a certain degree of expertise when it comes to ordering apéritifs, food, and wine, but, curiously enough, few people make any effort to partake of the amenities that represent the culmination of any gastronomic occasion—the postprandial Cognac and cigar. For years, I also eschewed these items as overrated, superfluous, and too time-consuming. Then, through gradual exposure, I became aware of their power to intensify and prolong the pleasures of the table, and today even the most dramatic feast fails to content me if I am denied my delectable Cognac and mellow cigar.

If my own past ignorance may serve as an example, I would suspect that many connoisseurs have deprived themselves of this ultimate reward mainly because of certain bewitching complexities. First, there is the popular tendency to choose as a *digestif* a sweet or blended liqueur over Cognac, as well as a cigarette or pipe over a cigar. Naturally it's a question of individual taste, but I can assure you that once you're in the habit of imbibing the most refined of distilled spirits while puffing on a full-flavored, aromatic cigar, all other options are out of the question. Second, acquiring a passionate taste for fine Cognac and delicious cigar smoke requires a good deal of time, patience, and, indeed, experimentation. The privilege is not unlike learning to walk or speak a foreign language fluently. Third, far too many people who do order a Cognac and cigar end up loathing the occasion only because the product is inferior in quality. To those honestly interested in spirits and tobacco, there's no substitute for self-gained knowledge and no excuse for not learning to determine the difference between cheap brandy and well-aged Cognac or between a crude cigar and one that is handmade by skilled craftsmen.

As in the case of selecting aristocratic Ports or clarets, dealing with Cognac can be a frustrating task for the uninitiated. Usually the labels on bottles read like hieroglyphics, and unless you familiarize yourself with the meaning behind all the colors, signs, stars, and nomenclature, you're in for trouble. Actually, the job is quite simple once you grasp the basic essentials. The main point to remember is that although Cognac is distilled wine, or brandy, not all brandy is Cognac. To qualify as authentic Cognac, the spirit must come from France, and, more specifically, from the chalky area around the western city of Cognac and the Charente River. Here the brandy is distilled only from Angoumois, Aunis, and Saintonge wine in simple copper pot stills, then aged in casks of precious Limousin oak. Brandy not registered by the Bureau National Interprofessionnel du Cognac is not, by French law, real Cognac.

The Cognac area, the soil of which resembles that of Champagne, is divided into six districts, and the quality of the brandy is determined not only by the period of aging but also by the soil of the exact district where the grapes are grown. The finest product, much of which is distilled on private estates, comes exclusively from the central district called Grande Champagne, where the soil is most chalky. The next best is produced from wine of the Petite Champagne. Beyond this district are the Borderies and three Bois, regions where the soil becomes progressively richer and the brandy more highly flavored. When Cognac from Grande Champagne and Petite Champagne is blended, the result is an excellent Fine Champagne. As the progression in blending continues outward to include brandy from the Borderies, Cognac begins to lose its unique finesse, and by the time the earthier wines of the Bois are added, the spirit is much less delicate.

As far as aging Cognac is concerned, federal control is even tighter. The legal minimum of time allowed in the Limousin barrels is two years. This is new, incomplete Cognac that rates no stars on any label. Cognac aged from three to five years is entitled by legal register to one, two, and three stars respectively, while that aged over five years can be officially designated as V.S.O.P. (Very Special Old Pale). From that point on, the law does not allow any firm to claim further aging—meaning, of course, you have no way of telling whether a V.S.O.P. is five or fifteen years old. If you're lucky enough to find Cognac bearing a vintage date, this signifies that it was matured outside of France (usually at the London docks) for perhaps twenty to thirty years. But do note, while searching out old dusty vintages, that after forty years Cognac loses much of its alcoholic strength and savor.

Selecting cigars is less complicated than assessing Cognac, particularly now that the American industry is making use of short-leaf tobacco and machine-processed binders. As any aficionado knows, a cigar is composed of blended filler that is held in place by a binder leaf before being encased in an exterior wrapper. Until fairly recently, the only distinguished cigars were those made of natural long filler and fashioned by hand. In the effort to manufacture domestic cigars that have more uniform flavor and a milder burn, however, the industry has introduced methods of machine pulverizing and handling that not only eliminate a good deal of high labor costs but also guarantee some very respectable products.

Of course, for purists there is still nothing more satisfying than a gracefully hand-tailored cigar full of rich long leaf and distinctive aroma. Connoisseurs have never quite recovered from the shock of '62, the year the absurd embargo was placed on that inimitable tobacco raised in the Cuban district of Vuelta Abajo. But most cigar smokers, unless they happen to be out of the country or on a foreign plane or ocean liner, have learned by necessity to do without their Montecristos, H. Upmanns, and Romeo y Julietas and to familiarize themselves with other superior handmade cigars. Fortunately, after Castro took power, many Cuban craftsmen were able to relocate, plant their seed in other countries with soil and climate similar to those of Cuba, and continue practicing their trade. Perhaps the most successful result of the endeavor is the noble Montecruz, a cigar composed of Brazilian, Dominican, and African Cameroon leaves and handmade on the Canary Islands in the Havana tradition. Jamaica produces excellent cigars (the Macanudo in particular), and here in the United States, Tampa's Shakespeare and La Corona make for very acceptable smokes.

We all have recollections of sublime moments of postprandial contentment, and one of the outstanding occasions that remains vivid in my own mind took place a few years back not in a French setting but aboard the superliner *Michelangelo*. Dinner one evening in the first-class dining saloon had involved a series of gastronomic superlatives, each lending itself to mounting appreciation. After single flutes of Gancia Spumante, my companions and I began with *sfogi en Saor* (sweet and sour baby sole), followed by an elegant molded risotto with Parmesan and chicken-liver sauce, washed down with a smooth '64 Brolio Riserva. The main course, truffled roast veal flavored with fresh sage, was served with feathery polenta, creamed *radicchio* with prosciutto, and a noble bottle of '62 Barolo. Then came a small salad of watercress and endive, a few crumbles of ripe Gorgonzola, and finally a delectable chocolate-and-rum torte known as a *tartufata*. The service had been expert, the conversation engaging, the spirits lively, but after two cups of espresso I was ready to enjoy the culminating moment in solitary splendor. And no place affords this opportunity any better than the *Michelangelo*'s first-class Pool Verandah.

As I made my way up to Lido Deck, I checked my inside coat pocket to make sure I hadn't left in my stateroom the leather cigar case that held the four precious Romeo y Julietas I had purchased on the ship. Entering the quiet lounge, I chose a comfortable black leather armchair on the starboard side overlooking the sea. A white moon spread its light across the calm water, the great vessel was riding smoothly, the mood was right. A waiter approached. *"Un Martell Cordon Argent, per favore,"* I directed.

When the Cognac arrived in a large-mouthed snifter, I cupped the glass in the palm of my hand and began swirling the golden liquid around the bulb, waiting for the warmth to release the spirit's essence. After a while, I raised the snifter so that the mouth encircled my nose, breathed deeply, and allowed the ethereal fragrance to penetrate all the nasal passages. My eyes remained on the sea as I took my first sip, held the liquid in my mouth, breathed deeply again, swallowed slowly, and became gradually aware how the Cognac was prolonging each and every flavor I had relished at dinner. Placing the snifter on the small table, I casually took one of the large Havana coronas from the case, removed the colorful romantic band, and clipped a V-opening at the pointed end. The cigar was tautly rolled, yet its body gave slightly when I squeezed and maneuvered it around under my nose. I placed it directly in the center between my lips, lit a match, allowed the sulfur to burn away, then held the flame slightly below the tuck. It took a few puffs to ignite the end evenly, but already my head was surrounded by an aromatic cloud of mild, clean-smelling smoke. The first huge draw I held in my mouth and played at inhaling. The taste of Cognac lingered, the two flavors were blending ideally, and my senses were fully aroused by the almost mystical communion of delicate alcohol and mellow smoke.

The ritual lasted about forty-five minutes or until I had flicked three one-inch white ashes from the slow-burning cigar into the ashtray and finished the Cordon Argent. As I sank deeper into the soft leather, I was fully content, satisfied, and unaware of time and the pressures of the world. Yes, the mighty sea and the majestic liner never failed to dispel worry, just as my faithful Cognac and cigar never failed to make complete a wonderful gastronomic experience and to consummate a perfect occasion.

## POSTSCRIPT

This is the first piece I ever wrote for *Town & Country*, and now, some 250 articles later, I can't help but be surprised at how little my temperament and view of things have changed since those innocent days. Nor can I help but wonder if, during these panicky times devoted to outlawing all forms of tobacco, there's a single magazine in this country that would print an essay extolling the merits of a good cigar. Although a nasty hiatal hernia forced me to virtually give up cigars about eight years ago, there is still no more sensuous postprandial experience than relaxing with a snifter of fine Cognac in a room where others are puffing on their aromatic Havanas (and *pace* the American health fanatic who would have all cigar enthusiasts cast into a leper colony). Let me also emphasize that most of the truly serious restaurants of the world (like La Tour d'Argent in Paris, La Caravelle in New York, and the Connaught in London) not only still allow cigar smoking but pride themselves on a noble selection presented dramatically in handsome hardwood humidors. Disapproving customers in these highly civilized places learn quickly enough either to cope or take their business elsewhere.

# PART IV
# THE FRENCH
# CONNECTION

My love of France and French cuisine is as intense today as when I was a young student of literature eager to learn as much about coq au vin as about the poetry of Baudelaire. There is still no place on earth where I'd rather dine out than Paris, and there's still no country where regional cooking is more diverse, more fascinating, more sumptuously delicious. If I seem to devote half my life to disclaiming loudly that reckless, destructive culinary movement of recent years known as *la nouvelle cuisine,* the other half is spent proclaiming the eternal merits of lusty bistro and brasserie food, Beaujolais, and great classic dishes in the tradition of Escoffier, Alexandre Dumaine, and Fernand Point.

Before I attended the Paris cooking school featured here, I thought I knew a lot about French cooking. Ha! No doubt I absorbed a great deal about the many culinary techniques that help to make French cuisine the most compelling approach to food in the world, but perhaps what was most exciting was my exposure to the veritable wealth of exceptional ingredients so difficult to find outside France: the flours and special yeasts we used in bread and pastry making; the delicate lettuces, Alpine potatoes, wild mushrooms, and strange beans used in all sorts of salads and vegetable dishes; the mountain hams, Bresse chickens, salt-marsh lamb, wild game birds, and Mediterranean fish that we stuffed, roasted, and poached; and the rich Norman creams, sweet butter, and fresh farm cheeses that we would sample in small neighborhood markets throughout the city. After cooking all the delectable dishes at La

Varenne and making my way nightly through the great Paris restaurants, bistros, and brasseries, I took off to really learn all about the exotic wolf fish along the Riviera, the blue-footed chickens and androgynous snails of Burgundy, the frogs' legs and foie gras of Alsace, and, indeed, the rare black truffles, fat geese and ducks, and lusty stews of the Southwest. The quest has been passionate, and I'm still at it.

# LOST IN PUFF PASTRY

1976

"*Vous êtes en retard, jeune homme,*" roars Chef Ferdinand Chambrette, glancing up from his work just long enough to comment on the fact that I'm exactly six minutes late to class. Having learned that no excuse is better than a feeble one as far as this particular French chef is concerned, I opt not to explain how the Paris Métro was late this morning and simply proceed to tie a long white apron around my distended gut, collect my personal set of knives, and hasten to join the chef-teacher and my fellow American students in the small kitchen.

Already my compatriots are gathered around the large wooden table: two males, six females, the same familiar faces I've been studying about six hours a day for the past week. As I join the group, Chef is opening a long cylindrical can. Removing the lid, he turns the tin upside down, punctures a small hole in the other end, and blows forcefully through the aperture, releasing onto a marble slab one huge luscious block of fresh truffled foie gras. We all gasp at the sight; then we gasp even louder as Chef slits the hunk of pure matter lengthwise, removes the fat truffles from the center, and casually tosses the precious goose liver onto a wire screen stretched across a mixing bowl.

"Work it through the sieve," he directs in French, handing Moyna a large wooden pestle, "every morsel of it." While she pursues this act of desecration, I begin my fifth puff pastry of the week (so far all unsuccessful), while others go about their assigned duties, carefully following the printed recipes we've received. Helene and Kathy tear the skin off chicken breasts and imitate Chef's method of deboning the meat; Sammy chops mushrooms for *duxelles;* Gloria makes Chantilly by beating sugar and kirsch with heavy cream; Cynthia cleans red snappers; Herb prepares the dough to make fresh noodles; Isabelle stands over a simmering stockpot, inwardly praying that her consommé will jell properly when later stirred over ice.

This is my last day at La Varenne, one of the best cooking schools in Paris, or, for that matter, in all of France. I'm here for a one-week advanced-level course, and my feet are killing me. Others have been around for three, four, six weeks and are fully acclimated to the strenuous schedules and the hard floor. Still others will remain in residence three months or more, and in all likelihood they'll leave as expert chefs. Upstairs on the second floor is the beginners class, conducted entirely in English. Once we leave our kitchen some four hours from now, the intermediates will move in to absorb the bilingual culinary wisdom of another French chef. We nine are taking the advanced course not only because we have a working knowledge of French, but also because for years we've been following the teachings of Julia Child and trying to reproduce recipes from *Larousse Gastronomique.* At times I feel like a dunce and wish I could take it slower and easier with the intermediate group. Then my soufflé rises perfectly, or my terrine comes out with a beautiful texture, or my sauce doesn't separate, and, at those proud moments, I'm glad I decided to take the full plunge into *la haute cuisine classique.* Furthermore, I'm now convinced anybody can do it who loves to cook and who's willing to work hard and learn.

Moyna's foie gras arm is exhausted, so, at the risk of suffering recriminations from the Chef, who for over thirty years has directed the award-winning kitchen at the Parisian restaurant La Boule d'Or, she lets up momentarily. Rolling out my dough and placing it in the refrigerator for the first of six fifteen-minute intervals, I glance about the room. Helene and Kathy are sisters from Long Island, young, energetic, both married, and both simply eager to master French cooking so they can entertain more gracefully when they return home to their families. Sammy, in his twenties, never has much to say but hopes one day to open a restaurant back in Oregon. Cynthia, from Pittsburgh, will tell you in no uncertain terms that she's been cooking for a large family for more than twenty years, that she's "done all this," and that there are a few things she could show Chef. So far Cynthia has broken specks of egg yolk in her whites, stuffed a fish from the wrong side, and destroyed an entire main course by confusing fish and beef stock. But we all love Cynthia, and we're jealous of her flawless soufflés. Isabelle is a Chinese girl from Indiana who's much more at ease in front of a copper mixing bowl than a wok. Herb was brought up in Georgia perfecting Brunswick stew; now he considers himself an authority on *filet de boeuf en croûte*. And dear Gloria. Nobody is quite sure exactly where Gloria is from since she's been wandering the European continent with her diplomat husband for years and, for some reason, doesn't care to discuss the last time she visited the States. Not one member of the class appears underfed, but Gloria, who apparently buys her stunning if rather snug cooking outfits at Dior and who is never without a few sapphires and a wedge of French bread coated with fresh butter, does undoubtedly have a slight weight problem. In all, it's a good group.

"*Au travail!*" Chef blasts in my direction, noticing my idleness. I grab a few endives and begin washing the leaves for a salad. "*Moyna, au travail!*" he repeats, staring at her.

"But, Chef, my arm's about to fall off," she protests. "This is worse than beating egg whites, and, besides, it seems it'll take forever to work all this foie gras through the wire. Surely there's an easier way."

"*Non, ma chérie,*" he snaps, "this is the only method, and I suggest you develop a little patience. *La bonne cuisine: c'est l'école de la patience,*" he continues, adding still another colorful aphorism from his repertory.

Today, like every day, we are preparing our own lunch—a hedonistic affair that in many respects could match the fare at Tour d'Argent. To begin there's mousse of foie gras in aspic. Then red snapper with *duxelles en papillote,* followed by ground boned chicken breast *pojarski* in heavy cream sauce, fresh noodles, watercress-and-endive salad, and, for dessert, *tarte aux fraises.* Sound simple? It's not. Chef assigns everyone a certain duty; the recipes we follow are not only in English and French but also in U.S. standard measures as well as in the metric system (although we work solely by the latter); and, if we're lucky, our 9:30 A.M. class will end over lunch about 1:30. Then it's back upstairs at 2:30 for a two-hour demonstration of methods that will be practiced in class the following session. And finally, for those with fortitude, there are often wine tastings or kitchen tours in the late afternoon, visits to pastry shops, cheese shops, or the new Les Halles market, and, in the evening, special meals in special restaurants. The same opportunities exist for students in the beginner and intermediate courses, and those lucky few who have the time and money to complete all three twelve-week levels will not only walk away with 1,100 mastered recipes under their arms, but will also be some sort of human encyclopedias on anything pertaining to the art of French cooking and eating.

Isabelle is worried about her brown aspic, which is to be chilled and used in molds for the foie gras mousse. Yesterday she began her stock, full of vegetables, gelatin, Madeira, and two egg whites for clarification (yes, we've learned how to clarify liquids with egg whites). Now she checks the hot broth. It's still not adequately clear, so she separates an egg and is just about to add another white.

"Stop!" shouts Chef. "It's too late now. That'll do absolutely no good, and all you'll end up with is a stringy mess. We'll have to make do with what you have."

"But, Chef," she tries to reason, "if we cook down the stock, why wouldn't the extra egg white help the clarification?"

"It just won't, and that's that. One of the mysterious laws of nature. All you could do is start again from scratch, and we don't have time for that. Besides, one of the important challenges in cooking is trying to work with imperfection when necessary in hopes of attaining perfection. Here, let me see what I can do."

With that he begins dipping spoonfuls of aspic from the stockpot into a small metal container. *"De la glace!"* he directs Gloria. "Stop eating all that butter—which is going to destroy your liver—and fill a large bowl with ice. And, Sammy, did you put those molds in the freezer? Good. Bring me one."

Everyone jumps except Cynthia, who's busy counting the folds of baking paper being wrapped airtight around a *duxelles*-covered red snapper.

*"Non, ma chérie,"* he says to arm-aching Moyna, "don't stop working that foie gras while you watch me! And, Kathy, that chicken's not ground fine enough. Run it through again, then beat it thoroughly with a wooden spoon till it's smooth."

All this time Chef is gently stirring the aspic over ice, glancing down from time to time to see if it's setting properly while simultaneously searching for unwanted particles that might surface when chilled. His massive hands, toughened and scarred from years of exposure to hot pans, stubborn dough, and misdirected knives, tend to conceal the innate delicacy of his technique and the refinement of his professional skill. But he studies the aspic with the love and intensity of a sculptor analyzing the first stages of a stone coming to life. His keen eyes seem to lose focus as he stares momentarily into the hypnotic golden liquid, waiting, just as the alchemist does, for that moment when the transformation of confusion into order begins. Chef is a craftsman, and he is an artist.

When the aspic starts to congeal, Chef spoons a little into the mold, then slowly turns and twists the mold in hopes that the aspic will adhere to the base and sides. It works (almost mysteriously), so he lets us coat the other molds.

*"Les truffes,"* he utters. Dead silence. *"Les truffes!* Where *are* the chopped truffles?" We freeze. *"Dieu,"* he swears, "don't tell me no one took the initiative to chop the truffles! Now everybody here has studied the recipe, everybody knows the mousse calls for specks of truffle, so why hasn't someone taken ten seconds to chop those truffles! Time wasted is the worst enemy of great cooking."

Two or three people grab knives, Gloria drops hers within one precarious inch of my foot, Chef glares, and by the time she's regained her composure, the cutting board is covered with black nuggets. Chef directs everyone to sprinkle the specks evenly around the molds, then explains how the molds must be refrigerated before a second coating of aspic can be applied.

Down the stairs comes an attractive middle-aged lady from the beginners class carrying in her arms an enormous casserole full of *coq au vin blanc*.

"*Excusez-moi, Chef*," she interrupts in half-French, half-English, "but our *frigidaire est complet*, and we were wondering if we could put this in yours for a while?"

"*Oui, oui*," he responds, throwing a hand in the air in mild irritation. "But *faites attention* to that *pâte feuilleté*."

*My God, my puff pastry! I should have rolled it the third time ten minutes ago!* I race to the refrigerator, grab the butter-stuffed dough, sling flour on the ice-cold marble, and begin rolling and folding in three.

"*Non, jeune homme*," Chef exclaims, springing from the main worktable over to my marble counter. "Look, you can see the butter through the dough, and if you don't close up those ends, you're going to lose half your butter in the baking." I stare closely, and sure enough, there are faint yellow patches on top, and the ends are loose. *Hummm, maybe that's why my puff pastry has been heavy as lard every day.* I cover the patches with flour, roll out, then seal the ends carefully with the rolling pin. *But how in heaven's name did Chef notice that from across the room?*

As soon as I give up the marble, Herb takes over, rolls out the dough for fresh noodles, and sets up the pasta machine. Back at the worktable, others are busy preparing the foie gras mousse and chicken mixture for the *pojarski*. Anyone obsessed with calories and cholesterol would suffer cardiac arrest over the huge slabs of fresh butter, cartons of *crème fraîche*, and tubs of heavy cream being added from all sides. (And not ten minutes ago Chef, with typical French sagacity, explained that the trouble with Belgian cuisine is that it's too heavy with butter and cream!) Here no one has ever heard of that absurd *cuisine minceur*.

Helene blends the ground chicken and cream with a large spoon, then stops when Chef moves in forcefully, expresses exasperation with a "*Mon Dieu*," crams his thick hands down into the bowl, and, in ten seconds, finishes mixing the ingredients with his fingers.

"*Ma chérie*," he sighs, "you must learn to use your hands whenever possible—for mixing, tasting, scraping, stirring, almost everything. Oh I know they consider this unsanitary in America, but, believe me, no Frenchman has ever died yet from mixing his steak tartare or green salad by hand. There's very little a spoon can do that two hands can't do better." He licks the feathery-light raw chicken from one finger. "Salt, it needs more salt."

Clunk! We all turn in horror, only to discover Gloria and Herb kneeling on the floor over a pile of sticky ribbon noodles.

"I told Herb we shouldn't have tried to dry the noodles like that," she explains to the group, "but he insisted we suspend that steel oven rack between that nail and this can opener, and now just look."

"Stop complaining, Gloria," Chef says sympathetically, "and learn to deal with the problem. All that matters is the results. *Ce n'est pas grave.* After all, those wet noodles aren't going to break, so you two simply restring them, attach the rack more sensibly, and get on about your work."

Chef now takes a pastry bag, fills it with handfuls of cream-enriched foie gras mousse, calls for the aspic- and truffle-lined molds, squeezes the bag till a little mousse flows (which he casually licks off), and artistically fills the first mold faster than the eye can follow. Everyone takes a turn, but nobody's mousse looks quite so exquisite as Chef's. *"Il faut de l'expéri-ence,"* he quips. A few more truffles on top of each, more aspic, and the glistening molds are returned to the refrigerator to chill.

Tension builds as the clock moves past noon, and once again we're made aware of what it's like in the kitchen of a great French restaurant or large home, trying to complete complex preparations on time. Chicken cutlets are formed, dusted lightly with flour, and sautéed slowly in butter before being flamed with brandy. The small red snappers, covered with *duxelles* and cloaked airtight, are made ready for the oven, where they'll bake in their own steam and retain every ounce of their succulent natural flavor. A large pot of water is put on to boil the noodles. Mushrooms are quickly sautéed, transferred to a bowl, and, along with lemon juice, white wine, and heavy cream, positioned so there'll be no time lost when the moment comes to finish off the chicken *pojarski.* Isabelle beats a vinaigrette for the salad, Helene checks the fresh strawberries for flaws, Kathy carefully stirs the delicate pastry cream she's prepared for the *tarte,* and I remain squatted at an oven door, peering through the small window and praying my puff pastry will rise to fluffy heights. Out comes the foie gras from the refrigerator for unmolding, and just as Sammy is about to plunge the bottom of one mold into hot water, Chef screams for the last time. *"Non, jeune homme!* What do you want: dribblings of hot water in your mousse?" And with that he takes a heavy dish towel, saturates it in the water, wraps it around the mold, and waits a few seconds. Out slides a masterpiece, smooth, firm, and glowing in black-speckled golden radiance.

Twelve-thirty, and we have cleared the long wooden table, set it with china, flatware, and crystal worthy of the sybaritic feast we've prepared, opened three bottles of vintage Corton-Charlemagne (there's no sou-pinch-ing at La Varenne), and begun devouring the luscious *mousse de foie gras en gelée.* At appropriate intervals, students get up to serve dishes for which they're mainly responsible: Cynthia and Sammy, the snapper; Helene and Kathy, *pojarski;* Herb, the noodles; Isabelle, the salad; and Gloria—well, Gloria helps everybody with everything. Chef doesn't budge from his seat, content in carrying on his profound discourses about everything from how to truss a partridge to the philosophy of Voltaire to the current political happenings in France—all subjects on which he's a self-acclaimed authority.

My feet sting so badly I can hardly enjoy the sensuous fare, but, while Gloria cleans away the cheese and salad and opens a little Champagne, I struggle up to serve my *tarte aux fraises.* It looks exquisite—a long, golden, beautifully risen, cream-filled pastry cradling giant fresh strawberries glistening with apricot glaze. Perfection. I wait for all to cut their first bites. Polite silence. Chef tastes and sits and stares at me. Then everyone glares, even Gloria. I taste. Something's wrong. But it can't be wrong, for the *tarte* looks perfect, and I'm proud I finally got my pastry to rise properly. "Salt," mumbles Moyna, breaking the deadening silence, "you left out the salt!" "Yes, salt," everyone chimes in, "there's not one grain of salt in this pastry; it's too bland, it needs at least a half teaspoon of salt, it . . . "

"*O.K., so I forgot the blasted salt. But what about the absolutely marvelous way my pastry rose?*"

"*Jeune homme,*" Chef interjects, "no doubt you've finally learned the trick to making puff pastry, but no matter how beautiful a dish looks, if the taste is not perfect, the dish is a failure. You didn't recheck the recipe and therefore forgot something so seemingly unimportant as salt. An accomplished chef can't afford to forget anything. It's all right to make mistakes as long as the end result is satisfactory. But there'll be plenty of other opportunities, so *ce n'est pas grave.*"

Chef and the others end up being very sympathetic, but, as I drag my swollen feet out the door and into the cool, sunlit streets of Paris, humiliation turns to fury. *Damn it, I'll show them. I'll simply prolong my stay in Paris, arrange to remain enrolled at La Varenne one more day, and come Monday I'll prepare puff pastry the likes of which would put even Paul Bocuse to shame. Yes, decided!* And with that I march back to the hotel, obtain permission to keep my room, put my feet to soak, pick up the phone, and tell the maître d'hôtel at Ledoyen I'll be in at nine sharp for the *feuilleté des langoustines.*

## POSTSCRIPT

La Varenne is still one of the most successful and professional cooking schools in Paris, and I don't regret for a moment the days I spent there familiarizing myself with many of the fine points of French cooking (this is the only cooking school I've ever attended). I am convinced, however, that the one and only truly valid way to learn to cook generally is to grab classic cookbooks like *Joy of Cooking* (which I still consult constantly), the first volume of *Mastering the Art of French Cooking* by Julia Child et al., and Marcella Hazan's *Classic Italian Cook Book,* get into the kitchen, and start reproducing as many dishes as possible. It may be true that only those born with exceptional talent can perform a Chopin étude really well or write a great novel. But it's equally true, I do believe, that anyone with determination and a modicum of imagination can become a very good cook after a reasonable amount of experience.

# THE BLACK DIAMONDS
# OF GASTRONOMY

*1981*

"*Cherche, Minou, cherche!*" commanded Monsieur Laroche, pulling his heavy sweater down over working blues, repositioning his faded beret, and grabbing a small basket off a hook.

"*Cherche, cherche!*"

Excitedly, the dog ran in circles around the farmyard, then shot through the old gate and down a dirt road, followed by the farmer and me. Normally the weather in southwest France is still relatively mild in December, but on this particular morning the air of the Périgord had an icy edge. On both sides of the road the terrain was rugged, with chalky soil, sharp rocks, stunted trees, and sparse vegetation that would have appeared to be partly scorched had it not been for a few scattered patches of moss. The scene hardly fulfilled anybody's romantic vision of La Belle France.

Suddenly Monsieur Laroche and I turned off the road and headed for a certain stretch of mossy woodland. Not far away, near a short oak tree that looked almost dead, Minou was pawing frantically at the ground as if she were trying to unearth a bone.

"*C'est ça, c'est ça,*" M. Laroche yelled to the mongrel, "that's right, Minou, show us where it is."

Directly over the spot where the dog was scratching, M. Laroche squatted, took a nail-like object from his pocket, and began carefully digging with his hands and the tool. Soon he rose with a lump of earth in his hand, flicked the mud off what looked like a walnut, sniffed the object, and tossed the eager dog a morsel of meat from his pocket. "*Une truffe,*" he mumbled disinterestedly, cleaning away more mud before passing the brownish, gnarled truffle to me to smell. I held it to my nose, noticed little more than a fungoid odor, laid it in the basket, and proceeded over to where Minou was again pawing.

Another truffle, then another. Some the color of earth, others grayish-black; some no bigger than a marble, others the size of a small egg. At one point the dog seemed to be almost out of control as she nosed the ground and scrabbled. This time what M. Laroche brought up was the size and color of an eight-ball. "*Ah, enfin, voilà une belle truffe,*" he exclaimed proudly, thrusting it at me. I rubbed, sniffed, flicked dirt, sniffed, and the more I fondled the large tuber, the more pronounced the aroma became. Lusty, earthy, cheesy, garlicky, ammoniated, decadent, obscene—no word could adequately describe the almost offensive odor, which was simply the unique fragrance of ripe truffle, the rare black jewel of gastronomy and the most expensive food delicacy in the world.

Having collected about a dozen truffles in less than an hour and run out of meaty rewards for Minou, we returned to wash and brush clean our valuable yield. Each specimen would fetch M. Laroche an incredible price the following Saturday at the market in Sarlat, yet he wrapped two large beauties in a handkerchief, generously dropped the treasure into my satchel, and put me on the road southward to Gascony, where my friends were waiting.

After twenty minutes in the closed car, I once again detected that elusive odor, faint at first, then pungent, then so overwhelming I had to roll down a window. Precariously untying the handkerchief while driving down the highway, I withdrew one of the fleshy truffles, studied it between glances at the road, sniffed it compulsively, caressed its warty surface, and finally gave in to curiosity and temptation. With one single indulgent bite my mouth seemed to explode with every glorious taste sensation I could imagine, lending full credence to the belief that, even though you think you've eaten truffles all your life, you've never really tasted truffles till you've eaten one fresh out of the ground. With total abandon I took another bite, then another, till I had consumed in seconds what, according to current retail value, was about $200 worth of truffle. Some have tried to describe its savor as rich, subtle, aromatic, unctuous, beefy, but it is linguistically impossible to adequately relate the gustatory details of this synesthetic experience. I can say that it was without question the most delicious thing I had ever tasted, and although I've since eaten truffles in many guises, the big black fresh one I so shamelessly devoured in the car that cold morning in Périgord remains in a class by itself.

Ever since the time of the ancients, truffles have been treasured by epicureans, adored by emperors and kings, praised in poetry, and endowed with all sorts of magical properties. The Romans referred to them as "children of the Gods" and dedicated them to Venus in the belief that "those who would lead virtuous lives should abstain from truffles." Whether or not it was Catherine de Medici's chefs who introduced the great truffles of nothern Italy to the noble tables of France and thus inspired the French to start digging is a topic for debate, but it is fact that François I appreciated the tuber for its supposed aphrodisiac virtues and that by the reign of Louis XIV the great chef François de la Varenne was incorporating a few truffles into his lavish dishes. The ultimate treat on the table of any French lord in the eighteenth century was a truffled turkey, and upper-class esteem for this aromatic food was so high in the early nineteenth century that one observer was led to write in 1825 that "nobody dares admit that he has been present at a meal where there is not at least one dish with truffles. However good it may be in itself, an entrée does not appear to advantage unless it has been enriched with truffles."

Brillat-Savarin called the truffle "the black diamond of cookery"; George Sand, "the fairy apple"; Alexandre Dumas, "the *sacro sanctorum* of epicures"; and others, everything from "the black pearl of gastronomy" to "the underground princess" to "the divine tuber." Although there are over three hundred varieties of truffles in countries all around the world, the most prized species are the two closely related black *Tuber malanosporum* and *Tuber brunale* found respectively in southwestern France and northern Italy and the rare ivory-colored *Tuber magnatum* from the Italian provinces of Piedmont, Tuscany, Romagna, and the Marches. Even after centuries of scientific research and experimentation, today we know little more than the ancients about the origin and cultivation of truffles. Over the years they have been loosely classified as a fungus, a mushroom, a tuber, a plant, a fruit, and a vegetable, but how they are born remains one of the great mysteries of nature. We know that truffles grow rootless underground in poor soil, generally in the vicinity of a certain species of oak tree—but also near filberts, chestnuts, poplars, and beeches. We suspect that truffles thrive symbiotically near the roots of these trees by means of widely-spreading, colorless, microscopic system of threads (hyphae) that absorb nourishment from the roots and soil and leave the terrain almost depleted of its moisture, minerals, and carbohydrates. We think that the ideal weather conditions for a good winter crop are a warm, wet spring followed by a hot summer, plenty of rain in late August, and a cool, clear fall. We have reason to believe that a truffle field that slopes slightly to the south yields the best tubers, and we've yet to find better means with which to locate the odorous underground fungi than the sensitive noses of specially trained pigs and dogs. (Traditionally, sows have been used in France and dogs in Italy, but since pigs love the taste of truffles and dogs don't, the French now use mostly canine sniffers.)

Over the years, every conceivable effort has been made to cultivate truffles. Acorns from "truffle oaks" (the scrub oaks around which truffles are most often found only after the tree is about ten years old) have been planted in productive fields of France and Italy with only negative results. Whole truffles or pieces of truffle buried in what appear to be perfect topical conditions have met with nothing but failure. And although nurseries sell pre-seeded saplings that promise 90 percent chance of good truffle growth, success has been negligible.

During harvest season, fresh black and white truffles are available in the United States through certain distributors and in the very finest delicacy shops of some large cities. Prices vary enormously, but it's rare to find fresh truffles for less than $400 a pound, and in really fancy stores with over-all inflated prices, the figure can reach $650. Ideally, fresh truffles should be consumed as quickly as possible (preferably within ten days) since they lose more and more savor the older they become. To preserve them as long as possible (I've held fresh black truffles up to a month), every medium for keeping them dry, from rice to sawdust to newspaper, has been suggested, and one Italian expert is convinced he's perfected a foolproof method of preserving fresh truffles indefinitely in a secret alcohol solution. So far the technique that seems to work best is the one recommended by the renowned distributor Urbani, whereby each truffle is wrapped loosely in newspaper, placed in an airtight container in the refrigerator, and re-wrapped each day. Fresh truffles can be frozen, but be warned that freezing causes them to lose about 30 to 40 percent of their aroma and flavor. Also be warned that since the aroma of fresh truffles is so incredibly powerful, failure to store them in containers that are absolutely airtight almost guarantees contamination of any and all other foods.

Contrary to what others might say, I've yet to taste a canned truffle that can equal one fresh from the ground, but, for those of us who love truffles, one from a can or bottle is better than none at all. The best canned truffles (which can often cost as much as the fresh) are washed, brushed, packed in natural truffle juice (made from damaged truffles), and heated long enough to satisfy European and American standards for preservation. The grading of preserved truffles is a long and complex matter, involving colorations, textures, brushings, peelings, and stages of boiling. To simplify matters, suffice it to say that the top two marketed grades are labeled "Extra" and "First Choice," designating not only the best black and white whole truffles but also those "peelings" and "pieces" derived from truffles that are either peeled for special clients, irregular in size, or damaged. The peelings and pieces are generally less expensive than the whole truffles and fine for preparing dishes that call for no more than chopped truffles.

As to the best way to prepare and eat truffles, I'm sure the only other subject in the entire field of gastronomy that evokes more debate, tension, and wrath is the best way to eat fresh caviar. In France, truffles are cooked whole in cinders (*sous les cendres*), slipped in slivers under the skin of roasted fowl, chopped into sauces, added to stuffings, inserted into foie gras, used to transform humble scrambled eggs and omelets into noble dishes, and, God forbid, even made into ice cream. For the Italians, there's hardly a dish that can't be enhanced by a small shaving of *tartufo bianco*, but remember that unlike the black truffle, which lends itself so beautifully to cooking, at least half the aroma and flavor of white truffles are lost when they are exposed to heat for any length of time.

In answer to the question whether any food is really worth $400 to $650 a pound, I might respond that this is strictly a matter of how much value you place on those few remaining world luxuries that add a novel (if transitory) dimension to one's life. The mystery of these strange tubers, their sensual texture, their haunting aroma, their magnificent savor, all contribute to a singular gustatory experience that defies comparison. Over the centuries, scientific, literary, and culinary sages have paid every tribute imaginable to truffles, and each time I'm exposed to their earthy glory, I believe with Brillat-Savarin that these jewels of gastronomy do indeed "make women more tender and men more agreeable."

## POSTSCRIPT
Just in recent years, great efforts have been made in the Pacific Northwest to cultivate genuine truffles. It's sheer folly, as far as I'm concerned, for the single example I tasted had absolutely no true truffle savor and resembled in flavor and texture, at most, a dried-out, dusty wild mushroom. No doubt hope springs eternal for certain adventurous souls, but it's not likely that even the most determined enthusiasts will ever succeed in an endeavor where the French and Italians have failed for centuries.

# CASSOULET:
# THE SOUL OF
# FRANCE

*1983*

W hile I have always expressed something more than a slight passion
for such delectable French stews as *estouffade de boeuf*, bouillabaisse, *coq au Riesling*, and *navarin d'agneau*, my involvement in that unctuous marriage of bean and meat known throughout the civilized world as
cassoulet approaches nothing less than an obsession. Once, on one of my
frequent gastronomic crossings aboard the S.S. *France*, I remained alone
two hours in the dining room during a force-ten gale, determined to finish
the crusty cassoulet that chef Le Huédé had spent two days preparing and
that had to be literally roped to the table. When Jovan Trboyevic an-
nounced a couple of years back that he had perfected a full-flavored "lean"
cassoulet at Les Nomades in Chicago, friends found it a bit eccentric when
I flew out, tasted the savory creation, and returned home the same evening
(with no indigestion). In southwest France, I'll drive a hundred miles out
of the way if so much as a mention is made of some cassoulet that is reputed
to be the best in the region. And it would be hard indeed to imagine life in
New York City without the prospect of consuming good cassoulet on a
regular basis at La Colombe d'Or and La Côte Basque (and yes, I eat as
much cassoulet in July as in February).

Of course the fact that cassoulet is probably the most complex, most
controversial, most heartwarming, and most delicious stew in the entire
annals of French culinary history does not necessarily mean that a genuine

version like the one featured here will appeal to all Americans. If, for example, you're governed by cholesterol counts or have an aversion to eating fat and garlic, you simply don't have the moral fortitude to deal with a real cassoulet. If you don't believe in spending a lot of time in the kitchen even for the most special occasion, this is not your dish. And if your idea of great French cuisine sadly happens to be a couple of pretty, perfectly sculptured anemic morsels from the nouvelle repertory, you'll surely find cassoulet too crude. If, on the other hand, you're really serious about food and care to go all out to serve a voluptuous dish that not only reflects the very soul of France but does wonders at dissipating all types of blues, nothing can equal a robust, addictive cassoulet chock-full of tender beans, earthy pork products, preserved duck or goose, and subtle seasonings.

That cassoulet's origins are shrouded in myth and mystery is confirmed by all forms of supposition down through the centuries. One enthusiast tried to trace the dish as far back as paleolithic times, while another, aware that the white haricot bean on which the concoction is based found its way to Europe only after the discovery of the New World, suggested that cassoulet might have been first made by the Incas or Aztecs. Was it perhaps the Moors of Spain who came up with the original recipe, or is the true ancestor the mutton stew made with beans that the Saracens introduced to the inhabitants of the Carcassé in southwest France about A.D. 720? Whenever and wherever cassoulet was conceived initially, it's for sure that the dish we know today is as closely linked to the soil of Languedoc in southwest France as the black truffle is to Périgord, that its first home was the town of Castelnaudary, and that its name was derived from the earthenware *cassole* made in the nearby village of Issel.

But, ah, now comes the great cassoulet war, the same strife that has been raging in and out of France for centuries, a gastronomic battle among three towns (and thousands of gourmands) that makes conflicts waged over bouillabaisse, Lancaster Hot Pot, and Texas chili seem like child's play. Referring to the area's three styles of cassoulet, gastronomic scholars speak irreverently of the Holy Trinity: God the Father, Castelnaudary; God the Son, Carcassonne; and God the Holy Spirit, Toulouse. Nobody denies that haricot beans and pork products were most likely first simmered together in Castelnaudary, but, after all, do these few peasant ingredients constitute an authentic cassoulet? Indeed they do, insist the inhabitants of Castelnaudary, who add no more to their beans than fresh pork, ham, pork rind, and sausage. By no means, retort the housewives a few miles away in Carcassone, convinced that no cassoulet is worth its fat that doesn't include a rack of mutton and, in season, a partridge. Absurd, scream the cooks in neighboring Toulouse, few of whom could imagine the dish with mutton or without salt pork, local pork-tripe sausages, tomatoes, and, above all, either preserved goose or duck simmered slowly in its own fat (*confit*).

Nor is all the heated discussion limited solely to the correct ingredients.

Everybody agrees that the most important component of any cassoulet is the white beans, high-quality beans that are to this stew what cabbage is to *choucroute garnie*, rascasse to bouillabaisse, and okra to Brunswick stew. But, alas, exactly which beans? There are good beans from the towns of Tarbes, Cazères, and Pamiers, as well as from the district of Charente. Some experts demand the tender-skinned *lingot* from the Vendée; others prefer the small, tough-skinned *lavelanet*; while the purest of the purists simply wouldn't prepare cassoulet without the gigantic, highly absorbent *haricot de maïs* from Béarn, which grows up the sides of corn stalks.

And what about the best oven and type of fuel? Important considerations, mind you. One chef from the Languedoc is perfectly satisfied with a reliable gas oven; another will tell you cassoulet cannot take on its distinct flavor unless it is baked in a classic baker's oven fueled with mountain gorse. Is it absolutely necessary to make cassoulet in the traditional low, oval, clay vessel? "Of course," insists the highly serious (and opinionated) Monsieur Bonnamy, spooning a preserved goose leg from the bubbly *cassole* at his wonderful Le Cassoulet restaurant in Toulouse. "How else can you expect to produce plenty of crust to break back into the stew!" Oh yes, the crust. There are those like the famous Jeanne-Marie Mourière in Quercy who add bread crumbs on top with a little goose or duck fat to ensure a crusty finish. Just the suggestion of such heresy riles not only Monsieur Bonnamy but also André Daguin over in Gascony and Toulouse-born Roger Lamazère (of Restaurant Lamazère) in Paris. "When baked properly," continues Bonnamy, "the crust of a great cassoulet forms naturally. Breaking all those bread crumbs and extra fat back into the dish just makes it that much heavier and more indigestible." And how many times should the crust be broken and reformed during the baking to produce that unctuous, silky, rich texture? Although tradition dictates seven times for absolutely perfect results, today most regional chefs break only twice for everyday eating, three times on holidays, and four times for marriages.

My recipe, which underwent numerous changes as I simmered beans, sampled enough garlic sausages to commit social suicide, and waded through duck fat, produces a very good cassoulet indeed. If you care to add pork to the simmering beans, substitute seasoned lamb shoulder for half the pork or preserved goose for the duck, or break the crust seven times, go ahead. To make the dish as digestible as possible, I've not only subjected the beans to three changes of fresh water but have also countered tradition by removing a good deal of fat once its essence has been incorporated into the stew. I suggest you do the same unless you enjoy Alka-Seltzer. Nothing is as good as homemade duck and goose *confit*, but if you refuse to wait the minimum of two weeks for it to mellow, you'd best try to find it (as well as duck or goose fat) in jars at specialty food shops. Remember, finally, that timing is all-important when cooking cassoulet, and that the stew's rich flavor and smooth texture are accomplished only by patient simmering. If you cheat, your cassoulet will suffer.

Since cassoulet is basically a hearty one-dish meal, what comes before and after should always be relatively light. At one of the world's greatest citadels of cassoulet, the Hôtel Fourcade in Castelnaudary, chef Michel Chabi suggests a sensible set meal: thin slices of mountain ham with tiny *cornichons*, the cassoulet, a simple green salad, and black-currant sorbet. At Le Cassoulet in Toulouse, most regulars start with either a delicate mousse of mussels and corn or an artichoke vinaigrette and end with a crisp green salad sprinkled with Roquefort. Cassoulet calls for sturdy wine with high acidity to balance the food. In Languedoc, they drink a racy Cahors or Madiran, but if neither of these is available, a good Châteauneuf-du-Pape would be eminently appropriate.

There are as many colorful stories about cassoulet as there are ingredients in the dish. In his *Histoire Comique,* Anatole France tells about a certain Mère Clémence who served nothing in her restaurant on rue Vavin in Paris but a cassoulet that never left the stove. Reinforced periodically with beans, *confit*, and sausage, the cassoulet simmered away consistently for no less than twenty years, halted only by the exigencies of World War I. Robert Courtine, France's most literate food journalist, remembers a certain tobacco shop in a tiny Languedoc village whose door handle, five or six times during the year, would be removed and whose customers would be met by a closed door and a curt note on it reading "Closed on Account of Cassoulet." But surely no commentary touches upon the romance and essence of this delectable culinary masterpiece any better than that of a hungry gastronome who, one frosty evening at a small inn between Toulouse and Castelnaudary, was served a glorious cassoulet prepared by an old grandmother: "The conclusion I reached after eating that wonder was that a great cassoulet needs not only good beans and sausage but also plenty of love—love for the cassoulet and love for those to whom you serve it."

# My Cassoulet

2 pounds boneless pork shoulder
2 ham hocks
 Salt and freshly ground pepper
2 pounds dry Great Northern beans
½ pound salt pork, cut into ½-inch slices
1 onion, peeled and stuck with 3 cloves
 Herb bouquet (bay leaf, parsley sprigs, 2 cloves garlic, and thyme tied in cheesecloth)
1 pound cotechino or other garlicky pork sausages
½ pound slab bacon, cut into ½-inch dice
3 tablespoons rendered duck fat from preserved duck (see following recipe)
 Pieces of 1 preserved duck (see following recipe)
½ pound fresh pork sausages
2 onions, peeled and sliced
2 carrots, cut into rounds
3 garlic cloves, minced
1 tomato, peeled and chopped coarse
3 cups beef stock or bouillon
2 cups dry white wine
 Duck cracklings (see following recipe)

*First Day.* Season the pork shoulder and ham hocks with salt and pepper to taste, place it in an earthenware or glass dish, cover, and let sit in the refrigerator 24 hours, turning once. Pick over the beans and wash and drain them. Place them in a large saucepan with enough water to cover and let them soak overnight.

*Second Day.* Drain the beans, rinse, and add fresh water to cover by at least 1 inch. Bring the beans to a boil, let them cook 5 minutes, drain, and add more fresh water to cover by 1 inch. Place the salt pork in another saucepan, add enough water to cover, bring to a boil, reduce the heat, simmer 10 minutes to remove excess salt, and rinse in cold water. Add the salt pork, studded onion, and herb bouquet to the beans, bring to a boil, reduce the heat, cover, and simmer 1 hour or till the beans are just tender. Let cool and refrigerate.

While the beans are cooking, prick the garlic sausages with a fork, place in a skillet or saucepan, and add enough water to cover. Bring to a boil, reduce heat, and poach 30 minutes. At the same time, blanch the slab bacon in boiling water about 3 minutes, drain, rinse under cold water, and pat dry with paper towels. Drain the sausages, let them cool, and cut them into chunks.

Heat the duck fat in a large, deep, heavy skillet, add the preserved duck pieces skin side down, cook them about 5 minutes or till lightly browned, and remove. Prick the fresh sausages with a fork, place them in the skillet, and fry till light brown. Cut the seasoned pork shoulder into chunks, place them in the skillet, and brown on all sides. Add the onions and carrots and sauté till the onions are soft. Add the ham hocks and slab bacon, increase the heat, and cook till the meats are slightly browned. Stir in the garlic and tomato, add the stock and white wine, bring to a boil, reduce the heat, and simmer, covered, about 1 hour or till the ham hocks are fully cooked. Add the preserved duck and chunks of garlic sausage to the ragout, cover the skillet, and place in the refrigerator overnight.

*Third Day*. Preheat the oven to 300° F.

Lift off most of the congealed fat collected on top of the ragout and discard. Remove the ham hocks from the ragout, cut the meat into chunks, discard the bones, and return the meat to the ragout. Remove the beans from the refrigerator, discard the herb bouquet, and bring the beans just to a simmer.

On the bottom of a 6-quart ovenproof casserole, arrange a layer of beans and salt pork, then a layer of ragout, dividing the meats as equally as possible and adding a few duck cracklings. Repeat with a layer of beans, then meat, ending with a layer of beans about 1 inch beneath the rim of the casserole. Add liquid from the ragout plus enough bean liquid just to cover the beans.

Place the casserole in the oven and allow the mixture to heat through for 1 hour. Increase the heat to 350° and bake about 30 minutes or till the cassoulet has crusted on top. Break the crust into the beans with a large spoon, reduce the heat to 300°, and continue baking about 20 minutes longer or till another crust forms. Break the crust again, add a little more bean liquid if the beans appear dry, and continue baking till a third crust forms. Remove the cassoulet from the oven and serve within 30 minutes.

Serves 10 to 12

# *Preserved Duck* (Confit)

(Advance preparation time: at least 2 weeks)

> 1 *fatty 4–5 pound duck*
> 4–5 *tablespoons coarse salt*
> *Freshly ground pepper*
> 1 *teaspoon dried thyme*
> 1 *teaspoon dried rosemary, crushed*
> 1 *bay leaf, crushed*
> 2 *cloves, crushed*
> 1 *garlic clove, minced*
> *Lard*

Remove wing tips from the duck, then cut up the duck into wings, drumsticks, thighs, and breasts (chopped crosswise into 3 pieces), reserving the heart and gizzard. Remove all peripheral and cavity fat and fatty skin from the pieces and the remaining carcass and set aside. Mix the salt, pepper to taste, herbs, cloves, and garlic in a small bowl, rub the mixture into the duck pieces, including the heart and gizzard, and pack into a large bowl. Weight down with a plate and heavy canned goods, cover with plastic wrap, and refrigerate 24 hours.

In the meantime, cut the reserved fat and skin into cubes, place in a saucepan with ¼ cup water over low heat, and render the fat slowly, about 45 minutes. Strain the fat into another bowl, continue frying the cubes till crisp (cracklings), transfer them to paper towels, and reserve for use in the cassoulet. When the fat is cool, cover and refrigerate till you are ready to use it.

Rinse the duck pieces in warm water and dry thoroughly with paper towels. Heat the duck fat in a large, deep saucepan or Dutch oven, add the duck pieces, and cook over moderate heat about 10 minutes or render more fat from the skin. If necessary, add enough lard to assure that the pieces are covered completely by liquid fat. Reduce the heat, simmer the duck gently and slowly for 1½ hours, and transfer the pieces to a plate.

Strain 1 inch of fat into a large terrine, crock, or wide-mouthed canning jars and place in the refrigerator about 30 minutes or till the fat congeals. Arrange the duck pieces on top of the fat, strain more fat over the pieces to cover completely, shake the container to distribute the fat evenly, add more fat if necessary, and let cool. When the fat has congealed, cover the container with plastic or a lid and store the *confit* in the refrigerator at least 2 weeks before using.

Under refrigeration, *confit* will keep 3 to 4 months and is delicious served by itself. Store any remaining fat in a covered jar in the refrigerator for making cassoulet, sautéing potatoes, browning meats for other stews, or enriching any number of vegetable dishes.

# SAVORING THE UPPER CRUST

*1988*

Of the many hundreds of recipes I've collected from round the world over the years, none is more important to me or evokes warmer memories than the one for *gratin dauphinois* scribbled in pencil almost thirty years ago at a small country inn called Rostang in the French Alpine village of Sassenage. At the time, I was a student of literature at the University of Grenoble in the province of Dauphiné, and although I was totally unaware that this charming, remote mountain inn not far from town also happened to be a two-star Michelin restaurant, the place's local reputation for fine (and expensive) food had inspired a young lady and me to save up our francs and drive up one day for lunch. After sipping a leisurely apéritif in the flowery outdoor garden, we moved into the rustic but well-appointed dining room, still neophytes to *la haute cuisine* but very curious to sample certain regional dishes we'd heard and read about for months. We marveled at her mysterious *ragoût d'écrivisses au Sauternes*; we tried to analyze the herby flavor of my *poularde à la crème d'estragon*. But what stunned us most, what we couldn't stop spooning onto our plates, what gave us much initial insight into the glory of French cooking was the rich, creamy, crusty gratin of potatoes placed automatically in the middle of the table.

"But aren't these something like our scalloped potatoes back home?" Pam whispered.

Well, yes, they were indeed *something* like our version in that basically the potato slices were layered in a deep dish, moistened with milk, cream, and butter, seasoned with salt and pepper, and baked till crusty on top. But to compare that gratin indigenous to the Dauphiné with standard scalloped potatoes was like comparing a genuine cassoulet from Gascony with ordinary baked pork and beans. As I was to learn some months later when I finally got up the nerve to ask Monsieur Rostang exactly how he prepared his regional classic, the potatoes in this gratin, first of all, were not just any variety but the hard, yellow mountain potatoes I'd so often seen displayed in Grenoble's open-air Marché des Maraîchers. Equally important were the luscious dairy products, all supplied by local farmers and all necessary to give the dish its unique flavor and unctuous texture. Elsewhere in France (as in America), potato gratins were generally cooked quickly in a fairly high oven, but Joseph Rostang baked his version at low heat no less than two and one half hours, adding additional cream at various intervals and basting the potatoes frequently. "You see," I remember his telling me, "all this probably began in the old days when there was only one bread oven in town. When housewives came down from the mountain to bake bread, they also brought their potatoes, cream, and butter and baked gratins slowly along with the batches of bread."

Eventually, in 1973, Jo Rostang moved on to Antibes on the Riviera to capture two Michelin stars at La Bonne Auberge, leaving his son Michel to continue the family tradition in Sassenage. Then, in 1978, Michel finally closed the small restaurant hidden in the Alps and opened his celebrated namesake in Paris. Both father and son have played important roles in the present revolutionizing of French cuisine, but the one dish neither has tampered with and the one that can be traced back through five generations of Rostang chefs is their *gratin dauphinois*. Over the years I must have prepared hundreds of different potato gratins, but to this day none compares to the crusted beauty I first savored so many years ago at that wonderful country inn and which I still prepare when I really want to show off the dish.

Although the origin of the word *gratin* is veiled in mystery, for centuries the inhabitants of both the Dauphiné and Savoy have prepared gratins not only with potatoes but also pumpkin, macaroni, wild mushrooms, Swiss chard, cardoons, celery root, crayfish, hashed boiled meats, and heaven knows what else. One common idea is that the concept stems from the word *gratter*, referring to the way one usually has to "scrape" part of the baked ingredients from the sides and bottom of the cooking vessel, but the little-known theory I prefer to believe is that the word *gratin* derives from the Latin name of the city of Grenoble, Gratianapolis. If the dish can indeed be traced back to Roman times, on the other hand, it's clear that what today is considered the prototype, namely the potato gratin, could not have been made till after this vegetable was introduced to Europe from the New World in the sixteenth century. Nor is it likely that any potato was gratinéed in France till the eighteenth century, since, until that time, the spud was generally thought to be poisonous. Once a certain scientist named Parmentier, however, proved that this tuber was not only safe but delicious to eat, the gratin quickly became associated with the superior Alpine potatoes, prepared in the Dauphiné with no more than milk or cream, butter, a bit of garlic, and seasonings, and in Savoy with meat stock and grated Gruyère or Parmesan cheese. From there the dish's popularity spread to every corner of France and eventually throughout the world, and today there's hardly a chef worth his butter who doesn't boast an exceptional *gratin de pommes de terre*. So elevated, in fact, has this essentially peasant dish become in the culinary repertory during modern times that today when one refers to the absolute top stratum of society, one speaks in French of *le gratin* and in English of "the upper crust."

Although general reference in French to *un bon gratin* usually implies potatoes served as a side dish, technically any ingredient or combination of components layered beneath a topping and baked or broiled to a crusty finish can be considered to have been "gratinéed." One of the most famous and sensuous dishes in all French cookery, for instance, is a *gratin de queues d'écrivisses*, crayfish tails bathed in a silky cream sauce, topped with grated Gruyère, run under the broiler, and presented either as an appetizer or main course. At the Auberge de l'Ill in Alsace, I've savored memorable gratins of mussels with saffron, salsify, macaroni with foie gras and truffles, and all sorts of fruits and berries. Across the border in Switzerland, two of the most sensational creations ever conceived are Fredy Girardet's gratin of trout with fresh tarragon and his orange *gratin Madame France* sprinkled with crushed pistachios. And what serious gastronome could imagine going to Venice without stopping by Harry's Bar for the splendid gratinéed *tagliatelle* with prosciutto? In this country, Julia Child has taught us how to make gratins with everything from leeks to shellfish to chicken to brains, and such other enlightened food experts as Wolfgang Puck, Paula Wolfert, and Marcella Hazan have shown how tomatoes and eggplant, potatoes and artichokes, and *gnocchi* pasta can be used to turn out splendid examples. So far, surprisingly, even the most innovative American restaurants rarely feature much more than the potato gratin in one guise or another, but no doubt as our creative young chefs continue to exploit various culinary concepts and the ever-increasing bounty of fresh native ingredients, the gratin will take on greater importance in professional kitchens.

The recipes featured here illustrate how all types of ingredients can be utilized to prepare gratins intended not only as side dishes but as major courses in meal planning. Nothing, of course, goes better with roasted meats or fowl and broiled fish than a large, piping-hot, classic *gratin dauphinois,* but combine the potatoes with ham, sausage, wild mushrooms and celery root, bacon and onions, or herbs and anchovies, and you have a simple but unusual luncheon dish that requires no more accompaniments than a mixed green salad and bottle of wine. Why always turn leftover chicken or turkey, mushrooms, and water chestnuts into an ordinary, rather bland pot pie when, by adding a chili pepper, a little Sherry or Madeira, bread crumbs, and plenty of fresh Parmesan, you can transform the dish into a pastryless, savory, main-course gratin worthy of the most sophisticated table? Shrimp, oysters, mussels, and crabmeat, either alone or combined with any number of compatible vegetables, mushrooms, and herbs, all lend themselves to spectacular appetizers or main courses when prepared au gratin, and what better way to present pasta in new dress than with spicy sausage or smoky meats under a golden cloak of crusted cheese? I love creamy gratins of cauliflower and goat cheese, celery knob and turnips, tomatoes and zucchini, leeks and pumpkin, and almost any variety of bean, and, although gratinéed desserts are still virtually unknown in this country, a gratin of oranges, grapefruit, bananas, apples, or any type of berry served with a sweet sauce adds considerable novelty to the coda of a great dinner.

Ideas about cooking gratins vary as radically as the ingredients that go into them, and the recipes that follow also demonstrate a few of the techniques. Among French chefs and housewives, for instance, nothing inspires heated argument more than the "correct" method for turning out an authentic *gratin dauphinois*. Should you first boil the potatoes before layering them in the dish or does this rob the spuds of the starch essential to thicken the liquid? Is it better to use all heavy cream or a mixture of light cream or milk and butter to produce a dish that has cheesy richness while actually containing no cheese? Is garlic permissible, or an egg yolk, or a little nutmeg, or a sprinkling of minced shallots? Should the gratin be baked quickly at relatively high heat or allowed to simmer slowly in a low oven so the potatoes can absorb as much liquid as possible? What about preparing a gratin in a heavy iron skillet as the lady chefs do at the famous Auberge de l'Âtre Fleuri in the Dauphiné, and does the *gratin Anna* (basically a potato cake) served at La Tour d'Argent in Paris qualify as a real gratin? Naturally, I'm convinced that my rendition here of the Rostang classic is faultless, sheer perfection, and without peer, but I'm not so smug as not to admit that on occasion I do sprinkle a bit of ripe Gruyère over the potatoes in the tradition of Savoy, or dust the layers with a suggestion of nutmeg, or raise the heat and reduce the cooking time slightly when I'm rushed. There are many, many ways to produce a good gratin, the only really unforgivable sin being a dish of old, bland, half-raw scalloped potatoes swimming in a watery milk bath.

While I am absolutely convinced that the king of gratins can never be overwhelmed by alien ingredients and must be baked gently if the full potato flavor is to shine forth and the texture is to be velvety from slow absorption of rich liquid, I'm hardly the purist when it comes to preparing other gratins, like the ones included here. Generally speaking, putting together a meat, seafood, vegetable, or dessert gratin should be a simple, uncomplicated procedure, one that leaves lots of room for experimentation and allows the home chef to serve a dish that is fun to make and delicious to eat. So long as you use fine ingredients and respect a few basic cooking techniques, there's no reason why the crusty gratin shouldn't add tremendous diversity and style to your menus. It's the sort of dish that evokes a wonderful tradition, inspires lots of inner warmth, and never fails to spark a hearty appetite.

## Gratin Dauphinois Rostang

1 garlic clove, peeled and cut in half
5 large russet potatoes (about 2½ pounds)
8 tablespoons (1 stick) butter
  Salt and freshly ground pepper
3 cups milk
2 cups heavy cream

Rub the bottom and sides of a large (2-quart), oval earthenware or ceramic gratin dish with the garlic halves and let dry.

Preheat the oven to 300° F. and spread a large sheet of foil over the bottom.

Peel and rinse the potatoes and cut them into ⅛-inch rounds with a mandoline or sharp knife. Grease the dish with 1 tablespoon of the butter and layer potato slices in the dish to within ½ inch of the top, adding salt and pepper to taste to each layer. Combine the milk and 1 cup of the cream in a heavy saucepan, bring almost to a boil, and pour over the potatoes. Dot the top with slices of the remaining butter, and bake the potatoes in the middle of the oven 1½ hours, breaking the bubbles and basting the potatoes with a large spoon from time to time. Add ½ cup of the remaining cream, baste, and continue baking 30 minutes. Add the remaining cream, baste, and bake 30 minutes longer or just till the potatoes are still moist and the top is golden brown.

Serves 6

## Gratin of Shrimp and Artichokes

8  *tablespoons (1 stick) butter*
1  *medium onion, minced*
2  *nine-ounce packages frozen artichoke hearts, cooked, drained,
   and cut in half*
¼  *cup flour*
1½  *cups half-and-half*
⅓  *cup Madeira*
½  *teaspoon dried tarragon*
   *Salt and freshly ground pepper*
1  *tablespoon Dijon mustard*
1½  *cups freshly grated Parmesan or genuine Swiss cheese*
2  *pounds fresh small shrimp, shelled and deveined*

In a large skillet, heat one-half the butter, add the onion, and
sauté over low heat for 2 minutes. Add the artichoke hearts, stir,
continue sautéing about 1 minute, and remove from the heat.

In a large saucepan, melt the remaining butter, add the flour, and
cook over low heat, stirring with a whisk, for 3 minutes. Add the
half-and-half and Madeira gradually, stirring. Add the tarragon and
salt and pepper to taste, increase the heat, stir, and simmer the sauce
3 minutes. Remove the skillet from the heat, stir in the mustard and
about one-half the cheese, and let stand.

Preheat the oven to 375° F.

Butter well the sides and bottom of a large oval gratin dish. Spoon
one-half the artichoke-and-onion mixture into the dish and arrange
one-half the shrimp on top. Spoon the remaining mixture over the
shrimp and arrange the remaining shrimp on top. Pour the sauce
evenly over the top, sprinkle with the remaining cheese, and bake
about 30 minutes or till bubbling and golden on top.

Serves 6 as lunch

## Gratin of Pasta and Sausage

1 *pound Italian hot sausages*
1 *cup heavy cream*
4 *tablespoons (½ stick) butter*
1 *egg yolk, beaten*
1½ *pounds dried fusilli pasta*
  *Salt and freshly ground pepper*
¾ *cup freshly grated Parmesan cheese*

Prick the sausages on all sides with a fork and place in a skillet with just enough water to cover. Bring to a boil, reduce the heat to moderate, and poach the sausages for 5 minutes. Pour off the water from the skillet, fry the sausages 15 to 20 minutes, turning, drain on paper towels, and cut into thin rounds.

Meanwhile, in a small saucepan, combine the cream, butter, and egg yolk over moderate heat. Simmer, stirring constantly with a whisk, about 1 minute or till the mixture thickens. Keep hot.

Preheat the oven to 325° F.

In a large pot, bring 6 quarts of salted water to a boil, add the pasta, stir, and cook till just firm to the bite. Drain the pasta, transfer it to a well-buttered large gratin dish, add the sausage and salt and pepper to taste, and stir till well blended. Pour the cream mixture over the pasta and sausage, sprinkle the cheese on top, and bake about 20 minutes or till the top is nicely browned.

Serves 6 as a main course

# THE CELESTIAL ORGAN

P aris never seemed so beautiful as on that crisp December evening
when I made my way toward the rue de Ponthieu. A light snow was
falling, the air was fresh and invigorating, and my spirits were soaring as
they always seem to do in Paris during the winter. Continuing down the
rue du Colisée, my thoughts returned to the rather frantic phone call I'd
received during the afternoon from a highly respected and even more highly
opinionated fellow gastronome with whom I disagree on almost everything.

"Guess what?" he had practically shouted. "Somebody just told me that
Lamazère is serving the season's first fresh foie gras. Let's get over there—
tonight!"

Such news travels fast in Paris, and when I arrived at the restaurant it
was pretty obvious from overheard conversations and mumblings that most
of the well-heeled customers waiting patiently had one thing and one thing
only in mind: the fresh liver of goose.

"Tonight we splurge," I said with abandon, directing the sommelier to
open a bottle of '67 Château d'Yquem.

"Not with my foie gras!" growled my companion, slapping the heel of his
hand against his forehead as an indication of my stupidity. *"Quelle bêtise,"*
he said to the wine captain. "We'll have a well-chilled Saran Nature."

"Champagne with fresh foie gras?" I exclaimed. "Never! I'll drink water
first."

"Then, *mon cher ami,* you drink your Perrier while I sip my still bubbly."

"No, *mon très cher,* I shall have my iced Sauternes with my foie gras. You may order your *blanc de blancs,* and may your own liver give out before the New Year."

Having resolved that all-too-familiar and friendly argument by requesting that the rather stunned sommelier open a bottle of each wine, we got down to the serious business of eating foie gras. The waiter arrived carrying a large platter, which he lowered for presentation with much the same ceremony as that of a high priest offering the sacraments. On it was a cylindrical giant liver that had been swaddled in cheesecloth, marinated for twenty-four hours with bay leaf, thyme, and Armagnac, and gently poached in stock to a subtle pink. After dipping a silver knife into a high porcelain cruet of hot water, he slowly cut away the first buttery slice, placing it directly in the center of a plain white china plate. Another dipping, another slice. Then we all three remained silent, reverently studying those delicately veined pinkish-beige slabs, those wondrous manifestations of an unholy organ raised to divine status by human gourmandise. This was foie gras in its purest form, spared all vulgar contact with truffles, lettuce, aspic, gherkins, anything at all but our forks and a few thin, delicate triangles of soft, warm toast. Even to attempt to describe the aroma, the flavor, or the velvety texture on the tongue would make a mockery of any language.

Few Americans have had the privilege of savoring absolutely fresh foie gras, and even the French will point out that the unadulterated dish is so special (and expensive) it can be enjoyed by most natives only at Christmas, the approximate time of year most of it is produced. (Today, France must import part of her annual two-thousand-ton goose-liver supply from Israel, Austria, Hungary, Czechoslovakia, and Luxembourg.) No doubt almost everyone has tasted at least one of the many varieties of goose or duck liver pâté distributed in tins, but, while a number of these products are delicious, to compare them with the supreme example served in staggering quantities throughout France during winter is like comparing processed domestic caviar with fresh beluga.

There is no adequate translation in the English language for foie gras (which literally means the monstrously fat liver of a force-fed goose or duck). Much too often, consumers, unable or unwilling to read the labels on tins, use the term erroneously when speaking of any pâté or terrine composed of any liver from chicken to pork to (perish the thought) beef. It's true that in the southwest of France certain locales supply a very flavorful duck foie gras, but, historically and linguistically speaking, genuine foie gras refers to the liver of the goose.

While the frescoes in ancient Egyptian tombs bear witness to the fact that geese were bred and force-fed as far back as 4,500 years ago, it was really the Romans who perfected the technique of overdeveloping goose livers by stuffing the birds on a diet of figs. Apicius, Cato, Horace, Juvenal, and other Latin writers make reference to *jecur ficatum,* or "goose liver fattened with figs." And most interesting of all is that, as the culinary term gradually displaced the original noun *jecur,* so did the French word *foie* (liver) derive from the Latin *figus* (fig). Who would deny that only the French (or, more precisely, their Gallic ancestors) could have named an organ of the body after an epicurean delicacy!

The Romans, like today's more ardent advocates, had such respect for foie gras that they refused to consume it any other way than whole, plain, and unadorned. As the tradition evolved in France, however, the dish underwent numerous changes, mainly in the cities of Strasbourg and Bordeaux. For centuries, the force-feeding of geese for majestic livers was (and still is) part of the culture in some parts of France (Alsace, Toulouse, Périgord, the Landes). There the prized breed of gray geese with white bellies has always proliferated under ideal environmental conditions, and there, after the introduction of corn from America in the eighteenth century, the production of foie gras became a veritable industry.

Then, in 1772, a chef by the name of Clause, attendant to the Alsatian Maréchal de Contades, came up with the idea of serving foie gras mixed with veal forcemeat in a pastry crust. Louis XVI tasted the dish and awarded Clause twenty-five *pistoles.* When the chef married a Strasbourg pastry cook, his *pâté de foie gras en croûte* not only made her shop a success but assured forever the city's link with the dish.

About the same time that Clause was wrapping his goose liver in pastry, Doyen, a chef in Bordeaux, was in the process of "giving foie gras a soul" by adding the embellishment of a truffle. To this day nothing causes more heated debate among serious gastronomes than the question whether the subtle, natural taste of foie gras is radically altered by juxtaposition with the strong flavor of this valuable fungus rooted from the earth of Périgord by keen-nosed pigs or specially trained dogs. Some argue that *foie gras truffé* represents the absolute ultimate in French gastronomy, whereas one reputed Gallic purist I know once became so enraged as to state: "Foie gras with truffles is merely an awful nouveau-riche creature with too many rings on its fingers."

All subjective emotions aside, no consideration of foie gras can be pursued without discussing the controversial force-feeding method man has perfected to satisfy his craving for the extraordinary dish. When a goose or duck is five months old, it is confined and allowed to eat its fill for approximately thirty days. Then come the weeks of force-feeding (*la gavage*), whereby the bird must digest fifty to seventy pounds of soft corn (and sometimes noodles) inserted by force down its gullet. Today in most areas, the method has been ingeniously streamlined by the use of electric "pumps," but on some southwest farms, tradition still dictates that someone (usually the housewife) straddle the goose or duck once a day, insert with one hand in its neck a tubelike mechanism full of corn paste, and, with the other hand, stroke the maize down its throat. Mammoth in size and literally stupefied, the bird is killed (usually after the first frost) and the large, firm, cream-colored liver, weighing up to four pounds, is removed, cleaned, and eventually poached, sterilized for canning, or sold fresh in bulk.

Although I know of no federal law in the United States that prohibits the force-feeding of geese and ducks for foie gras, it's for sure that anyone in this country who conspicuously practiced the trade would attract the gimlet eye of the Society for the Prevention of Cruelty to Animals. Fortunately or unfortunately—depending on your convictions—in France those in the regions of production not only have no qualms about the method used for obtaining this luxurious comestible but actually take great pride in their work. In his classic book *Simple French Cooking*, my friend Richard Olney—who has lived in southern France for the past thirty years—relates what must be one of the most revealing accounts of this phenomenon:

"I once listened in amazement to a Périgord farmwife describing—in what was intended to be a vehement denial that the raising of geese destined to produce *foie gras* involves cruelty to animals—the tenderness and gentleness with which the birds are treated. With mounting enthusiasm and in the most extraordinarily sensuous language, she described the suspense and excitement as the moment finally arrives to delicately slit the abdomen, lovingly to—ever so gently—pry it open, exposing finally the huge, glorious, and tender blond treasure, fragile object of so many months' solicitous care and of present reverence. One sensed vividly the goose's plenary participation, actually sharing in the beauty of the sublime moment for which her life had been lived."

Since laws governing the labeling of tinned foie gras are stringent, all the consumer need know is how to read. Succinctly summarized, *bloc*, *parfait*, and *lingot* denote pure goose or duck *foie gras naturel*, the finest. *Purée*, *mousse crème*, *tombeau*, and *pâté* indicate that the goose or duck liver has been mixed with pork, chicken, lard, eggs, corn flour, onions, milk, or any other ingredients that a producer may choose to add. Some of these blends can undoubtedly make for delightful eating; others are intimidating disasters. I've tasted some superb mixtures labeled *Tombeau de Foie Gras Truffé*, *Rouleau de Purée de Foie Gras*, and the like. I've also reeled back in horror after opening such lyric-sounding cans labeled *Rillettes de Confit d'Oie*, *Mousse de Foie Gras*, *Pâté de Foie du Périgord*, and (perish the memory) Party Pâté with Truffle Juice. Labels are tricky (even if legitimate), and the consumer who fails to notice the deletion of or substitute for a single word (e.g., *Pâté de Foie* with no *Gras*, or *Oie* instead of *Foie Gras*) is asking for trouble. There's one rule of thumb, however, that applies as much to the quality of foie gras and pâté as to that of caviar: the more expensive, the better—alas.

Fresh foie gras—often available in the finest gourmet shops during the Christmas season—can be kept as long as a month when it is carefully wrapped in aluminum foil or plastic and stored in the refrigerator. Some people don't hestitate to freeze the item, but, by testing, I found thawed foie gras not only virtually tasteless but also broken down in texture. The canned varieties are extremely perishable, spoiling in a matter of days after opening, even when kept covered and well refrigerated. When you plan to serve one, the best idea is to choose a size that can be consumed in a single meal, open it two or three hours before serving, cover it tightly with plastic wrap, and refrigerate.

When should you eat this delicacy and what are the best ways to serve it? Needless to say, pure foie gras (either fresh or canned) is a luxury food, which, like caviar, should be treated graciously and not gulped down at any and every occasion. A popular custom in certain uneducated circles is to place a plate of foie gras on the coffee table to be smeared in large quantities on crackers while sipping cocktails and apéritifs. I find this casual practice nothing less than barbaric, not only because it demonstrates a certain lack of style and respect for the delicacy but also because consuming too much richly concentrated foie gras can totally destroy any great dinner (and, yes, believe it or not, induce that very real French ailment known as a *crise de foie*). As far as I'm concerned, the one and only time to savor the dish (and this means no more than a two-ounce slice) is right at the beginning of a very special meal, a conviction shared by none other than the legendary "Prince of Gastronomes," Curnonsky:

"Its very richness demands that *foie gras* be served at the start of a meal, when the appetite is fresh and joyful, and not when the stomach is overloaded with other food. Only then, at the start, can its full taste and flavor be appreciated."

Foie gras requires no adornments to be fully enjoyed—nothing more, in fact, than a white china plate, a small silver fork, and a few soft, thin pieces of plain toast slightly warmed and served under a linen napkin. (And remember: it should be cut only at the moment of serving, with a knife dipped in hot water each time a slice is made to avoid tearing the liver.) As to which wine to pour, different connoisseurs have different opinions. Some prefer a Champagne *nature*, with no sparkle, others like a golden Tokay, and still others insist on a very old Port. But I know of nothing that goes better with foie gras than a freezing-cold Sauternes, preferably a regal Château d'Yquem.

If the French seem to get a bit carried away with foie gras, it's only because they're reveling in a grand tradition of which the rest of the world can only be envious. Over the centuries, France has developed a glorious cuisine composed of a countless number of delectable dishes that defy challenge. Of course we all have our favorites, and each of us likes to point out those that bear keenest testimony to the art of great eating. But, after all, when human imagination has been stretched to its utmost potential, it's difficult to deny that foie gras remains the most magnificent flower of French gastronomy, the absolute quintessence of gustatory joy and refinement.

## POSTSCRIPT

Anyone familiar with the occasional glories and rampant abuses of the nouvelle cuisine since I published this article over a decade ago can't help but be aware of the stellar role played by foie gras on both French and American menus. Today, the delicacy is blended into every salad imaginable, sautéed with every known vinegar, and served sprinkled with every member of the onion family, turned into custards, flans, and mousses, and heaven knows what else. One reason for the current popularity of foie gras in this country is that a very respectable fresh domestic product is now being made with the livers of moulard ducks and distributed by the highly reputable firm of D'Artagnan in Jersey City, New Jersey. Exactly how this foie gras is produced remains something of a secret, but, delicious as it can be, I've yet to sample any that equals the luscious terrines made from force-fed geese in southwest France. On the other hand, American duck foie gras is, after all, available fresh year round, and there can be no doubt that the product is getting better and better as experimentation continues.

# THE BISTRO BOUNTY OF PARIS

*1985*

W hen I am asked if I can pinpoint the origin of my passion for France and French cuisine, I never hesitate for a moment to relate the details of my first meal at Allard when I was a student in Paris almost thirty years ago. Curiously enough, what brought me and two fellow "literati" to the bistro that chilly fall evening was the pursuit not of food but of literary history: the great dramatist Jean Racine had lived on this same site in the Latin Quarter between 1680 and 1684, and the narrow old rue Saint-André-des-Arts had been the setting for George du Maurier's romantic nineteenth-century novel *Trilby*. After sufficiently venerating the immediate neighborhood, we peeked through the barred, lace-curtained windows of the bistro, deciphered at least part of the posted menu scribbled in purple ink, and decided we could afford dinner.

Inside it was warm, customers around the long zinc bar were laughing and drinking and speaking the language we were yearning to master, and the aromas from the small open kitchen were like none we'd ever known before. Patiently, the veteran waiter in his impeccable white shirt and long black apron helped us with the menu and tolerated our halting French before shuffling back across the sawdusty floor to fetch us a bottle of red wine. I recall every dish we ordered that night: sizzling *escargots de Bourgogne*, *jambon persillé*, grilled fresh sardines, rich coq au vin, pink *gigot d'agneau aux flageolets* (roast leg of lamb with small beans) and tender, moist roast chicken with strange mushrooms. We ate cheese that smelled awful but tasted wonderful; we studied the delicate salad greens that were so different from the iceberg lettuce back home; we sampled our first luscious chocolate charlotte and strawberry tart mounded with slightly sour *crème fraîche*; and we marveled at the fresh, fruity wine we later learned was Monsieur Allard's special Beaujolais from the cask. Before the evening was over, the wine that loosened our tongues and the cognac that tenderly burned our throats encouraged us to communicate with the French party at the next table, intelligent, engaging strangers who, in little more than an hour *chez* Allard, would teach us three young Americans more about French life than we would learn in a year in the classroom.

Since those faraway days, my love for the venerable bistros of Paris only intensifies each time I return to the city, resulting, over the years, in an intimate acquaintance with such beloved names as Benoît, l'Ami Louis, Joséphine, Chez Pauline, Le Paillon, Cartet, Moissonnier, Gérard, La Grille, and, to be sure, Allard. And what never ceases to astonish and baffle me is that most Americans simply don't know these places, where, at minimum cost, you savor the sort of unadorned, old-fashioned, no-nonsense regional cookery that has nourished the French for centuries. Just ask the average visitor returning from Paris where he or she dined, and what you generally get is a list composed of several astronomically priced, Michelin-starred temples, tourist havens like Maxim's or Fouquet's, and at least one of the trendy nouvelle haunts specializing in such ephemera as minuscule nuggets of lobster with strawberries, stuffed pasta colored with squid ink, veal with pistachio sauce, and fish bleeding at the bone.

Ask, on the other hand, French natives (including most chefs from the famous three-star restaurants) or serious American gastronomes to cite the places in Paris where they truly love to eat, and rest assured that the vast majority will say bistros (many of which are not even listed in the guides, much less bestowed with stars and toques).

For me the most trenchant testimony to how Parisians really feel about the food they consume was a comment made not long ago by a very sophisticated lady with whom I struck up a conversation while finishing a *baba au rhum* at Gérard. What, I asked, did she think about *la nouvelle cuisine*? *"Qu'est-ce que c'est?"* she snapped, picking the last morsel of marrow out of a large bone in her pot-au-feu.

The point is that you can go through all the legendary three-star restaurants, check out the most fashionable brasseries, and attempt to appreciate the laboratory food prepared by the latest young turks. But when you want to savor the real, unadulterated cuisine the French love so much, you still head for the bistros. What is served in these relatively small mom-and-pop places scattered about the city is what French food is really all about: unpretentious, home-cooked, soul-warming, sensibly-priced fare you can eat every day. I find it ironic that so many Americans travel to Paris only to dine night after night with other Americans and foreign visitors only in the best-known restaurants, unaware that even if the French could afford these inflated bastions of so-called *haute cuisine*, most would never frequent them on a regular basis. Don't get me wrong. A stylish lunch at Pré Catelan in the Bois de Boulogne or a glamorous dinner at La Tour d'Argent or Faugeron can provide a memorable experience, but not, for heaven's sake, meal after meal. At the right bistros, on the other hand, you can not only enjoy some of the best food and ambience Paris has to offer but can do so without the aid of Alka-Seltzer, and without the fear of going broke.

Of course, everyone has his or her impression of exactly what a genuine Paris bistro is, and indeed the phenomenon is not that easy to define linguistically and historically. Most likely the word *bistro* derives from *bistouille*, a derogatory term for cheap wine once served in a public drinking house. From all indications, the word was first used in its modern connotation shortly after the French Revolution to denote an establishment somewhere between a café (where only beverages were served) and a restaurant. Today most people think of a typical bistro as a cozy hideaway with a handwritten menu, dim lighting, dark wood, an impressive zinc bar, frosted-glass panels and plenty of hearty food, a *boîte* where the husband or wife does the cooking while the other watches over a rather raffish clientele. In authentic Paris bistros such a description is still pretty valid, but when you make the rounds year after year as I have, you come to appreciate other features that help give these wonderful places their special identity.

First, what distinguishes a great bistro from a dive (Paris is full of dives that many people irreverently refer to as bistros) is the setting and the clientele. Places like Benoît, Aux Lyonnais, La Grille, and Chez Dumonet (still affectionately called Joséphine by old-timers) are masterpieces of Art Nouveau or Art Deco design from the twenties and thirties, and even bistros of more recent vintage, such as Savy, Chez Gramond and Chez Gorisse, boast some of the most-appealing décors in Paris. If you still linger under the impression that bistros are patronized only by destitute students and customers who haven't knotted a necktie in years, you haven't observed the well-heeled crowds at Chez Pauline, Au Cochon d'Or, Chez Georges on the boulevard Péreire, and Moissonnier. Even when the food is delectable at La Croque au Sel, La Fontaine de Mars, and other such raunchy hangouts in the Latin Quarter, the noise, smoke, and dress can make you want to flee; but the first-rate bistros, though basically informal, are run with the same pride and respect for their customers as are the finest restaurants.

It's also true that the most reputable bistros are still family enterprises, some of which go back two or three generations. A Sousceyrac, for instance, was opened in 1923 by Adolphe and Ida Asfaux, was sustained by their son Gabriel and his wife, and is now run by grandsons Luc and Patrick, who are apprenticing their sons to continue the tradition. At Chez

Pauline, Paul Génin works closely with his son in preparation for the future, and although Jacqueline Libois, owner of Ty-Coz for thirty years, no longer has a husband minding the books, there can be no doubt that her standards for impeccable seafood will be upheld by daughter Marie-Françoise. Age forced Marie Cartet finally to place the bistro that has borne her name for more than three decades in the capable hands of Raymond and Marie-Thérèse Noaille, but even now Madame Cartet comes around to keep an eye on things. At Chez Albert, Marcel and Suzanne Beaumont have shared the responsibilities for over a quarter of a century. Chef Louis Moissonnier and his lovely wife Jeannine preside at Moissonnier, as do Jean-Claude and Jeannine Gramond at Chez Gramond. At Pierre Traiteur, Guy Nouyrigat receives and pampers guests in the style his mother taught him. "Family tradition is what the true Paris bistro is all about," says Fernande Allard, who runs the kitchen at Allard exactly as she did for years before her husband, André, died. "If this tradition goes, the soul of the bistro goes."

As much a part of the bistro tradition as setting, clientele, and family involvement, of course, are the classic, never-changing, copious regional dishes that have nourished Parisians for more than two centuries. Culinary innovation is virtually unheard of in a real bistro, so if your idea of great French cuisine is tiny portions of rare duck breast with raspberry vinegar served on fancy, oversize plates accompanied by two or three colorful vegetable purées, stay away from the bistros. What you find there is savory pâtés and terrines served with large jars of *cornichons*; the shredded meats and poultry enriched with fat known as *rillettes*; garlicky hot sausage flanked by vinegary potato salad; and lusty stews such as *blanquette de veau*, *daube de boeuf*, *canard aux navets* (duck with turnips), *navarin d'agneau* and bouillabaisse.

No bistro worthy of its name would fail to provide a vinegary *frisée au lard* (curly endive and bacon salad), a juicy entrecôte steak accompanied by thin *pommes frites* fried in lard, and either a *sole meunière* or *raie beurre noire* (skate with black butter). At serious bistros there's always a pink *gigot* (roast leg of lamb) surrounded by unctuous *flageolet* beans, a well-seasoned *boudin noir* (black sausage) served with applesauce, grilled *pied de cochon* (pig's foot) or jellied *tête de veau* (calf's cheek), some spicy version of *andouillette* (chitterling sausage), a creamy potato gratin, plenty of thin green beans sautéed in plenty of butter, and the sort of *mousse au chocolat* and *crème caramel* that make a mockery of those found in the so-called bistros of America. Some say the quintessential bistro dish is pot-au-feu (beef and vegetables with bone marrow); others single out cassoulet or *râble de lièvre* (saddle of hare in a coal-black pepper sauce); others salivate at the very mention of *petit salé aux choux* (pickled pork with cabbage); while still others insist it's that legendary rich, earthy, mouth-watering, dark beef stew called *boeuf bourguignon*—in Paris, by the way, served always with fresh noodles. I order them all, I eat them all, I love them all.

Most of the better bistros not only offer *plats du jour* that often reflect delectable seasonal ingredients but also prepare certain dishes only once a week—*petit salé* on Monday at Chez Pauline, *blanquette de veau* on Tuesday at Benoît, *gigot* on Wednesday lunch at Chez Dumonet, for example. The daily formula at these places has not changed in years; it never will. Remember, also, that most bistros close down Saturday and Sunday, and that few accept credit cards. Don't go to any bistro expecting to find a highly sophisticated wine list. When the great growths of Bordeaux and Burgundy are available, it's true that you can usually savor them (as well as vintage Champagnes) at a fraction of their cost in high-class restaurants, but generally nothing goes better with this type of food than an honest Beaujolais, a full-bodied Côtes-du-Rhône, or a sturdy wine from the southwest.

Perhaps it's a sign of a jaded palate or an increasingly stubborn respect for truth and solidity, but the more I roam the great City of Lights and study her gastronomic trends and changes, the more I distrust those fashionable restaurants whose reputations revolve more often than not around the fickle whims of celebrity chefs, manipulative food, and a gullible public forever impressed with the superficial ratings of guidebooks and self-appointed restaurant authorities. I much prefer the warm laughter, friendly service, and pungent aromas of a bistro to the bland austerity of a Michelin shrine. I like a basket of crusty fresh bread and a large slab of sweet butter considerably more than a puny slice of walnut toast proffered with a few silly curls. And I find infinitely more virtue in an earthy *terrine de lapin*, a pot of aromatic steamed mussels, a sensuous veal stew, and a jug of *crème fraîche* for my fruit tart than in a mosaic-like fish pâté, sculptured vegetables, and a pretentious hot flan of foie gras with oysters and crayfish afloat in a pool of overreduced sauce. For decades enthusiasts of every persuasion have sung the glories of the bistro, but no one ever penned more succinct, meaningful advice about this Paris institution than Miss Marlene Dietrich: "When you are really hungry, / When you don't want to dress up, / When you want to feel at home, / Go there."

## POSTSCRIPT

Even the great bistros of Paris are not immune to certain inevitable changes, as evidenced during the past year by the death of octogenarian owner-chef Antoine Magnin at the venerable l'Ami Louis mentioned in the essay. The good news is that, much as this legendary veteran will be missed, Magnin's bistro is still going strong since, while still alive, he took certain important steps to ensure that the tradition continues. For decades, the *Guide Michelin* has refused so much as to acknowledge l'Ami Louis, obviously because the bistro's shabby décor, spartan table appointments, and primitive toilet facilities have always given the impression of being in a basement of some war zone. But the world's glitterati who flock there for the greatest foie gras, roast chicken, and potato gratin in all France have never seemed to give a hoot about the surroundings. So let's hope the place continues to function as if Monsieur Magnin were still tending his wood fire and teaching the populace what real bistro food is all about.

# BRASSERIES:
# PARIS WHERE IT
# SIZZLES

*1984*

W hen it comes to really eating well in Paris, there is little doubt that much of the major action is in that noisy, glittery, aromatic phenomenon known as the brasserie—a *sui generis* Parisian institution that is somewhere between a café and a restaurant. Of course, dinner at the legendary three-star Taillevent or La Tour d'Argent still makes for a very special occasion; the bourgeois dishes at Allard, Chez Pauline, and Le Petit Saint-Benoît are as savory and delicious as they've been for decades; and nobody can fault the innovative but intelligent creations of a new-breed chef like Alain Dutournier at Au Trou Gascon. But, as anyone knows who roams the avenues and side streets of Paris, the great brasseries are still in full swing, attracting a stylish, fun-loving clientele and serving some of the most memorable food the city has to offer.

Needless to say I'm not referring to the hundreds of small, third-rate haunts that are visible from every corner in the city and boast the word *brasserie* on their awnings, but rather to those fathomless enclaves of polished brass, dark woodwork, painted panels, potted palms, and ornamental mirrors where Parisians congregate to enjoy an informal, relaxed atmosphere, savor platters of fresh oysters, grilled meats, *choucroute garnie,* and pot-au-feu at low cost, and to wash it all down with glasses of malty lager and carafes of simple wines. Many of these brasseries, such as Flo, Bofinger, and the fabled Lipp, have scarcely changed in a hundred or more years and retain their original Art Nouveau décor, while others, like Baumann-Ternes and Chez Francis, have been carefully reconstructed in accordance with *fin de siècle* architectural tastes. That the great brasseries of Paris have somehow managed to survive the changing social and economic trends of the twentieth century is something of a miracle. That they are now experiencing a remarkable rebirth in popularity can most likely be attributed both to the dreams of a few dedicated individuals and to the sizable portion of the fashionable French public that is finally rejecting the exorbitantly expensive classic or pretentious nouvelle restaurants in favor of more down-to-earth, convivial settings where they can enjoy traditional, honest, sensibly-priced fare. That many of these splendid brasseries have so far been rediscovered only by savvy Parisians and remain virtually unknown to tourist mobs can only be considered a blessing.

Dining in one of these voluminous saloons requires a certain attitude on the part of the customer (especially a newcomer) if the experience is to be fully appreciated. Conviviality and noise, for example, are elements as important to the setting as the painted lamp shades, black-tie waiters, and elevated racks of fresh oysters on the table. Most brasseries do accept reservations, but even if you have booked a table, prepare for a short, moderate, or long wait, since no party is ever coaxed to rush through a meal. Waiters are highly efficient but tend to be brusque at first. Accept it all with a smile, and by the end of the meal you may be offered an extra dessert or complimentary bottle of mineral water. Remember that these institutions are French to the core, meaning that menus are never translated (and even the handwritten French can be difficult to decipher) and the staffs are not required to speak English. On the other hand, make even the slightest effort to communicate in the native tongue, and before you know it you will have won the respect of even the most intolerant waiter and will be helped to understand what most of the menu is all about.

What you must be aware of, above all, is that brasserie cuisine is based on a menu formula that has proved successful over the decades and is therefore rarely modified. You simply don't go to a brasserie to sample the latest in French culinary sophistication or to explore vintage wines as you would in a luxury restaurant. Nor are you expected to follow the normal dining procedure of beginning the meal with an apéritif and following through with an appetizer, main course, cheese or salad, dessert, and digestive. Brasserie food involves platters of fresh shellfish, usually arranged at a savory stand or counter right on the premises, hefty steaks and chops with nice sauces, *gigot* served with unctuous white beans, lusty stews, simple grilled fish with perhaps a hollandaise or *beurre blanc* sauce, rich chocolate mousse and *crème caramel* the likes of which disappeared from fancy restaurants years ago, and, of course, mountains of non-acidic sauerkraut studded with every pork product imaginable.

Anything goes in a brasserie: an *oeuf en gelée* followed by a grilled entrecôte with *frites*, a bouillabaisse or cassoulet with bread and salad, a *choucroute* and nothing more. To drink, there are simple, inexpensive bottles or carafes of house wine, plenty of mineral water, and delicious Alsatian and German beers on draft. You learn quickly that a regular glass of beer is called a *demi*, a half-liter a *sérieux*, and (for trenchermen) a full liter a *formidable*. If you decide in the middle of the meal that a plate of *frites* or *haricots verts* is in order, you simply signal the waiter. *"Une portion de frites, s'il vous plaît."* More beer or another bottle of Riesling? Yes, indeed. And what's that scrumptious cake at the next table? In seconds a slice arrives. This is what a Parisian brasserie is all about, and eventually, as you eat and relax and talk and quaff, you realize that you have never had so much fun or savored such delicious French food anywhere.

"It is clear," writes French epicure Robert Courtine in a celebration of brasseries, "that however much we have succeeded in modernizing the bistro and neonizing our restaurants, nothing has been able to impinge on the style of our brasserie: the dim waiters with their shuffling feet, that slightly sharp aroma of beef, sauerkraut, and sawdust, the banquettes with their dark patina acquired from acquaintance with the peccant side of so many lives, and even down to those ladies quietly waiting, always so modest, beaming, blooming, of a certain age that guarantees experience, and whose visible flesh seems to have borrowed its pink tint from the pork butcher's window."

The ambiguous term *brasserie* was used for centuries in France to designate those firms given the legal right to brew beer. In the eighteenth century, the expression came to signify not only a brewery but also a social place where people could share good food and tankards of suds. Until the French Revolution, breweries had a federal monopoly on both the production and sale of beer, but after 1791, when all corporations were suppressed, the floodgates were opened to individual enterprise. Brasseries, like public cafés, flourished all over France, and beer became almost as popular a beverage as wine—especially in Alsace and Lorraine, the provinces near Germany.

What accounted for the creation of so many fashionable brasseries in Paris toward the end of the nineteenth century was the large numbers of skilled *brasseurs* from Alsace-Lorraine who fled to the capital after France lost its northeastern territory in the Franco-Prussian War of 1870. Bofinger, Lipp, Floderer, Mollard, Zeyer—they all arrived to make their fortunes, ushering in what can only be called the golden age of Parisian brasseries and creating a social stage on which would unfold much of the glamour and frivolity of that legendary era known as *La Belle Époque*. This was a highly ornamental period devoted to self-indulgence, leisure, and beauty, and Paris was its most promiscuous playground—where gentlemen died in the arms of mistresses, where the tightly-laced demimondaines of the dance halls, cabarets, and brasseries sported elaborate clothes and shook their peacock fans in the face of rigid Victorian values, and where the likes of Stravinsky, Proust, Diaghilev, Sarah Bernhardt, and Cézanne altered the artistic world forever. To grasp the spirit of this wondrous moment, try to imagine the crowd at Brasserie Flo exclaiming over the mounds of *choucroute garnie,* clinking glasses, and joining in on the chorus of *"Paris, c'est une blonde qui plaît à tout le monde."* It's been said that this privileged, oblivious society danced its way into World War I; but it also created a jubilant lifestyle in Paris that made all those to follow pale by comparison.

Although most *Belle Époque* brasserie owners never forswore the hearty Alsatian dishes that have remained the foundation of brasserie cuisine, they did abandon the ponderous Germanic décor of their establishments back home to embrace the highly liberated precepts flourishing in the decorative arts. Interiors caught the mood of the times with an elaborate display of hand-carved woodwork, elegant marquetry, beveled mirrors, and naïve frescoes depicting everything from the sensual delights of Rhine maidens to the adventures of the prodigal son. The establishments featured exquisite stained-glass ceilings and cupolas, intricate brass and wrought-iron fixtures, subtle globe lighting and deep-tufted banquettes—all of which still exist in one form or another at such landmarks as Bofinger, Flo, Lipp, Julien, and Vagenende. After the First World War, the newest brasseries began to assume a slightly different but equally enticing decorative façade as the floral style of Art Nouveau gave way to the more rigorous dictates of Art Deco, the results of which we can admire today at La Coupole, Vaudeville, and Le Dôme.

From the twenties straight through World War II and the fifties, the brasseries thrived as arenas of brilliant social discourse, political intrigue, and artistic revolution. Figures like Sartre, Camus, Hemingway, and Picasso often spent the wee hours at La Closerie des Lilas, La Coupole, Le Dôme and Lipp. Some places (Chez Jenny, Hansi, Terminus Nord) continued to honor their Alsatian heritage by serving nothing but the traditional *choucroute, boudin noir,* pigs' knuckles, Münster cheese, and plum tart, while others began to add items that over the years would also become standard brasserie fare: Baltic creamed herring, sardines with butter, *gigot à l'ail* (garlicky leg of lamb), *boeuf gros sel* (boiled beef with coarse salt), steak *béarnaise,* and *sandre au beurre blanc* (fish in butter sauce).

With all the social and gastronomic changes of the sixties, however, not even the wonderful food and low prices could prevent the temporary decline of the brasseries. Gradually they lost their popularity as the old interiors began to fade, the banquettes became ragged around the edges, and the clientele transferred their interest either to spiffy restaurants serving the new style of French cuisine or to a crazed night life of *discothèque.* Fortunately, the brasseries didn't disappear altogether, but by the seventies it was pretty obvious to everyone that most of these hitherto sacred institutions (the almost mythical Lipp, of course, being the one eternal exception) had lost more than their flair. They had lost their very soul.

Enter Jean-Paul Bucher, a ruddy-cheeked, energetic Alsatian from the village of Molsheim, the man without whom many of the famous Parisian brasseries might today be no more than a memory. Arriving in Paris about fifteen years ago, Bucher first took a job at Hansi preparing standard brasserie dishes before moving on to the hallowed classic kitchens of Maxim's and Lucas-Carton. When the Brasserie Flo, hidden away on one of the more ominous streets of Paris and in sad disrepair, went up for sale, Bucher, with Riesling in his veins, decided to gamble on the old Art Nouveau palace. He depleted his savings, laboriously restored the breathtaking interior, and established a traditional menu he felt certain would work. After the first year profits had doubled, and by 1979 Jean-Paul Bucher had performed his miracles not only at Flo but at Terminus Nord, Julien, and Vaudeville. Today a seat at any one of his brasseries is at a premium. His secret of success? "There's really no big secret," he confesses. "You simply offer people a beautiful setting, welcome them like friends, provide them with well-prepared food at reasonable prices from a limited menu, and never, ever, forget for an instant that they are here to take their time, relax, and have fun."

Encouraged by the success of Bucher, other entrepreneurs followed suit during the seventies and early eighties. Georges Alexandre and his wife, Marie-Louise (who met while working at the Brasserie Lutétia on the rue de Sèvres), acquired Bofinger (supposedly the oldest brasserie in Paris) from none other than Eric de Rothschild. Within a year, natural light was once again filtering through the magnificent stained-glass cupola; the rich woodwork, brass, and leather glistened; the restored murals had regained their soft colors. The entire place became the perfect setting for chef René Schwéri's incomparable foie gras, seafood pot-au-feu, and *andouillette à la ficelle* (poached chitterling sausage). At La Coupole, René Lafon (who created the brasserie in 1927 with his brother-in-law Ernest Fraux) had the Othon Friesz frescoes cleaned, added more giant flower arrangements, and instilled fresh life by turning over more of the brasserie's management to his sophisticated sons, Pierre and Jean. At Le Dôme, Claude Bras had his own in-house fish market constructed and set about transforming the brasserie into one of Paris's finest seafood spots. At Chez Jenny, the new owner, Christian Chrétiennot, not only had the brasserie completely renovated but also added a *Weinstube* where customers could savor grilled *boudin, frites*, and pitchers of Alsatian wine well into the late hours of the night.

When Chez Francis began to go on the rocks, owner Jean Richard decided simply to close the brasserie and start over from scratch. He engaged Slavik (the talented designer who did the interiors of Le Muniche, Baumann-Ternes, Baumann-Baltard and Le Dôme) to produce a stylish

brasserie in a reminiscent mode. As for Guy-Pierre Baumann, this aggressive Alsatian wasted no time building the two flamboyant brasseries bearing
his name and adding a new dimension to brasserie cuisine by offering no
fewer than thirteen different preparations of *choucroute,* including one
made with seafood. And what about the Brasserie Lipp? Well, let's just say
that nothing—no change in fashion or government, no war, no gastronomic
upheaval—nothing has affected the success of Lipp in a hundred years.
"Republics come and go," writes one observer, "but Lipp remains."

Anyone who ventures to visit this most mythical of all Parisian brasseries
(and nobody should die without the unique experience) must realize that
the Lipp, in the heart of St.-Germain, is possibly the most exclusive public
club in the world. Getting into the Connaught Grill in London, Taillevent
in Paris, or Le Cirque in New York is mere child's play compared to landing
a table at Brasserie Lipp. Here, in the Art Nouveau shrine of wooden
paneling, antique mirrors, moleskin banquettes and Fargue ceramics has
sat every French President within memory, every member of the National
Assembly, every entertainment star, every artist, writer, and composer of
note, every important banker, lawyer, and doctor in the French capital.
Purchased in 1920 by Marcelin Cazes from Léonard Lipp and passed on to
Marcelin's son, Roger, in the mid-sixties (a nephew, Michel, is now heir
to the dynasty), the brasserie is run with an almost tyrannical sense of
authority that assures no break in tradition but seems calculated to ruffle
the feathers of all but the privileged few who rarely have to wait for tables
either in the front bar or rear main-floor dining room.

There Monsieur Cazes stands like Cerberus every day and night (except
at Sunday lunch, when Michel holds guard, and Monday, when the brasserie is closed), inspecting all who arrive, jotting down notes on strange
round cards, and deciding in an instant who gets seated, when, and where.
What determines a candidate's status remains a mystery: dress, political
conviction, degree of celebrity, speech, who knows? Monsieur Cazes (and
I've never heard *anyone* address him as Roger) is familiar with 85 percent
of the clientele during the busiest hours (after one o'clock at lunch and
after nine in the evening), and it is rumored he's informed of important
political and economic happenings even before the Élysée Palace and the
*bourse.* The other 15 percent who manage to get seated upstairs (Siberia)
either endure an interminable wait or have the sense to show up when the
brasserie is virtually empty (before noon and at six in the evening). The
single English statement "No Salad as a Meal" printed in red on the menu
lets the American tourist know exactly where he stands from the start
("Few tourists understand our tradition, customs, and food," sulks Monsieur Cazes between puffs on his Havana), and should you not approve of
dining in the presence of dogs or settling the bill in hard cash, stay away.
For years I was rejected by Monsieur Cazes with the cold proclamation
that, no, there would be no table available at eight, nine . . . midnight.

Then, after I lunched and dined very early on a few occasions, he agreed finally to let me have a dinner table in the back room "at 9:30 sharp, not before." Now, when I arrive around eight, he politely shakes my hand, glances at my companions and those ever-present white cards, and . . . well . . . perhaps if we could *prendre un verre* in the café he might find us a table in the front room in about thirty minutes.

Why tolerate the indifference, insolence, indignity? For the simple reason that I happen to love the Lipp and can't help but respect Monsieur Cazes and the old tradition he's determined to maintain in a world devoted to mediocre standards, meager convictions, and the quick buck. So, yes, I shall always wait my turn at Lipp if for no other reason than to sink momentarily into a soft banquette, do justice to a little creamed herring and the best *boeuf gros sel* on earth, and venerate the spirit of a brasserie that symbolizes the very soul of Paris.

## POSTSCRIPT

There was occasion for universal grief in 1987 when Roger Cazes rejected his last dubious customer at Chez Lipp, took a final puff on his Havana, and moved to the celestial banquette to share *boeuf gros sel* with his illustrious cronies. Since his death, the brasserie has been run by his cousin Michel Cazes and niece Mme. Perrochon, experienced professionals who've made people a bit nervous with talk of renovating the place but who seem to respect tradition as much as their mentor. I've been back to Lipp once since the younger members of the family assumed management and could detect no changes whatsoever in the vibrant social scene or delicious cuisine. So far, thus, continuity persists at what must still be considered the world's greatest brasserie.

The other big news since I published this essay is that Jean-Paul Bucher, the forty-eight-year-old entrepreneur responsible for revitalizing Brasserie Flo, Terminus Nord, Julien, and Vaudeville, recently expanded his empire even more by purchasing the historically famous La Coupole. And how does he explain the brilliant success of his various brasseries: "Quality, quality, quality," he cries, "and remember that gastronomy isn't for millionaires only!"

# PART V
# A PRIVATE VIEW OF
# THE PUBLIC ARENA

It's no exaggeration to state that the only evenings I am not perched
in one restaurant or another somewhere on the globe is when I'm
preparing food and entertaining at my country house in East
Hampton on weekends. The public restaurant is indeed my most
important arena, the location where my ideas and opinions ferment, the field where I search for perfect gustatory satisfaction,
the place where I'm most comfortable. I will travel hundreds of
miles to sample a particular dish in a restaurant; I will risk friendship, reputation, life, and liver attempting to get a recipe or learning more about the internal workings of a great restaurant; and I
will order every dish on a vast menu to determine a kitchen's
strengths and weaknesses. Once, I went so far as to work as an
undercover captain in a luxury French restaurant (Le Perroquet
in Chicago) just to see firsthand how the dining public is observed
from behind the scenes, and I'd still love nothing more than to
experience the agony of actually running a restaurant for . . .
well, maybe a week or so.

In this section, I first try to portray what I visualize as restaurant perfection, then conduct something of a tour through certain
establishments that manifest many of those very special (and often
indefinable) virtues I'm forever seeking. What is perhaps most
interesting in this section is that every single restaurant included
is still as successful, intriguing, and important as at the time the
essay was published (or even more so). Does this mean that the simple food at Mortimer's is, in its own way, as compelling as the classic international fare in the Princess Grill aboard QE 2? Is the
service by Alsatian locals at the Auberge de l'Ill as polished as that

by highly trained professionals at Le Cirque and The Four Seasons? Is it really so important that a peppermill is automatically placed on every table at Mortimer's, that jacket and tie are absolutely *de rigueur* at Le Cirque, or that all guests at the Auberge de l'Ill are served complimentary *amuses-gueule* with their apéritifs? I let the essays speak for themselves.

# IN SEARCH OF THE
# PERFECT RESTAURANT

*1983*

A lthough my quest for the perfect restaurant often takes on quixotic dimensions, I have no more intention of abandoning this quest than of abandoning my patient wait for that blessed moment when I actually have my fill of fresh white truffles. Night after night in country after country I search, forever hopeful that the ideal is no farther away than my next dinner reservation. I can't help but feel it most likely exists in some deluxe French citadel of haute cuisine, but I'm also receptive to the possibility that the ultimate dining experience might be realized within the confines of a stylish Burgundian country inn, amid the splendor of Venice, in the grill room of a distinguished London hotel, or even at an all-American steak house.

No restaurant is too distant when there's rumor of perfection, and no address is beneath serious consideration. My search involves as many aesthetic as gustatory principles, and while I'm not so naïve that I don't sometimes wonder if my demands can actually be met, I nevertheless know without a shadow of doubt what that very special occasion will be like if and when it occurs.

Let's say the name of this restaurant is Amboise—simple, dignified, graceful. When I call for a reservation a few days in advance, I know the place is serious when a polite Frenchwoman requests that I reconfirm by 6 P.M. on the appointed evening. (I respect even the finest restaurant's need to combat the suicidal problem of no-shows, but I find the increasingly popular protective device of asking guests for a phone number both arrogant and insulting.) Amboise's location in a metropolitan center is identified by no more than a modest plaque, and the second my companion and I arrive, we know instinctively we've hit upon something that could prove extraordinary.

The cloakroom attendant steps out of the roomy *vestiaire* (no crushed herringbones here), helps us remove our coats, waves us on when I ask about a check, and watches to see where we are seated. Waiting to introduce himself is Monsieur Beauchamps, the stout, bold, lordly owner and host, who has been in the profession at least twenty years, who wouldn't be caught dead in any attire other than a well-tailored, dark-blue, double-breasted suit, and who bears resemblance to Robert Meyzen at La Caravelle in New York and Raymond Oliver at Le Grand Véfour in Paris. There's no bar to be seen up front, only two upholstered period chairs in the foyer for those who might prefer to await friends there before being seated at table. At Amboise, a reservation at eight-thirty means that the table is ready at eight-thirty (and yours for the entire evening). None of that "Would you care to have a drink at the bar?" business that you can encounter in even the most reputable restaurants.

Amboise has a nice feel and murmur—no offensive kitchen odors or stark lighting, no loud voices, no clinking of silver and china, no background music, but enough life to make you feel warm and at ease. The walls are paneled with rich, waxed wood, the oil paintings are unobtrusive, and it's obvious immediately that the properly dressed clientele is here for serious dining.

Monsieur Beauchamps escorts the two of us to a spacious leather-banquette table for four, pulls out the table so we can both sit facing out, then introduces us to our black-tie captain, André. *"Peut-être un petit apéritif ou cocktail?"* When Madame orders a light Kir, André identifies the white wine for her approval, as I remember happening once at Commander's Palace in New Orleans; when I order my Bourbon Manhattan, he asks if there's a particular brand of whiskey I prefer. Bowing and stepping back, he quietly relays the order to a waiter, asks if we'd care to study the menu over drinks, then signals to a busboy, who removes the two extra place settings, opens the complimentary bottle of mineral water, serves bread, and places on the table a plate of miniature appetizers. I'm impressed.

Nibbling on the tiny canapés of foie gras, fresh caviar, and cured ham rolled in cucumber, we take time for closer study of the establishment. Most impressive is the spaciousness of the dining room, enabling guests to discuss the best-kept state secrets without being overheard and captains and waiters to serve without falling all over themselves and the diners. There's no chatter among the floor staff, most of whom can perform their various jobs without any oral communication whatsoever and all of whom have been trained to react instinctively to even the slightest need at table —a spill (to be covered with a fresh napkin), a fork dropped on the floor, a snuffed-out cigarette, an empty wine glass.

The captains wear unwrinkled dinner jackets, and there are no ball-points sticking out of their pockets; waiters and busboys wear white uniforms without food stains; the wine steward sports an embroidered gold grape cluster on his left lapel, not a neck chain; and all have clean-shaven faces, nicely combed hair, and polished shoes. Above all, everyone on the serving staff appears proud, and when Monsieur Beauchamps approaches for one reason or another, I sense the same respect and friendship that exists between Mr. Chambers and his loyal staff in the Princess Grill aboard *Queen Elizabeth 2* or Jovan Trboyevic and his team at Les Nomades in Chicago.

The table appointments are classic, yet each reflects the owner's impeccable taste and individuality: a starched white linen tablecloth with a single blue stripe down one side, large damask napkins with the restaurant's monogram embroidered in one corner, heavy antique silver, a colorful ceramic pot with exactly four perfect fresh blooms, small blue-and-white porcelain ashtrays, a low table lamp with a handsome silk shade, and just the sort of expensive, pocket-sized silver peppermills that tempt some dolts to steal. Resting in an attractive wire-mesh basket is a fresh loaf of sliced bread wrapped loosely in linen. In place of those silly nuggets of hard butter frozen in ice, the soft unsalted slabs fitted into special silver trays here remind me of those placed on the tables at La Bonne Auberge in Antibes, France. A nice substitute for pottery bowls bursting with white and pink packets of sugar and saccharin is a crystal frog whose back is filled with superfine sugar (if guests at Amboise must have a sugar substitute, it's delivered to the table in a small china cup). The white service plate and china bear no more than the restaurant's crest in blue, while the sensible-sized water glasses and thin-stemmed wineglasses could have easily been supplied by Baccarat.

Within minutes the drinks are served by the waiter, Georges (I ask his name, having learned how this simple gesture can affect service dramatically), who waits for us to sip and nod our approval. André arrives with the menus, but, unlike a less-professional captain, who begins reeling off daily specials before you've had time to absorb the regular offerings, he tells us he'll return shortly to answer any questions and discuss the dinner. Since nothing disconcerts me more than one of those heavy, laminated, tasseled folio menus capable of tipping over every blessed glass on the table, it's a relief to be handed the neat, manageable two-page example.

Some luxury restaurants observe the unnecessary practice of offering a menu bearing prices only to the host; Amboise is above all that pretension. Many other expensive places have the gall to demand a hefty prix fixe, then tack on supplemental charges to half the appetizers, all grilled meats, and coffee. Here the cost of the entire meal is a flat sixty dollars per head. Period. I express relief when a frantic perusal of the menu reveals no foie gras salad, lobster with julienne of leeks and orange rind, rare duck breast with multicolored peppercorns, asparagus with pineapple beurre blanc, lamb with Roquefort sauce, kiwi with sour-cherry sabayon, and all those other idiotic nouvelle conceits that make a mockery of *la haute cuisine* and drive serious gastronomes up the wall.

The menu at Amboise is basically classic but by no means tedious, and I doubt if the owner and chef have even heard of that trendy folly known as a *menu de dégustation* (this is a restaurant, not a food laboratory). There's game pâté en croûte, fresh turbot with mustard sauce (at Amboise there's no need to spell out on the menu that the fish is fresh, since customers assume that everything here is fresh), *estouffade de boeuf*, and medallions of lamb with truffles and Madeira sauce. But there's also crabmeat sausage in a sauce faintly accented with Pernod, a ragout of sweetbreads, crayfish, and morels, roast pigeon with garlic sauce, and a glazed orange confection that brings to mind Fredy Girardet's splendid *gratin d'oranges Madame France*. Obviously the chef at Amboise is at once a traditionalist and an intelligent innovator who understands the chemistry of food, the antithesis of today's star-struck amateur who feels it his mission to introduce us to such egomaniacal fantasies as fillet of beef with cucumber balls and chicken stuffed with stuffed squash blossoms and who enjoys nothing more than the dubious habit of leaving the kitchen periodically to roam around the dining room soliciting compliments from guests.

André returns to describe the specials and supply advice. My companion and I have already debated the merits of pike-and-salmon terrine, pigeon mousse with endive sauce, a simple *oeuf en gelée*, roast chicken with tarragon, grilled salmon with apple and horseradish cream, veal kidneys with Armagnac sauce, and baked rabbit in a red-wine sauce, only to have the captain begin describing a gratin of herbed snails and oysters, preserved goose as an appetizer, a venison steak with fresh cèpes, and scallop quenelles in sauce Nantua. "Now this," I remark quietly, "is what I call an interesting menu!"

With agonizing bliss the final decisions are made. We want to just taste one of the pâtés, but which one? *"Pas de problème,"* André informs. He'll bring us a sliver of each—plus a dab of pigeon mousse. Afterward, Madame will have the unorthodox half-portion *confit d'oie* followed by a whole grilled turbot, whereas I, for whom the ultimate test of any restaurant (and a rare treat, indeed) is roast chicken, will take a golden bird after the special seafood gratin. In place of salad after the main course, André suggests we substitute exactly two buttered asparagus apiece, followed by a little cheese. Dessert soufflés (any flavor, of course) are included on the menu at no extra cost, but at Amboise no guest is asked to order one any earlier than after the main course. André completes the order, hands copies to the waiter and wine stewards, and bows away.

Jean, the experienced, dignified sommelier, immediately hands us *each* a small, leather-bound, neatly printed wine list. There are no ridiculous travel pictures or labels glued on under plastic, no tassels, no ludicrous poems or quotations celebrating the beauty of the grape, no flowery descriptions of the wines. Most of the best French, Alsatian, and California vintages are well represented, but there are also an impressive number of much less expensive second- and third-growth *petits châteaux* from good years, testimony to Monsieur Beauchamps's and Jean's knowledge of and involvement in wine.

After allowing us a few minutes to study the list, Jean glances at what we've ordered, then, in the same manner as Renzo at Laurent in New York, discusses how certain medium-priced bottles might be appropriate with the food. Only when I suggest a noble and expensive white Burgundy to complement the gratin, fish, and chicken does he address the various possibilities, but, alas, what about the confit? The sturdy Burgundy should hold up against the dish, he assures, but why not also a bottle of something like the '74 Lynch-Bages? The wine is priced right at $28, he explains, it's fully mature, with an intriguing iron aroma of Pauillac, it's still aggressive enough to take on the confit, yet it has developed an almost silky texture, which could prove interesting with the chicken and later on with cheese. Jean speaks with authority without being haughty, with concern without becoming over-familiar, with grace without pretension. He's a rare breed, fast disappearing.

Just as the assortment of pâtés is being served, Jean returns with both wines and one glass, opens the white, sniffs the cork, places it on the table only so that I can see it's not dry, and pours for me to taste. Unlike the vast majority of wine stewards, who would automatically stash any and all whites in a wine cooler to be numbed by ice, he knows this Burgundy is sufficiently chilled and simply sets it on the table. He next opens the claret, sniffs, asks if he might check the color, nose, and flavor in his glass, then pours a few drops in *each* of our glasses for approval. Since the wine is fine but needs air to develop, he proceeds to fill the glasses a third full instead of following the common but totally useless practice of letting the wine stay in the bottle. And, since Amboise doesn't even own one of those inane wine baskets, Jean merely places the red next to the white, asks whether or not we'd prefer to pour our own wine throughout the meal (we do), and bows back. This entire interchange takes place in less than one minute.

The pâtés and mousse, served with an attractive jug of cornichons, are everything they should be: extremely light or full-textured, subtly seasoned, aged enough to yield good flavor but not in the least rancid, and, miracle or miracles, not ice cold. When mustards (note, plural) are offered, they're served in small ceramic crocks and descriptions are given for each.

The nugget of boned preserved goose leg, flanked by a spoonful of soft white beans, is proof of the chef's ability to deal properly with fat, while the herbed *gratin aux escargots et aux huîtres* would be a masterly symphony of taste contrasts even if it were not served in a miniature silver skillet.

The evening is now in full swing, but still the restaurant guests maintain their decorum, the staff move swiftly but never frantically, and forever wandering amid it all is the watchful figure of Monsieur Beauchamps. Just as the turbot and chicken are brought to the serving table for final preparation, a busboy refills our water glasses, replaces the butter, and offers us clean napkins. André formally presents the whole turbot in an oval copper skillet, asks if Madame would like the fish filleted, then lowers the platter containing my golden plump *poulet rôti* for me to admire.

Back at the serving table, *patron* and captain go into action, Monsieur Beauchamps deftly disjointing the chicken while André removes the bones from the turbot. Within seconds the fish is heated over an unobtrusive, odorless flame, transferred to a warm, not hot, medium-sized plate (who could imagine a sophisticated place like Amboise using those gaudy, lattice-edged monstrosities now imitated from one restaurant to the next world-wide?), garnished with a half lemon wrapped in a bib similar to those at the Cipriani in Venice, and whisked off by Georges to my companion. Ditto one chicken breast, placed directly in the center of the plate and graced with no more than a single sprig of watercress. Would Madame prefer her mustard sauce on the side? And Monsieur?

Vegetables do not assume the form of baby food at Amboise. Rather, each of us is served a side dish containing a few glazed turnips, Sugar Snap peas like the memorable ones sautéed in butter at The Four Seasons in New York, and *roesti* potatoes. André's careful eye watches from a distance as we begin. The turbot is ethereal: flaky but tender, moist but not raw in the center, full-flavored but with no hint of fishiness. As for the chicken (of free-range pedigree, to be sure), I moan in ecstasy when my teeth sink into the first tarragon-scented morsel, so crisp on the outside and juicy inside. Not since I had my last buttery roast chicken at Chez L'Ami Louis in Paris have I tasted a bird with such savor, such dewy moistness, such voluptuous character. Yes, thank you, Georges, I will indeed have another serving. He smiles.

As the wine works its gustatory and psychological wonders, our conversation becomes even more animated, our involvement in the outside world seems almost negligible, and our sense of being in some microcosmic universe of gastronomic precision and perfection is nearly confirmed. Monsieur Beauchamps leans down for one second to ask if everything is satisfactory, a consoling contrast to the supercilious owner at another deluxe emporium the week before, who spent the better part of the evening sitting and *dining* with friends.

Once, no other legitimate grandee than the late Charles Ritz corrected me when I took knife and fork to some prized purple Italian asparagus that had arrived at his famous hotel in Paris. But even if I had not learned the hard, embarrassing way how to eat the vegetable properly, the finger bowls with warm water laced with lemon slices placed next to the fat beauties at Amboise would make me think twice. We're also thinking twice about cheese and dessert, having already given André a negative on the soufflé. *"Mais il y a une très belle triple crème ce soir,"* he whispers. We defer, only to have our appetites rekindled when he produces a wicker basket displaying not only the splendid Brillat-Savarin but also a fully ripe Camembert, a moist, deep-veined Roquefort, an assertive Pont l'Evèque, a supple St.-Nectaire, and an assortment of fresh chèvres—all fully exposed, no tacky wrappers or packages. Elsewhere I cringe at the sight of a captain who cuts into Roquefort, then desecrates a beautiful Camembert or Brie by using the same knife. André has a separate knife for each cheese. Without asking, he quickly peels a ripe pear, places two slices on each cheese plate, and directs Georges to offer us bread and wafers.

I've never had much use for those gigantic dessert trolleys overladen more often than not with dried-out cakes, soggy tarts, and mushy macerated fruits, so once again I welcome the menus. We're tempted to try either the raspberry *bavarois, the pavé glacé Montmorency,* or imaginative crêpes that bring to mind (after André's description) the sumptuous *crêpes Mireille* made with apricot and pear preserves and flamed with kirsch at the Auberge de l'Ill in Alsace. But, of course, Georges has to appear with a glorious apricot tart that, he says, is served with a *bowl* of *crème fraîche,* and André begins to list off sorbets of gooseberry, ginger, Champagne, and mango, and . . . yes, Jean, a bottle of bubbly is in order to wash down the dessert and exquisite petits fours placed on the table, and thank you, Georges, we would appreciate another bottle of mineral water.

Coffee at Amboise is taken to mean espresso, and espresso at Amboise does not mean one puny cup. Whereas a less fastidious establishment might place one of those cheap, dented, metal pots on the table, here the coffee is served in a lovely blue-and-white china pot large enough to hold at least six cups. If you linger and the coffee gets cold, no problem, since Georges's hand is on the sides of that pot every time he refills. And such aromatic, strong, delicious coffee it is, especially when sipped along with snifters of framboise. We linger euphorically. I wish the evening could go on forever, but I know that the bill will never be offered before being requested. André presents it in a simple leather folder. The total is $214 before tax and gratuities. Expensive. Since I'm not sure whether the captain and wine steward will receive a split of the tip if I enter it as one lump sum on the credit card slip, I fill in a percentage only for Georges and the busboys. As we leave and shake hands with André and Jean (both of whom kept their distance till it became obvious we wanted to thank them), I palm each what I think is appropriate—and, believe me, I have reason to be generous with these pros. Up front the *dame du vestiaire* already has our coats ready, and Monsieur Beauchamps has stationed himself here, smiling, to thank us, kiss Madame's hand, and say that he hopes we'll return soon. The evening has cost me a fortune, but as I offer the lady my arm and we move out into the crisp night of reality, I'm convinced more than ever before that no price is too high for perfection.

## POSTSCRIPT

When this fantasy essay first appeared in *Cuisine* some five years back, reader response was nothing less than phenomenal, lending full credence to the supposition that no topic today fascinates the American public more or inspires more heated debate than what does and does not constitute a great restaurant. Most people wrote in about their own personal experiences and favorites; others suggested altogether different views than mine on restaurant perfection; and a few lashed out at me for being too élitist. Whatever the reaction, I do think my profile proved that, for perhaps the first time in our history, Americans are now keenly serious about where and how they dine out and demonstrate a level of sophistication that could hardly be imagined just twenty years ago.

The basic ideas, principles, and personal preferences outlined in the essay are still as valid for me as when I sketched them out. Only some of the nonfictional heroes referred to have changed. The great Robert Meyzen, who left Henri Soulé at Le Pavillon to create La Caravelle in 1960, sold his interest in this noble restaurant a few years ago to his famous chef, Roger Fessaguet, and André Jammet of the famous Hotel Bristol family in Paris. Now, M. Jammet is the sole owner, and while this veteran professional, along with his gifted young American chef, Michael Romano, has given La Caravelle renewed brilliance, the dynamic presence of Robert will not be forgotten for many years. Raymond Oliver, alas, is no longer with us, a sad reminder that even in Paris the loss of certain gastronomic traditions and standards makes my search for restaurant perfection more and more difficult.

# THE SEASONING OF THE FOUR SEASONS

1983

W hen I'm asked about New York's top restaurants, I invariably mention Le Cirque, La Caravelle, Il Nido, and The Coach House. But
always firmly fixed in my mind is that venerable social and gastronomic
force on Park Avenue that almost defies objective appraisal. Like Tiffany's,
the Frick Collection, and Brooks Brothers, the lofty Four Seasons is now a
veritable New York institution contributing as much to the city's celebrity
and energy as the brokerage firms on Wall Street and the fashion houses of
Seventh Avenue. But perhaps the key to the mythic aspect of The Four
Seasons is that, like so much in people's fantasies about Manhattan, it is
larger than life.

I've dined at The Four Seasons ever since it opened almost a quarter
century ago. I watched the restaurant bloom, founder into near oblivion,
then resurge ten years ago under the new ownership of Tom Margittai and
Paul Kovi to become the temple it is now. Like thousands of other devotees,
I know Tom and Paul, along with the veteran bartenders, captains, waiters, and managers, and I've tasted each dish on the ever-changing menus.
Returning to The Four Seasons is always like going home, yet each time I
climb that broad, somber staircase and view the Bar Room's grand sweep of
space, each time I'm led down that wide corridor past the large Picasso
tapestry into the regal vastness of the hushed Pool Room, and each time I
bite into that first morsel, I experience a new thrill, a sense of utter awe.

The Four Seasons is often referred to as the quintessential New York restaurant, symbolizing for the city what La Tour d'Argent is for Paris and the Connaught for London. I'll go a step further and state that, for many like myself, The Four Seasons *is* New York.

Pick any day of the week except Sunday and the scene at the restaurant is about the same. As early as 8:30 A.M., the phones upstairs at the main desk start ringing, while downstairs in a minuscule niche near the cloakroom, one employee does nothing but call customers all morning to reconfirm advance reservations for both lunch and dinner. By ten o'clock, Tom or Paul, their managers, and various other staff members are working the phones steadily, listening to frantic demands for certain tables, trying to explain politely why the Pool Room must be booked two weeks in advance for Saturday dinner and the Bar Room Grill two days in advance for lunch, and dealing patiently with customers who want to change either the time of their reservations or the number of people in their party. Names are studied and logged on the large reservation sheet along with seating requests, phone numbers, and all sorts of colorful stars, lines, and hieroglyphics comprehensible only to the staff. Tables are assigned, changed, then changed again; and eventually individual cards on every party are made out to be delivered to captains in the appropriate dining room. Mistakes in seating are extremely rare.

By noon, the staff is in black tie or seasonal uniform, tables have been set, carpets vacuumed once, twice, three times, bartenders are poised for action, and the blasting phones at the desk are shut off. Up the stairs they come: three ladies sporting this season's Saint-Laurent, Calvin Klein, or Givenchy; a major New York publisher accompanied by an influential literary agent; a smiling young couple obviously in town for a holiday; New York's foremost real-estate developer with one of the city's top lawyers; a trickle of recognizable celebrities (Bill Blass, Jackie Onassis, Tom Brokaw, Liz Smith). Managers Julian or Alex greet unfamiliar faces with utmost courtesy and escort them to tables in the Pool Room for a quiet, leisurely lunch. The famous and powerful, by contrast, shake hands with or peck the cheeks of Tom and Paul, exchange a few words, and head for their tables in the Bar Room Grill to transact business over no more than perhaps a light galantine of capon and sweetbreads, a thin slice of calf's liver with scallion butter, a paillard of veal, and a little white wine. On any given day, The Four Seasons management knows over 90 percent of those who lunch in the Grill. They are regulars, important regulars. They represent the leading players in the worlds of advertising, publishing, banking, law, architecture, and fashion. This room is their unofficial club. Here at noon high-powered executives gather, hefty contracts are negotiated, pressing corporate issues are settled, fortunes are increased or diminished, and waistlines remain slim. While guests back in the Pool Room linger over elegant desserts and espresso until 3 or 3:30, the Grill regulars talk, eat, and are back at the office by 2.

In the early evening, action shifts to the bar and the Pool Room. For thousands of New Yorkers and out-of-towners alike, there simply is no after-work watering hole like the great black upholstered bar at The Four Seasons—no matter that they must pay five bucks a drink for the privilege of standing under Richard Lippold's stunning brass-rod sculpture, sipping one of Jimmy's or Henry's expert concoctions, and nibbling on the fanciest of mixed nuts. The enlightened also know that the best pre-theater feast in town can be enjoyed in the Pool Room for half the cost of a regular dinner, which I suppose explains why by 6:30 The Four Seasons has already served more people than most other deluxe restaurants will accommodate in an entire evening.

At about eight o'clock, the bar has begun to thin out as tipplers either leave for dinner elsewhere or move into one of the dining rooms. If it's a week night, the impeccable Pool Room crowd tends to be at least half local, and it's not unusual to see Rudolf Nureyev, Jackie O., or Rex Harrison downing smoked salmon rillettes, quail and lobster ragout, and sweetbreads in mustard crumbs at one of the eight highly sought-after tables around the pool fountain. Customers with smaller appetites prefer a less dramatic dinner of fried Camembert, deviled chicken with lemon compote, or simple charcoal-grilled fish in the Grill. Now that people have learned they can drop by the Grill after the theater for a little pasta, an elaborate cheese tray, or a Bourbon soufflé, the room buzzes until midnight. On Saturday evenings, when the Grill is closed, the Pool Room is packed with tourists, the regulars having fled either to the privacy of their townhouses or to the wilds of Connecticut or Long Island. Some of the glamour that helps make The Four Seasons what it is might be missing on the weekends, but there is always the superbly inventive cuisine, the allure, and the big-city tone that crystallize an overall impression that the restaurant is in a class by itself.

That The Four Seasons can now boast the prestige and popularity once enjoyed by such auspicious havens as Café Chambord and Le Pavillon is 100 percent attributable to the determination, professionalism, and taste of Tom Margittai and Paul Kovi, the charming, urbane, shrewd impresarios who took a big chance when they purchased the restaurant a decade ago. The partners have distinctly different but complementary personalities. The quieter, gentler Tom (who comes from Transylvania) has a style that is courteous, caring, low-key, and he is attentive to the last detail. Hungarian-born Paul, the more naturally outgoing and impetuous of the two, has the stance of an athlete, talks with a touch of bravado, and makes a fuss over the ladies by greeting them with a kiss on the hand. While Tom always wears a conservative dark suit, Paul's customary dress is blue blazer with a distinctive tie pin as a finishing touch. What the two men primarily have in common is an unfailing graciousness, a ready smile, and an almost uncanny knowledge of food. Today they are the image of success, but the rise to the top was neither quick nor easy.

The Four Seasons was opened by Restaurant Associates (a corporation specializing in various theme restaurants) in 1959 as part of the impressive Seagram Building, designed by Ludwig Mies van der Rohe and Philip Johnson and hailed in its day as the paragon of modern architecture. Johnson's influence brought twenty-foot French rosewood-paneled walls soaring upward around immense open spaces, undulating looped brass and coppery chain curtains covering floor-to-ceiling smoked-glass windows. The appointments were (and still are) an unprecedented blend with spectacular impact: furniture by Mies van der Rohe, works by Picasso and Richard Lippold, a twenty-foot Carrara marble gurgling pool in the main dining room, silver hollowware and glassware by Ada and Garth Huxtable, Belgium-flax tablecloths and napkins, and full-size trees virtually dwarfed by the 24,000 square feet of floor space and high ceilings. The plants, the staff uniforms, and, most significantly, the menus changed four times a year with the seasons. The eclectic menus combined the rich bounty of America with numerous international culinary concepts and techniques, making The Four Seasons a veritable pioneer of what would years later be termed the New American Cuisine.

When the restaurant first opened, the country's most creative restaurateur, Joe Baum, assumed direction of the operation; the celebrated chef Albert Stoekli was hired to supervise the kitchen; and even James Beard was brought in as a food consultant. The establishment therefore should have developed into a gastronomic landmark during the sixties. It didn't. Yes, the décor was captivating, the cuisine could be exciting, and service was exemplary. But New Yorkers stayed away, serious gastronomes stayed away, the social leaders stayed away; everybody, in fact, stayed away except the tourists. People found the place cold, haughty, intimidating. As corporate management took less and less interest in the facility, The Four Seasons seemed to be gasping for breath by the early seventies, and there seemed little hope for survival.

Ironically, Paul Kovi became director of The Four Seasons toward the end of this sad period, and even more ironically, his associate (then his boss) Tom Margittai, who was vice-president of Restaurant Associates, had been given the responsibility of unloading the restaurant. "The early seventies was one of the bleakest economic eras in New York's history," recalls Tom, "and there's no doubt The Four Seasons was becoming more and more a loser. At that time, the fashion in the restaurant business was simply to get out of town, and having been in this field for years, Paul and I were ourselves thinking seriously about leaving and opening a restaurant in some other city. But where? We talked and talked, debated and debated, then finally we came to the conclusion that here was one of the world's potentially greatest restaurants up for sale and just waiting to fall into the right hands. So we decided to take the plunge ourselves and make one last stand in New York. Purchasing The Four Seasons back then was, in many respects, a vote for New York. The city had to recover, we figured, so why not at least try to pump fresh blood into this magnificent restaurant, give it a new soul, and develop it into the cultural landmark it was always intended to be? Whether or not we made the right decision, suffice it to say that over the years we've turned down handsome offers to open Four Seasons restaurants in Chicago, Houston, Los Angeles, Paris, Tokyo, you name it."

Investing every dollar they could in the enterprise, these ambitious, highly respected gentlemen set out against all odds in 1973 to create their dream restaurant. First, however, they had to rid themselves of The Forum of the Twelve Caesars, another failing property of Restaurant Associates and one that had been included in The Four Seasons deal. As much as many of us loved and respected The Forum, there was simply no viable way Tom and Paul could handle both restaurants. Fortunately, The Forum sold fairly quickly, and within a year volume doubled at The Four Seasons.

Physically, the place remained as monumental and elegant as ever, but suddenly there was new internal vigor and warmth without a trace of pretension. Margittai hired Swiss-born Joseph (Seppi) Renggli, who had already worked with him in one capacity or another for eight years, to devote himself full-time to the kitchen, and in a matter of months the quality of the cuisine improved dramatically. Paul commenced work on the wine list, laying the foundation for what would become not only one of the finest cellars in the world but also the first comprehensive collection of California wines in the East. At first, the food critics were aloof, apprehensive, challenging, but before long even the most bitterly hostile skeptics were raving about the improvements. Local food and wine societies began to book the restaurant for special occasions; winemakers chose The Four Seasons as the ideal setting in which to hold tastings; Tom and Paul inaugurated a series of small private dinners given four times a year to celebrate the beginning of each season with their most loyal customers; and in 1975 the first of the California vintners' barrel-tasting dinners—and considered the country's most important annual wine event—took place.

The Four Seasons seemed to be weathering well. Eventually, world-renowned chefs like Paul Bocuse, Alain Chapel, Michel Guérard, and Marcella Hazan came to demonstrate their talents for the public. The Pool Room was dotted with more and more celebrities. One evening there would be Arthur Rubinstein, Eudora Welty, Halston, and Moshe Dayan; the next, Philippe de Rothschild, Margot Fonteyn, Lillian Hellman, and Betty Ford; and the next, Courrèges, Woody Allen, Sir Laurence Olivier, and Truman Capote. Exclamations over the food and wines resounded around the world, prompting Tom, Paul, and Seppi to publish in 1980 one of the most innovative cookbooks ever produced. No sooner had they decided to begin serving a light, grill-style lunch in the virtually unused area behind the bar than the room became the noontime confluence point of some of New York's most powerful figures. Despite its enormous overhead, the restaurant gradually began to turn a decent profit, but unlike so many other superior establishments that slip now and then into mediocrity, The Four Seasons never compromised its strict professional standards. Above all, Tom and Paul established at the start that every guest—no matter what his or her pedigree—was to be treated the same. "We're not and never have been in the snob-appeal business," Tom asserts. "We're in the business of deluxe quality, no more, no less."

If it's true that The Four Seasons has evolved into a social bastion for many New Yorkers, it's equally true that success has not affected the originality and quality of the cuisine. In the fall, there's pasta with fresh wild mushrooms, roast partridge with kale, and marinated pheasant with Gorgonzola polenta; winter brings knob celery-and-fennel soufflé, wild-turkey consommé, linguine with hare sauce, and roast saddle of venison with juniper sauce. In spring, it's chilled asparagus-and-cucumber soup, fiddlehead ferns with soy sauce, rabbit in spring cabbage, and mousse of trout with fresh crayfish tails. And, in summer, there's fresh tomato-and-basil soup, pâté of salmon and crabmeat, striped bass baked in sea salt, a luscious lobster soufflé, and without doubt the world's greatest roast duck, served with delicate peaches. Needless to say, nobody is ever bored by the food at The Four Seasons.

Any attempt to explain why this stately restaurant functions internally as well as it does would certainly have to mention that no waiter is eligible for a job until he or she has had at least three years' experience in a similar first-class location, that any chef hired in the kitchen must undergo training in every facet of food preparation ("In an emergency," says Seppi, "my chefs can assume control of any station"), and that Tom and Paul deal with no fewer than three hundred purveyors on the various levels of operation. I'm convinced, however, that the true secret of the restaurant's triumph revolves, as in most viable businesses, around the owners' almost paternal relationship with all members of the staff and the employees' firm sense of loyalty toward both their employers and the institution itself. Yes, those who work at The Four Seasons no doubt take home top pay, and with this type of experience on their records, they could most assuredly land other jobs anywhere on earth. But there's obviously a more subtle motivation— call it pride, respect, or fidelity.

Jim Kelly, for example, has headed the bar for thirteen years, and, before that, he worked for Margittai at Charlie Brown's. Seppi, whom Tom and Paul have known eighteen years, was previously executive chef for Restaurant Associates, then for The Forum; chef Christian Albin (better known as "Hitch") is a twelve-year veteran Tom first encountered at Tav-

ern on the Green. Maître d'hôtel of the Pool Room, Oreste Carnevali, has
been associated with the owners for nineteen years, one year less than Pool
Room captain, Gino, who began his career under Tom at Tower Suite.
Kurt, Damien, Steve, and Italo, also captains in the Pool Room, have been
on the scene ever since the restaurant changed hands, and even younger
members of the staff, like managers Alex von Bidder and Julian Niccolini,
can already claim between six and seven years of uninterrupted service.
"It's true," says Paul, "we've had very little turnover in staff, but, after all,
we are a team."

Whatever might account for The Four Seasons' lofty reputation, two
gentlemen have managed to create an eminently civilized restaurant that is
completely in tune with the times, one that is at once formal and friendly,
worldly and reserved but comfortable—in other words, a New York restaurant with true contemporary flair. In another era, Manhattan was epito-
mized by the exclusive elegance and rigid perfectionism of Le Pavillon, The
Colony, and Café Chauveron, classic epicurean shrines that reflected both
the societal spirit of the times and the personalities of the brilliant individuals who gave them life and luster. A decade ago, Tom Margittai and Paul
Kovi were perhaps the first to realize that public tastes were changing
radically, and they've since had the insight to temper their operation in
accordance with current social styles and gustatory demands: a relaxed
dress code, a more casual relationship between staff and customer, lighter
and simpler food with a definite American accent, and the never-ending
effort to stock the most varied selection of the finest domestic and foreign
wines for a clientele increasingly educated and demanding along these
lines. Catering thus to people from many walks of life, these persevering
entrepreneurs nurture The Four Seasons with such discrimination that its
interpretation of excellence appeals to all, from the seasoned gastronome to
the most timid customer venturing into this citadel who is made to feel
perfectly at ease. Perhaps nothing sums up the spirit better than the dedication Tom and Paul include in The Four Seasons Cookbook: "This book is
lovingly dedicated to all those who delight with us in the joys of food and
wine and to all who toiled with us over the years to make The Four Seasons
a restaurant loved by so many."

## POSTSCRIPT

What never fails to utterly amaze me about The Four Seasons is how the
restaurant continues to move with the times, catering as easily to curious
tourists and suburbanites as to sophisticated gastronomes, modifying the
eclectic menus as dining trends evolve (even a Spa Cuisine is now available), upgrading the décor, table appointments, and staff uniforms, and, to
be sure, forever matching its stratospheric prices with the elevated econ-
omy. Equally impressive (and certainly indicative of something extraordinary) is that virtually every major staff member mentioned in this article is

still on the job: Jimmy and Henry at the bar, Oreste and Gino and Damien in the Pool Room, Alex and Julian at the front desk, Seppi and Hitch in the kitchen, and, of course, Tom and Paul everywhere. Today, the owners estimate that they now know 99 percent of those who lunch in the Grill, and if, indeed, I've noticed any general change at the restaurant over the past months, it would have to be the ever-increasing popularity of the newly decorated Grill in the evening. I must say that some of the updated, "lighter" dishes seem to contradict what I've always held sacred about the cuisine, but so long as I can order those earthy game terrines and that inimitable roast duck with peppercorn sauce, and the crusty apple charlotte, The Four Seasons will remain a very special arena.

One of the greatest regrets in the food and wine industry was Tom and Paul's decision a few years back to discontinue the celebrated California wine-barrel-tasting dinner held annually at The Four Seasons. The reason given was that the event had simply outgrown even the capabilities of this huge restaurant, but I suspect that the real truth was that management just couldn't tolerate any longer a very touchy ticket demand that equaled that of the hottest Broadway sellout.

# THE MYSTIQUE
# OF MORTIMER'S

1984

G lenn Bernbaum, already in his sartorial best and still agonizing over recent withdrawal from three packs of cigarettes a day ("It's like losing your oldest friend"), is pacing the floor at Mortimer's, one of the most wildly fashionable restaurants in Manhattan and one virtually unknown to any but savvy New Yorkers.

"What *am* I going to do with all those flowers!" he groans, gesturing to the bar crowded with pots of lilies of the valley that, the previous evening, had adorned tables for a private party given by a French socialite. "Steve," he calls to the head chef out in the kitchen, "let's taste the cold beef special you're putting on for lunch today, and, oh yes, how's that rhubarb sherbet coming along for the Bill Blass party?" Then, glancing down at a dinner check he's been fumbling with, he addresses a headwaiter: "Joel, are you absolutely sure these are the wines they ordered last night? I just can't believe they ordered this much wine! Check it and double-check it."

"Glenn, it's the *New York Times* on the phone wanting to know who gave the dinner last night that Joan Collins attended," the bartender informs. "Yes, can I help you?" Bernbaum answers softly, cupping the phone under his jaw. "I'm sorry, but we don't give out information on any of our customers. I hope you understand. Thank you." Picking up a large reservation ledger, he proudly ticks off to me a few names expected for lunch or dinner: Pat Lawford, Mike Wallace, Ann Slater, Vincent Fourcade, Gloria

Vanderbilt. "You know, we don't take reservations at Mortimer's—except, of course, for our friends." The beef and sherbet arrive. "Fine," he says of the beef. But of the sherbet, "God, that is awful, dreadful, absolutely *inedible!* Much too much wine, and it needs sugar . . . or something. Work on it some more." Then, after calling Nan Kempner just to check on how the party she gave for her mother-in-law the previous night at the Cosmopolitan Club went, after consulting with the chef on the details regarding a new pasta to be included on the dinner menu, and after setting up an appointment to determine which decorations should be used for a very important upcoming private party being given by Bill Blass and Oscar de la Renta for Glenn's old friend Diana Vreeland, he relaxes momentarily with a can of Tab and continues to peruse the reservations.

As I glance around the clubby front room with its dark brick walls, huge wood-framed mirrors, simple bentwood chairs and discreet globe lighting, I wonder for the hundredth time exactly what it is about Mortimer's that has made the restaurant home to so many famous and well-heeled personalities since the day it opened in 1976 at the corner of Lexington Avenue and 75th Street. Everybody's heard of Elaine's, "21," the Grill Room at The Four Seasons, and a couple of other places that are more clubs than restaurants, but, unlike them, Mortimer's has somehow managed to maintain its quiet, dignified profile without attracting the tourists. Here on Manhattan's chic Upper East Side, there are at least a dozen similar saloons within a five-block radius, each designed in basically the same manner, each catering to a stylish crowd, and each respectfully successful. Yet none has the mystique, the cachet, the social clout of Mortimer's. Living only a block away, I witness the action day and night: the stretch limos parked two-deep along Lexington, the lines of spiffy locals waiting at noon each and every Sunday for the doors to open for lunch, the greats of the fashion, art, and entertainment worlds casually sipping apéritifs at the outdoor café on 75th Street, and the best-placed names of New York society sharing crab cakes with friends in the evening or throwing parties in the back room for some of the best-placed names of European society.

Thus, there's never a time here that isn't conducive to seeing and being seen. On any given day, for example, Pat Buckley may be observed lunching with Nan Kempner, C. Z. Guest and Fernanda Niven (daughter-in-law of late actor David Niven) at 1B—the much-sought-after window table; Mike Wallace with Shirley MacLaine; or Mike Nichols with Jackie O. While the unknown, upwardly mobile youngsters wait their turn for tables at the bar, headwaiter Robert Caravaggi (whose father was, for years, the famous co-owner of Quo Vadis) greets regulars like Felix Rohatyn, Lee Radziwill, Gian-Carlo Menotti, Countess Donina Cicogna, and Paloma Picasso and shows them to "reserved" tables. In the rear dining room, there may be a private party, such as the one given by Reinaldo and Carolina Herrera for England's Princess Margaret, the one King Juan Carlos of

Spain arranged for his family, the one for Yves Saint-Laurent by Jacqueline de Ribes, or the one Katharine Graham threw for the entire *Newsweek* staff. This is their sanctuary, their watering hole, and Glenn Bernbaum— owner, manager, demanding boss, godfather—is the one who feeds, protects, consoles, entertains, and provides the unique style, taste, and ambience that simply don't exist in many other places. "I think I spend more time at Mortimer's than in my own apartment!" exclaims Ann Slater, New York socialite *par excellence*. "The place is really home."

The success of Glenn Bernbaum and Mortimer's is hardly typical of the New York restaurant scene. For twenty-one years, Bernbaum was part-owner and operator of The Custom Shop chain of shirtmakers for men. Then, as he tells it, one morning he came to the realization that what he really wanted was a small restaurant where he and his friends could enjoy simple but good American food and have fun. When the building on the corner of Lexington and 75th became available, he bought it, began construction of the café, and got a few people from The Custom Shop to help decorate it. The problem of a name was solved one day after he'd just spoken with Stanley Mortimer II of Tuxedo Park (married at one time to Babe Paley) when in walked the head of The Custom Shop, Mortimer Levitt, and . . .

"I knew exactly what I wanted from the start," says Bernbaum. "A casual, unpretentious atmosphere, a neighborhood clientele, a very simple menu with basically uncomplicated American food, old-fashioned music from the forties, and a top-notch, loyal staff who understood my way of doing things. Well, the very first day, old friends like Bill Blass, Kenneth Lane, Jerry Zipkin, and Tom Margittai from The Four Seasons came in and brought others. Then Diana Vreeland (bless her) showed up one Sunday for lunch and Sundays were never the same afterwards. And, finally, Jackie Onassis arrived. One day, Bill Blass said to me, 'Do you realize you've got every celebrity in New York coming to this place?' I didn't recognize half the crowd at that time, but I did feel we must be on the right track."

The rich and famous did keep coming, and Bernbaum, who had continued to hold down his responsibilities at The Custom Shop during the day, decided in 1980 to devote his entire time and energy to the restaurant. A second room was added; food experts were hired as consultants to come up with exciting off-the-menu specials and keep a check on the kitchen ("I discovered almost immediately that in this business you must constantly be trying to improve the food just to *stay afloat*," notes Glenn). In addition, a small sidewalk café was opened along 75th Street where guests could have brunch or afternoon tea in the open air, and Bernbaum even moved into an apartment upstairs. Eventually, unable any longer to ignore this trendy saloon, which featured such low-brow items as chicken liver pâté, grilled sardines, hamburgers, and chicken hash, the powerful restaurant critic for the *New York Times,* Mimi Sheraton, showed up, glanced about, tasted, and wrote wickedly that "middle-aged preppies with tired stomachs can count on bland, soft, minimally decent food to see them through lunch and dinner at Mortimer's." She had, of course, totally misunderstood what the restaurant was all about, and her review carried about as much weight with Bernbaum's crowd as a bottle of cheap champagne.

The truth about Mortimer's food is that it is, indeed, quite good for what it is: simple, fresh, honest fare that is intended to satisfy, not astound. Vegetables come only from Manhattan's prestigious Butterfield Market, fish and shellfish from three different seafood suppliers, and meats from no fewer than four of the city's finest butchers ("The competition keeps each on his toes and ensures quality," says Glenn). Not a day passes that Bernbaum and his chef don't discuss which seasonal foods might be prepared as specials (asparagus, soft-shell crabs, venison, rhubarb). But, when one of Glenn's friends wants to throw a party, it's usually left to the boss to decide which dishes should be served. "I know what we can do well and when we're trying to go beyond our capabilities," he emphasizes, "so why attempt some fancy dish that's not going to impress anybody here when what our friends really want are puff-pastry pizzas, great chili, crab cakes, or a perfectly roasted rack of lamb? I mean, the people who come regularly to Mortimer's are also regulars at places like Le Cirque, The Four Seasons, and La Grenouille, so when they drop by here for dinner or want to give a party, the last thing they want is more *haute cuisine.*"

Contrary to what the relatively short menu might imply and to what outsiders might think, the food at Mortimer's is forever uppermost in Bernbaum's mind. Conceptually, the regular offerings at lunch and dinner have not changed in the eight years since the restaurant opened, meaning there's probably not another menu formula in town that has worked so well for so long. There's creamy Senegalese soup, crisp whitebait, giant hot mushroom caps with a delicious herb dressing, small twinburgers with fresh, crunchy shoestring potatoes, a copious *salade niçoise,* grilled calf's liver, chicken curry, buttery snap peas, and a different pasta and fish every day. By far the most popular items are the gravlax with mustard dill sauce, the paillard of chicken, and for dessert the crusty crème brûlée. Personal tastes, of course, vary. Pat Buckley prefers the chicken salad, crab cakes, and rich profiteroles; Nan Kempner loves the grilled flounder; and Fernanda Niven favors the Salad Mortimer (smoked chicken, sliced avocado, mushrooms vinaigrette, and potato salad), most likely because it was her private chef who created the dish for a potato contest held a few years back at the family's summer house in Southampton. While Bernbaum will tell you that the secret of success at Mortimer's is the no-nonsense food or the comfortable, well-bred atmosphere, or the way each and every member of the young staff instinctively understands how to protect and communicate with those customers who expect a bit more out of life than most people, ask anyone who knows the place intimately and it becomes perfectly obvious that the one and only secret to the restaurant's popularity is Bernbaum himself. "Yes, the balance between formality and informality, the lighting, people, staff, food—all that is on target," declares Fernanda Niven, "but let's face it, Mortimer's *is* Glenn Bernbaum, and Glenn is Mortimer's. If something happened to him, the place would fold up in a week." To C. Z. Guest, Bernbaum is simply "very special"; to Pat Buckley, he is "one of the last true gentlemen, who really knocks himself out to do things right and make sure a customer's privacy is never invaded"; and to Bill Blass, he is "our best friend, a gentleman who cares."

New York social arbiter Nan Kempner, who calls Mortimer's alternately her "clubhouse," "canteen," and "annex," is no less emphatic with regard to Bernbaum's abilities and considerations. "The man is unique. He keeps his eyes, ears, and mouth open to everything that's happening in this town —and in London, Houston, and God knows where else. When a certain seasonal food comes on the market, Glenn is the first to have it. When a good customer happens to be entertaining at home and can't get the quality of meat or fish that's needed, a phone call to Glenn puts her in touch with one of his own purveyors. And, when at times I realize I just can't cope with giving another reception or dinner party at the apartment, Glenn comes to the rescue and no demand is too much."

It's one o'clock on Saturday afternoon, and they're still piling through the door for lunch. At a front table, Bernbaum, beer in hand, is participating in, of all things, a professional sardine tasting when, suddenly, in walks Claudette Colbert. Her table's not quite set, so Glenn invites her to sit at our table momentarily amidst piles of oily cans while he proceeds to read the riot act to whichever waiter was responsible for the delay. Across the room is George Hamilton, bronzed from the tropics, and at the table next to him is Gloria Vanderbilt, looking stunning. And next to her is John Bowes-Lyon, nephew of the Queen Mother and one of the many Brits who think nothing of ringing up in the morning from Heathrow to ask Glenn to hold a table for a late lunch. The place is buzzing as film producer Ray Stark makes his way gingerly through the crowd toward the back room, hesitating once to peck the cheek of some starlet decked out in what could only be a Trigère casual. Waiters, balancing bottles of Perrier and platters of puffy omelets, chicken hash, and strawberry tarts, apologize incessantly as they wedge themselves between the crush of well-dressed bodies, and Bernbaum, when he's not jumping up to shake a hand or deal with a problem only he can somehow detect through the maze, samples another brand of sardine, sips his beer, and surveys his social empire.

"Glenn," I finally burst out, "how in heaven's name do you take this days and night? Aren't you exhausted?"

"What do you mean?" he retorts. "This is what it's all about: my friends all having fun and eating good food and drinking good wines and . . . I mean, do you think I'd rather be selling shirts!"

## POSTSCRIPT

It would be interesting to report how Mortimer's has evolved socially and gastronomically since I wrote this four years ago, but the truth is that absolutely nothing has changed: not the faces (but do add Fergie to the British contingent), not the décor, not the reservations policy, not the basic menus, and certainly not the raging success of the place. Glenn Bernbaum has become something of a superstar himself in the pages of those publications devoted to the lifestyles of the rich and famous, sponsoring various benefits for worthwhile causes, lending his last name to the naming of two rare monkeys (Bern and Baum) given by some of his celebrated customers to the Bronx Zoo as his birthday present, and even hobnobbing in black tie with cronies *outside* his own restaurant. Yes, Mortimer's is indeed a phenomenon unique to our age, and so long as Bernbaum is around to console and coddle and dictate, the saloon will undoubtedly continue to make headlines.

I do question my own sanity when I realize I failed to so much as mention one of the supreme, unquestionable, and unalterable reasons for Mortimer's success: the cheap prices. "You must never forget," I've heard Bernbaum whisper, "that the rich don't like to spend a lot of money."

# LE CIRQUE:
# DROP-DEAD GLAMOUR AND
# FOUR-STAR FOOD

*1987*

A round 10:30 on a hot summer morning in New York, tension is building at Le Cirque as captains and busboys and bartenders and chefs go about their appointed tasks in preparation for still another glittering lunch at Manhattan's premier restaurant. Owner Sirio Maccioni is restless and wound up as he makes every effort to stay seated while explaining his restaurant's revised menu. The subject of attention is black bass wrapped in potato with red wine sauce, a sensational new dish created by Le Cirque's young chef, Daniel Boulud, but one that still worries Sirio a bit. Does black bass have the right texture for this innovative concept, or would red snapper work better? Exactly how crisp should the potato casing be, and is the *heurre rouge* perhaps too intense a sauce? For me and for everyone I know who has sampled the fish, it is sheer perfection, and I say so. Sirio cracks a quick, nervous smile but wonders nevertheless if the dish could be improved.

Spying a thread or minuscule piece of paper on the carpet, he leans down instinctively to pick it up, then, abandoning the black-bass problem, commences to tell why, at lunch on alternate Thursdays, Le Cirque's famous *bollito misto* has been replaced by Daniel's inspired pot-au-feu. Ears attuned to every sound in the room, he suddenly jumps up and darts to the front desk, where a captain, who has been manning three phones ever since I arrived, seems to be having problems with a reservations request.

The pitch is high as the two rave in Italian, hands flying in the air. On his way back to the table, Sirio bangs his knuckles angrily against the side of the exquisite cold buffet being set up by the staff. "You never hesitate one second when dealing with a reservation in this restaurant. *Never!* No maybes, no suggestion to please call back in one hour, no long explanations. You make the decision instantly and just say yes or no. When you hesitate, you've got trouble."

Eventually, after spending fifteen impatient minutes on the phone to Italy confirming advance October orders for fresh white truffles and *porcini* mushrooms, and after rejecting the design for some new crystal glassware, and after a long discussion with his veteran maître d'hôtel, Romeo, about which tables at lunch or dinner will be assigned to the likes of Gianni Agnelli, Ann Getty, Diane von Furstenberg, Prince Rainier of Monaco, Paul Bocuse, Pauline Trigère, Gloria Vanderbilt, the Duke of Bedford, Nancy Reagan, and any number of other socialites, monarchs, ambassadors, royals, and three-star chefs, Sirio once again calms down. To most of the public, he is the tall, suave, composed, hand-kissing gentleman who has greeted guests since he opened Le Cirque in 1974. But inwardly this is a man driven by an almost compulsive craving for perfection, by the very private need for fame and success, and by a set of strict personal and professional values that has made him and Le Cirque veritable legends in their own time.

Uncanny in his ability to please the most-demanding customer, obsessed with quality on every level, and stubborn in his refusal to compromise his principles, Sirio can be compared in many respects only with the late Henri Soulé, even as Le Cirque must now be considered, both socially and gastronomically, to be Le Pavillon of the eighties. Sirio does, to be sure, disdain the dictatorial role that Soulé assumed toward clientele and staff alike in his effort to create America's finest restaurant (Soulé, for example, was always Monsieur Soulé, whereas few can even spell Sirio's last name), and I doubt that any kitchen in the country could ever again produce the number of spectacular classic French dishes that were perfected during the fifties and sixties at Le Pavillon. But there can be no doubt that Sirio has developed Le Cirque into the most glamorous social arena New York has known since Soulé died over twenty years ago, just as there can be no question that his extraordinary culinary standards simply don't exist today in many other deluxe restaurants.

Another significant link between Sirio Maccioni and Henri Soulé is the fact that Sirio, like his French predecessor, has already spawned a colony of young restaurateurs and chefs who at one time or another worked at Le Cirque, then moved on either to open their own restaurants or to assume major positions in some of the New York area's leading establishments. Such past and present gastronomic citadels as La Caravelle, La Grenouille, La Potinière du Soir, Lafayette, La Seine, La Toque Blanche and Le Périgord-Park were all opened by graduates of Le Pavillon. Just as those disciples of Soulé sustained and enriched one glorious tradition, so are many of Sirio's former employees and associates demonstrating elsewhere much of the professional expertise they acquired at Le Cirque. Camille Dulac, for instance, who worked as a captain and later as assistant maître d'hôtel for almost two years at Le Cirque, is now co-owner of the illustrious Le Chantilly, while Michel Jean, a captain under Sirio for five years, is currently operating his own busy Provence in Greenwich Village. Sylvain Farieri and David Bouley—owners, respectively, of La Metairie and Restaurant Bouley —cut their teeth at Le Cirque, and who knows where such accomplished chefs as Pierre Baran (Le Cygne), André Gaillard (La Réserve), Jean-Louis Todeschini (Fatso & Co. in Wayne, New Jersey), and Jacques Thiebeult (La Grange at The Homestead Inn in Greenwich, Connecticut) would be today without their experience in the kitchen at 65th Street and Park Avenue.

Benito Sevarin, who started as a waiter at Le Cirque and eventually was promoted to be assistant maître d'hôtel, has been instrumental as manager in the recent restructuring of the elegant Café Pierre in the Hotel Pierre; and when it was revealed last spring that headwaiter Bruno Dussin was leaving Le Cirque after a tenure of thirteen consecutive years to run the show at what has become Harry Cipriani's wildly successful Bellini by Cipriani, the news spread about town like fire. Of course, nothing inspired more gossip and conjecture than the announcement that Alain Sailhac, head of the kitchen at Le Cirque for eight and a half years and one of the most brilliant chefs in the nation, had accepted the position of executive chef at the renovated "21" Club, a move that could finally transform the landmark into a serious restaurant.

Sirio opened Le Cirque at a time when New York's gastronomic scene was undergoing tremendous change, when the classic cuisine of such old-guard restaurateurs as Charles Masson (La Grenouille), Roger Chauveron (Café Chauveron) and Gene Cavallero Senior (The Colony) was being modified radically by practitioners of the revolutionary nouvelle cuisine. A new restaurant like Le Cirque had to determine its direction quickly. Sirio initially attracted much of his luminous clientele at Le Cirque by soliciting regulars he had served as a young maître d'hôtel under autocratic Cavallero at the old Colony (at one time Le Pavillon's arch-rival), and since then he has fed not only the most famous social, cultural, and business personalities of our era but also two American Presidents (Ronald Reagan's dinner at Le Cirque in 1981 was a heralded event, and Richard Nixon is still a regular). It's hardly news that tables at Le Cirque must be booked days, often weeks in advance (unless, of course, you know Sirio personally); that the staff is one of the highest paid in the world; that the recipes for such signature dishes as *pasta primavera* (created by Sirio himself), beef *carpaccio, goujonettes* of sole, coconut macaroons, and crème brûlée have been sought by every chef from Paul Bocuse on down; that on the only occasion the distinguished Swiss chef Fredy Girardet left Europe it was to cook at Le Cirque for two days; and that when a favored customer goes a spell without showing up at the restaurant, it's normal procedure for Sirio to pick up the phone or drop an inquiring note.

"Yes, yes, that's all people ever talk about," snaps Sirio when reminded of reasons for his and Le Cirque's celebrity. "But what they don't understand is that my primary goal, my reason for having this restaurant and tolerating this impossible way of life, is to provide the finest cuisine and service in America. Glamour is secondary. Other restaurateurs come in here, look around at all the fashionable faces, and think 'Ah, so that's what it takes for success; if only I could draw a crowd like that.' Well, let me tell you, that crowd is not stupid, and if I didn't make the constant effort to maintain the reputation of our food and service, Le Cirque would disappear."

While nobody who has frequented Le Cirque over the years could ever doubt the importance of the restaurant's vibrant social scene, it's equally true that never once has Sirio allowed his culinary standards to drop—even the most fastidious arbiters award him the highest accolades (Le Cirque is one of the few restaurants in New York patronized openly by such powerful critics as Mimi Sheraton, Gael Greene, Craig Claiborne, and Christian Millau). It is true he's been severely (and sometimes justifiably) criticized for packing too many people around a mere thirty-five tables ("If I removed five tables," he retorts, "that would reduce my business twenty-five percent and prices would have to soar"), for directing unknown customers with reservations to the bar for an irritating wait ("What am I supposed to do when a party is one hour late and I've given their table to others?" he says with frustration), and for holding the "best" tables in the house for friends ("Regulars who come here four or five times a week—and I know close to seventy-five percent of my clientele—have the *right* to special favors"). But, when it comes to the menu, service, and setting at Le Cirque, few would disagree that Sirio runs a tight ship. He has been known to cross the Atlantic to track down a head chef he wanted (Alain Sailhac) and to convince another (Daniel Boulud) that the executive position in Le Cirque's kitchen is more attractive than that offered at Lutèce. He considers it absolutely essential to maintain a kitchen staff of thirty and a restaurant brigade of one maître d'hôtel, six captains, sixteen waiters, and five busboys; he thinks nothing of paying a great chef well into six figures and making it possible for a top-notch waiter to pull in over $1,000 a week; and, out of an annual gross revenue of $6 million, no less than $60,000 is spent each year just on flowers. "Whether it's a question of a chef or a waiter or caviar or an ashtray," he insists, "I have got to have the very best available, no matter what the cost."

Beside the fact that Le Cirque's successive head chefs (Jean Vergnes,

Alain Sailhac and Daniel Boulud) happen to be three of the finest in the profession, I do think much of the restaurant's culinary success is due to the way Sirio has always maintained a sensible balance on his French-Italian menu. He never discards such proven classics as Vergnes's duckling and foie gras terrine with pistachios, lobster bisque, broiled flounder with mustard sauce, and whole roasted saddle of lamb, while encouraging the creation of new concepts like Sailhac's fresh pasta with *langoustines* and his delectable *noisettes d'agneau* topped with garlic purée, or Boulud's herbed chicken baked under weights and his improbable but credible beef tenderloin with snails in red-wine sauce. That certain calorie-conscious customers—forever satisfied with the same safe diet of *carpaccio*, chicken *paillard*, and grilled Dover sole—never have and never will present a challenge to the kitchen hardly deters Sirio and his chef from allowing the menu to evolve along more ambitious lines.

When domestic foie gras became available a few years ago, Le Cirque was the first to sauté it lightly and serve it with a vinegar sauce. Let Sirio hear about a new breed of duck or type of lettuce or variety of wild mushroom on the market and you can rest assured it will be featured at Le Cirque in one form or another weeks before it appears in other restaurants. Just recently, Sirio or Daniel or somebody came up with the revolutionary idea of serving a cold bouillabaisse with sweet garlic toast during the warm months. The dish was tested in the kitchen, tasted, revised, tasted again, tested on a few loyal customers and eventually offered as a special. Some loved the dish; others raised an eyebrow. As always, Sirio observes, listens, and makes decisions. If enough people take to the dish, on the menu it stays; if too many balk, off it goes. "You see, we don't invent dishes at Le Cirque," Sirio points out sternly, "since I'm convinced that there's really been nothing new since Escoffier—despite what all those inexperienced young chefs think today. But sometimes we do try to modify certain classic concepts, especially when a new product comes along. And why not? Often the dish fails, but when it works, it's very exciting."

It does seem that, in addition to the many other disciplines to which Sirio's alumni were exposed while working at Le Cirque (the absolute necessity of being on the job at all times, the importance of giving every customer the same standard of service, developing superhuman patience and tolerance, and learning that nothing can be accomplished without intimate teamwork), it is this sense of management flexibility that surfaces most when former employees discuss their mentor and his restaurant. "I think I mellowed working at Le Cirque," says Camille Dulac. "At first I had my own inflated ideas about how to deal with demanding customers and temperamental chefs; then gradually I learned from Sirio that you must always bend a little while maintaining the role of authority, give of yourself while never allowing the utter seriousness of your position to be denigrated."

Alain Sailhac explains that "Sirio pushes, pushes, pushes like a locomotive, but in the kitchen he needs someone to interpret what he has on his mind. It's not easy to communicate with this man who demands so much and hates excuses, but Sirio recognizes a good chef and bows to his own limitations when it comes to just what that chef is capable of accomplishing. Sometimes people think Sirio's a little crazy. Well, he's never crazy; he's intelligent and shrewd and knows exactly what he's doing at all times." Michel Jean concurs: "Sirio can be tough, very tough, but he realizes when and how to keep his distance from an employee he respects. He's always there when you need help and advice, but, while I was at Le Cirque, I learned the most just by simply *watching* him work. He's an amazing man and one who will always be in a class by himself."

It's late on a Tuesday night, and Sirio is tired. This evening he has greeted and pampered almost two hundred of the *beau monde*, resolved a dozen crises with Romeo and captains Renato and Rémy, orchestrated the menus for a dozen tables, and is now dividing his time between telling stragglers goodnight and trying to grab a bite to eat at the back table with old pals Pierre Franey (former chef at Le Pavillon) and Roger Fessaguet (former sous chef at Le Pavillon and co-owner of La Caravelle). The irony of this trio dining together titillates the imagination. Once the last Givenchy dresses and Kenneth hairdos and bespoke Dunhill suits have made their way to the street and I'm left alone with a few busboys and my glass of *grappa* in the deserted room, Sirio sits down for a moment. I want to know what really drives him, what keeps him year after year at a job that deprives him of a normal family life, prevents him from traveling the world, and makes it virtually impossible for him to enjoy his financial prosperity.

"It's very simple," he answers directly. "So long as Le Cirque is a success, I know that I can be totally independent, and that I can help my three sons, Mario, Marco, and Mauro, avoid the sort of early life I had—moving around from one hotel job to the next in one country after another. That's why I live in terror of losing a single customer, and that's why I set standards so high that even I have a hard time meeting them. On the other hand, don't forget that we Italians (and I've never been more proud than now to be Italian) are not easily impressed and have learned the hard way to take everything with a grain of salt. Yes, I want Le Cirque to be the greatest restaurant in the world, but, if something happens, I want to be able to say that I always aimed for the top and put every ounce of effort and energy I had into the place."

Bringing up the analogy of Le Cirque and Le Pavillon, I remind Sirio how Soulé had once said that "No one is indispensable except Soulé; without Soulé there is no Pavillon." Sirio produces one of his squinty, modest smiles. "Basically I disagree. No one at Le Cirque is indispensable, including me. And by that I mean that if somebody else can work longer and harder and dress better than I do, that person deserves to run this restaurant. Actually, I'll be so presumptuous as to say that we're better now than Le Pavillon ever was, since our foundation is so strong that the restaurant could function for quite a while without any given chef or maître d'hôtel or me."

That's a noble statement, to be sure, but ask any man or woman who's ever worked for Sirio and knows the luxury restaurant business in New York, and the first point emphasized is that Le Cirque without Sirio is as inconceivable as Fifth Avenue without Tiffany or Cartier. Ask, for that matter, any one of a hundred longtime loyals like Jerome Zipkin or Elizabeth Taylor or Mrs. Douglas MacArthur or Woody Allen. What most people don't know, however, is that even now Sirio has each of his three young sons not only working through the ranks of certain three-star restaurants in France, but also putting in time at Le Cirque periodically. So who knows if a small dynasty is in the making, and if, as always, Sirio Maccioni is determined to sustain the legend of Le Cirque in any way he knows possible? What I do know is that today in the restaurant world, hardly a month goes by that I don't still hear what Craig Claiborne has referred to as a timeless refrain: "You remember him; he worked under Soulé." I also know that a month rarely passes now that I don't show up at one new restaurant or another in New York, try to figure out where I've seen the young, dignified individual who ushers me gracefully to a table, or the faintly familiar face who serves with such professional expertise, and am told in a discreet whisper: "Remember me? I worked for Sirio."

# L'AUBERGE DE L'ILL: THE GREATEST RESTAURANT IN THE WORLD?

*1988*

Nestled between the Vosges Mountains of eastern France and the Rhine in the tiny, remote village of Illhaeusern (population: 517) is what many consider to be the finest restaurant in the world. In this restaurant, there is no pompous maître d'hôtel in starch-fronted dress shirt and tails, no grand crystal chandeliers or polished antique sideboards overloaded with heavy silver, no elaborate floral arrangements or dinner plates, no bizarre dishes of the nouvelle persuasion, and, indeed, no superstar chef parading around among the guests. What you do see is a short, neatly dressed man at the entrance who always greets customers as if they were old friends; discreet pale green walls with handsome bleached wood panelings and tastefully framed watercolors; and great expanses of windows overlooking a small stream bordered by old weeping willows and manicured gardens. There are crisp beige linens, fine glassware, a collection of attractive decanters, and small vases of fresh country flowers; local waiters and waitresses who never stop smiling while demonstrating their impeccable training; and both classic and updated regional dishes so ingenious in concept, so beautifully balanced, so precisely cooked, so indescribably delicious that even the most jaded epicure can't help but feel utterly stunned upon leaving the table.

The Auberge de l'Ill, owned and operated by the Haeberlin family, has had three Michelin stars for over twenty years, and should that famous tire

company of omnipotent culinary arbitration ever have reason to acknowledge the absolute ultimate in restaurant excellence by introducing a four-
star category in its prestigious guide, no doubt that reason would be this
basically simple, unpretentious, rustic auberge tucked away in the bucolic
hills of Alsace. Although I, like many other obsessed gastronomades, have
been making the pilgrimage to Illhaeusern on and off since at least the mid-
sixties, virtually no British, very few Americans, and not even many of the
French know the restaurant the way they do such other more-accessible
three-star French temples as Paul Bocuse, Alain Chapel, and Le Moulin
de Mougins.

True, over the years the Haeberlins have fed the likes of Jean-Paul
Sartre, Orson Welles, England's Queen Mother, Marlene Dietrich, and
Montserrat-Caballé, but never has the Auberge been a regular target for
most tourists in search of superlative French dining. "Alsace is just too far
away from everything else in France" is the tiring refrain I've always heard,
an excuse that might make sense if the region didn't just happen to be one
of the most unspoiled and beautiful in all Europe and if the Auberge de l'Ill
didn't represent the apogee of *la grande cuisine française*. As a result, the
vast majority of majestic Jaguars, sleek Mercedeses and Citröens, and family Peugeots that pour into Illhaeusern's single winding street year after
year, cross the little bridge over the River Ill, and park somewhere between
the village church and the restaurant come from Germany, Belgium, Switzerland, and, just thirty-six miles away, Strasbourg. These people are not
out to visit museums or gaze at monuments or sightsee. Their one and only
objective is the Auberge de l'Ill, where, ever since Fritz Haeberlin began
serving his frogs'-leg soup, eel stew, and *beckeoffe* over a century ago,
serious gastronomes have come to relax under the willows, sip fruity Alsatian wines produced in the surrounding vineyards, and savor delectable
food that, in current Michelin vernacular, is "worthy of a special journey."

Today there are three generations of Haeberlins involved in the Auberge. Marthe, the ninety-three-year-old matriarch of the family, still
makes her rounds of the dining room and supervises the laundry. Paul, her
oldest son, is the stocky, shy, almost withdrawn chef responsible for the
restaurant's distinguished culinary reputation, while his multi-talented
brother, Jean-Pierre, is the comparably slight, affable, well-tailored gentleman who not only has directed the front of the house since 1950 but also is
the mayor of Illhaeusern, a professional engineer and landscape artist, and
the accomplished hand behind the charming watercolors that grace the
menu and walls. After apprenticing at such citadels as Lasserre in Paris,
Bocuse, and Troisgros, Marc, Paul's thirty-four-year-old son, returned
home in 1976 to join his father in the kitchen, adding brilliant new dimension to the regional specialties and assuring that the family tradition would
continue well into the next century. The Auberge de l'Ill received its first
Michelin star in 1952, its second in 1957, and its third ten years later. In

1980, the prestigious Ordre National du Mérite was bestowed upon both Paul and Jean-Pierre by President Giscard d'Estaing.

My own close association with the Auberge began when the restaurant had only two stars and guests often arrived without a reservation to wait their turn for a table. In those days, there were no more than a few waitresses and no sommelier; an elaborate three-course lunch with wine was rarely more than about $15; and it was never unusual to spot Jean-Pierre shortly before noon finishing up work in his garden before quickly changing from jeans and a pullover into a dark suit. Quite often I and my companions would sit as long as an hour on the flower-trimmed outdoor terrace, gazing at swans gliding peacefully across the water, drinking a crisp Muscat d'Alsace or bubbly Moët et Chandon, and studying the fascinating menu.

Perhaps the first indication always that we were in a very special restaurant was the total absence of potato soup, *choucroute garni*, pig's feet, dumplings, heavy stews, and other such traditional hearty Alsatian fare, which could be absolutely delectable in the appropriate setting but which was simply not Paul Haeberlin's style of cooking. Instead, we were confronted with a whole fresh black truffle coated with foie gras, baked in puff pastry, and served with a burnished Cognac-and-truffle sauce; a delicate effusion of cream, egg yolks, frogs' legs, Riesling, and watercress, called simply *le potage de grenouilles au cresson;* small salmon fillets concealed under a pike soufflé with an ethereal cream sauce *(le saumon soufflé);* roasted local pheasant stuffed with foie gras, mushrooms, and cabbage in a truffled Madeira sauce; and a voluptuous white peach poached in vanilla syrup and served in a chocolate "butterfly" with pistachio ice cream and a Champagne sabayon sauce. Incredibly, the cuisine was sumptuous but not overwhelming, highly imaginative without being contrived, fully regional in nature but classical in execution. Once, over tiny glazed plums and snifters of mirabelle brandy, I asked Paul to describe his food in general. "What I produce is no more than German-style dishes cooked with a bit of French subtlety and refinement" was his triumph of understatement.

I suppose what continues to astonish me most about the Auberge de l'Ill is how little the spirit of the restaurant and cuisine has changed over the years. It's true, of course, that today customers have to book tables up to three months in advance (and reconfirm those reservations forty-eight hours prior to arrival), that the same inimitable salmon soufflé that cost me 30 francs in 1974 is now priced at 125 francs, that Marc's innovative influence in the kitchen is more and more pronounced, and that three-star status demands the extraordinary knowledge and talents of a sommelier like Serge Dubs (recent winner of the Meilleur Sommelier de France). But basically the restaurant is much the way it's been for decades, never giving the impression of having developed into some sort of culinary and social factory like so many of its peers throughout France.

There's Jean-Pierre, a little older and balder but still kissing locals on both cheeks, welcoming newcomers with true Alsatian warmth, coaxing his large canine, Upso, away from the entrance, and forever rambling about his garden and dining room. Today there's as much of that precious commodity called space between tables as twenty years ago; the charming waitresses and handsome waiters speak French (like the Haeberlins themselves) with an almost incomprehensible Alsatian accent; and delectable *amuses-gueule* are still served gratis on the terrace with your Champagne Cassis, as are the addictive postprandial confections known as *mignardises*. Although Paul remains as invisible as always in his kitchen, Marc is somewhat more outgoing, leaving his domain on occasion to answer the questions of an inquisitive guest and often standing by the door in late evening to bid friends goodnight and thank strangers for coming. As in the old days, much of the foodstuff is still supplied by locals: fresh bread from a bakery down the road; dairy products, fruits, and vegetables from small nearby farms; wild game and mushrooms from hunters; and the runny, orange-crusted, sensuous fresh Münster cheese made by J. Haxaire in the small town of Lapoutroie. The Auberge has always boasted an impressive listing of wines and white fruit brandies indigenous to the region, but I think it's safe to assume that today the restaurant's collection of Alsatian wines and *eaux-de-vie* is the most extensive in the world.

Being resolutely convinced that the reputation and longevity of any great restaurant is based at least partially not on an eclectic menu that changes daily according to the frivolous whims of the chef but on certain steadfast dishes that have been tested and perfected over a period of time (pressed duck at La Tour d'Argent in Paris, English mutton chops at Jack's in San Francisco, *bollito misto* at Del Cambio in Turin), I can state that the primary reason most epicures return to the Auberge de l'Ill is to savor again and again those specialties whose names have become virtually synonymous with this restaurant. Where else, for instance, can you order a sybaritic foie-gras-and-truffle soufflé, a silky timbale of creamed pike with boned frogs' legs poached in Riesling *(la mousseline de grenouilles)*, buttery chunks of tender lobster with shallots braised in Champagne and *crème fraîche (le homard Prince Wladimir)*, and an elaborate saddle of rabbit stuffed with vegetables and baked in puff pastry *(le râble de lapereau)?* I know one passionate gastronome who travels a long distance to the Auberge for the sole purpose of feasting on nothing but a slice of *brioche de foie gras* in golden aspic and the famous salmon soufflé, and once I drove all the way from Baden-Baden in Germany (a bit panicky during the cure I was undergoing) just to perch at a window table and consume Paul's sophisticated fish stew of eel, perch, trout, and mushrooms *(la matelote d'Illhaeusern au Riesling)* enhanced by Hügel's spicy Gewürztraminer. Most of these magnificent specialties have been around as long as anybody can remember, classic dishes that give real meaning to the idea of culinary perfection and that never fail to make an indelible impact on both the palate and the soul.

If it's true that no three-star restaurant in France champions and respects family tradition like the Auberge de l'Ill, it's equally true that Paul and especially Marc are forever experimenting with new culinary concepts, different textural and flavor combinations, and various methods for adding further distinction to their regional dishes. This is not to say, indeed, that either father or son has ever endorsed that dubious school of cooking known as *la nouvelle cuisine,* only that both are always seeking ways to redefine much of the food that is their heritage and give it exciting new flair without altering its basic character. "We never fell into the nouvelle trap," Marc insists. "Sure, it's fine to serve beautiful food, but never, never at the expense of flavor. No matter what we prepare, there must always be logic and harmony." And what about the tendency today all over France (and the world) to impose on guests lighter and "healthier" dishes? "There's nothing wrong with light food, and our food can be quite light," snaps Jean-Pierre, "but it's not our business at the Auberge to put people on diets."

So exactly how do Paul and Marc go about modifying a regional specialty and transforming basically peasant dishes into highly refined classics that are easy to digest but still packed full of flavor? Surely no item serves as a better example than Marc's brilliant *petit beckeoffe aux truffes.* Traditionally, *beckeoffe* (or "baker's oven") is a heavy, robust stew involving layers of highly seasoned marinated pork, beef, pig's feet and tail, potatoes, and onions that are assembled in a large earthenware casserole and cooked slowly with white wine for hours—in olden times during Monday-morning washday. In the updated version, however, a mini terrine is composed of delicate layers of lamb, pork, and leeks, enriched with fresh truffles, and simmered just long enough to produce a savory dish that has a number of distinctly individual flavors yet is discreet enough to be included in the orchestration of a complete menu. Today in France, it seems that every trendy restaurant serves the same prosaic warm lettuce and foie gras salad vinaigrette, but by combining pig cheeks, goose liver, and green lentils, nestling the mixture on top of oak leaf lettuce, and crowning it with both a sautéed slice of foie gras and a tiny fried quail's egg, the Haeberlins not only pay homage to their region but also demonstrate imaginative and delectable touches that give the appetizer salad totally new meaning. For years one of Paul's most celebrated creations was his *côtelette de perdreau Romanoff,* an elaborate partridge preparation with truffles and foie gras. To commemorate the investiture of his father and uncle with the Ordre National du Mérite, young Marc created a similar dish by marinating squab breasts in Port and Cognac, layering them between cabbage leaves and a forcemeat of pork, chicken, foie gras, and shallots, baking the package in puff pastry, and anointing it with a truffled *sauce périgueux.* Who knows how the President of France reacted when the complex dish was placed before him at the Auberge, but there's no doubt that Marc's innovative *feuilleté de pigeon-neau* will go down in the annals of French gastronomy as a veritable jewel in the classic repertory.

Although it is fully possible to have a memorable three-course meal at the Auberge de l'Ill for about fifty dollars a head (including a simple bottle of Riesling and service), one of the best values in all France is the restaurant's eight-course menu at 475 francs (approximately eighty dollars) featuring small portions of various seasonal dishes. Normally, I loathe this sort of *dégustation*, which can drag on for hours and totally corrupt one's stamina, palate, and memory bank. But at the Auberge, the production not only moves with incredible swiftness but illustrates Paul's and Marc's inimitable expertise at formulating menus with perfect balance. During my most recent visit, I and my cohorts, sated from a typically overindulgent gastronomic romp through several French provinces, opted to settle for no more than six courses, a decision that led to one of the greatest and most soothing meals ever. After washing down a few *flammekueche* (small Alsatian onion-and-bacon tarts) with a fresh Muscat d'Alsace on the terrace, we were served first a luscious squab-and-foie-gras salad surrounding a small potato filled with creamy potato purée and truffles. Next came an extraordinary chilled consommé in which were suspended pieces of poached mackerel, carrots, tomatoes, and fresh dill, an ingenious concept enhanced even more by a poached quail egg hidden on the bottom and a dollop of caviar on top. Next were sumptuous crab claws stuffed with a mousse of sea bass, followed by a full-flavored fillet of venison served with both a pocket of cabbage stuffed with forcemeat and wild mushrooms and that wonderful Alsatian spaetzle-like pasta known as *Wasserstriwla*.

From the elaborate array of cheeses on the handsome Cristofle trolley, we chose only the fresh, crusty, mildly assertive, sensational Münster produced locally, and for dessert we engaged in a "symphony of plums," some layered in puff pastry, others wrapped in frozen cream and folded into crêpes with crushed almonds, and still others incorporated in a delicate sorbet. With the salad and fish courses, we drank an exceptional full-bodied Bott Frères Riesling '83; for the venison, Serge introduced us to Hügel's fascinating '83 Pinot Noir; with the runny Münster, we polished off a spicy '81 Gewürztraminer made a few miles away in the village of Éguisheim. To complement the small pastries and chocolates served with coffee and to observe a proud Alsace tradition, we lifted icy snifters of raspberry brandy. "And that, my dear friends," I volunteered, "is what the real three-star dining experience in France should be all about."

On more than one occasion, I've heard Jean-Pierre Haeberlin say that the most difficult job for him and his brother is "to constantly create perfection," and I have no doubt that this obsession with and devotion to quality on every level is what primarily has allowed the Auberge to maintain its lofty reputation. On the other hand, I can't help but feel that much of the restaurant's success has always been due to the familial, almost dynastic solidarity that has sustained the Auberge for generations and continues to serve as its very backbone. Today, for instance, Paul's wife, Marie, handles the floral arrangements, and their daughter, Danielle, helps grandmother Marthe with the laundry and supervises table appointments. In turn, it is Danielle's husband, Marco, who takes over at the front when Jean-Pierre is away or needed elsewhere as town mayor, while Marc's wife, Martine, deals with all the complex bookkeeping. Continuity is manifested even further by the non-Haeberlin chefs, waiters, and waitresses who've been at the Auberge for ten, twenty, thirty years, loyal veterans who are virtually part of the family and who are gradually replaced by younger locals proud to contribute their energy and talent to the tradition.

If it is true that a great restaurant is the reflection of the devoted souls behind it, then I am indeed ready to believe that the Auberge de l'Ill is and will remain in a class by itself for many years to come. As to whether or not it is the finest dining experience anywhere, I can only urge you to make the special journey to Alsace, perhaps spend a morning or afternoon roaming through the verdant hills and vineyards, show up at the restaurant in time to unwind on the terrace overlooking the serene river, let the Haeberlins work their magic, and form your own opinion. What I strongly suspect is that you'll yearn to return time and again to savor not only a rare gastronomic occasion but also a soft way of life that most people think disappeared long ago.

# QE 2'S PEERLESS PRINCESS

*1986*

There's nothing more frustrating, more bedeviling, more agonizing in the life of a professional gastronome than the realization that restaurant perfection is as elusive as the savor of fresh truffle. Occasionally, you hit upon a place that appears to be the ultimate in setting, service, wine selection, and food preparation. You return a second, third, perhaps a fourth time, convinced you've finally found the ideal refuge where the palate can be forever gratified, the aesthetics guaranteed, the soul warmed. But then there's always the inevitable occasion when the fatal flaw rears its head: a stained napkin, an indifferent table captain, a bottle of wine that remains unpoured, a sauce without breeding, a dinner check presented before being requested. Suddenly, gloom descends, and, taking the last sips of a lukewarm espresso, you know the search must begin again.

Given this fact of life, it should be clear why, when asked to name the finest restaurant in the world, I cringe in hesitation. Racing through my brain are visions of a sturdy English breakfast amid the polished wood and brass of London's Connaught; a dreamlike lunch of salmon soufflé and *feuilleté* of squab with cabbage at the Auberge de l'Ill overlooking a small stream in Alsace; and an impeccable risotto graced by copious shavings of fresh white truffle at Del Cambio in Turin. I picture myself in the shady garden of Commander's Palace in New Orleans, yearning for another order of shrimp rémoulade or sautéed buster crabs. I visualize one of the elder black-tie waiters or motherly waitresses at Wilton's in London as he or she deftly removes the moist, succulent flesh from the bone of a Dover sole and garnishes the plate with a bibbed lemon half. I think of Jovan Trboyevic escorting me into the dining room of Chicago's Les Nomades, the most civilized in America; of Egon von Fodermayer personally explaining to every guest each tempting appetizer on the trolley at Zu den Drei Husaren in Vienna; of headwaiter Oreste Carnevali carving the most celestial duck *au poivre* at The Four Seasons in New York; and of Monsieur Vrinat taking all the time in the world to detail the preparation of the *selle d'agneau en rognonnade* at Taillevant in Paris.

Despite all these delicious memories, however, I always know deep down that, everything considered, for me there is still no experience that quite equals dining in the Princess Grill aboard *Queen Elizabeth 2* during a transatlantic crossing. By my latest count, I've made forty-one voyages on that magnificent liner since she began plying the North Atlantic between Southampton and New York back in 1969, dining initially as a frugal tourist-class passenger in the Britannia (now called the Mauretania) Restaurant, then as a more affluent traveler in the regular first-class Columbia Restaurant, and eventually as an unabashed hedonist in the first-class Queen's Grill, reserved for top-paying passengers. It was not till some time later that I became a habitué of the Princess Grill, the smallest, most intimate, and, in my opinion, most splendid of the three first-class saloons on *QE 2*. Because of its secluded location up a circular staircase from One Deck, the vast majority of passengers never even know it exists. Only those with "D" grade staterooms are entitled to this particular luxury, and even those in the more expensive upper-grade suites and staterooms cannot move from the Queen's Grill to the Princess unless there happens to be a vacant table in the latter—which is very rare.

What places the Princess in a class by itself is first the ambience created by its private bar hidden at the bottom of the gracious staircase, where diners have cocktails and postprandial coffee and cigars; then the clublike aroma of the restaurant's original burgundy leather and velvet chairs and banquettes (this is the only dining saloon on the ship that has never been subjected to major modification); the sweeping views of the sea from every table; the basically British staff of top-notch professionals; and the fashionable but serious clientele. The feeling is that of old-fashioned, unadulterated, quiet exclusivity—a place where the term "first class" has real meaning. A small brass plaque at the entrance reads, "Gentlemen are requested to wear jacket and tie in the restaurant," a polite way of saying that black tie is all but *de rigueur* except the first and last evenings at sea.

From the first step up the staircase for the first dinner after embarkation, the Princess Grill works her powerful charms. Like all Princess passengers, I am greeted first by Mr. David Chambers, the Grill's veteran maître d'hôtel, correctly attired in white tie and black tails with a white carnation in his lapel. Looking around, I see the same experienced waiters I've known for years, each sporting a spanking white jacket trimmed with burgundy facing that matches the room's décor. With great good fortune, we are seated at my favorite table, #138, where long-time waiter Michael Hey rushes up to shake hands, welcome me back, and confirm that I'll be having my usual double portion of fresh caviar this and every other evening. Michael, who served none other than Her Majesty at Buckingham Palace before joining Cunard, is, in my opinion, the most attentive, polished, and professional waiter I've encountered anywhere—*anywhere*. I see once again the splendid silver trolley that displays whole joints of beef and lamb, the shiny brass railings that elegantly ring the room, and the four statues of Air, Fire, Water, and Earth that add a subtle flair. The setting is correct without being stuffy, the lighting low but sufficient.

Within minutes, we're sipping Taittinger and studying the copious offerings on the menu. Like as not, seated against a plush banquette at a nearby table is Meryl Streep or Jeremy Irons, or at the prized table #164 near the entrance there is a quartet of instantly recognized names and celebrated faces. Probably only a few passengers who sit at the corner window table, #114, realize that theirs is the table Queen Elizabeth II herself chose shortly after her namesake was launched. The ship begins to sway soothingly as she heads for the North Atlantic, the murmur in the room picks up as passengers relax, and all the tableside service commences.

Since this is the first night at sea, almost everyone orders from a regular menu, one that might appear a bit limited to some epicures but that makes those in most other deluxe restaurants pale by comparison. To start, there are such items as fresh Scotch smoked salmon with dilled horseradish sauce, pure foie gras, sliced Matjes herring and onions in sour cream, and a delicate double consommé served with a julienne of vegetables and truffle. Next, perhaps, a small broiled fillet of lemon sole with avocado and chervil butter, or poached fillets of sea bream with shrimp and lobster sauce, or a delectable risotto with tomato *coulis,* followed by the tenderest grilled sweetbreads on garlic croutons with a light pepper sauce, a whole golden roast chicken *à l'anglaise* enhanced by bacon and *chipolata* sausages, or silky smoked ox tongue glazed with Madeira sauce. The waiter will arrive at the table with an array of vegetables, such as cauliflower Mornay, sautéed courgettes with basil, and puffy potatoes *fondants.* Of course, if all this sounds too sturdy for a first dinner at sea, you always have the option of choosing no more than a few slices of meat from the cold table, a salad, a raspberry soufflé or Black Forest gâteau, and perhaps a savory of Scotch woodcock. Whatever you choose, the regular Princess dinner menu— which changes daily and is only a suggestion of things to come—manages quite nicely to placate the tensions of embarkation and set the mood.

It is no secret to regulars, however, that head chef Karl Winkler and his three senior chefs can and will prepare virtually any dish imaginable in the international repertory with a little advance notice, just as it is no secret that a first-class Grill passenger can also savor unlimited amounts of fresh Iranian caviar three times a day if so desired (Cunard remains the world's largest purchaser of fresh caviar, and on a typical *QE 2* five-day transatlantic voyage, no less than eighty pounds of the precious stuff is served to first-class passengers). Eating well is such serious business in the Princess that at breakfast we peruse lunch menus, at lunch we study dinner menus and discuss special orders with Mr. Chambers, and at dinner we may even determine what particular dish we would like the following day at breakfast or lunch. No sensible demand, no logical ingredient, no sane recipe is beyond the scope of this kitchen.

Although dinner in the Princess is the most dramatic of the meals, breakfast and lunch certainly can never be considered minor repasts. At eight in the morning, Mr. Chambers is attired in morning dress and red carnation, and waiters are wearing their daytime gray jackets and straight neckties; the tables are set with the same damask linens, eight pieces of silver per person, Royal Doulton white china with the Cunard crested gold lion, cut crystal glasses, peppermills, and silver finger bowls as in the evening. No sooner are you seated with a hot cup of coffee than a young *commis* first presents a gigantic platter loaded with at least a dozen different fresh pastries—including Scotch baps, muffins, croissants, brioches, and biscuits—then returns with a trolley laden with various marmalades, jams, and honeys. Orange juice, of course, is freshly squeezed, pineapples and melons are cut before being placed on the table, and toast is served in handsome silver racks. There are ten varieties of cereal (including hominy grits), eight different egg preparations, all types of bacon and sausage, and seven items on a cold buffet. You can order grilled kippered herring or lamb chops, onion soup, a minute steak, poached finnan haddock in milk, or corned-beef hash. Or perhaps just scrambled eggs with caviar or smoked salmon and a bottle of bubbly. Most remarkable of all is that, even after consuming an Olympian English breakfast aboard *QE 2* at 9 A.M., by eleven you're all ready to be served a cup of hot bouillon at your deck chair.

These days I control myself at lunch since I know in advance exactly all that my liver will be subjected to in the evening. While in more youthful and resilient days I thought nothing of knocking off a terrine of duckling, a braised brisket of beef with sauerkraut, and apple-and-rhubarb pie Chantilly at noon, I now settle for little more than my double sevruga slowly spooned on toast and perhaps a chilled half-lobster or tender crayfish with mustard mayonnaise. Most others in the saloon, by contrast, go the limit. They start with spiced potted shrimp, perhaps, or assorted French and Italian sausages, and proceed to a puffy asparagus omelet (I've never had omelets, even in France, to equal those turned out by the dozens in the Princess) or fried river smelts with rémoulade sauce. Then there are split lamb's kidneys on toast with *sauce diable*, barbecued chicken and shrimp kabobs on rice pilaf, or stuffed roast veal in puff pastry. Dessert? By all means. Just a little apricot custard pudding, or *Apfel Strudel* with apricot sauce, or *millefeuille*, or perhaps simply pineapple sherbet with tile cookies. It's amazing how this kitchen produces such a variety of mouth-watering dishes for lunch, and it's even more amazing that a humble club sandwich or cheeseburger is prepared and served here with the same concern for quality and flair given the most exotic *poppodums*, sweetbreads, and seafood pastas.

Over the years, I've had numerous dishes in the Princess that I would consider flawless (juicy poached turbot topped with mussels in a light saffron sauce, braised duck with olives, *gnocchi* with Gorgonzola sauce, an authentic French *navarin d'agneau*, pheasant Souvaroff, roasted grouse on toast points, *Wiener Schnitzel* with fresh *cèpes*, and calf's brains sautéed in black butter are some of the more memorable, but nothing sticks so indelibly in my memory as one particular dinner that was centered around a pot-au-feu. It was the third night at sea, the ship was struggling valiantly against an eight-force gale, and although hundreds of less-seasoned passengers were suffering the agonies of the damned in their staterooms, the Princess was filled to capacity with tuxedos and bejeweled gowns and functioning on a heroic scale. The previous day at lunch, I had asked Mr. Chambers if the chef would be willing to produce the classic French dish of boiled meats with marrow bone and vegetables for our table of four, a preparation that, when executed correctly, requires lots of manual labor and hours of simmering. No problem. This evening the tablecloths had been wetted down slightly and the fiddles (table railings) raised to prevent everything from toppling into our laps as the ship lunged. We had luscious beluga caviar with iced vodka, we had silky smoked salmon carved tableside, we had fat, garlicky *escargots*, and each was exemplary. But the pot-au-feu was a culinary spectacle the likes of which would have stunned even Monsieur le Huédé, head chef on my beloved S.S. *France*. Out it came in a gigantic deep copper vessel tended by two waiters, who began to secure it with heavy twine to a serving table as if this precarious procedure were carried out nightly. Then, while the noble liner heaved from side to side, Mr. Chambers carved the steaming beef, chicken, and pork, a captain spooned marrow bone and sculptured vegetables onto each plate, and the two waiters served.

Yes, it was an exemplary pot-au-feu, as juicy and flavorful as I'd ever had, but what impressed me most was how, under the worst of circumstances, the kitchen and staff had demonstrated the sort of professionalism rarely found today in even the most competent restaurants in the world. No storm kept fresh flowers and finger bowls off the tables, no ocean swell prevented our veteran wine steward from steadily replenishing our glasses with Chambolle-Musigny, no emergency dissuaded Mr. Chambers from delivering the lemon soufflé he'd promised. Once again the Princess Grill upheld the Cunard tradition for excellence, and, as we rolled with this last great superliner, nibbled on delicate petits fours, and coddled snifters of old Armagnac, I realized once again what a special privilege it was to be dining in a style that always attains a lofty degree of perfection and that one day will be no more than a nostalgic link to a glorious past.

## POSTSCRIPT

When *QE* 2 was subjected to major refitting in 1986–87, I shivered at the thought of what might be done to the Princess Grill. Imagine my relief, therefore, when I discovered not only that this classic jewel of a dining saloon had been left basically intact but that the service and cuisine (under the executive direction of a brilliant new chef, Rudolf Sodamin) was even more glorious than before. Of course, a few of us old fogies, loath to accept today's rapidly changing social patterns and relaxed enforcement of rules everywhere, almost dropped our soup spoons one day at lunch when a couple in jogging suits arrived with small children in tow, but even this sort of breach of propriety is soon forgotten once this remarkable room is in high gear and the feasting is well under way.

# PART VI
# A NEW LOOK
# AT OLD FAVORITES

In much the same way that I wrote about fried chicken, meat loaf, hamburgers, and gumbo in *American Taste*, here I champion still more gastronomic underdogs, forever insistent that such traditional and wonderful dishes as simple boiled beef and baked beans can still hold their own against the silly conceits of the so-called New American style of cooking and convinced that the great potential of staples like potatoes and onions has only begun to be exploited by adventurous cooks. I enjoy nothing more, for example, than extolling the merits of something like the humble sardine, tracing its importance throughout various countries, and showing how it can be utilized in numerous different ways to create new and exciting dishes. I always find it ironic and absurd the way our young, inexperienced American superstar chefs search so desperately for novel ideas and exotic food combinations in other cuisines when, all the time, there's so much inherent in their own gastronomic culture just waiting to be exposed or reinterpreted.

# THE UNSUNG SARDINE

*1984*

At the fashionable Brasserie Lipp on the Boulevard St.-Germain in Paris, a svelte young French socialite sits in the front room chatting with her companion, sipping a *vin blanc cassis* (known in less-sophisticated circles as *un Kir*), and checking out the crowd. When the black-tie waiter approaches to take orders, she doesn't hesitate. *"Les sardines beurre,"* she directs, *"suivies par la sole meunière."* Sardines and sautéed sole, simple and uncomplicated, perfect for a light dinner. Within minutes, her first course arrives: four fat sardines glistening in their olive-oil bath and flanked by a little parsleyed potato salad. In much fancier Parisian restaurants, the sardines might be served in a long, elegant, narrow porcelain dish *(un ravier)* or directly in the tin fitted into a specially designed sardine holder *(une sardinière)*, but the savvy Lipp clientele hardly expects such lavishment. The lady cuts one sardine in half, spears the morsel with a fork, spreads a little sweet butter on top, and proceeds as if she were savoring the first bite of fresh foie gras. After taking a sip of heady beer, she gently rolls the next portion about in the thick oil, and the next she smears with hot mustard. Obviously she has performed this ritual hundreds of times before; obviously she loves and understands sardines.

Of course most Americans would be totally baffled by this gastronomic scene, which occurs year-round in homes and restaurants all over France. Sardines? Ordinary, common, lowly canned sardines actually being approached as something of a delicacy? Well, the French do relish sardines in ways others just don't understand, but, as anyone who's ever ordered them in a French bistro or brasserie knows, there's a world of difference between the firm, scintillating, unctuous beauties that are produced in Brittany and the less noble examples we pick up occasionally in the super-market to eat casually as snack food. Don't get me wrong. For those who take the time and have the fortitude to seek out and sample every variety of French, Portuguese, Norwegian, Baltic, Brazilian, and domestic sardine that appears on the market, there are indeed great rewards to be reaped, gustatory surprises that most Americans would never guess existed. No doubt the French appreciate sardines more than anyone else on earth (to the tune of 200 million tins annually), but now that significant efforts are being made in America not only to import the very finest brands from Europe but also to upgrade the quality of sardines produced in the state of Maine, it does seem that it is time for us to consider seriously a neglected food that is highly nutritious, blessedly inexpensive, and delectable to eat simply by itself or incorporated into numerous dishes.

Exactly what, you ask, constitutes a great canned sardine, and how do you go about locating the best of the dozens and dozens of brands stacked on the shelves? Perfect sardines are neither too large (over five inches) nor too small (under two inches), and the size of the fish in the can is uniform in length and width. Perfect sardines are tightly and evenly layered, firm-fleshed, well-gutted but unbroken, and with both bright, silvery skins and creamy-white backbones that separate easily from the ideally pinkish flesh around the soft bone. The oil (whether olive, peanut, cottonseed, or soy-bean) is heavy and clear, the aroma when opening the can is mild and pleasant, and the rich, smooth, slightly salty flavor indicates that the sar-dines have been allowed to age and ripen in the can at least twelve months. Contrary to what most people believe, there are excellent sardines that are not necessarily skinned and boned, and some of the finest are even packed with the tails intact. Curiously enough, price is no guarantee of the quality of sardines. A tin of French Rödels (considered the Lafites of the sardine world) can cost as much as $8, but an equally great can of Port Clydes from Maine can be found for less than one dollar. There's only one way to locate perfect sardines: by opening can after can, studying, and tasting.

Technically, the sardine is any one of several species of young, small herring that are fished primarily in the Mediterranean and off the coasts of North Africa, Spain, Portugal, France, Yugoslavia, Norway, and the state of Maine. The principal species used for canning by the French and Por-tuguese, for example, is the pilchard (*Clupea pilchardus*) that migrates an-nually from the South Atlantic up the coast to Brittany, while in Norway, it's the brisling or sprat (*Clupea sprattus*), around Sardinia (the fish's name-sake) the Mediterranean pilchard (*Sardinia sardina*), and off Maine the sild or musse (*Clupea harengus*). Sardine lovers will argue interminably about which is the finest species, but the truth is that the quality of a sardine depends not so much on its lineage as on its size, age, processing, and the amount of time it's left in the can to ripen. That some producers choose to can older six- to seven-inch sardines instead of the younger three- to four-inchers, to steam or smoke instead of grilling them before packing, to debone and skin instead of leaving the fish intact, and to pack in soybean oil instead of the best-grade olive oil definitely has lots of effect on texture and taste.

The French Bretons (who have dominated the European sardine business for centuries) control not only the canning industry in France but also a good deal of the production in North Africa and Portugal. As a result, the likely reason certain brands of Portuguese sardines (such as Marie Elizabeth) taste so much better than others is that they're processed in accordance with French standards. So demanding, in fact, are the Breton canners around Concarneau, La Turballe, and Dounarnenez that even when additional olive oil must be imported into France from Italy or Greece to meet the packing standards, nothing will do but to have the oil refined in Marseille in line with strict specifications. The French, unlike so many other producers, have established and maintained such quality control for sardines that there's little wonder connoisseurs go out of their way to lay hands on prestige tins of Rödel, Gravier Aîné, Les Savoureuses, and Phillipe et Canaud. Certainly the most popular way of eating these luscious sardines in France is directly out of the can with a little mustard or butter, but by no means does the passion stop there. Throughout the provinces (but especially in Brittany and the south), both fresh and tinned sardines are grilled, turned into fritters, stuffed, used to enrich sauces, marinated, battered and sautéed à la meunière, added to casseroles, and even included in at least one version of bouillabaisse.

While the French remain the uncontested arbiters of sardine refinement, these small fish also play an important role in any number of other cuisines around the world. In Portugal, for instance, no dish is more loved than sardinhada, traditionally a dozen grilled small sardines served with boiled potatoes and a composed salad of tomatoes, onions, and peppers. In Spain, there seems to be a different sardine pie for every province, while throughout North Africa one of the most popular preparations is a scabech of chilled sardines with garlic and vinegar. A standard appetizer in Greece is canned sardines mashed with eggs and anchovies and spread on strips of pita; in Sardinia itself, almost every restaurant serves a savory combination of sardines baked with tomatoes and herbs; and anyone who's ever sampled the pasta with sardine sauce (pasta con le sarde) found throughout Sicily will understand why epicures consider this dish one of the world's finest culinary creations. In Brazil, tiny sardines are soused with numerous spicy ingredients; in Japan, they are threaded on skewers, dipped in soy sauce, and grilled; and one of the joys of an authentic Scandinavian smorgasbord is the rows of delicate sardines adorned with bracelets of sliced red onion, feathers of fresh dill, and colorful sprinklings of chives and chopped hard-boiled eggs.

The English, whose predisposition for quality sardines is surpassed only by that of the French, have developed over the years what amounts to a unique form of sardine cookery. They mash the fish with hard-boiled eggs, anchovy paste, mustard, minced onion, and butter to serve as a basic sardine butter for multiple canapés. They add sardines to red peppers, diced apple, sliced oranges, and lettuce to make a tasty luncheon salad and mix the pilchards with mashed potatoes and vinegar to produce a different version of fish cakes. They nestle them in baked potatoes before sprinkling with cheese and running under the broiler, coat them with egg batter and bread crumbs to deep-fry as fritters, slip them under a blanket of Cheddar for a nice variation of Welsh rarebit, roll them in bacon to grill for a postprandial savory, and, at teatime, serve them hot on toast points with a dash of English mustard and a few capers. And who says the English have no culinary imagination!

That we in the United States do not look upon the sardine with equal fervor is most likely due to the fact that this inexpensive, readily available, canned snack food has never enjoyed anything close to the snob appeal linked with such supposedly luxury items as bottled caviar, packaged smoked salmon, and processed *pâté de foie gras*. (The same could be said for tuna fish, which, as a canned product, has always been held in low esteem by gourmets but which now, so long as it is readily available in fresh form and expensive, is highly popular with chefs and the public alike.) But what never ceases to surprise me is how those of our generation so obsessed with good health and weight control will ignore such nutritious, wholesome, and tasty sustenance as an inexpensive can of sardines. Ounce for ounce, sardines provide more calcium and phosphorus than milk, more protein than steak, more potassium than bananas, and more iron than cooked spinach. Low in fat and high in nutrients, sardines contain less sodium than most processed foods, and medical studies have shown that a certain fish oil in sardines (EPA) can reduce the risk of heart disease even when included in a diet otherwise high in fats. There are no more than about two hundred calories in a drained can of sardines packed in oil, and the calories drop even lower if you choose sardines packed in tomato, mustard, chili, or one of the other sauces that do not contain oil (personally, I can't imagine eating sardines with no oil).

Sardine aficionados are as serious about the object of their gustatory passion as oenophiles are about wine, and surely none in recent memory was more involved than Vyvyan Holland, the son of Oscar Wilde. Mr. Holland founded a society in London devoted to the collecting and tasting of vintage sardines. After sampling brilliant specimens of Rödel, Peneau, and Amieux from the years 1914, '21, '24, and '29, he and his cohorts reached the extraordinary conclusion that since the finest vintage sardines happened to correspond in year to the greatest French wines (especially Sauternes), then this must imply that the best years for wine are the best years for French olive oil.

Unfortunately, nobody during the last couple of decades has had the spirit to pick up where Vyvyan Holland and his society left off, a predicament that leaves many a sardine fancier wondering about what was produced in such memorable wine years as '66, '70, and '75. And what a noble idea that would be: to purchase excellent sardines by the case, turn them every year to redistribute the oil, age them to full maturity, and eventually determine, as with wine, the rare vintages. Of course, it's not a hobby to be undertaken by everyone, for, as Mr. Holland pointed out, "It may be twenty years before a young enthusiast will reap the full benefits of his industry." Still, the results of such enterprise could be rewarding, and the delectable but neglected sardine might finally receive the tribute it deserves.

## Sardine Pâté

1 cup (2 sticks) butter, softened
2 four-ounce cans boneless, skinless sardines,
   drained and chopped
2 tablespoons minced onion
2 tablespoons minced celery
¼ cup minced black olives
2 hard-boiled eggs, chopped fine
3 tablespoons lemon juice
   Freshly ground pepper
   Pinch of ground fennel

Place the butter in a mixing bowl and cream with an electric mixer till light and fluffy. Add the sardines gradually and continue beating with the mixer till well blended. Add the onion, celery, olives, eggs, lemon juice, pepper to taste, and fennel, and blend thoroughly with a wooden spoon. Transfer to a mold, cover with plastic wrap, and chill at least 4 hours.

Serve the pâté on toast strips with cocktails or mounded on small plates with toast strips on the side as an appetizer.

Serves 6 to 8

## POSTSCRIPT

It took exactly three years for Frank Zachary, my editor-in-chief at *Town & Country* and a veritable sardine fanatic, to convince me that this topic was worthy of extensive investigation. Actually, ever since my lean student days in France, I myself had developed something of a passion for these delectable little fish we used to devour with sweet butter in inexpensive bistros and brasseries, but, I mean, a full-length serious essay on canned sardines for our upscale audience! Well, suffice it to say that, like so many other of Frank's ideas that have given me pause initially, the sardine piece was one of the most successful food stories we ever published. And, furthermore, shortly after the article appeared and other food journalists about the country began predicting that sardines would become a trend, sure enough, sales sky-rocketed. Now, if only we could convince someone somewhere to start marketing a steady supply of those wonderful, fat, *fresh* sardines that are grilled, baked, stuffed, and fried in countries all around the Mediterranean.

# E PLURIBUS ONION

*1985*

W hen that most sagacious of Victorian culinarians, Mrs. Beeton, spoke rather cryptically of "the alliaceous tribe," she was referring to none other than the ancient and noble members of the lily family known in kitchens round the world as onion, scallion, leek, shallot, chive, and garlic. I don't suppose it would matter that many cooks today are hardly aware of the close affinity the common bulb onion we take so much for granted has with these other vegetables of the genus *Allium*, but it does bother me how Americans underestimate the versatility of the onion and how so few give a second thought to exploiting the potential of its aromatic relatives. More often than not, the onion itself is considered no more than a flavoring agent in soups, stews, stocks, sauces, salads, and sandwiches. Though I'd be the last to deny that nothing awakens the gustatory senses or inspires the soul like the aroma of onions simmering in a lusty stew or the crunch of a few sweet, odoriferous slices on a juicy hamburger, it would be nice to see the onion highlighted in ways other than the all-too-familiar fried rings and creamed dishes.

As for scallions, about the only time you encounter these peppery "green onions" is when they are mixed into Oriental food, placed on a plate of nouvelle cuisine for garnish, or added raw to salads for zest. And how many cooks can taste the delicate yet distinct difference between genuine shallots and tiny yellow onions? The only people who've learned about the many uses of fresh chives are those who grow them, and the social status of leeks is still so dubious in this country that the likelihood of finding an ample fresh supply in the supermarket (and I'm talking about really fresh, good-looking leeks) is about as remote in most areas as spotting a bunch of impeccably fresh sorrel. Fortunately, garlic as a seasoning has gained wider acceptance in our cookery over the past few decades (there's even an annual garlic festival every June near San Francisco), but only now are adventurous chefs learning about the gustatory advantages of baking, roasting, and braising whole cloves of this surprisingly sweet member of the onion family.

From the sweet white Bermudas to the zesty Spanish giants, the mellow purples of Italy, the tiny silverskins that lend themselves so well to creaming, the exotic beauties from Walla Walla (Washington), Vidalia (Georgia), and Maui (Hawaii), and the ubiquitous Ebenezer and Globe yellows, the tear-producing bulb onion has every right to be treated with more culinary imagination than it has received throughout the twentieth century. If we in America have never really given the bulb fair tribute, it nevertheless has been extolled in many other cuisines over the years as a vegetable worthy of endless experimentation. Some of the more famous results, of course, are the cold, crisp sweet-and-sour onions of China; the curried creamed onions and eggs and the caramelized roasted onions of the British Isles; the pickled purple onions served with *cochinita pibil* (pig roasted in banana leaves) in Mexico's Yucatán; and, in France, the savory onion tarts, *pissaladières,* onions stuffed with various forcemeats and other minced vegetables, and the classic *soubise* sauce spooned over sweetbreads, fish, and poultry. Less known are the mounds of delicately crumbled fried onions the Indonesians and Vietnamese sprinkle on any number of their dishes the way we sprinkle chopped parsley; the onion *tajines* of Morocco enhanced with everything from lemon to honey to black raisins; the fat onions stuffed with kidneys in England and the onion cakes of Wales; the onions braised in red wine with brown sugar, bacon, and vinegar and served cold with pâtés in Burgundy; and the delectable onion *daussades* spread on crusty bread along the French Riviera. In these and many other dishes, the noble globe commands center stage, boasting its ability to stand on its own merit and adding very special character to the international repertoire.

If the bulb onion has been simply underrepresented on American menus these past many years, its mighty cousin, the leek, has remained virtually nonexistent except at the most sophisticated tables. Usually relegated to the soup or stock pot when it's used at all, the leek, with its non-bulbing white stalks, has got to be one of the most subtle, delicious vegetables on earth, lending itself beautifully to being marinated, braised, glazed, puréed, stuffed, creamed, made into soups and tarts, and even pan-fried. Often referred to as "the poor man's asparagus" and technically available throughout the year, the leek, like the onion, has been cultivated as far back as our knowledge goes, leaving forever in question whether its origins are Mediterranean, Irish, Welsh, or Scottish. Today the leek is the national emblem of Wales, and such is the cult in England's Northumberland that each year leeks are shampooed, combed, polished with oil, and proudly displayed in a hot competition. Cock-a-leekie soup, that unique concoction of fowl, leeks, and prunes, is a veritable staple for the Scots, while one of the most beloved dishes throughout northern England is steamed leek pudding flavored with bacon and sage. The Belgians show off the vegetable in a tart called *flamiche,* the Italians in a braised preparation by the name of *porri in umido,* the Basques in an earthy stew made with goose fat, and the Spanish in a red-pepper-enriched vinaigrette. As for the United States, there are signs that the popularity of leeks is rising, owing primarily to their ever-increasing availability at greengrocers, specialty food shops, and carriage-trade supermarkets. So far, the stalks are still relatively expensive (I've paid as much as two dollars for a single leek), but as consumers learn of the vegetable's many merits and distribution widens, prices should one day reflect what could be a very bountiful crop (leeks are incredibly sturdy and can be grown in vast quantities almost anywhere).

Contrary to what many believe, the scallion is not the same onion as the shallot (though the two are often used interchangeably), nor is the scallion technically identical to what is generally called the spring onion (though the two are certainly very close sisters). There's hardly any need to go into the complex genealogical differences between such species of scallions as the White Lisbon, Welsh onion (the popular scallion in Oriental cookery), and French *ciboule,* or such varieties of shallots as the Giant Red, French Epicurean, and Yellow Multiplier. It is important to know that scallions and spring onions are usually raised from seeds of the common bulb onion and grown for their immature, mellow stems, not for their potentially pungent bulbs. Shallots, on the other hand, are highly prized for their mature bulbs, which grow in clusters like garlic and yield an even more delicate flavor than scallions. Deriving its name from the town of Ascalon in ancient Palestine (a prime onion-producing area of the ancient world), the shallot was called the Ascalonian onion by both the Greeks and Romans and played an important role in the development of both cuisines.

Since the Middle Ages, the shallot has been most closely associated with the French wine center of Bordeaux, where the nutty-tasting reddish variety is still cultivated in great profusion and simmered with claret to make a flavoring base for a number of steak sauces. (Elsewhere in France, the shallot is a key ingredient in such classic sauces as *beurre blanc, Bercy, marchand de vin,* and *béarnaise.*) Since most of the planting bulbs are imported from Europe, shallots are still very costly on the American market, a fact that explains why so many chefs choose to use the relatively inexpensive scallion in recipes that call for shallots. Although I have grown my own shallots (a pound of expensive bulbs will yield about six or seven pounds of shallots), I must say that, unless you are preparing a highly refined sauce that demands only the most subtle ingredients, small, slim scallions will probably make a satisfactory substitution.

The most delicate and neglected member of the onion family is the nippy chive, a hardy perennial herb for the garden or flowerpot that I underestimated as much as other Americans did until the day the well-known French chef Pierre Franey uprooted a clump in his East Hampton garden and told me to replant it. Over the next months, I clipped the fine, hollow green spears for use in the kitchen, separated the clump for replanting, allowed some of the plants to maintain their beautiful lavender blossoms, and eventually transplanted enough in pots to see me through the winter. Native to the Orient, chives have been cultivated for almost five thousand years, often for medicinal uses (it's said they aid the digestion of fatty foods), occasionally for fortune-telling rites (they supposedly drive away diseases and evil influences), but mostly for culinary purposes. While the common chive has tubular, bright-green, mellow-tasting leaves that grow up to a foot long, the less-known garlic or Chinese chive found in Oriental markets has flat, grayish leaves that grow up to two feet and have a distinctively stronger flavor.

Traditionally in this country, snipped chives (usually frozen) are found sprinkled only on vichyssoise or a baked potato anointed with sour cream, or mixed with cream cheese on a bagel, but those of us who've taken to cultivating the herb have now learned to utilize it in ways we simply never thought about before. Used in conjunction with chopped parsley, chervil, and other herbs, cut chives add a whole new personality to salads, scrambled eggs, omelets, and pasta dishes. Incorporate them into vegetable purées or mashed potatoes; scatter them over buttered carrots or peas, marinated leeks, and steamed vegetables; add them to stir-fried meat and poultry dishes; and make compound butter to spread over sizzling steaks and chops. A delectable chive soup can be made in no time by combining cooked potatoes, a handful of fresh chives, chicken stock, light cream, and seasonings in a blender or food processor. Reduce a little vinegar and lemon juice in a saucepan, whisk in plenty of sweet butter, stir in lots of snipped chives, and you have an elegant sauce that complements any number of vegetable dishes. Creamy tarts, quiches, and pies highlighting onions, leeks, or scallions never fail to woo guests, but when prepared with the more unusual fresh chives, they assume an originality that coaxes everyone to beg for the recipes.

It is important to remember that, since all onions can undergo marked transformations during storage and when later subjected to any form of heat, the way in which they are kept and the precision with which they are cooked are always of primary concern. Generally, you should store ordinary globe and Spanish onions in a cool, dry area (not in the refrigerator) and use them immediately if they begin to sprout. If shallots are nice and firm when purchased, they keep well for months in dry storage. Leeks and scallions are much more perishable, but if you wrap them in plastic, store them in the bottom of the refrigerator, and trim back the outer green leaves periodically, they can last up to two weeks without spoiling or losing much of their savor. As for the actual cooking of most onions, remember that brief sautéing both tames and enhances flavor, that longer simmering in butter or oil produces a rich, sweet taste as the natural sugar content begins to caramelize, and that lengthy baking or stewing results in an even sweeter, mellower flavor. Particular care must be taken not to expose scallions and chives to direct high heat, and be warned that if shallots end up frying and browning when no more than a light sauté is called for, they become bitter.

Often, when I separate the leaves of a leek or peel back the pristine skin of a baby scallion or savor the aroma of yellow onions and shallots being slowly sautéed in butter, I wonder how the art of cooking could ever have developed over the centuries without these distinctive vegetables. It's said that the Egyptians regarded the concentric rings of the globe onion as symbols of heaven, hell, earth, and the universe, and if you ever study, really examine, the inside of an onion, you'll realize why it is truly one of nature's most amazing masterpieces.

## Vidalia Onions Stuffed with Ham and Mushrooms

  6  *large Vidalia (or Spanish) onions (about 4 pounds)*
  8  *tablespoons (1 stick) butter*
  4  *medium scallions, trimmed of all but 2 inches of green tops and finely chopped*
  1  *garlic clove, minced*
  4  *dashes Tabasco*
  3  *cups fine-chopped fresh mushrooms*
  2  *cups fine-chopped cooked ham*
½  *cup fine-chopped parsley*
    *Pinch of rubbed sage*
    *Pinch of ground cinnamon*
½  *cup heavy cream*
  1  *tablespoon dry Sherry*
    *Salt and freshly ground pepper*
  1  *cup dry red wine*
  1  *cup beef broth*
  4  *tablespoons minced fresh parsley*

Remove the skins from the onions, and, working at the stem ends, scoop out the center of each with a melon-ball scoop or sturdy spoon, leaving a ¼-inch shell. Chop fine enough of the centers to measure 1

*(continued)*

cup. Bring a kettle of salted water to a boil, add the onion shells, and cook over moderately high heat for 5 minutes. Invert the onions on paper towels and drain.

Preheat the oven to 350° F.

In a large skillet, heat one-half the butter, add the chopped onions, scallions, garlic, and Tabasco, and sauté over low heat for 5 minutes, stirring. Add the remaining butter, mushrooms, ham, parsley, sage, and cinnamon. Increase the heat to moderate, and continue sautéing, stirring, about 5 minutes or till the mushrooms are soft. Add the cream, Sherry, and salt and pepper to taste, stir well again, and let cook 5 minutes.

Sprinkle the onion shells with salt and pepper to taste, arrange them open side up in a casserole or baking dish just large enough to hold them, and divide the stuffing among them, mounding it. Combine the wine and broth in a bowl, pour enough around the onions to reach 1 inch up the sides, cover with foil, and bake 1 hour, basting once or twice. Transfer the onions with a slotted spoon to a heated serving platter and sprinkle the tops with the minced parsley.

Serves 6

## Creamed Leeks with Italian Sausages

½   pound Italian sweet sausages
10   leeks (about 3 pounds)
2   tablespoons butter
2   garlic cloves, minced
1½   cups heavy cream
     Salt and freshly ground pepper
     Pinch of nutmeg
¼   cup bread crumbs
3   tablespoons melted butter

Prick the sausages on all sides with a fork and place in a skillet with just enough water to cover. Bring to a boil, reduce the heat to moderate, and poach the sausages about 3 minutes. Pour off the water from the skillet, fry the sausages 15 to 20 minutes, turning, drain on paper towels, and cut them into thin slices.

While the sausages are frying, trim the leeks of all but about 2 inches of green tops, slice the whites down the middle almost to the root end, and rinse the leaves thoroughly under cold running water to remove all grit. Chop the whites crosswise at 2-inch intervals.

Preheat the oven to 400° F.

In a large saucepan, heat the 2 tablespoons of butter, add the garlic, and sauté over low heat 1 minute. Add the chopped leeks, increase the heat to moderate, and cook, stirring, till the leeks are wilted. Add the cream, salt and pepper to taste, and nutmeg. Return the heat to moderate, and cook 10 to 15 minutes or till the leeks are tender. Pour the leeks into a large, shallow baking dish and arrange the sausage rounds on top. Sprinkle on the bread crumbs, drizzle the crumbs with the melted butter, and bake 20 minutes or till the top is golden brown.

Serves 6

# USING THE OLD BEAN

L et's consider the current status of baked beans. I can recall when dozens of restaurants in Boston, the legendary "home of the bean," offered baked beans on their menus at breakfast, lunch, and dinner. But today in that city of culinary revolution, the only places to savor this regional specialty are tourist-mobbed Durgin-Park in Faneuil Hall Marketplace, Locke-Ober Café during Friday's lunch of baked beans and codfish cakes, occasionally Restaurant Jasper, and The Colony—where an innovative baked-bean dish is regularly featured. There was a time when the lusty bean eaters of the Pacific Northwest derided eastern baked beans as effete (one enthusiast from Oregon even persuaded Julia Child to change her recipe), while natives of the Southwest, disdaining the use of molasses and maple syrup to sweeten the beans, boasted about their regional version of fiery baked beans seasoned with garlic, fresh coriander, and chili peppers. Michigan has traditionally produced more beans than any other state, but finding a restaurant or inn there that serves a crock of sensuous pea beans still bubbling from hours in the oven is almost as difficult today as finding a barbecue house in Atlanta that serves genuine Brunswick stew. As one major Boston food writer said recently: "What with all the new sophisticated restaurants in this area, most of the public now considers baked beans just too plebeian."

Of course I find all this ridiculous, for, plebeian or not, nothing stimulates the appetite more on a brisk morning than the intoxicating aroma of beans simmering ever so slowly with a mixture of onions, salt pork, mustard, brown sugar, and molasses. Served with homemade coleslaw, sturdy rye or black bread, perhaps a light fruit tart, and washed down with apple cider or beer, crusty baked beans make for a meal that not only is simple to prepare but also provides the sort of inner warmth that takes us back to childhood.

The multitudinous varieties of this protean vegetable—including haricots, garbanzos, limas, and lentils—known collectively as beans have for thousands of years been one of the major food staples of the world. It's therefore little wonder that beans have been dried and baked in virtually every country since man first learned to dig a hole in the ground, place a container inside, and build a fire around it. Over the centuries, almost every nation has developed its own version of baked beans, utilizing every dried legume imaginable. One of the oldest British dishes, for example, contains the broad (or fava) beans and pork that have sustained life through many a cold winter, and so steeped in history is that magnificent French concoction of white beans baked with pork and preserved goose or duck, cassoulet, that all hope of pinpointing its origins disappeared ages ago. In Italy, Tuscans still love nothing more than *cannellini* (white kidney beans) baked with pork and vegetables in a special earthenware *creta*, while in Spain and Brazil, those earthy baked-bean, sausage, and meat stews called *fabada* and *feijoada* have become national dishes. The Dutch bake brown kidney and lima beans with bacon and serve them traditionally with fried onion rings, while the German dish *Blindhuhn* consists of navy beans baked with apples, carrots, and potatoes. In India, where every color of lentil has been cultivated and dried since ancient times, barbecued red lentils are a special treat; and serious gastronomes traveling through central China go out of their way to savor baked lentils and pork, deftly seasoned with ginger, chili peppers, and exotic spices.

At home, of course, one of the most famous dishes in our culinary repertory is Boston Baked Beans, that classic combination of pea beans, salt pork, dry mustard, brown sugar, and either molasses or maple syrup. I still have doubts that this remarkable dish was a colonial invention, since native Indians were baking beans with molasses in their "bean holes" long before colonists arrived, while the earliest Yankee rum and molasses dealers surely must have been exposed to the pea beans cooked with the exact same ingredients on many Caribbean islands. (Jamaica baked beans, usually spiked with dark rum and numerous spices, are still a great specialty of that island.) In any case, baked beans have been closely identified with New England cookery ever since the days when Puritan housewives, forbidden to prepare food on the Sabbath, simmered their beans on Saturday to be served throughout the weekend. That such a classic regional dish should be pushed aside in favor of greater "culinary sophistication" is as sad as the gradual disappearance of baked beans and limas from the Pacific Northwest, baked spareribs and pintos from the Southwest, and spicy baked garbanzos from Texas.

So what are new possibilities with baked beans? Over the years, I've prepared such dishes as baked black-eyed peas with ham hocks, red beans with oxtails, a southern white bean pie redolent of spices and rum, and gratins of everything from flageolets with cubed lamb to limas with mushrooms and walnuts to white beans with *chorizo* sausage. Why not, in addition, try baking lentils enhanced with chutney, red beans with snails, sweet and sour limas or chickpeas chock-full of leftover pork, or even a "New England cassoulet" with Boston baked beans, duck, and sausages? Besides the traditional seasonings for baked beans—onions, salt pork, molasses, maple syrup, brown sugar, and mustard—an exciting new dimension can be gained by the use of honey, chili peppers, exotic vinegars, ground nuts, spirits, cheeses, and fresh herbs.

The only potential problems with baking dried beans are the initial soaking to restore lost moisture and the length of cooking time. To assure proper texture and avoid the slight risk of toxicity, all dried beans (with the possible exceptions of lentils and split peas) should be either soaked in water for a long period or blanched and soaked about an hour before baking (commonly referred to as the quick method). Ideal soaking time depends on the age of the bean, but since there's no way to determine when a package of beans was processed, more often than not you have to go by instinct. The safest procedures are to soak the beans at least six hours in cold water (removing loose skins) or simmer them ten minutes and let them stand one hour or till plump and softened.

The correct cooking time for baked beans depends on the type of bean and how you like them. I've baked pinto beans for as long as ten hours without having them lose their "bite," but once, when I cooked limas and navy beans about five hours, I ended up with a pot of mush. No matter which baked-bean dish you decide to prepare, the rule to follow is taste, taste, taste, not only to check periodically for texture but also to assure that the beans remain fully moist and seasoned throughout the simmering process.

It is also important to invest in a top-quality earthenware or stoneware bean pot or crock. You can turn out respectable beans in a cast-iron pot or heavy casserole, but for a vessel that distributes heat evenly on all sides, maintains the constant temperature so important for slow simmering, and is virtually scorch-proof, nothing beats a vitrified stoneware pot or, even better, a partially vitrified earthenware pot that has been glazed only on the inside with the outer surface left bare for greater heat absorption. *Do* beware of the cheap clay pots found at flea markets and tourist traps around the world. Some of the finest cooking pottery I own was purchased in villages near the town of Vallauris in southern France (where Picasso obtained clay for ceramics); the pots you find in most such places, however, are usually pretty to look at but, because of poor porosity and glazing, a disaster in the kitchen. For the best bean pots and crocks on the market in this country, look for pottery by Karen Karnes and the late Bernard Leach.

## Jasper White's Boston Baked Beans

1  pound dried navy or Great Northern beans, picked over and washed
8  ounces salt pork, half cut into ½-inch dice, half cut into thin strips
1  medium onion, cut into medium dice
4  garlic cloves, chopped fine
2  medium tomatoes, peeled, seeded, and cut into medium dice
1  teaspoon salt
2  teaspoons freshly ground pepper
¼  cup Coleman's mustard
⅓  cup maple syrup (or maple sugar)
⅓  cup molasses
2  bay leaves
2  tablespoons cider vinegar

Place the beans in a pot, add water to cover, and let them soak overnight. Drain the beans.

Sprinkle the diced salt pork and onion over the bottom of an earthenware bean pot or crock and add the beans. In a saucepan, bring 1 quart of water to a boil, add the garlic, tomatoes, salt, pepper, mustard, maple syrup, molasses, bay leaves, and vinegar. Reduce the heat, simmer 1 minute, and pour the mixture over the beans.

Preheat the oven to 250° F.

Arrange the strips of salt pork over the beans, cover the pot, and bake 4 hours, adding more boiling water halfway through the cooking if necessary to keep the beans covered. Uncover and bake 1 hour longer.

Serves 6 to 8

## Brendan Walsh's Southwestern Baked Beans

1½ pounds dried Great Northern white beans
1 smoked ham hock
2 medium onions, minced
5 garlic cloves, minced
2 large ripe tomatoes, chopped
½ pound slab bacon, cut into ½-inch pieces
1 jalapeño chili pepper, seeded and minced
½ cup brown sugar
2 bay leaves
2 whole cloves
Pinch ground cinnamon
3 tablespoons top-quality chili powder
1½ teaspoons cumin
¼ cup top-quality barbecue sauce
2 tablespoons balsamic vinegar
3 tablespoons Worcestershire sauce
2 tablespoons Tequila
Salt and freshly ground pepper to taste
Chicken stock or broth
1 bunch fresh coriander (cilantro), chopped fine

Place the beans in a large saucepan with enough water to cover and bring them to a boil. Reduce the heat, blanch the beans 10 minutes, and drain. Meanwhile, place the ham hock in another large saucepan, add enough water to cover, bring to a boil, and blanch 10 minutes.

Preheat the oven to 325° F.

Transfer the beans to a large bean pot or large, heavy casserole, add all the remaining ingredients except the stock and coriander, and stir till well blended. Fit the ham hock down in the beans, add enough stock to cover the ingredients completely, cover the pot, and bake 3 hours, stirring the beans every 30 to 40 minutes and adding more stock if necessary.

With a slotted spoon, transfer the ham hock to a cutting board. Remove the meat from the bone and chop it fine. Stir the chopped meat back into the beans, and continue baking till the beans have absorbed most of the liquid and are very tender.

When ready to serve, stir the coriander into the beans. Serve the beans in bowls as a side dish or spoon them around roasted or grilled meats on large serving plates.

Serves 8

## Craig Claiborne's Baked Black Beans in Rum

1  pound dried black beans
1  large onion, chopped
2  garlic cloves, minced
2  ribs celery, diced
1  carrot, scraped and minced
   Small herb bouquet (bay leaf, thyme, and parsley tied in
   cheesecloth)
   Salt and freshly ground pepper
3  tablespoons butter
6  tablespoons dark rum
   Sour cream

Place the beans in a large pot with enough water to cover by 1
inch, and bring to a boil. Cook 2 minutes, remove from the heat, and
let soak 1 hour. Drain the water from the pot and add 6 cups of fresh
water. Add the onion, garlic, celery, carrot, herb bouquet, and salt
and pepper to taste, stir, and bring to a boil. Reduce the heat, cover,
and simmer 1½ hours or till the beans are almost tender. Remove and
discard the herb bouquet.

Preheat the oven to 350° F.

Transfer the beans and liquid to a bean pot or casserole, add the
butter and 3 tablespoons of the rum, cover, and bake 2 hours. Add
the remaining rum, stir well, and serve in deep soup bowls with sour
cream on the side.

Serves 6

# THE LORDLY SPUD

_1983_

O f the many wonderful foods that have been either denigrated or neglected amid all the fervor and innovation of the gastronomic revolution in America, surely none has suffered the ignominy of the humble white
potato. Rice (especially wild rice) has assumed new culinary importance in
the fanciest restaurants; pasta served in every manner imaginable is the
carbohydrate rage with professional chefs and home cooks alike; whole
trout, exotic fruits, fiddlehead ferns, and who knows what else are wrapped
with crèpes of all sizes; and the amount of puff pastry being used to produce
turnovers, patty shells, tarts, and cakes or to envelop any ingredient from
creamed frogs' legs to truffles to goat cheese is enough to add three inches
to the national waistline in less than a year's time. But the common potato?
Never. Yes, simple baked and fried potatoes are forever staples at steak
houses throughout the nation, but even to suggest that serious efforts have
been made to elevate the tuber's role in our more creative style of cooking
is ludicrous.

Considering the fact that the spud's primary function throughout history
was as a foodstuff for the poor and fodder for livestock, its current social
status comes as no great surprise. Cultivated originally by Indians in the
high Andes of Peru and first transported by conquistadors from the New
World back to Spain in the early sixteenth century, the white potato traveled for two hundred years from Galicia to Italy, from Switzerland and the

Low Countries to France, and finally to the British Isles before being reintroduced to America (in New Hampshire) by Irish immigrants. Until well into the nineteenth century, the European upper classes were not particularly receptive to potatoes. Even some of the common folk refused to partake of the bountiful crop, unable (or unwilling) to make a distinction between leprosy and a minor skin rash often brought on by a large amount of the mildly toxic substance known as solanine contained in certain potato strains.

The French found harmony with the spud only after an eccentric eighteenth-century agronomist named Parmentier planted potato fields in the Bois de Boulogne in Paris and convinced Louis XVI of the vegetable's many merits (eventually Louis became so enthusiastic that he sported potato flowers on his robes for the court to admire). In England, it was not until 1832 that the authorities decided to recognize the wholesomeness of the potato and amend the Bread Acts so that potato flour could appear in that food without forfeiture of its legal right to be called bread. In 1740, potatoes literally staved off famine in Ireland, but in Scotland they were considered ungodly by the clergy since they were not mentioned in the Bible. Although the potato had become a field crop by 1762 in the northeastern part of the United States and was later planted by Thomas Jefferson in Virginia, a *Farmer's Manual* from the mid-nineteenth century still recommended that "potatoes be grown near the hog pens as a convenience towards feeding the hogs." Even in the early twentieth century, one cookbook writer continued to advise housewives to throw out potato water for fear it was poisonous.

An average potato, consumed without all the butter or sour cream or cheese sauce, contains less than one hundred calories and boasts many valuable nutrients plus lots of fiber. Anyone who's ever tasted either boiled new potatoes right from the ground or a hefty fresh Idaho baked *without foil* and sprinkled with no more than salt, pepper, and a little chopped parsley or fresh herbs can't help but be aware of the spud's potential as a noble vegetable worthy of limitless experimentation. Over the past century, at least a few enlightened culinary minds have produced potato dishes that will most likely remain in the repertory for ages to come, but these serve only as a starting point. Most noteworthy would be Switzerland's crisp *roesti* (a fried shredded potato pancake); Germany's potato bread, pancakes, hot potato salads, and dumplings; Britain's Colcannon (fluffy mashed potatoes and kale fried in bacon fat till crisp) and earthy hot pots (stews built on a variety of meats and potatoes); and, to be sure, France's luscious gratins, *duchesse* (silky-smooth puréed potatoes used to decorate all types of classic dishes), oniony *lyonnaise, sarladaise* (a truffled potato cake), and puffy *pommes soufflées*. The United States can certainly take credit for such tasty staples as hashed browns, cottage fries, O'Briens, home fries, Saratoga chips, and twice-baked stuffed potatoes, but, except for that elegant soupy marriage of potato and leek called vichyssoise (which was actually created by French chef Louis Diat at the old Ritz-Carlton Hotel in New York), it can hardly be said that America has contributed a great deal to the refinement of potato cookery.

Let's investigate ways that the spud can be utilized to produce new, imaginative creations and any number of interesting luncheon or light main-course dinner dishes. What, for instance, could be more different and delectable at noon than a savory potato and feta cheese soufflé served with a simple meat salad and a nice white wine, followed by a fruit tart? A classic potato gratin that would normally have no more importance than as a side vegetable takes on new interest when enriched with sweet turnips and salty country ham, while a seemingly ordinary baked-potato skin assumes a certain elegance when used to encompass a delicate poached egg graced with rich lobster sauce or tangy creamed oysters spiked with fresh horseradish. If marinated shrimp and a touch of curry contribute dramatic flair to potato salad, no less intriguing would be the addition of such components as bean sprouts and red peppers, blue cheese and bacon, artichoke hearts and cucumbers, sausage, flounder and green peppers, or curried mussels. The potato lends itself to dozens of hot and cold main-course possibilities, inspiring the seasoned chef to experiment on numerous taste and textural levels with our rediscovered bounty of native ingredients and allowing the host or hostess to serve stylish, economical dishes that require minimal preparation and provide plenty of nutrition.

The United States produces, without question, the finest potatoes in the world (some 160 different varieties, in fact), but what happens to those potatoes is often enough to discourage the most ardent champion. Just forty years ago, all the potatoes Americans ate (about 150 pounds per person annually) were fresh, most coming directly from the fields. Today, however, a good one-third of the crop is processed into chips, sticks, wafers, and every type of pre-cut, frozen, freeze-dried, dehydrated produce imaginable. Not only is a good deal of flavor and nutrition lost in any processing, but quite often growers abandon our very best potato varieties in favor of those that sell best to processors seeking the highest yields and profits. " 'French fries' say the menus," complains columnist Russell Baker, "but they are not French fries any longer. They are a fuzzy-textured substance with the taste of plastic wool."

It is indeed sad that one of nature's best-designed products, capable of sustaining a shelf life of many months, must fall victim to both the abuses of modern technology and human laziness. But those who are really serious about potato cookery still have plenty of opportunities to benefit from the best we have to offer. True potato connoisseurs can distinguish between Irish Cobblers, Kennebecs, Red Pontiacs, and Colorado Longs the way professional oenophiles can pinpoint the subtleties in different zinfandels. But the everyday consumer need only be aware of the five basic categories (russets, round whites, round reds, long whites, and new potatoes) and the reasons for selecting one over the other for various cooking purposes. Without doubt the finest baking potato on earth is Idaho's Russet Burbank, a thick-skinned, mealy, starchy, fluffy-textured spud that owes its name to its developer, Luther Burbank, and its celebrity to the volcanic soil and ideal climate in which it grows. Other large russets, such as the Long Island, have lots to offer those who love great baked potatoes, crisp French fries, and twice-baked skins. But when it comes to ideal flavor, nothing equals a fresh, authentic Idaho produced in the state of Idaho.

Lower in starch and higher in moisture than the russets, round whites such as Maine Superiors and Nebraska Triumphs are excellent for roasting alongside meat, for sautéing, and for mashing. Firm, thin-skinned round reds, such as Pontiacs and Norlands, should be boiled for salads, sliced for gratins, fried, and used generally for dishes that require low-starch potatoes that hold their shape. Waxy long whites, developed in California and often curiously mistaken for genuine Idahoes in all supermarkets, are perhaps the most versatile of all—though I personally find these all-purpose potatoes a little too watery and lacking in flavor. New potatoes are exactly what the name implies (small, fresh, tender potatoes harvested at the start of the summer season), and to serve these flavorful unskinned beauties any way but simply boiled, salted and peppered, and perhaps buttered, is downright criminal.

While starch and moisture content are a major consideration when choosing potatoes for certain preparations (the only thing more unappetizing than potato salad made with mealy potatoes is a low-starch, soggy baked potato), nothing is more important than making sure your spuds are fresh and storing them in the proper manner. When buying potatoes, make sure the body is firm, the skin smooth, and that there is no sprouting, discoloration, or spotting. The depth of the eyes of a potato has absolutely no effect on its quality, though deep eyes do make cleaning and peeling more difficult. Stored in a dark place at an ideal temperature of between 45 and 50 degrees, potatoes will maintain their flavor and texture for months. If kept at too high a temperature, they will soften, shrink, and sprout; at too low a temperature (in the refrigerator, for example), the starch will convert to sugar, making the potatoes undesirably sweet.

Writing about the potato, James Beard once commented that "what is so remarkable is that it is France, England, and Germany that have given the world the greatest recipes. The country of its origin (South America) has contributed not a single potato dish of any renown, nor have we developed many good potato dishes in the United States—although what we have can be exciting if done well." Today, during a period when every food in America is being reinterpreted in terms of its potential in our new gastronomy, no vegetable deserves more immediate attention than this one that is so readily available and that lends itself to so many levels of experimentation. For centuries the potato has quietly but efficiently served society in a

capacity that can only be defined as noble. Now this same spud demands to
be honored in a lordly fashion.

## Potato and Feta Cheese Soufflé

4  *medium boiling potatoes*
4  *eggs, separated*
½  *cup milk*
¼  *cup half-and-half*
5  *tablespoons butter*
1  *small onion, minced*
1  *rib celery, minced*
1  *cup finely crumbled feta cheese*
   *Salt and freshly ground pepper*

Place the potatoes in a large saucepan with enough lightly salted
water to cover. Bring to a boil, reduce the heat to moderate, cover,
and boil about 30 minutes or till the potatoes are very tender. When
they are cool enough to handle, peel the potatoes, transfer to a large
mixing bowl, and mash with a ricer or fork. Add the egg yolks, milk,
and half-and-half and beat to a smooth purée with an electric mixer.

Preheat the oven to 400° F.

In a small skillet, heat 3 tablespoons of the butter, add the onion
and celery, sauté them over low heat about 2 minutes or till soft, and
add to the potato mixture. Add the cheese and salt and pepper to
taste, and stir till well blended.

Grease the bottom and sides of a medium (7- or 8-inch) soufflé dish
with the remaining butter. In another large bowl, beat the egg whites
with a pinch of salt till stiff, fold one-third of the whites into the
potato mixture, then fold the mixture into the remaining whites. Pour
the mixture into the prepared dish, place the dish on a baking sheet,
and bake 40 to 50 minutes or till puffed and golden brown.

Serves 4 as a main luncheon course

## Oyster-Stuffed Potatoes with Horseradish

4 large Idaho potatoes
6 tablespoons (¾ stick) butter
1 small onion, minced
½ pint shucked oysters
¼ cup dry Sherry
  Salt
  Pinch of allspice
⅓ cup heavy cream
⅓ cup freshly grated horseradish

Preheat the oven to 425° F.

Wash, scrub, and dry the potatoes, prick each several times with a fork, and bake 1 hour or till soft.

In a saucepan, heat one-half the butter, add the onion, and sauté over low heat about 2 minutes or till the onion is soft. Add the oysters (reserving the liquor), cook about 1 minute or till the oysters curl, add the Sherry, bring to a boil, transfer the oysters to a bowl, and reserve the cooking liquid.

Slice the tops off the potatoes lengthwise, scoop out the pulp, and place half in a mixing bowl, reserving the remaining pulp for another use. Add the remaining butter, salt to taste, and allspice to the pulp in the bowl, mash with a fork till smooth, and spoon equal parts of the mixture onto the bottom and up the sides of the potato jackets. In a saucepan, bring the oyster liquor to a boil, reduce to about 3 tablespoons, add the cream, and cook 1 minute. Remove the saucepan from the heat, add the oysters and half the horseradish, and stir. Spoon the oysters and sauce into the prepared potatoes, reheat the stuffed potatoes, and when ready to serve, sprinkle the top of each with the remaining horseradish.

Serves 4 as a main course

## Twice-Baked Potato Skins with Cheese and Bacon

4 very large Idaho potatoes
⅓ cup melted butter
  Freshly ground pepper
6 strips cooked bacon, crumbled
¾ cup grated Swiss or Parmesan cheese

Preheat the oven to 425° F.

Wash, scrub, and dry the potatoes, prick each several times with a fork, and bake 1 hour or till soft. Cut the potatoes in thirds lengthwise, scoop out all but about ¼ inch of pulp from each piece, and reserve the pulp for another use.

Place the shells skin side down in a large baking dish, brush liberally with melted butter, and season with plenty of fresh pepper. Sprinkle the bacon and cheese on top of each piece, place the potato skins in the oven, and continue baking about 15 minutes or till the tops are golden brown and the skins are crisp.

Serves 4 as a light lunch with salad, or 6 as a side vegetable

# BOILED BEEF: VARIATIONS ON A NOBLE THEME

1986

I f, in my stubborn quest to savor real, unadulterated food in today's
kiwied world, there is one dish I go out of my way to eat, it would have
to be boiled beef, in any style, shape, or form. When prepared and served
properly, boiled beef is one of the most succulent dishes ever conceived by
man. Just the thought of confronting a steaming platter of pot-au-feu
chock-full of tender meat, marrow bones, leeks, and carrots is enough to
get me on the next plane to Paris. In London, I search out the handful of
old-fashioned English restaurants that still offer up on the silver trolley a
giant boiled silverside of beef served with flavor-packed dumplings, fresh
horseradish, and coarse salt. A trip to San Francisco wouldn't be complete
without a stop at either the venerable Tadich Grill for the best corned beef
and cabbage this side of Dublin or the elegant Fournou's Ovens in the
Stanford Court hotel for a slab or two of rare poached fillet with julienne
vegetables. Even when I'm taking a periodic cure at the luxurious Brenner's Park Hotel in Baden-Baden, Germany, I somehow always manage to
sneak out to a small Stube or country inn for a little lusty *Rindfleisch* with
a few browned potatoes and herby Frankfurt sauce on the side. A month
never passes (no matter the season) that I don't serve in my home the same
boiled short ribs of beef on which I was weaned in the South, and my best
Yankee friends know I never feel so privileged as when they go all out to
prepare an authentic New England boiled dinner complete with moist,

thick slices of corned beef, small white onions, new potatoes, earthy cabbage, and the youngest beets, accompanied by plenty of mustard and pickles.

Boiling has always been one of the simplest and most successful methods of making meats and numerous other foods palatable. During the Middle Ages, there wasn't a household, court, or monastery that didn't utilize at least one great cauldron in the preparation of meats, vegetables, and puddings. It is said that even Charlemagne himself, when told by his doctors that boiled meats were much better for his health than roasted meats, developed a passion for beef that was slowly simmered with vegetables and herbs in an aromatic stock (i.e., the ancestor of French pot-au-feu—or "pot on the fire"). Over the centuries, virtually every nation in the world has come to boast one style or another of boiled beef (Danish *sprengt oksebryst*, Czechoslovakian *houezi maso*, Romanian *cacuta*, Italian *bollito misto*, Russian *otvarnaia govyadina*, Spanish and Mexican *cocido*, German *Rindfleisch*, Argentine *puchero*, Chinese aromatic boiled beef, Irish corned beef and cabbage), but surely no one has loved and respected the dish more than the English, the Austrians, and the French.

In Elizabethan times, even the finest tables in England were not properly appointed without an imposing boiled silverside (similar in cut to our rump and round roasts), a salted brisket boiled with spices in ale, a platter of chilled spiced beef (rolled, pressed boiled brisket), or an elaborate boiled roast stuffed with oysters, streaky bacon, and parsley. In his delightful book *Blue Trout and Truffles,* the late Joseph Wechsberg devoted an entire chapter to the celebrated boiled beef of Vienna, relating how, during the city's golden age, the greatest beef was produced from steers fed only on molasses and sugar beets and how truly serious gastronomes patronized a certain restaurant solely for the privilege of being able to choose from no fewer than twenty-four varieties of boiled beef. "In Vienna," he states, "a person who couldn't talk learnedly about at least a dozen different cuts of boiled beef didn't belong, no matter how much money he'd made or whether the Kaiser had awarded him the title of *Hofrat* or *Kommerzialrat.*" As for the French, the great Escoffier himself summed up his nation's feelings about pot-au-feu: "In France, the pot-au-feu is the symbol of family life . . . a comfortable and thoroughly bourgeois dish which nothing can dethrone."

Because of today's trendy eating habits, scouting out restaurants even in Paris, London, and Vienna—much less New York—that still prepare some genuine version of boiled beef is no easy task. But such blessed places do indeed exist. In Paris, there's *boeuf gros sel* (boiled beef with coarse salt) every Thursday at Chez Pauline, *boeuf aux carottes* (boiled beef with carrots) every Friday at Allard, and Chef Leonetti's sumptuous pot-au-feu at a remote bistro called Gérard. Classic Italian *bollito misto* (which is virtually nonexistent in Italian restaurants in the United States) might include other boiled meats besides beef. But since at such fine restaurants as Cesarina in Rome, Tre Galline in Turin, and the incredibly popular Fini in Modena each meat is presented and served separately from a special silver trolley, purists can relish a sensible and delicious meal by ordering no more than the boiled beef, a few vegetables, and, of course, that zesty confection of conserved fruits known as *mostarda*.

A bit more spectacular is the *costato di bue* at Savini in Milan, a delectable boiled standing rib roast with *salsa verde* that I've devoured on more than one occasion but never managed to get the recipe for until Craig Claiborne brought off that coup a few years back. In Vienna, no sensuous experience can quite match taking in a few hours of fine opera, then repairing to the Hapsburg splendor of the Sacher Hotel's dining room to savor the wonderful *Tafelspitz* served with horseradish-spiked applesauce. And in London connoisseurs of boiled beef can appease their craving either at Rule's in Covent Garden or in the stately confines of the Grill Room at the Dorchester (where a classic poached fillet of beef is served with numerous vegetables and a vinegary mustard sauce).

How well I remember the tender, meaty boiled short ribs of beef nestled in a bed of fresh noodles at the old Lüchow's on 14th Street in New York, a plebeian dish that required as accompaniment only a tart green salad, a few slices of dark pumpernickel bread, steins of heady German beer, and dulcet strains of Strauss from the small string orchestra. Lüchow's as we know it is gone, but we boiled-beef fanciers can take solace in the knowledge that at Gallagher's Steak House on West 52nd Street the short ribs (still available only at lunch on Tuesdays) are as copious and meaty as ever; that the boiled tenderloin with pungent dill sauce and bread dumplings at the Czechoslovakian Ruc on East 72nd Street is always on the menu; and that even the distinguished Four Seasons offers a sensational *Tafelspitz* as a special of the day periodically throughout the fall and winter months. Some of the best boiled beef anywhere is the Old World flanken and *cholent* served in the great New York Jewish delicatessens. Prepared from a special cut of short ribs, flanken (for some odd reason pronounced "flunken" by deli habitués) is a meal in itself, consisting of a chunk of boiled beef plunked down in a large bowl of vegetable soup. There's not a hint of sophistication about the dish, but consumed, as it traditionally is, with fresh rye bread and Dr. Brown's Celray Soda, there's really nothing like it to restore the soul and add warmth on a cold winter's day. *Cholent*, which is boiled brisket simmered for hours with barley, white beans, and eggs, is an equally delicious and popular Jewish dish with a rich history, and perhaps its most fascinating culinary feature is the way in which, even after eight hours of simmering, the yolks of the whole eggs nestled among the vegetables somehow come out soft and creamy.

Of course the most logical place to enjoy boiled beef is at home, not only because it's so easy to prepare but because the leftover meat can be used to concoct any number of tasty salads, hashes, sandwiches, and cold plates. Generally the best (and most economical) cuts of meat for boiling are brisket (both regular and corned), short ribs, shin (foreshank), and chuck and blade pot roasts, all readily available in supermarkets (genuine flanken, a cut that yields the meatiest short ribs, usually has to be ordered specially from butchers). These meats require long, slow simmering (or poaching) if the texture and flavor are to be ideal, and any effort to serve them rare can only result in disaster. Conversely, rump or round roasts, standing rib roasts, and whole fillets can be boiled with spectacular success as long as they are not overcooked (medium-rare is preferred for these cuts), and, as one boiled-beef expert, James Nassikas of the Stanford Court in San Francisco, has repeatedly emphasized: "Few people are aware that the best-tasting beef is poached, not roasted." Furthermore, unless you intend for some of the meat's flavor to leach out to other ingredients in the pot, don't start the beef in cold water or stock (as in pot-au-feu or the New England boiled dinner). Rather, lower it directly into boiling liquid so that its savor is quickly sealed (as in *Tafelspitz* or *boeuf à la ficelle*—beef fillet on a string). Standard accompaniments to any boiled beef are zesty mustards, coarse salt, horseradish, caper and herbed green sauces, and tart pickles, but so simple and flexible is this dish that anything from fresh vegetables to sauerkraut and pickled red cabbage to even a garlicky *aïoli* sauce can only enhance the overall gustatory experience.

The most memorable boiled beef I have ever enjoyed was the *boeuf à la ficelle* I used to order on the much-lamented S.S. *France*. The beef was the pride of Chef Henri Le Huédé and beautifully demonstrated how, in the right hands, even the humblest dish can be transformed into both a culinary and visual masterpiece. Out from the galley it came, this unadorned, slightly undercooked whole tenderloin still in its bouillon, suspended by string from a large wooden spoon placed across the edges of a tall, cylindrical, shiny copper marmite. Working tableside, our captain immediately transferred the meat to a cutting board while a waiter set about quickly reheating small bundles of sculpted carrots, turnips, leeks, and celery in the hot broth. The aromas were intoxicating. After the fillet was sliced and the juicy pink slabs were arranged across the center of large heated dinner plates, the waiter untied the steaming vegetables and distributed them artistically around the rosy, mouth-watering beef. The captain supplied the table with ramekins of coarse salt, hot mustard, and French *cornichons;* added a few grinds of fresh pepper to the meat; asked whether we'd like a little hot broth or horseradish sauce spooned on top; and watched as we took those first luscious bites and nodded approval. This was boiled beef in all its unpretentious and natural glory, the same type of beef I continue to seek out today, the same beef that inspired the late James Beard to offer this trenchant comment on the dish's appeal: "It's simple, certainly, but it is precisely the simplicity of preparation and the honest, appetizing flavors that make this one of the outstanding gastronomic treats of all time."

## Viennese Tafelspitz *with Horseradish Sauce*

One 3- to 4-pound boneless bottom round roast
1 large onion, peeled
3 carrots, sliced
3 celery ribs, sliced
3 parsnips, peeled and sliced
3 small leeks, rinsed well under running water, sliced in half lengthwise, and trimmed of all but 2 inches of green leaves
   Herb bouquet (½ teaspoon each dried marjoram and ground nutmeg, 2 bay leaves, 4 cloves, and 3 sprigs parsley tied in cheesecloth)
   Salt and freshly ground pepper
2 pounds sauerkraut, cooked according to package directions
¼ cup chopped parsley

Sauce:

2 tablespoons butter
2 tablespoons flour
½ cup cooking broth
½ cup milk
½ cup heavy cream
   Salt and freshly ground pepper
⅓ cup freshly grated horseradish

Tie the roast securely with kitchen string, place it in a large kettle, add enough boiling water to cover by 2 inches, and skim off any scum that rises to the surface. Add the vegetables and herb bouquet, salt and pepper to taste, heat the water to a low boil, cover, and simmer the meat 3 hours or till tender.

To prepare the sauce, heat the butter in a saucepan, add the flour, and stir briskly with a whisk. When they are well blended, add the cooking broth from the kettle and, stirring rapidly, also the milk. When the mixture is thickened and smooth, add the cream, stirring constantly. Add salt and pepper to taste and stir well. Add the horseradish, stir till well blended, and keep the sauce hot.

To serve, cut the meat into ½-inch-thick slices, arrange the slices down the center of a large heated platter, and surround the meat with

(continued)

hot sauerkraut. Sprinkle parsley over the top and serve with the sauce plus bowls of coarse salt and assorted mustards on the side.

Serves 6 to 8

## Chilled English Spiced Beef

One 4-pound thin-cut brisket of beef
3 tablespoons fine-chopped parsley
½ teaspoon dried sage
½ teaspoon dried thyme
½ teaspoon ground cloves
½ teaspoon ground allspice
½ teaspoon ground nutmeg
Salt and cayenne pepper

Rinse the brisket well under cold running water. Combine the herbs and spices in a small bowl, add salt and cayenne pepper to taste, mix well, and rub the mixture over all surfaces of the meat. Roll up the meat lengthwise as tightly as possible, bind firmly with kitchen string, then wrap in cheesecloth and tie securely. Wrap again in plastic wrap and place in the refrigerator for 6 hours.

Remove the plastic wrap, place the rolled beef in a kettle just large enough to hold the bundle, and cover with cold water. Bring the water to a boil, reduce the heat, cover, and simmer the beef for 5 hours, adding more water if necessary to keep the beef covered.

Transfer the beef to a deep bowl, pour a little cooking broth on top, fit a plate atop the meat, then place 8 to 10 pounds of weights on the plate (large canned goods, bricks, etc.) to press the meat down. Place the bowl in the refrigerator and chill for 12 hours.

To serve, remove the cheesecloth and string, cut the cold beef against the grain in thin slices, and serve with potato salad, blanched chilled vegetables, an assortment of mustards, and pickles.

Serves 6 to 8

## Short Ribs of Beef in Ale

 8  *meaty short ribs of beef*
 2  *twelve-ounce bottles of imported ale*
    *Salt and freshly ground pepper*
16  *small whole white onions, peeled and scored on root ends*
14  *small red new potatoes*
 1  *large can whole tomatoes*
    *Beef stock or broth (optional)*

Place the short ribs in a large saucepan or casserole, pour on the ale plus enough cold water to cover the meat by 1 inch, and add salt and pepper to taste. Bring the liquid to a boil, reduce the heat, cover, and simmer for 3 hours, adding more ale or water if necessary to keep the meat covered. During the last 20 minutes of simmering, add the onions. Rinse the potatoes and cut away a strip of skin around the middle of each, then add them to the liquid during the last 15 minutes of simmering.

Preheat the oven to 375° F.

Transfer the meat to a shallow baking dish and, with a slotted spoon, place the onions and potatoes around the meat. Add the tomatoes and their juices. If the baking dish is not three-quarters full, add water or beef stock, salt and pepper the dish to taste, and bake about 30 minutes or till the top is slightly crusted.

Serves 6 to 8

# RUMINATIONS ON RISOTTO

*1987*

I f I had to single out the one dish that best exemplifies the brilliance of northern Italian cuisine and the ebullient spirit of Italian gastronomy, that dish would have to be risotto. Often considered the pasta of Lombardy, Piedmont, and the regions around Venice, this unique method of preparing rice has no equivalent in any other country; nor, in my opinion, is there a pilaf, jambalaya, paella, or Oriental rice specialty that even approaches the subtlety of a great risotto.

Risotto is made by simmering special Italian short-grain rice with specific quantities of stock or wine and incorporating other flavorful ingredients at the last minute—a basically simple but tricky procedure that requires patience and constant attention. Little by little, hot cooking liquid is ladled into the pot, allowing the rice to slowly absorb each addition. To attain ideal texture—at once creamy and al dente—you must not only maintain a steady simmer while adding liquid but also stir the rice constantly for up to twenty-five minutes. If the heat is too high and the liquid evaporates too quickly, the rice will not cook evenly; if the simmer is not vigorous enough, the rice will become gummy. The Italians speak of perfect risotto as being *all'onda*, or "rippling," meaning that each puffy grain of rice should remain separate and whole while still clinging to the others. Furthermore, risotto must be served immediately, preferably right from the pot. It takes practice to produce a genuine example, but once you've mastered the technique and experimented with adding all sorts of cheese, seafood, meats, vegetables, mushrooms, wines, and herbs, you have a dish that makes a luxurious first course, a stylish lunch, or—served with no more than a tart salad, crusty loaf of bread, and fine bottle of wine—a gratifying main course at dinner.

When traveling in Italy, I'll make any detour to sample a recommended risotto, and, indeed, there have been memorable occasions. For my taste, the finest *risotto alla milanese*, that classic combination of rice, saffron, Parmesan cheese, and often bone marrow, is the one I've had so often at Savini in Milan, a restaurant that also excels in its rendition of *risotto al salto* (leftover *milanese* that is quickly sautéed as a pancake). I visited Verona a few years back for the sole purpose of sampling a *risotto con le seppie* (with cuttlefish and its ink) at 12 Apostoli and an elegant salmon risotto at the Hotel Due Torri. Once, three of us showed up at Del Cambio in Turin to share a colorful *risotto spinaci spumanti Cinzano,* a rich, sensuous *risotto alla finanziera* (with sweetbreads and chicken livers), as well as a brutally expensive risotto christened with the pungent shavings of one whole fresh white truffle. At Il Cigno in Mantua, it was an intriguing pumpkin risotto; at Dante in Bologna, the rice was enhanced by earthy wild *porcini* mushrooms; and in Venice, I always make it a special point to savor the exquisite mixed seafood risotto at the Gritti Palace (preferably on the terrace overlooking the Grand Canal), as well as the creamy vegetable risottos featured at Harry's Bar and the Cipriani Hotel.

Contrary to popular belief, rice was not introduced to Italy by Marco Polo on his return from Asia but by the Saracens during the Middle Ages. Today, no country in Europe produces more rice than Italy, and despite the Italians' love of pasta, they are one of the largest European consumers of the grain. Cultivated almost exclusively in the northern Po and Ticino valleys, the types of rice traditionally used to make risotto are Arborio, Vialone Nano, and Canaroli: shorter, rounder grains than American short-grain rice and the only ones with enough starch to yield the creamy texture characteristic of fine risotto. Some people say they've had success substituting our unconverted long-grain rice; I never have. Arborio (and, unfortunately, only Arborio) is now available at specialty food shops throughout the nation in *sacchetti* (small canvas or muslin bags) and boxes, so if you're determined to make extraordinary risotto, make every effort to obtain the special rice.

This method of preparing rice is practiced not only in the north of Italy but throughout virtually all the provinces, each highlighting various foods and wines indigenous to the particular area. In Emilia-Romagna (and especially in Bologna), for instance, you find numerous risottos featuring the region's famous hams, sausages, wild game, and, of course, Parmesan cheese. The Ligurians and Neapolitans utilize their abundant supplies of fresh seafood, olives, and herbs; chefs in and around Padua incorporate their superior varieties of local fowl; and in Umbria one of the most popular risottos is flavored with a local wine called *solleone*. Everything from octopus to calves' liver to radicchio to tiny wild artichokes goes into the risottos served in the Veneto, while throughout Piedmont and Lombardy, traditional ingredients include frogs' legs, crayfish, salmon, lavender asparagus, wild mushrooms, white truffles, Barolo wine, and all sorts of well-aged cheeses. It's not hyperbole to suggest that one of the best ways to study certain gastronomic differences among the Italian provinces is to sample the many regional risottos.

Since risotto lends itself to boundless variations, it is curious that there are so few Italian restaurants in the United States that feature appetizing versions of the dish, and that even the majority of our most innovative, creative young American chefs continue to neglect risotto in favor of still another tired pasta salad, stuffed ravioli, or trendy pizza. No doubt the necessary timing in cooking risotto can cause problems in restaurants with impatient customers (restaurants in Lombardy often keep four or five pots of rice simmering at ten-minute intervals), but even this obstacle does not prevent serious professionals from turning out some real beauties.

Although I've watched highly experienced native chefs make acceptable risottos by adding most of the liquid at one time and simply simmering the rice for about twenty minutes, I've met with nothing but gluey disaster whenever I've tried to cheat by doing what the Italians call "drowning the rice." Don't attempt it. Since many variables can affect the way the rice cooks (the size and thickness of the pot, the amount of exposed surface, whether gas or electric heat is used, the consistency of the stock or wine, the temperature of the added ingredients), for best results I strongly recommend that you abide by the classic technique outlined earlier—patiently adding liquid by the half cupful; maintaining a steady, slightly vigorous simmer; stirring constantly with a wooden spoon; and watching, watching, watching to make sure the rice never sticks to the bottom or dries out completely. And the more I prepare the dish, the more I prefer a risotto that remains quite moist, almost soupy, to one that is dry.

Since rice is a complex carbohydrate rich in B vitamins and fiber, low in fat and calories, and containing no cholesterol, risotto is as soundly nutritious as it is delicious. So, seek out a few bags of Arborio, take out your heaviest pot and sturdy wooden spoon, use lots of imagination with ingredients, and present family and guests a delectable dish that is sophisticated to serve and healthy to consume.

## Risotto with Sausage and Zucchini

½  pound Italian sausage (hot or sweet), casings removed
6  tablespoons (¾ stick) butter
1½ pounds zucchini, scrubbed and chopped coarse
8  cups beef consommé (fresh or canned)
3  tablespoons olive oil
2  small onions, chopped fine
2  cups Arborio rice
1  cup fine-chopped parsley
1  cup freshly grated Parmesan cheese
   Salt and freshly ground pepper
3  tablespoons butter, cut into pieces

Crumble the sausage in a small skillet, fry over low heat, stirring, till well cooked, and drain on paper towels. In another skillet, heat 3 tablespoons of the butter, add the zucchini, sauté over moderate heat 2 minutes, stirring, and transfer to a plate. In a saucepan, heat the consommé and keep it at a bare simmer.

In a large, heavy saucepan, heat 3 more tablespoons butter and the oil. Add the onions, and sauté over low heat 2 minutes, stirring. Add the rice, increase the heat to moderate, and cook, stirring, 2 minutes or till the rice is translucent. With a ladle, add about ½ cup of the hot consommé, reduce the heat to a vigorous simmer, and cook, stirring with a wooden spoon, till most of the liquid is absorbed. Maintaining the heat at a steady simmer, continue to add consommé, ½ cup at a time, stirring constantly after each addition till the liquid is almost absorbed (about 20 minutes). Add the sausage, zucchini, parsley, and final ½ cup of consommé and cook about 3 minutes longer, stirring, or just till the rice is al dente but still very moist. Remove the pan from the heat, add the cheese, salt and pepper to taste, and the 3 tablespoons of butter cut into pieces. Stir till well blended, and serve immediately.

Serves 6

## Risotto with Shrimp and Peas

    1  pound fresh medium shrimp
    1  celery stalk, cracked into 3 pieces
    ½  lemon, seeded
    5  black peppercorns
   10  cups water
    6  tablespoons (¾ stick) butter
    3  tablespoons olive oil
    1  medium onion, chopped fine
    2  cups Arborio rice
    1  cup dry white wine
    2  cups cooked peas (fresh or frozen)
    ½  teaspoon powdered fennel
    ½  cup freshly grated Parmesan cheese
       Salt and freshly ground pepper

Place the shrimp, celery, lemon, and peppercorns into a large saucepan and add the water. Bring to a boil, remove from the heat, let sit 1 minute, and with a slotted spoon transfer the shrimp to a colander. When cool enough to handle, shell and devein the shrimp and cut each in half. Return the shells to the saucepan, bring to a boil, reduce the heat, cover, and let simmer 1 hour. Strain the broth through a double thickness of cheesecloth into a clean saucepan and keep hot.

In a large, heavy saucepan, heat one-half the butter and the oil, add the onion, and sauté over low heat for 2 minutes, stirring. Add the rice, increase the heat to moderate, and cook, stirring, 2 minutes, or till the rice is translucent. Add the wine and cook, stirring with a wooden spoon, till the wine is absorbed. With a ladle, add about ½ cup of the shrimp broth and cook, stirring, till most of the liquid is absorbed. Maintaining the heat at a steady simmer, continue to add broth, ½ cup at a time, stirring constantly after each addition till about 7 cups are almost absorbed (about 20 minutes). Add the shrimp, peas, and fennel. Stir well, and continue cooking, stirring, about 3 minutes or till the rice is al dente but still very moist. Remove the pan from the heat, cut the remaining butter into pieces, and add to the rice. Add the cheese, salt and pepper to taste, stir till well blended, and serve immediately.

Serves 6

# THE ROMANCE
# OF CHESTNUTS

*1982*

R oasted over an open fire, braised with fresh vegetables, added to stuff-ings for poultry and game, ground into flour, and puréed for any number of garnishes and elegant desserts, the versatile chestnut has played a very special role in world gastronomy throughout modern history. Who could imagine, for example, Christmas in France without those rich, lux-urious *marrons glacés*, or the banquet table in England without a sumptuous chestnut pudding, or, as a matter of fact, the American Thanksgiving or Yuletide season without a golden bird bursting with chestnut stuffing? So universal is the association of this unique palate-pleasing nugget with the year-end festivities that there's hardly a country where it doesn't enhance the various gustatory rituals.

In Italy, "drunken chestnuts" (roasted nuts soaked in wine) are an integral part of cold-weather feasts, and it is not unusual for Japanese connoisseurs to send to distant cities for the exact type of chestnut they prefer on their New Year's menus. The Greeks would hardly invite friends over to celebrate the season without serving plenty of boiled chestnuts kept warm under a heavy cloth cover. And even New Yorkers seem to find temporary respite from their misanthropy when the chill in the air is perfumed by the aroma emanating from Fifth Avenue's chestnut carts. Of all the attractions France offers in the fall, no aspect of the country evokes more nostalgia in me than the majestic chestnut trees that fill the forests, garland the fields, and line the city streets and highways. Heaven knows how many times over the years I've driven mile after mile down rustic roads at lunchtime searching for the perfect *marronnier* as an appropriate picnic setting for zesty loaves of bread, sweet butter, earthy *pâté de campagne*, Gruyère, fruit tarts, and Beaujolais. I pity those who have never been lulled to sleep by the gentle sound of rain on big chestnut leaves outside a simple French country inn, and how could I not relate foraging for truffles in Périgord to the prickly chestnut burs that must first be swept aside before still another mysterious diamond of gastronomy can be lifted from the earth? Once, under the mammoth *marronnier* at the two-star Chapon Fin outside of Thoissey, chef Paul Blanc demonstrated the best way to swat chestnuts out of the courtyard tree—the same nuts, in fact, used later that evening in a luscious casserole of sweetbreads and wild mushrooms. And come late October or early November, I, like the French, never pass a candy shop—especially the two-century-old Tanrade one block east of the Madeleine—without glancing to see if the inevitable sign has been posted: "*Vos Marrons Glacés Sont Arrivés.*"

The main reason I attach more sentimental value to the chestnuts of Europe than to those found in the United States is that the trees are now virtually nonexistent in this country. Growing up to one hundred feet tall and over forty inches in girth, these magnificent giants once covered America, providing inspiration for nineteenth-century writers like Thoreau and Longfellow, as well as lumber for houses, masts for clipper ships, railway ties for a nation pushing westward, poles for telegraph and telephone lines, fences for livestock, tannin for leather, and certainly a popular sport for chestnuting enthusiasts. Eager to experiment with the prized European species (or Spanish chestnut), American horticulturists began importing saplings in the late eighteenth century, and by 1805 the French émigré Éleuthère Irénée Du Pont had acres of healthy trees on his estate in Delaware. For over a century, the chestnuts multiplied all along the East Coast, in the Midwest, and throughout the Pacific states. Then, in 1904, it was discovered that saplings imported from the Far East and planted on Long Island had brought with them a fungus (*Endothia parasitica*) deadly to chestnuts in America. The blight spread in all directions. Even the most advanced scientific efforts failed to check its destruction, and by the 1940s the entire natural range of the American chestnut—some nine million acres—had been completely devastated.

Although today devoted specialists in northwestern Michigan continue experimentation with eight groves of chestnuts (including twelve seventy-year-old patriarchs) that have somehow survived the infection, the likelihood of ever seeing vast chestnut forests in the United States is still remote. Fortunately, however, close to 20 million pounds of succulent European chestnuts are imported each year, enough to satisfy the American demand. Some come from France and Corsica, others from Spain and Portugal, but the vast majority are harvested in southern Italy and processed in Avellino, near Naples. All are of the *Castanea sativa* species, the largest and richest chestnut on earth, and all can be purchased fresh, canned in water or vanilla syrup, dried, frozen, soaked in spirits, ground into flour, and—most luxurious—candied. When the crop has been good, fresh chestnuts cost about a dollar a pound; in a bad year, the price runs as high as three dollars a pound. *Marrons glacés*, those candied beauties that serve as the harbinger of the Christmas–New Year's season in France and whose complex preparation involves sixteen separate laborious operations, can easily cost $15 the dozen.

Since Biblical times, the bountiful chestnut has provided both basic nourishment for the poor and some of the most lavish dishes for the wealthy. Legend has it that the nut's generic name *Castanea* derived from the Thessalonian town of Castan, from where, at some point, saplings were taken and transported to western Europe. Highly prized by the patricians of Rome for certain exotic preparations, and a veritable staple for the populace in the form of flour, the chestnut was most likely spread throughout Europe by Roman legions. The nut became popular in France by the thirteenth century, and during the Renaissance the native chestnuts produced around Lyon were being served at the royal table not only in France but in England. Whether or not *marrons glacés* were actually first made by a confectioner trying to win the favor of Louis XIV is debatable, but it does seem probable that these glazed sweetmeats were quite the rage at Versailles and, as tokens of love and friendship, played a delicate role in many a courtly liaison.

Technically and linguistically, there are two types of edible European chestnuts: the *châtaigne* and the *marron*, both of which are of the same *Castanea* species and almost universally referred to by their French names. The *châtaignier*, a tree that grows wild, yields two or three nuts per bur that have a rather bland flavor and are generally boiled, ground into flour, or fed to livestock. The *marronnier*, on the other hand, is simply a cultivated *Castanea* that yields burs each with a single large and sweet nut. Unbeknownst to most of the world, the ornamental chestnut trees lining the streets and *allées* of Paris have never produced edible kernels, being of the *Aesculus hippocastanum* species and referred to in English as horse chestnuts. (The French compound the confusion, however, by officially labeling these white flowering trees *châtaigniers* and then casually referring to them as *marronniers*.) Today the center of the French *marron* industry is in the department of Ardèche in northern Languedoc, where a century ago the citizens of Privas conceived the plan of industrializing the production of chestnuts in order to counteract unemployment brought on by a slump in the area's silk industry. Of course, chestnuts are a major crop throughout Brittany, Périgord, Limousin, and Corsica, but when gastronomes the world over are curious to witness the production of *marrons glacés*, they still visit one of the four large plants in Privas. Although most Italian chestnuts are grown in the South, some connoisseurs insist that the most glorious specimens are those that are collected in the Piedmont.

Exactly what role chestnuts assumed in American cookery during the nineteenth century is not easy to determine, but today it's clear that all but the most adventurous chefs do little more than mix them with Brussels sprouts or cabbage, add them to stuffings, and perhaps whip a little purée into a cream dessert. By contrast, Europeans use natural and sweetened chestnuts in pâtés, spreads, soups, soufflés, stews, compotes, jams, fritters, croquettes, and myriad holiday cakes, logs, pies, and other festive desserts. Since the chestnut is unique as both a savory and a sweet, there's no reason why Americans shouldn't exploit the nut's many possibilities as they continue to move full force in the development of a new national style of cooking.

While fresh imported chestnuts are generally available in our larger cities from late October through January, remember that there's absolutely nothing wrong (except perhaps the higher price and absence of romance) with the various packaged products marketed year round throughout the country. Frozen chestnuts, stocked widely in supermarkets under the Napoli label, are of identical quality to fresh, cost about the same, and can be stored almost indefinitely without risk of rotting or drying up. Fresh chestnuts, on the other hand, are highly perishable, lasting less than two weeks.

Preparing the fresh variety for use presents problems calling for skill and patience, for the nut has a very hard outer husk and a rough, bitter inner skin that must be removed. People all over the world have different ways of shelling chestnuts, but I've found the following technique produces ideal results: With a very sharp paring knife (or special chestnut knife with a hooked blade), cut a deep X on the flat side of each nut. Toss the nuts into boiling water, boil 10 to 15 minutes, and, with a slotted spoon, transfer them to a plate. When they are just cool enough to handle but still hot and wet, remove both the shell and brown inner skin, dipping stubborn nuts back into the hot water before trying to clean them thoroughly. One and one-half pounds of fresh chestnuts in the shell yield approximately one pound of peeled nuts. Prepared chestnuts in cans and jars (packaged whole or in pieces, dry-roasted or in water or syrup) require no more effort than opening the container. Unless the nuts are intended for use in a sweet dessert, make sure to purchase them unsweetened.

"It was very exciting at that season," wrote Thoreau in *Walden*, "to roam the then boundless chestnut wood of Lincoln . . . with a bag on my shoulder and a stick to open burs with in my hand, for I did not always wait for the frost, amid the rustling of leaves and the loud reproofs of the red squirrels and jays, whose half-consumed nuts I sometimes stole, for the burs which they had selected were sure to contain sound ones." Although Americans may never again be able to experience Thoreau's autumnal thrill of wandering through native chestnut forests, at least they can still gather all the beautiful nuts they desire in just the time it takes to make an outing to the market. And, among those with spirit and imagination, all the romance of chestnuts is there for the plucking, a romance of American heritage that filters into kitchens along with some delectable aromas and serves to inspire plenty of old-fashioned cheer.

## Chestnut Soup with Ginger

   1  *pound chestnuts, shelled and peeled*
   1  *small onion, chopped fine*
   1  *teaspoon sugar*
   2  *teaspoons grated lemon rind*
  ½  *teaspoon salt*
 2½  *cups chicken stock or broth*
  ½  *cup milk*
  ½  *cup heavy cream*
      *Pinch ground ginger*
   1  *egg yolk, beaten*
  ¼  *cup Sherry*

Place the chestnuts in a large saucepan with enough water to cover, add the onion, sugar, lemon rind, and salt, bring the liquid to a boil, reduce the heat, cover, and simmer about 35 minutes or till the chestnuts are soft. Transfer the mixture to a blender or food processor and blend to a purée. Transfer the purée back to the saucepan, add the chicken stock, milk, heavy cream, and ginger. Bring to a boil, and stir. Gradually stir a little of the soup into the beaten egg yolk, add the mixture to the saucepan, add the Sherry, and reheat, making sure not to let the soup boil.

Serves 4 to 6

## Chestnut Fritters

1  cup flour
¼  teaspoon salt
1  cup beer
2  teaspoons vegetable oil
2  eggs, separated
1  cup canned chestnut purée
2  tablespoons heavy cream
1  teaspoon sugar
¼  teaspoon vanilla
    Vegetable oil for frying
    Confectioners' sugar

Sift the flour into a bowl and, stirring constantly, add the salt, beer, and oil in a slow stream. Strain the batter into another bowl, cover with plastic wrap, and let stand 3 hours.

Stir the batter, beat the egg whites till stiff, and fold the egg whites into the batter. In another bowl, combine the chestnut purée with one beaten egg yolk, the heavy cream, sugar, and vanilla. Mix well, and shape into small ovals. In a deep fryer or heavy saucepan heat about 2 cups of oil to 375° F. Dip the ovals into the batter, fry in batches till golden brown, and drain on a paper bag. Sift confectioners' sugar over the fritters and serve with fruit preserves for breakfast or as a dessert.

Serves 4

# ELEGANT BURNT CREAM

1986

I am absolutely passionate about crème brûlée, and the way I happened to savor one of the world's most glorious versions at the Savoy Grill in London was not exactly a coincidence. For a number of years, a rather eccentric English gastronome and I had made a point of dining together whenever I was in the city, an arrangement that gradually led to the sampling of numerous examples of England's legendary queen of desserts (also known as burnt cream, Trinity or Cambridge cream, or grilled cream) in some of London's finest restaurants. I had first raved over the silky, cool custard, topped with its crunchy, caramelized crust, at Ma Cuisine in Walton Street. "Ah yes, very good pudding indeed," my esteemed colleague agreed, "but have you had the crème brûlée at Savoy Grill, with its absolutely smooth, slightly spotty caramel?" I was in ecstasy at Langan's Brasserie as the spoon broke through the golden crust in the ramekin to reveal an almost liquid baked cream with just the slightest aroma of vanilla. "Yes, excellent texture," my fellow taster declared, "but, mind you, at Savoy Grill they would never dream of preparing crème brûlée in these rather absurd little individual cups. Takes away all the drama from the pudding, wouldn't you say?" At still another testing at Walton's restaurant, I wondered aloud whether the addition of a little lemon zest to the custard had enhanced that celebrated restaurant's interpretation of "burnt cream." "Sacrilege, my dear boy, unadulterated sacrilege," was the hushed but outraged response from across the table. "At Savoy Grill, they would most surely discharge the chef if he tampered with this classic in such fashion."

After being bombarded with such strong proclamations about what had to be the city's quintessential crème brûlée, I eventually allowed the fanatical Brit to set up a dinner at Savoy Grill, making it perfectly clear to the veteran headwaiter that our party of four was there primarily to sample the restaurant's crème brûlée. Of course, everything about this famous dining room was as impeccable as I had remembered: the hushed dignity, the polished woodwork and deep, royal-blue banquettes, the heavy silver and starched napery, the highly professional black-tailed staff. For starters, we had delectable smoked Scotch salmon, unctuous potted beef, an elegant pâté of sweetbreads and lobster, and rich *oeufs en cocotte Petit Duc*. Next, there was a sumptuous roast saddle of lamb carved on the silver trolley, moist grilled Dover sole on the bone, crisp Norfolk duck roasted with apples and almonds, and a ragout of fork-tender veal kidneys, all washed down with vintage white Burgundy and a full-bodied second-growth claret.

Then came the long-awaited moment. Our captain wheeled in a table bearing a copper gratin dish about eighteen inches long—certainly twice as large as the regular crème brûlée on the dessert trolley. Proudly he lifted the pudding and tilted it toward us for our perusal. The hard, caramel crust, smooth as a piece of glass and completely covering the soft custard beneath, sparkled, its golden hue highlighted by a few slightly darker, "burnt" tones. Then, with one powerful, dramatic stroke, the captain shattered the thick crust with the back of a large, heavy silver spoon, exposing a luscious, creamy custard the color of light egg yolk. On each plate went two spoonfuls of custard, topped with a chunk of crust. Slowly we tasted, my English sophisticate almost in a trance. Never had I savored a custard so velvety, so subtle, so rich in flavor; never had I bitten into a burnt-sugar crust that provided such harmonious counterpoint; and never had I known any dessert that married so beautifully with the sweet Barsac the sommelier poured. On every count, this was indeed the crème brûlée by which all others had to be measured.

Since that memorable evening, my fascination with this almost ceremonial dessert has only intensified, while my never-ending research into its mysterious origins and history has become increasingly futile. Some food historians like to say that crème brûlée can be traced back centuries to a Catalan dish called *crema cremada* ("cremated cream"); others insist it was introduced to the British Isles from France by Mary, Queen of Scots; and none other than Julia Child has classified it as a Creole dessert. Since there is not one shred of solid evidence to support these and many other theories, I am fully satisfied that, contrary to popular belief and despite the name, crème brûlée is not and never has been a French dish (it's not even mentioned in *Larousse Gastronomique*, Escoffier, Pellaprat, Alexandre Dumas, Brillat-Savarin, and other authoritative French sources). Burnt cream is

English to the core, period. And, since at least the seventeenth century, its *locus classicus* has been one or more of the colleges at Cambridge, where it is still prepared and served with the utmost love and respect. It is "a phoenix dish of our cookery that rises again and again into popularity," writes the eminent English culinarian Jane Grigson. "It appears first in 17th-century, then in 18th-century cookery books, and then disappears to bob up at the beginning of this century at Trinity College, Cambridge." (Today, burnt cream is served with great ceremony at most of the twelve annual feasts prepared for Trinity's distinguished fellows.) Who knows when and why "burnt cream" was Gallicized as "crème brûlée," and who really cares? "Just another linguistic affectation," I was told by head pastry chef Roy Barlow in the Trinity kitchen. "I've been cooking for students and fellows at Cambridge for over thirty years, and we've always referred to the dish by its proper English name—burnt cream."

Whether we speak of crème brûlée, burnt cream, or Trinity pudding, what matters is that this incomparable dessert, which graces the table regularly at such august addresses as 10 Downing Street, Buckingham Palace, and the Houses of Parliament, has been prepared for centuries in the finest kitchens of England in basically the same way. Recipes differ as to the number of egg yolks and amounts of sugar and cream, as well as to how much sugar is needed to caramelize the top, but essentially crème brûlée is made by whisking hot cream into sugared egg yolks, cooking the mixture on top of the stove or baking it slowly in a traditional shallow, round 9-inch dish (a special burnt-cream dish was once designed by Copeland-Spode Company for the kitchens at Cambridge), chilling the custard till it is firm, sprinkling the top with a thick layer of castor sugar (similar to, but not the same as, our superfine sugar), and caramelizing the sugar to a hard, even, golden-brown crust. Whereas years ago caramelization was done with a special metal hand tool known as a salamander, today most chefs merely run the sugared pudding quickly under a broiler or, in truly experienced, expert hands like those of the chefs at Trinity College and the Savoy, sometimes just boil the castor sugar down to an amber syrup and pour it directly over the chilled custard.

Americans are now raving about all the trendy crème brûlées served at who knows how many upscale restaurants in this country, and I suppose some of these custards are just fine (though, purist that I am, I have absolutely no respect for any crème brûlée flavored with ginger or maple or coffee or filled with berries). The problem is that I've not yet encountered one that can match the crème brûlée offered at the Savoy Grill and other respected dining rooms throughout England. And the reasons are simple. Consider farm-fresh English eggs, their orange yolks. Taste a spoonful of England's dense, satiny, incredibly rich double cream with no less than 48 percent butterfat. Touch to the tongue a fingertip of Tahitian vanilla extract that the English import and notice the intense flavor. Feel the smooth, almost floury texture of genuine castor sugar, which caramelizes so evenly. Like many other great dishes, genuine crème brûlée demands ingredients that are hard to duplicate away from home ground—which is as good a reason as any to book the next Concorde to London.

While the only way you're likely to produce a true English crème brûlée in the United States is by seeking out English double and single creams in deluxe food shops, finding farm-fresh eggs from barnyard chickens, and laying hands on imported castor sugar, this doesn't mean that a respectable pudding cannot be made from domestic ingredients. After working with the chefs at the Savoy Grill and Trinity College and acquiring the recipes featured here, I must have made at least two dozen crèmes brûlées, utilizing every type of domestic cream, sugar, and egg and almost every cooking utensil and vessel. Some of my puddings were utter disasters; others were truly magnificent. What I did learn is that no matter which ingredients you use or what cooking technique you decide to follow (the recipes illustrate two distinctly different but classic methods), a great crème brûlée must be made in a dish wide enough to give the pudding real drama (I prefer a large, shallow gratin dish); the custard, flavored with a hint of good vanilla, must be velvety soft, almost liquid in texture; and the caramel crust must be at least one-quarter inch thick and smooth as glass. As long as you follow directions carefully and pay close attention to what you're doing, either of the recipes should produce a glorious dish that not only bears witness to a proud English cooking tradition but also adds flair to any dinner table.

## Trinity College Burnt Cream

3 *cups heavy cream*
8 *egg yolks*
6 *tablespoons superfine sugar*
1 *teaspoon vanilla extract*
1½ *teaspoons cornstarch*
1½ *cups superfine sugar*

In a large saucepan, bring the cream to just below the boil. Meanwhile, combine the egg yolks and 6 tablespoons of sugar in a large mixing bowl and beat rapidly with a wire whisk till foamy. Beating constantly, add the hot cream to the egg mixture; whisk till well blended. Pour the mixture into the saucepan, and cook over very low heat a few minutes or till the mixture has thickened, stirring constantly and never allowing the mixture to boil. Add the vanilla and cornstarch and mix till well blended. Strain the mixture through a fine sieve into a 9-inch round glass baking dish, filling the dish to within 1 inch from the top. Let it cool, cover with plastic wrap, and chill the custard at least 3 hours or till very firm.

Preheat the oven broiler.

Sprinkle the 1½ cups of sugar evenly over the top of the custard and carefully spread it out with a fork to cover the custard evenly and completely. Place the dish as close under the broiler as possible and let the top caramelize to a golden brown, watching the pudding carefully and, if necessary, turning the dish so that the caramelization is even. Remove the dish from the broiler and let it stand 10 minutes or till the caramel has cooled and hardened.

To serve, crack the crust with a heavy silver spoon and serve the custard and crust on each plate.

Serves 6 to 8

## Savoy Grill Crème Brûlée

2  *cups heavy cream*
1  *cup half-and-half*
½  *cup superfine sugar*
5  *egg yolks*
2  *teaspoons vanilla extract*
1½  *cups granulated sugar*
½  *cup water*

Preheat the oven to 300° F.

In a saucepan, combine the heavy cream and half-and-half, bring just to a boil, and remove from the heat. Meanwhile, in a large mixing bowl, combine the superfine sugar and egg yolks and beat rapidly with a wire whisk till foamy. Add the vanilla and whisk till well blended. Whisking the egg mixture rapidly (never stopping for a second), pour on the hot cream mixture and continue whisking briskly till the mixture is well blended and smooth. Strain the mixture through a fine sieve into either a 9-inch round glass baking dish or a medium gratin dish, filling the dish to within 1 inch of the top. Place the dish in a baking pan, pour hot water into the pan till it is three-quarters full, and bake 25 to 30 minutes or till a straw or small knife inserted in the middle comes out just barely sticky. Remove the dish from the water bath; let the custard cool. Cover the dish with plastic wrap, and refrigerate at least 3 hours or till the custard is well chilled and the top has formed a skin.

About 1 hour before serving, combine the granulated sugar and water in a saucepan and stir. Boil 7 to 10 minutes or till the syrup just begins to darken slightly but is not burnt, brushing the sides of the pan with water if crystals begin to form. Pour a thick, even layer about ¼ inch thick over the chilled custard, tilting the dish carefully so that any bubbles disappear and all traces of custard are covered with caramel. Let the dish stand 10 minutes or till the caramel has cooled and hardened.

To serve, crack the crust with a heavy spoon and serve the custard and crust on each plate.

**Serves 6 to 8**

# STRAWBERRY SHORTCAKE

*1988*

W hat really confirmed my long-time conviction that we've got serious gastronomic troubles in this country is the incredible, daunting, threatening discovery I made recently that there is no formal recipe in *Joy of Cooking* for strawberry shortcake—not to mention in a multitude of other well-known American cookbooks. I mean, it was like going to the *Larousse Gastronomique* and not finding directions for preparing *mousse au chocolat*, or to Mrs. Beeton and not learning all about plum pudding. Needless to say, I never so much as hoped that a wonderful, old-fashioned classic like strawberry shortcake might be included in today's trendier cookbooks laboriously devoted to the virtues of flourless chocolate tortes, berried crèmes brûlées, and quaint tea sorbets. But to realize that the dish is not even listed in the index of America's culinary bible, the tome on which most of us were weaned, the very chronicle of our eating habits, is enough to convince me that the American sweet tooth is increasingly doomed to be gratified by no more than ultra-light mango mousse and low-cal pumpkin flan.

Over the years, I've championed the noble cause of baked beans, Brunswick stew, succotash, well-aged country ham, hash, johnny cakes, corn pudding, and dozens of other great all-American dishes so scorned and neglected by the snazzy practitioners of the "new" style of cooking. Now I must speak out for strawberry shortcake, that dense, rich, luscious concoction that was once served in all civilized homes during the summer months and that should be right up there with fried chicken, potato salad, and apple pie as a veritable icon in the repertory of authentic American cookery. Who over the age of thirty can help but remember the ecstatic thrill of eating this sensuous dessert fresh from the kitchen? Out it came, two thick discs of buttered biscuit pastry or sponge cake separated and slathered with warm crushed and sugared ripe strawberries that dripped in rivulets down the sides. If you wanted to be fancy, you spread a layer of whipped cream over the top and garnished the cake with a few perfect whole berries, but serious shortcake lovers demanded no further enhancements than pitchers of more crushed berries and thick cream to pour on at will. Over the years, enthusiasts have attempted in every possible way to describe the sensation of savoring great strawberry shortcake, but nobody records the experience with keener passion than the New England gastronome John Thorne: "A bite of real strawberry shortcake is a mouthful of contrast. The rich, sweet cream, the tart juicy berries, and the sour, crumbly texture of hot biscuit all refuse to amalgam into a single flavor tone, but produce mouth-stimulating contrasts of flavor—hot and cold, soft and hard, sweet and tart, smooth and crumbly. The mouth is alert and enchanted at once."

It's true that today strawberry shortcake should well be considered the quintessential American dessert, but, as much as I'd love to relate how the confection was created by some early nineteenth-century Georgia housewife or industrious New York chef, I have every reason to believe that the cake's origins are as British as gingerbread, the sandwich, pancakes, and corned-beef hash. The idea of making pastry "short" (i.e., crisp) by the use of lard or another fat, for instance, can be traced in England as far back as the fifteenth century, and in 1599, none other than Mr. Shakespeare himself mentions "shortcake" in his *Merry Wives of Windsor*. Short pastries such as shortcake, shortbread, biscuits, and scones have been popular staples throughout the British Isles for centuries, and while there's no evidence to prove that an Englishman or Scot was the first to scatter crushed strawberries (probably the wild variety) over a split cake or scone and moisten the combination with fresh cream, it is fairly obvious that a direct historical link can be established between this confection and the ancient British tradition of smearing strawberry preserves and thick double or clotted cream over warm scones and other forms of short pastry. Even today when visiting Devon or Cornwall, the only treat I enjoy more than a fluffy split scone covered with strawberry preserves and clotted cream at teatime is a juicy wedge of strawberry shortcake from the trolley at dinner.

Wherever and whenever strawberry shortcake might have evolved in Britain, it's clear that its reputation as something of a national treasure in America had taken root by the mid-nineteenth century, when "shortcake" referred to a rich short pastry used to enclose fruit, and was well-established by 1883 when Mary Lincoln directed how to prepare griddle strawberry shortcakes in her *Boston Cook Book*. The dessert figured prominently in Fannie Farmer's *Boston Cooking School Cookbook* of 1896; it was featured regularly in such pioneering regional volumes of the South as the 1908 *Woman's Club Cook Book* of Charlotte, North Carolina; and even in that naïve children's classic of early Americana, *Rebecca of Sunnybrook Farm*, author Kate Douglas Wiggin posed a question that must have stirred the minds and appetites of hungry young readers all over the country: "Who would not rather make a delicious strawberry shortcake than play 'The Maiden's Prayer' on the piano?"

Now for the very sensitive and touchy question as to whether genuine strawberry shortcake should be made with biscuit or scone dough or sponge cake. Most Southerners and Midwesterners simply could not conceive of eating real shortcake not made with some form of short pastry; Yankees, who've never really understood what biscuits are all about, generally maintain that shortcake is synonymous with sponge cake; and I'm resolutely convinced that today's inhabitants of the West Coast (where, ironically, the world's greatest strawberries are produced) couldn't care one way or the other. Since I must say that, over the years, I've savored some very decent strawberry shortcake prepared with sponge pastry (most memorably at the old Lindy's in New York), I'd almost be willing to attribute high status to this version were it not for one important culinary fact: the word "shortcake" indicates automatically that shortening (or some form of fat) is a major ingredient in the pastry, and since sponge cake contains no trace of fat, it cannot qualify as an authentic foundation for the dessert. (On the other hand, I choose not to try to explain why most modern-day strawberry shortcake found in England is made with . . . yes . . . sponge cake!)

Given all the historical and linguistic confusion connected with strawberry shortcake, I say let's just forget the dialectics, entertain all sensible options, and concentrate primarily on restoring the popularity of a delectable dish that should symbolize the very soul of American cuisine. Although I personally believe that the ultimate strawberry shortcake is made with a rich scone pastry and nothing less than double or clotted cream (increasingly available as British imports in our finest specialty food shops), I can certainly endorse other versions so long as they are prepared properly with high-quality fresh ingredients (and this does not include the use of commercial biscuit dough or sponge cake, frozen strawberries, and those disgusting artificial cream substitutes).

Nothing makes for a more spectacular presentation than a whole two-layer shortcake lovingly decorated with fat berries and dramatic swirls of whipped cream and cut into wedges. Yet, there's something so homey, so comforting about serving small individual shortcakes intended to be saturated with berries and rich cream according to guests' appetite and inspiration. Traditionalists insist that no strawberry shortcake is worth its calories unless the pastry, berries, and even the cream are warm. Nonsense. I do agree that, for textural contrasts, it's quite extraordinary to bite into crisp hot short pastry covered with warmed strawberries and lukewarm cream, but I must also admit that some of the best shortcake I've ever put in my mouth was served with each component at room temperature—and sometimes slightly chilled. Fortunately, strawberry shortcake is one of those compelling desserts that essentially makes no greater demands on the human palate than on the cook who prepares the dish.

The recipes here illustrate not only four different variations of shortcake but also the subtle ways this basically simple confection has evolved in our culinary history. Although my absolute favorite is the sinful beauty made with scone dough, I wouldn't hesitate one second to prepare and serve any one of the other versions, confident that guests would wolf down every morsel of pastry, every berry, and every drop of cream in sight. So the next balmy morning, why not set out early for the market, select the ripest strawberries and freshest cream you can find, get out that trusty mixing bowl, and produce the sort of sumptuous strawberry shortcake that would make our ancestors proud and that adds such a joyful touch of old-fashioned flavor to the summer table?

## *Strawberry Scone Cake*

3  cups unbleached flour
1  tablespoon baking powder
¾  cup superfine sugar
¼  teaspoon salt
6  tablespoons (¾ stick) butter, cut into small pieces
2  eggs, lightly beaten
1  teaspoon vanilla
1  cup heavy cream
4  pints ripe fresh strawberries
3  tablespoons melted butter
2  cups clotted, double, or heavy cream

Preheat the oven to 375° F.

Sift together the flour, baking powder, ¼ cup of the sugar, and salt into a large mixing bowl, add the pieces of butter, and work with the fingers till the mixture is crumbly. Add the eggs, vanilla, and cream and mix lightly just till the dough is soft, adding a little more cream if necessary. Turn the dough out onto a lightly floured surface and pat it gently with floured hands into a thick round about 9 inches in diameter. Place the round on a lightly greased baking sheet and bake about 30 minutes or till the scone is just golden.

While the scone is baking, stem the strawberries, cut each in half, and place them in a large saucepan. Add the remaining ½ cup sugar and toss the berries well with a fork, crushing just till they begin to juice. Heat till just slightly warm.

Trim the edges of the hot scone till even, carefully slice it in half horizontally with a sharp knife, and brush the soft surface of each half with melted butter. Position one half soft side up on a cake plate and spoon enough strawberries over the surface to cover. Gently place the other half on top soft side down, and spoon berries and juice over the top, allowing both to drip down the sides. Pour about one-half the cream over the top and serve immediately in wedges with the remaining cream and any remaining strawberries in pitchers on the side.

Serves 6 to 8

## Mary Lincoln's Griddle Strawberry Shortcake

2 cups all-purpose flour
½ teaspoon baking soda
½ teaspoon cream of tartar
½ teaspoon salt
4 tablespoons (½ stick) unsalted butter, cut into small pieces
1 cup sour cream
3 tablespoons melted butter
4 pints ripe fresh strawberries, stemmed, sliced, and tossed with ½ cup superfine sugar
2 cups clotted, heavy, or whipped cream

Sift together the flour, baking soda, cream of tartar, and salt into a mixing bowl, add the butter, and work with the fingers till the mixture is crumbly. Add the sour cream and cut it into the mixture till just blended. Transfer the dough to a floured surface, pat it (with floured hands) into a flat cake, turn it over, and roll it out gently ½ inch thick.

Preheat a lightly greased griddle over low heat.

Cut the dough into 3-inch rounds or into wedges, gather up the scraps, roll out, and cut more rounds or wedges. Brush one side of each round lightly with melted butter and grill the buttered sides about 8 minutes or till the rounds are puffed. Brush the other sides with butter, gently turn the rounds over, and grill about 8 minutes or till golden brown and fluffy inside when partly pulled open.

To serve, place on the table one bowl of the strawberries and one

(continued)

of the cream and let the eaters split the warm shortcakes with their fingers and lavish the halves with strawberries, juice, and cream.

Serves 6


## Southern Strawberry Shortcake

2½ cups unbleached flour
1 tablespoon baking powder
1 tablespoon sugar
4 tablespoons vegetable shortening
1 cup milk
3 tablespoons melted butter
4 pints ripe fresh strawberries
½ cup superfine sugar
2 cups heavy cream

Preheat the oven to 450° F. and grease two 8-inch layer-cake pans.

Sift together the flour, baking powder, and sugar into a mixing bowl, add the shortening, and work with the fingers till the mixture is crumbly. Add the milk and stir with a wooden spoon just till the dough is soft, adding a little more milk if necessary. Turn the dough out onto a lightly floured surface and, with floured hands, press into a ball. Cut the ball in half and press each half into a cake pan. Bake the cakes about 15 minutes or till golden, transfer to a rack, and brush the tops with the melted butter.

While the cakes are baking, pick out about 12 large strawberries, stem them, and set them aside. Stem the remaining strawberries, cut them in half, and place in a large saucepan. Add the superfine sugar, toss the berries with a fork (crushing them slightly), and heat them till just slightly warm and juicy.

Whip the heavy cream, spoon it into a pastry bag, and pipe a border of cream around the edges of one cake positioned on a cake plate. Spoon the warm berries inside the ring of cream, gently place the other cake on top, buttered side up, pipe another border of cream, and pile the remaining berries inside the ring. Pipe the remaining cream over the strawberries, and decorate the top with the reserved whole berries. Serve the shortcake in large wedges.

Serves 6

## Strawberry Sponge Cake

6  *eggs, separated*
1½  *cups superfine sugar*
1  *teaspoon vanilla*
1  *cup cake flour, sifted*
1½  *teaspoons baking powder*
¼  *teaspoon salt*
4  *pints ripe fresh strawberries*
2  *cups heavy cream, whipped*

Preheat the oven to 350° F.

In a large mixing bowl, beat the egg yolks with an electric mixer till very light and gradually add 1 cup of the sugar and the vanilla, beating constantly till the mixture is thickened. Gradually add the flour, baking powder, and salt, beating constantly till the batter is well blended. Beat the egg whites till just stiff but not dry and gradually fold them into the batter. Spoon the mixture into 2 lightly greased 8-inch layer-cake pans and bake about 30 minutes or till golden and spongy. Transfer the cakes to a rack and let cool.

While the cakes are baking, pick out 12 large, unstemmed strawberries and set them aside. Stem the remaining berries, cut them in half, and place in a mixing bowl. Add the remaining ½ cup of sugar and toss the strawberries well with a fork, crushing them till they juice.

Position one cake on a cake plate and spoon half the crushed berries and juice over the surface. Gently place the other cake on top and spoon the remaining berries and juice over the surface, allowing both to drip down the sides. Spoon the whipped cream evenly over the top and decorate with the reserved berries. Serve in large wedges.

Serves 6

# PART VII
# NOT BY BREAD ALONE

Although my interest in wine and booze has never been quite as spirited as my devotion to food, I have discoursed over the years on every alcoholic topic from California boutique wineries to rum to Champagne Rosé to the divine evils of the Martini. Unlike certain of my more fragile friends and colleagues who somehow find great virtue in casually sipping Kirs, domestic Chenin Blanc, and Perrier water, I'm of that nearly extinct breed who still down real cocktails, who drink as much sturdy French Burgundy with food as can be afforded, and for whom no major dinner is ever complete without an elegant digestive. I am a member of no wine society, I never attend the multitude of formal wine tastings to which I'm invited (finding the idea of tasting forty Chardonnays in thirty minutes downright embarrassing), and I remain resolutely convinced that the State of California will never produce a wine that inspires the swoon I experience each and every time I lift a Bonnes-Mares, Corton-Charlemagne, or Margaux to my lips. In other words, I am the ultimate wine snob.

# A WEE DRAM

1974

I t was one of those rare sunny days in the Highlands of Scotland, an almost unreal day to Scot and foreigner alike. The soaring peaks of the Grampian Mountains displayed majestic profiles which served as dramatic backdrops for the great spreads of fragrant heather, prickly gorse, and golden bracken. The lochs shimmered with a primordial radiance, the secluded glens seemed especially serene, and even the otherwise brooding pines added luster to the breathtaking landscape. Enveloped by all this remote splendor as we drove along the narrow highway that leads north from Glasgow, I couldn't help but recall a moving verse by Robert Burns committed to memory many years back:

> When Death's dark stream I ferry o'er
> (A time that surely shall come),
> In Heaven itself I'll ask no more
> Than just a Highland welcome.

My driver, MacRoberts, was a ruddy Scotsman—keen, proud, thick-brogued, and a veteran expert on sheep, Aberdeen cattle, golf, and of course, Scotch whisky. He talked of Scottish history, clans, tartans, and feuds. Directional signs indicated place names I couldn't identify, much less pronounce. Ardlui, Loch Awe, Ben Cruachan, Lochan Nah-Achlaise, and now and then I heard the calls of curlews and grouse. At Loch Ness I asked if the legendary monster did indeed exist, and with an authoritative "Aye!" MacRoberts assured me it did. Further on we passed the site of the Battle of Culloden, and I saw where Bonnie Charlie met his sad downfall and the white rose of the Jacobites withered forever.

By dusk, we'd reached the borders of Moray Firth, and my map told me we were nearing the heart of the region that produces Scotch whisky. The air was crisp and clean, the silence almost frightening, and had it not been for barking sheep dogs rounding up large herds of woollies, I might have believed I'd prematurely met my last reward. Passing through the small town of Nairn, MacRoberts pulled over in front of an old inn he'd obviously known for years.

"How 'bout a wee dram?" he queried. "Ye know, just a tip to warm up the body before the last leg of the trip. A very nice place here with a fine selection of whiskies."

Seated next to me at the small bar was a brawny old red-cheeked character decked out in a green-and-yellow-plaid kilt, and next to him on the floor was his hefty towser, begging for another chip or bit of salmon canapé.

"What'll it be?" asked MacRoberts.

The array of Scotch whisky behind the bar was enough to stagger the imagination. Naturally I recognized such distinguished brands as Grant's, Cutty Sark, Ballantine, Chivas Regal, Dewars, White Horse, J & B, Haig, and Johnny Walker, but I was nothing less than dumbfounded trying to place Highland Queen, Mortlach, Laphroaig, Strathconon, plus God knows how many names with the prefix "Glen." Suddenly my eye caught the label of a whisky I'd never tasted but which I'd heard was the father of all Scotch.

"Glenlivet," I told the attractive barmaid, "with ice and soda."

"Nae on ye blessed life!" belted the kilted and unsteady Hercules with the boxer. "Glenlivet and soda? Never, me fine lad! D'ye realize what yer drinking? That's no baby whisky, Jimmy [everyone's "Jimmy" to a Highlander], that's a prize of a single malt, one of the best in the Highlands, and nae will I sit here calmly and watch ye dash it with seltzer! Better ye should take a blend than be disrespectful to The Glenlivet."

"Look, Jimmy, ye see this empty water pitcher?" he said, reaching over the bar. He grabbed the large pitcher, picked up a spoon, and cracked it against the resounding glass. "Aye, now that, me good man, is the sound ye hear when ye drink a noble malt with no more than a wee bit of pure water. It's got character, and it talks to ye as it goes down. Whereas this," he went on, tapping a small shot glass, "now this is the echo of one of those blended whiskies full of seltzer, ice cubes, and the good Lord knows what other terrible properties. It's almost silent, that's what it is. Ye can play around with the blends, lad, but nae with the malts."

Although I had no doubt the old gentleman was indulging in more than a little exaggeration, he was the first of many northern purists I encountered during my week in Scotland who are the living manifestations of the passionate romance that has existed for centuries between the Scots and their whisky. He was also the first to give me some insight into the important difference between the rare single malts foreigners scarcely know and the blended whiskies, which find their largest market in the United States. Time and again I was reminded by rough old-timers of the Scottish expression: "There are two things that Highlanders like naked, and one of these is malt whisky," just as time and again I met those who argued vehemently that the most admirable aspect of the Scotch industry is the ability of gifted native blenders to take numerous whiskies and produce a consistently distinctive high-quality spirit. But whatever a Scot's conviction, it's for sure that the national drink is still as intimately associated with the ways of all the people as it was when a traveler once wrote: "They administer it in colds, fevers, and faintings, and it is a frequent prayer of theirs that 'God may keep them from that disorder that whisky will not cure.' "

"*Slàinte mhath*," the old Scotsman pronounced, slugging down the last of his drink, then tossing another piece of salmon to the dog.

"*Slanja va*," responded MacRoberts, holding up his glass to toast and directing me with his eyes to do the same.

Both expressions momentarily suggested to me that Celtic might still indeed be a living language. But figuring they had something to do with good health, I raised my Glenlivet garnished with one ice cube and a touch of water, repeated what the old fellow had said, and took the first sip. My palate tingled. My first impression was it couldn't be Scotch, or at least it wasn't like any Scotch I'd ever tasted! It was more like an exotic *digestif*, or something that should be sipped after a gréat meal. Rich, smooth, and mellow, with a velvety body, it was as resonant as a *grande fine* Cognac. Exquisite.

"Too peaty for ye, lad?" inquired the veteran. "Aye, I can tell ye never had a good drink of whisky, one with a fine heavy nose."

Without doubt, peaty was the right word to describe the overall distinctive aroma and flavor of the spirit, but there was so much more to the whisky, some sort of noble quality that could best be defined as having robust character with subliminal finesse.

Once we'd tipped another dram and were again making our way eastward toward Teacher's Glendronach distillery at Forgue, MacRoberts began to fill me in on a number of essential facts pertaining to the Scotch whisky industry in general. I first learned there are two kinds of Scotch: malt whisky, made in relatively small amounts only from malted barley and processed in pot stills; and grain whisky, made in much greater quantities from malted and unmalted barley, as well as corn, and processed in what is known as the "Coffey continuous-operation column still." The malts are divided into four distinct groups according to the geographical area of the distilleries (more than one hundred in all) where they're made. Highland malts are produced north of an imaginary line from Dundee on the east to Greenock on the west and are highly respected for their patrician subtlety. Lowland malts are distilled south of the line, while the two heaviest-flavored whiskies are made on the island of Islay and at Campbeltown in the Mull of Kintyre. Although each differs considerably in flavor, all are aristocratic spirits, whose individual characters depend primarily on the soft water, the peat used to roast the barley, and the climates of their geographical locations.

The opposite is true of the gigantic patent still, which was invented in 1831 by Aeneas Coffey in Ireland, which produces a clear, odorless, nearly tasteless spirit and which can operate as efficiently on the Cromarty Firth as on the Firth of Clyde. Blended Scotch whisky (the drink known through-out the world) consists mainly of grain whisky (called the pad) flavored with as many as forty different malts (referred to as "top dressing"). Many Old Guard Highlanders are convinced that blended whisky was developed for those with bland tastes, and more than a few will snicker out loud when reminded that American sophisticates (who "drink with their eyes instead of their palates") think they can tell a radical difference between one blend and another. I was later to find out that some professionals in the business consider this viewpoint absurd, while, interestingly enough, others place a good deal of credence in the idea. (I was also later to conduct a couple of blind tastings back home with lifelong Scotch drinkers, only to discover that very few could consistently choose correctly their supposedly favorite brands from a selection of five different labels. It was even more interesting that no one expressed any strong objection to any brand, a phenomenon that would lend lots of support to the contention that most all blended Scotch is good whisky.)

Continuing through the great Scotch-producing county of Aberdeen-shire, MacRoberts began to discourse on the various theories pertaining to the origins and development of the industry. From him I learned that the term "whisky" (or wiskie) derives from the Gaelic uisge beatha, translated from the Latin aqua vitae (water of life), and that the art of distillation was most likely brought to Scotland by Christian missionary monks. Later I discovered that the earliest historical reference to whisky occurs in the Scottish Exchequer Rolls for 1494, where there is an entry of "eight bolls of malt to Friar John Cor wherewith to make aqua vitae." From that point on the manufacture and selling of whisky grew steadily, to such a degree that in 1660 the authorities imposed an excise tax "on every pynt of aqua-vytie or strong watter," a move that would set off the two-hundred-year Whisky War between the revenue agents and the illicit mountain distillers (and one, by the way, that would eventually account for the fact that in our own day the Scots pay between 75 and 85 percent duty on a bottle of whisky). Every year more and more whisky was made in the Highlands, but because slow pot-still production could barely meet even the local demand, the malt remained virtually unknown outside Scotland till the early nineteenth century—meaning, of course, till the era when machines would change everything.

The new continuous-operation still that was brought from Dublin to Glasgow in 1832 by a group of Lowland industrialists was capable of enormous production. The only problem, however, was the shortage of barley to feed the giant machine. Faced with this dilemma, the operators turned to grain, the resultant alcoholic liquid being what is called today "grain neutral spirits." Unfortunately, this could not be passed off as whisky, and were it not for a clever individual in Edinburgh named Andrew Usher, the Scotch whisky industry just might have remained nestled in the Highlands, mainly along the banks of the River Spey. Usher's idea was simply to blend a little of the fragrant malts from the Highlands with the bland grain spirit being distilled down south, a revolutionary concept that ultimately brought about not only the international triumph of Scotch but also a fierce fifty-year feud between Highlander purists and Lowlander capitalists determined to use the term "whisky" in labeling the blends. Eventually the Lowlanders won the struggle by obtaining a royal commission, which ruled that any spirit distilled on Scottish soil from barley or grain in pot or column stills could be labeled Scotch whisky. But anyone who thinks the battle is now forgotten might like to bring up the subject with a Highlander!

The boom had begun, and everyone wanted to "be in whisky." Distilleries and new firms opened almost overnight, competition among strongly independent Scots was strong, and by 1900 such leaders as John Walker, John Dewar, John Haig, William Teacher, Matthew Gloag, George Ballantine, William Grant, James Buchanan, and MacDonald & Muir had inscribed their names on labels for posterity. The need, however, for capital expansion appeared inevitable almost from the beginning, and in May, 1877, four of the distillers amalgamated to form a single combine, eschewing for the sake of pride whatever advantages the D.C.L. (Distillers Company Limited of Edinburgh) might offer in the way of raw materials, production, and overall financial security.

By the time I spotted at Glendronach the same pagoda-type kiln roof I'd seen at so many other malt distilleries along the way, it was almost dark. Here we were in the heart of the Highlands and, while I knew from the dots on my map that we were surrounded on every side by dozens of distilleries hidden in the folding hills, nothing in sight suggested we could be anywhere but in some unfamiliar paradise. Now the air was quite chilly, a light fog had begun to spread over the miles and miles of moors and grazing turf, and the engine of the car was the only audible sound in the otherwise mystical quiet of the countryside. As we approached The Glen House (a stately guesthouse adjoining the distillery), I caught a glimpse of Dronac Burn, the small peaty-brown stream that flows directly under the distillery and without which the glory of Teacher's Scotch would be non-existent. There to meet us was Bill Thom, a short, cheerful Scotsman who's spent the majority of his forty-some years as manager.

"Aye, I see ye made it, lad," he almost sang, shaking my hand. "Yer room's ready, peat's on the fire, and ye'll find plenty of whisky on the shelf. A wee drop or so after dinner might give ye a few extra winks. But remember, lad, old Mrs. Finch comes over to serve breakfast at 8:00 A.M. sharp, and she can be a fiery dragon of a woman if she has to reheat yer porridge. After breakfast I'll show ye how we make the malt—the old-fashioned way —aye, the only way, as far as I'm concerned."

Entering the Glendronach distillery, I was first intrigued by the number of cats scurrying about.

"Mice," explained Bill Thom. "They're everywhere, trying to feast on the barley, ye know. Some places use pesticides. Not us. We prefer cats."

Inside the malting room I witnessed the first stage in the lengthy and complex production of whisky. The floor was covered with wet barley, and men in traditional blue overalls were scooping it up with large wooden shovels and throwing it through the air with an expertise that defies description. This would continue for a week or more, twenty-four hours a day, seven days a week, until germination had developed. (At other distilleries, more and more of this work is being done by machinery.) Next, the "green malt" is transferred to the kiln to be dried over a fire of peat and coke, a procedure that governs the peaty or "smoky" taste and aroma of whisky. After mixing hot water with the finely ground malt (grist) to extract the sugar, workers pour the resultant liquid, or wort, into giant wooden vats to ferment. Here yeast is added, the living enzymes attack the sugar and convert it into low-strength crude alcohol (wash), and after about seventy-two hours the liquid is ready for distillation.

Highland and island malts are traditionally distilled twice in large copper pot stills, while in the Lowlands, it's not unusual for a distinguished malt to be distilled three times. Distillation is a complicated process—an art— that can be carried out only by seasoned experts. Suffice it to say that the first distillation does no more than separate the alcohol from the fermented liquid, and that from the second distillation only the middle fraction (or cut) is of high enough standard to be collected for maturing. The third distillation of a Lowland malt is really a concentration and further refinement of the output of the previous still. At all stages of production the distillate is controlled from the spirit safe, a padlocked copper-and-glass container where workers can inspect and test the liquid without having access to the spirit itself, which, at all times in the distillery, is duty-free and therefore under strict surveillance by the resident officer of Her Majesty's Customs and Excise.

After distillation the whisky, whether it be malt or the lighter-flavored grain out of the continuous still, is filled into casks made of oak and stored duty-free at the distillery warehouse until it's either bottled as a single malt or blended. (Both manager and customs officer have keys, and one cannot open a warehouse without the other.) Although British law dictates that all whisky must be aged at least three years, most companies leave their malts down twice that long, and some age a whisky fifteen years or longer. Exactly what occurs in the cask remains one of the great mysteries of Scotch, but in principle the permeable oak allows air to pass in, evaporation takes place, certain undesirable constituents in the new spirit are removed, and in due course the whisky becomes mellow.

It's also in the cask that Scotch takes on some of its color and additional flavor, and herein lies one aspect of the industry that Scots don't care much to discuss. The truth is that the great majority of casks utilized in the aging of Scotch whisky are either old Sherry casks or used Bourbon barrels received from the United States, and obviously the impregnated wood of both affects the character of the spirit. Last year alone close to one million Bourbon casks were shipped to Scottish distilleries at a fraction of their original cost, since, according to our federal law, all Bourbon must be aged in *new* white-oak barrels. It's a point to be made—for who knows, were it not for the seasoned casks, a good deal of Scotch whisky just might taste a bit different. Such influence on the color, however, would in the long run be minimal, since blenders, who aim at uniformity in their products year after year, bring their whiskies to a definite standard color by adding, if necessary, a small amount of coloring solution prepared from caramelized sugar.

Time passes too rapidly in the Highlands, as in all Bonnie Scotland, but by the time I'd spent a week moving from one distillery to the next, chatting with great names in the industry, and watching proud individuals at work producing the spirit, I'd developed many new opinions and learned a good deal about a drink that seems to gain more popularity every day. Certainly nothing impressed me more than the aristocratic single malts, which because of their limited production have so far remained unknown to most Americans, but which are the very essence of Scotch whisky. It's interesting that distillers are beginning to bottle larger quantities of this original Scotch in anticipation of a lucrative export market; and, if the statistics are correct, I have no doubt that eventually in America the pungent single malts will become a new status drink—if not before meals, then certainly as a postprandial one.

One reputable Scottish liqueur, Drambuie, which is made with the finest Scotch whisky, has always been a favorite after-dinner spirit in this country. But how many people have ever gone a step further and tried a dram of Lochan Ora, Dalmore, or Glenfiddich, comparable to The Glenlivet and made by the house of Grant? Just recently I've noticed that liquor stores are stocking more Glenfiddich, and I don't consider it insignificant that from The Glenlivet's yearly output of 1.35 million gallons more than four thousand cases of the famous twelve-year-old malts are now being distributed nationwide in the United States. The message seems clear, and once Scotch lovers develop more sophisticated palates and agree to pay from ten to thirteen dollars for a pure malt whisky, the new trend should prove to be exciting.

As for the blends, the market continues to explode. Americans now consume half of all the whisky produced in Scotland and, while I do find it sad indeed that so many appreciate a brand more for its lofty social status and price tag than for its gustatory merits, I feel confident that sales can only increase steadily. For one thing, more and more brands are being imported in barrels at 100 proof, cut with distilled water, and bottled here —a factor that affects not only the amount of Scotch that can be distributed but also, because of lower taxes, the prices customers pay. Second, some producers feel greater profits are realized by marketing more "private-label" whisky, which can be shipped under contract to individual liquor stores, bottled and labeled by the buyers, and sold to customers at cheaper prices. This means, of course, that it's quite possible for a consumer who doesn't care about prestige labels to buy a blend and pay considerably less than he would for the internationally known brand name. But most fastidious Scotch drinkers will still shell out for the security of a brand name and the words "Bottled in Scotland."

Trends and marketing and public tastes are indeed important aspects that the industry must constantly consider, but after all is said and done, I prefer to believe that the overall reputation and, yes, the romance of Scotch are enough to ensure its continuing appeal to those who love and respect great spirits. From its ancient beginnings in the remote Highland glens, through centuries of strife and turmoil, up till the present day, Scotch whisky has played an integral role in the development and prosperity of a proud country. The drink has received many an accolade, but surely no one has summed up more succinctly its esteem in the eyes of the Scottish people than a certain old-timer by the name of James Hogg:

"If a body could just find oot the exac' proper proportion and quantity that ought to be drunk every day, and keep to that, I verily trow that he might leeve for ever, without dying at a', and that doctors and kirkyards would go oot o' fashion."

## POSTSCRIPT

All modesty aside, it is gratifying that my prediction many years ago that the single malts would eventually win over a large segment of the Scotch-drinking American public has finally come true. In fact, while sales of blended Scotch have plummeted in the last couple of years, the figures for the malts have improved steadily. And sophisticated tipplers are not only sipping The Glenlivet and Glenfiddich as cocktails but also ordering them as postprandials in place of Cognac, sweet liqueurs, and the like.

# AT THE BODEGAS

*1975*

*S*ubdued, I thought, racing my small Seat 127 along the narrow stretch of coastal highway that connects continental Spain's southernmost town of Tarifa with the ancient Andalusian port city of Cádiz. *Yes, everything here is so subdued, tempered, almost naturally mollified. I know that no more than a couple of kilometers to the west is the raging Atlantic, that the great black bulls quietly grazing to my right are as potentially dangerous as lightning, that the rather ordinary-looking ponies galloping in pastures up ahead will one day develop into noble Carthusian stallions, and above all, that out there, somewhere, are the vineyards that produce one of the finest wines in the world.*

In a way it all baffled the imagination, but my homework assured me I was in the heart of Spain's most romantic and historically fascinating region —despite the conspicuous absence of tourists. Here the Phoenicians had wandered fifteen hundred years before the Greeks fought the Persian Wars. Nearby, Tartessus (known as the Athens of the West) had flourished as a cosmopolitan community, only to disappear with hardly a trace 2,500 years ago. The Carthaginians, the Hebrews, the Moors, and finally the Christians—all had inhabited this verdant area at some point.

But now it was as though no civilization had ever existed, and as the brilliant sun began to fade, the scenery and mood became even more magical. The landscape took on the same haunting quiet that follows a doleful flamenco canto; it appeared that the giant cacti along the road were being caressed by jasmine and eddies of autochthonous yellow wildflowers; and in the distance the old whitewashed Moorish towns seemed to float on the edge of mountains, invoking the soul-touching tones of a nearly forgotten verse of García Lorca, Andalusia's most celebrated poet:

> *On the lonely mountain*
> *A village cemetery*
> *Appears like a field*
> *Sown with seeds of skulls,*
> *And cypresses have flowered*
> *Like gigantic heads,*
> *Which, with empty eyeholes*
> *And green hair,*
> *Pensively and sadly*
> *Contemplate the skyline.*

Those who do visit Andalusia come for any number of reasons: the warm sun and impressive vistas of mountain and sea, the proud horses and bulls, the vibrant flash of the flamenco guitar and colorful dancers. This is the land of *torreros, caballeros,* polo matches, century-old castles perched atop huge rock cliffs, cork plantations, and, along the coast, fishing villages where natives and visitors alike spend afternoons casually talking over tables piled high with fresh sweet prawns and crawfishlike *cigalas.* This is the unspoiled Spain of legend, a territory full of blue-blood aristocrats and a region still endowed with the mystical powers to produce that elevated spiritual sensation known locally as a *duende.*

It also happens to be one blessed section of the world where, within a minuscule triangle area, nature has allowed the production of a distinguished wine—Sherry. Even if Andalusia did not offer so many other attractions, it would be worth the trip sixty miles south of Seville just to visit the famous *bodegas* (enormous sheds where shippers store and age their Sherries) in Jerez de la Frontera, Puerto de Santa María, and Sanlúcar de Barrameda. These are three relatively small towns, located no more than fifteen miles apart, which supply virtually every ounce of genuine Sherry consumed throughout the world.

Although many people don't realize it, Sherry is not a generic word referring to wine but a name that stems from an archaic pronunciation of Jerez, the major center of production. The original Arabic name of the city was Seris, but throughout centuries of various ethnic influences the word gradually evolved from Seris to Xeres to Scherrisch and, finally to Jerez, the appellation granted by King Don Juan I in a royal decree of 1380. Later the spelling was modified further by the British, who for more than three centuries have exercised a dominating force in the trade and whose influence is still visibly and linguistically pronounced. Technically, Sherry is the official name of a particular geographical site, and it is only here, in the area designated by the Control Council for the Protection of the Name "Jerez-Xeres-Sherry," that the wine may be made.

As I entered the outskirts of Jerez, my first impression was of a quiet city, basically a conglomeration of block-long *bodegas* separated by large, regal private homes with wrought-iron balconies, spacious patios, and colorful gardens. (It has been said that the two most inconspicuous millionaire-inhabited towns on the globe are Reims, in France, and Jerez de la Frontera.) Suddenly the prestigious Spanish and English names are all there, proudly painted in black along the sides of enormous whitewashed warehouses: González Byass, John Harvey, Garvey, Díez Hermanos, Pedro Domecq, Sandeman, Williams & Humbert, Zoila Ruiz-Mateos. Inside these dim, cool sanctuaries—each of which resembles a vaulted, clerestory-windowed cathedral and, in accordance with tradition, faces southward to the sea—rest the broad-chested oak casks (or butts) of aging Sherry. The sight is impressive and, if the wind happens to be blowing across the *bodegas,* the aroma of wine in the air inspires a synesthetic sensation experienced nowhere else in the world.

Passing one *bodega* after another (there are more than 130 in Jerez alone), I ended up in the center of the old town, having failed to locate the Hotel Jerez. The narrow cobblestone streets were filled with young and old, well-dressed locals who—during what I came to realize was Holy Week—had left their houses to attend the hours-long religious procession through the town and then, as is customary, gather in "fellowship" in the *tascas* (bars) before solemnly observing Good Friday.

When I approached the crowded counter of one bar to ask directions to the hotel, the barman, ignoring my beckoning *"Por favor, señor,"* automatically placed in front of me a small tulip-shaped glass *(copita),* a half-bottle with a label reading *"Fino—Jerez Muy Seco,"* and a plate of *tapas*—crumbled white cheese, tiny fried fish, octopus, olives, prawns, and a slice of cured regional ham. Filling the glass three-quarters full, I held the pale golden liquid up to the light, then sniffed its subtle, clean-smelling nose, then sipped. This was Sherry? It couldn't be! But indeed it was—the genuine thing, the fabulous dry *fino* I'd heard about, the crisp fresh wine you rarely find outside of Spain and which can hardly be compared with the sometimes stale, overly sweet bottled product in other parts of the world. (To my knowledge only the British import Sherry by the cask.)

Watching the gestures of others at the bar, I followed suit, pouring a second, a third, a fourth glass of *fino* and spearing the *tapas* with a toothpick. The atmosphere reeled in gaiety, unknown fingers tipped their *copitas* to me as a symbol of hospitality, and before long, radiant in spirit, I was carrying on lengthy conversations in a language in which my vocabulary is limited to a well-chosen dozen words. Such was my introduction to Jerez, the town and the wine, and by the time my fellow tipplers had drawn me a map to the hotel, I already had some notion of what it was like to experience Andalusian *duende*.

"There's a gentleman waiting for you in the bar," said the desk clerk. "Oh, no worry about the time. He said the plans were for you to call him after your arrival but that he'd decided to come on over and have a *copa*." (In Jerez there's never an occasion—religious, business, or social—that doesn't call for two or three glasses of Sherry.)

Seated at the bar with a split of La Ina *fino* in front of him was a suavely dressed figure who bore close resemblance to a Velásquez nobleman.

"Ah, welcome to Jerez," he greeted. "I'm José Ignacio López de Carrizosa y Domecq. How was the trip up?"

"Fine," I replied, "just beautiful." Then I froze. *The name! What was that name? I certainly got the Domecq part, but how should I address him? Don José? Señor Domecq? Oh, the hell with it, I'll simply ask.*

"Just call me Ignacio," he responded with a friendly smile. "That's what I'm called in the family and at the Consejo Regulador (the Sherry Control Council), where I work. Around town it's usually Don José Ignacio, depending on where I am and with whom. But don't let our Spanish names bother you, although—since you ask—their formation is really quite simple. The *Don* signifies a certain breeding and education, the equivalent of your *gentleman*. The first names are the same as those of my father and uncle. Carrizosa is my paternal family name, and my mother is a Domecq. Now that you've got that straight, how about a little *fino?*"

While it was completely obvious that my host was extending to a foreign visitor the type of courtesy implicit in *noblesse oblige* (or, as the Domecq coat-of-arms reads, *Domecq Oblige*), it was equally evident later on that under normal circumstances Ignacio, like all other members of aristocratic families associated with the Sherry empire of Jerez (the Terrys, Gonzálezes, Osbornes, and Carrizosas), observes a refined social protocol and enjoys an exclusive lifestyle rarely witnessed today on so large a scale. Most can trace their bloodlines back centuries; intermarriage within the various Sherry families is as common today as it was two hundred years ago. As in the case of the powerful Domecqs (who number some four hundred), it is not unusual for cousins to marry, generation after generation. The result is not only a highly centralized industry controlled by numerous closely knit private families but also an almost feudal society within which the nobility play the most important roles in the civic, political, cultural, and religious activities of the community.

When Ignacio said the Sherry sovereigns share many mutual interests, he wasn't exaggerating. Above all, these aristocrats work, and they work hard—running the family business, fulfilling their duties as civic leaders

("I'm sort of expected to serve as the town's next mayor," confides Ignacio), and devoting hours of their time to outsiders like me who express a serious interest in their industry. On the other hand, they spend their leisure time in activities indicative of the landed gentry. In town they socialize with each other at the exclusive Club El Lebrero, where women and children are forbidden except during formal celebrations. Most entertain regularly in stately homes with gorgeous flower-adorned patios, or in medieval and Renaissance palaces staffed with brigades of servants.

After attending a number of austere, almost medieval religious ceremonies with members of different Sherry families (and after recovering from a typical Spanish midnight dinner party given by a grandee) I was introduced by Ignacio to all the complex but fascinating procedures involved in the production of what has to be the world's most intriguing wine. My education began in the vineyards, which are hidden away on low hills stretching westward in a small triangle from Jerez to Puerto de Santa María and Sanlúcar.

Here, in what is officially known as the Sherry Zone, the amber-colored palomino grape (the variety from which 90 percent of Sherry is made) flourishes in three types of soil: *albariza* (a white chalk soil, which, since it protects the vine from summer heat by forming a baked crust beneath which moisture is retained, is classified as the finest), *barro* (containing chalk, clay, and sand), and *arena* (composed of sand and silica). Exactly why one hill of earth is white *albariza* and the adjoining one *barro* nobody knows, but because the quality of the grape is in large part determined by the particular soil that nourishes the vine, soil regulations are tough and assessments are constantly being made by the control council. Anyone who might doubt the important influence of soil on the grape need only bite into a few palomino clusters plucked from different areas: the *albariza* grapes are subtly dry in taste compared with the *barro* and *arena* varieties, which are much sweeter. Without these flavor differences, Sherry simply could not be developed into the unique wine it is.

September is the month of the harvest, or *vendimia,* and it is during this time that Jerez springs to life. Grape pickers arrive from all over Andalusia and occasionally even from different parts of the world. In the daytime they work hard and fast, removing the fat golden clusters with primevally short, curved blades and transporting them by burro or truck to the various *lagares* for pressing. The Pedro Ximénez grape, an extremely sweet variety utilized primarily for blending, is usually sun-dried on large flat mats before being pressed to an almost raisinlike state. For centuries—or until just a decade ago—the scene of workmen crushing the grapes with hobnailed boots was not a rare sight. Today, alas, machines do most of the work, pressing every drop of juice from the grapes and transferring the must to mammoth American-made white-oak butts for fermentation.

From the moment the must undergoes primary fermentation (whereby yeast converts sugar into alcohol) till the finished wine is stored to age, mysterious natural phenomena affect the development of Sherry in ways that can't be explained to this day. Surely the most magical feature of all has to do with the way Sherry develops naturally into different styles. After a few months of fermentation, the wine is tasted to determine whether it will be light or heavy, and what's so curious is that butts with identical backgrounds can turn out to be surprisingly different. Why? No one knows. The wines are then put aside: the lighter to develop into delicate dry *finos* and possibly rare amontillados, the heavier ones into rich olorosos.

It is also intriguing that while other wines (the single exception besides Sherry being those of the Jura region of France) cease fermenting at about fourteen or fifteen degrees of alcohol—at which point the flowering yeast is killed—in *fino* Sherry the strange Spanish yeast (*flor*) of this area can survive inexplicably up to twenty percent alcohol, thus assuring a wine with practically no sugar content. Furthermore, whereas other wines spend their youth carefully protected against destruction by air, *fino* not only depends upon this agent for development and optimum character but, ironically, begins to lose its freshness when bottled at the *bodega*. Thus, the reason for the inhabitants of Jerez to drink from half bottles or small, unsealed glass containers in wicker.

Much has been said concerning the marked differences between drinking *fino* directly from the butt in the *bodega* and from the bottle, and all I can add is you have to undergo the experience personally to appreciate it. There you stand on damp, moldy earth inside the dark, high-ceilinged, solemn storehouse, surrounded by endless stacks of butts and virtually overwhelmed by the sensuous presence of wine. Up walks the *capataz* (manager) carrying a four-foot-long *venencia* of whalebone with a silver beaker attached to the end. He approaches a butt—and plunk, down he plunges the wand through the *flor* into the precious Sherry. Withdrawing it, he takes a glass, holds it at arm's length, then lets the gold liquid stream through the air directly into the narrow glass. (Sounds easy? Don't try it if you value the clothes you're wearing.)

Hesitating for a moment to study the *flor* drifting on top, you check the nose. It's elusive. Can something actually smell dry? Or is it perhaps like the scent of daisies in the wind? Or maybe a waft of lemon? Apple! Yes, that's it, a freshly picked apple. You sip, breathe in through the mouth, swallow, sip again, spit on the damp ground, taste, and wonder. The wine is dry, a bit salty, clean, crisp, fresh, balanced; you're at a loss for vocabulary. You then sip a little *fino* poured from a bottle. Nice, okay, good— but . . .

One hour later you're in Sanlúcar to taste *manzanilla,* a separate class of *fino*, which, when sampled right in the town, has even greater finesse, saltiness, and delicacy than the Sherry you just sipped—but which, if transported even the short fifteen miles to Jerez, loses its unique character-

istics and becomes a regular *fino*. Again, why? Still another secret nature
has concealed for more than two thousand years. You'd like to take a few
bottles home to share with friends. Fine. The wine travels beautifully,
since those in the trade know how to add a small dose of alcohol to keep it
in good condition for shipping. But remember, like the standard *finos,* the
*manzanilla* will lose more and more of that edge of perfection you admire.
In fact, once you're away, you'll swear it's a *fino*. It is, and there's nothing
you or any other human being can do about it. If you become addicted to
*manzanilla,* there's only one earthly solution: move to Sanlúcar.

If Sherry has not evolved as a *fino* (or *manzanilla*), it is registered by the
*capataz* (with chalk marks on the butt) as either a potential amontillado or
an oloroso (the Sherry on which all the sweet cream and milk Sherries are
based). Whereas delicate *finos* are aged no more than two or three years to
safeguard freshness, amontillados remain in the oak six, seven, or—in the
case of a truly rare natural example left unsweetened—nineteen or twenty
years. Basically the same is true of oloroso, the richest, most full-bodied of
the Sherries. If it's smoothed out with sweet Pedro Ximénez and aged five
or six years, it's the good but rather ordinary wine so beloved by most of
the sweet-toothed world outside Spain. Conversely, an unsweetened oloroso left to mature for years and develop its characteristic nutty flavor is a
true ceremonial wine for the gods. Having now tasted these old baronial
amontillados and olorosos, I'll never be quite satisfied with a cream or milk
Sherry.

Aside from the special amontillados and olorosos put away to age indefinitely, all Sherry is produced in *bodegas* by an elaborate system known as
the *solera,* which in principle is a pyramid constructed of four to six butts.
The *solera* itself is the oldest cask, at the bottom, the only one on which a
date is indicated; the butts above (*criaderas,* or nurseries) contain, progressively upward, younger and younger wine. As the wine is drawn in small
quantities from the bottom row of casks they are refilled from the tier
above, and so on, up and up. In this way the younger Sherries assume the
characteristics of the older wines below, ultimately acquiring the flavor of
the oldest butt at the bottom and thus assuring wines of consistent quality
year after year. After the Sherry is drawn from the *solera* it is checked by
professional tasters (often the company owners themselves), enriched with
a little old wine, and possibly blended with small amounts of *vino dulce* or
*vino de color* to perfect the taste and color characteristic of a particular
brand. Needless to say, the role of the taster is one of the most crucial in
the overall production and represents the point when man is allowed to
improve on nature.

A few hours before my train was due to leave Jerez for Madrid, I was
invited to the Carrizosa country house for an informal Sunday lunch with
the family and friends (meaning, of course, relatives). Present on the large,
shaded patio was a scattering of Domecqs, Terrys, Osbornes, and Gonzá-

lezes, five or six *marqueses, duques* and *duquesas* (all addressed by their titles), and who knows what other distinguished guests. First everyone was served various old amontillados ("You 'water the arena' with amontillado," explained Ignacio), then *copitas* of *fino* drawn from a cask. Soon the tables were stacked high with thick loaves of homemade bread, local cheeses, fruits, meats, and a fantastic assortment of boiled fresh crustaceans spread out on paper.

As the Sherry flowed and the food was slowly consumed, spirits soared. Suddenly someone grabbed a guitar, sat down, and strummed out what must have been—by the look on everybody's face—a sad song of love, a ballad that echoed within the warm, whitewashed, unreal confines of this rustic paradise. Then he broke into a frenzied flamenco, snapping the strings with the agility of a professional performer. Everyone clapped to the beat, a few shouted, *"Olé!"* from time to time, and at one point a young, dark beauty lifted her skirt slightly to the knees and began beating out the rhythm on the tile floor. I stood in the background, sipped my *fino,* marveled at the myth, and finally realized fully what it means to have *duende.*

## POSTSCRIPT

I've returned to Jerez only once since the initial visit described here and still cannot get over how time stands virtually still with regard to both the centuries-old production of Sherry and the noble lifestyles of the great families. Sure, there were a few Domecqs and Terrys and Osbornes who had either passed on or retired as "gentlemen of leisure," but in their places were younger Domecqs and Terrys and Osbornes, all continuing the family traditions, all members of the Club El Librero like their fathers and uncles, and all entertaining in a grand manner more suggestive of the Renaissance than the 1980s. And have I yet ever tasted in the U.S. or England or anywhere a *fino* to equal that sipped right in Jerez or Sanlúcar? Never.

# THE LIQUID MIRACLE OF
# BURGUNDY

*1981*

O ne of my most vivid memories of first living in France was the frequent drive I'd make with friends from Grenoble to Paris, a trip that
led straight through the heart of Burgundy and was invariably highlighted
by a meal at Alexandre Dumaine's Hôtel de la Côte d'Or in Saulieu. As
naïve Michelinless students of literature, we, of course, had no idea that
we were eating in a three-star restaurant or that the short, rotund chef
who would sit and speak French with us after the meal was already a living
legend in the world of gastronomy. All we knew was that never in our lives
had we tasted such luscious food or drunk such superb wines as in this
simple roadside inn.

On one occasion, when I had made the trip alone and had just devoured
some unforgettable roasted *jambon du Morvan*, Monsieur Dumaine approached the table with a bottle of red wine, eyed the inexpensive Beaujolais I was drinking, and asked if I'd like a glass of '49 La Tâche. I studied
the unfamiliar label, sniffed the vigorous bouquet, and, as we sipped, a
whole new world opened up to me. Why had I never tasted it before—not
even something like it? Where did it come from?

"Where does it come from!" exclaimed Dumaine. "Why, right here in
the Côte d'Or, *naturellement*, just up the road from the Clos de Vougeot.
Surely you've visited the Côte d'Or!"

La Tâche, La Côte d'Or, Clos de Vougeot—the names were meaningless to me. Sure, I had been aware of the vineyards all along Route N-6 (in the Beaujolais and near Mâcon), but what I didn't realize was that, by never having cut off to N-74 in the direction of Beaune and Dijon, I'd completely missed seeing that minuscule area of Burgundy that produces some of the world's greatest wines.

"Ah, *jeune homme*, tomorrow morning you'll visit the Côte d'Or with Dumaine," insisted the chef, and, sure enough, the next day at the crack of dawn we squeezed into the small car and headed southeast. At N-74 we turned north, and suffice it to say that in just a few hours I received an education that would benefit me the rest of my life and significantly influence my future.

Meursault, Pommard, Aloxe-Corton, Nuits-St.-Georges, Vosne-Romanée, Vougeot, Chambertin—no sooner had we zipped by one great vineyard or wine commune than we were at the next. From time to time, Dumaine would stop at a farmhouse to give me the opportunity to meet a grower and sample his wine. I was told about the soil, grape varieties, weather, vinification, and all the age-old mysteries involved in the production of burgundy. In the end, I actually understood very little, but that gentle, kind man (who I'd later learn was known worldwide as "Alexandre the Great" and whom I would see only once again before his death) had instilled in me an excitement that would gradually nourish my knowledge and appreciation of the wine I, to this day, value over all others.

Since those early days, I've visited Burgundy more times than I can recall, forever fascinated by the region's hard-working, colorful inhabitants, the lusty, rib-sticking cuisine, and, of course, the rare and expensive wines (the total production of Burgundy is only one-third that of Bordeaux). Just as Paris is the brain of France and Champagne the soul, Burgundy is the stomach. The very mention of this ancient duchy, which stretches from Dijon southward almost to Lyon, evokes memories of fat *escargots*, richly aromatic coq au vin, toothsome *jambon persillé*, zesty *lapin à la dijonnaise*, juicy slabs of Charolais beef, Bresse chickens—dishes that could only be classified *à la bourguignonne*. And who could imagine savoring these specialties without also drinking aristocratic Chambertins, sturdy Nuits-St.-Georges, or simple Beaujolais? "For more than two thousand years," writes Alexis Lichine in his *Guide to the Wines and Vineyards of France*, "Burgundians have been planting the vine continuously in the same soil, devoting themselves to its care, making and drinking magnificent wines, and shipping them all over the world. From father to son the tradition has been passed, from nobleman to priest to peasant. Over the centuries, the finest vineyard sites have been discovered; the best vines for the soil have been found and planted there and cherished with loving care. The result is Burgundy as we know it today."

One aspect of Burgundy that I continually find fascinating is that, considering all her former glory and riches, the province is remarkably rustic.

The vast majority of growers are still people of the soil who live in what amount to small farmhouses on land used almost as much for the cultivation of grain and raising of cattle as for pinot noir and chardonnay grapes. First-time visitors to the Côte d'Or, for instance, are always surprised (and a bit disappointed) not to find as many spacious country estates and regal châteaux as in the Bordeaux region. And the reasons are simple. From Roman times until the late eighteenth century, the vast majority of vineyards in Burgundy were owned and operated by the Church, but with the wave of anticlericalism that followed the French Revolution, the land was seized by the state and eventually parceled out to the people. The result was a system of small ownership whereby the vineyards remained entities but were divided among individuals. Today, there are only a few families who've managed to acquire large tracts of land. Most domains are made up of fragmented plots from any number of widely scattered vineyards (the Clos de Vougeot, for example, has over sixty growers in its 124 acres).

Burgundy is divided into six wine-producing districts that make up an Appellation Contrôlée area less than half the size of New York City (or about 75,000 acres): Chablis, the Côte d'Or (composed of the Côte de Nuits and the Côte de Beaune), the Chalonnais, the Mâconnais, and the Beaujolais. Although the visual and geographical characteristics of each district can be as distinct as the individual wines, the growers themselves seem to have a lot in common. For all the nobility of their wines, the Burgundians are down-to-earth, fun-loving people, who have little trace of the pretension and stuffiness all too often encountered around Bordeaux and who enjoy nothing more than welcoming strangers into their midst to discuss and taste wine. From Chablis southward to the Beaujolais, signs reading "Vente Directe" ("Direct Sales") are displayed everywhere, encouraging enthusiasts to visit the courtyards and cellars in Vosne, Meursault, Gevrey, Fuissé, and Fleurie, have a glass of wine, perhaps meet the proprietor, and, of course, purchase a few bottles.

Each year in Beaune, Burgundy's quaint, cobblestoned wine capital, peasants and noble growers alike sponsor a huge public wine auction on the third Sunday of November, the proceeds of which are donated to the town's fifteenth-century charity hospital (Hospices de Beaune). The day before the auction, people come from all over the world to celebrate the event. In the great hall of the Clos de Vougeot, five hundred robed members of the Confrérie des Chevaliers du Tastevin (the colorful society that promotes the wines of Burgundy) hold a Rabelaisian-type food and wine revelry that makes even the most elaborate parties around the world pale by comparison. For those who can stand up to all the drinking and merry-making, a Hospices weekend is an unforgettable experience.

No less indicative of the Burgundian lifestyle are the numerous private social affairs thrown periodically by growers throughout the region. Any serious oenophile would jump at the chance to attend a formal dégustation (wine tasting) given at Chambertin by Jean Trapet (a fourth-generation grower whom Alexis Lichine has referred to as "the greatest"); or in Georges Blanc's three-star restaurant at Vonnas near Mâcon; or at Marquis François de Roussy de Sales's magnificent Château de la Chaize built in the Beaujolais in 1676 by none other than the famous Mansard. The September *dégustation* of fine burgundies given by Madame Lalou Bize-Leroy at her spacious farmhouse near Nuits-St.-Georges might not be the most publicized annual event in France, but for those who love and respect great wine, it's certainly one of the most prized invitations. After all, Lalou is co-owner of all the Romanée-Conti and La Tâche vineyards, plus parts of Richebourg, Grands-Échézeaux, Échézeaux, and Montrachet, and, unlike the pretentious, silly bread-and-cheese wine tastings thought to be so chic throughout America, this informal spectacle at the Domaine d'Auvernay is an exercise in sheer hedonism. To be sure, guests are dead serious about the privilege of drinking '29 Les St.-Georges, '38 La Richemone, '45 Nuits-St.-Georges Premier Cru, '49 Clos des Argillat, and some thirty other rare burgundies. But of equal importance is Lalou's food spread copiously across four huge oak refectory tables: earthy pâtés and rillettes, buckets of foie gras, baronial hams and beef roasts, lobsters with chervil, prosciutto and *Bünderfleisch*, avocado mousse with chopped radishes and garlic, cold trout and eel, deviled chicken wings, and pounds of chocolate—yes, chocolate! When guests are not tasting or consuming delicious food, they're taking strolls around the grounds and casually socializing. "What would they think in the United States about eating garlicky food with these wines and cleansing the palate with chocolate?" snickered a French chef at one event. "Notice that the single item nobody has touched is the cheese," observed another guest. As elsewhere in Burgundy, tasting wine at Lalou's is not intended to be a lesson in chemistry but rather a means of accomplishing and experiencing many levels of human enjoyment.

No matter where you travel in Burgundy, the fundamental question is what makes one vineyard (or *climat*) more valuable than another, one wine better than the next? What explains, for instance, why Chambertin–Clos de Bèze is superior to Charmes-Chambertin, located right across the road, or why a First-Growth Beaujolais like Juliénas is longer-lived than the Saint-Amour produced two kilometers away? For centuries, experts have studied the soil, the tilt of the slopes, the temperature, the rainfall, and the wind direction. Yet the mystery of these great wines remains.

As with all reputable French wines, Burgundy is subject to strict Appellation Contrôlée laws, whereby the number of vines in a given *climat*, the yield per hectare, and the methods of pruning, growing, fertilizing, vinifying, and aging are so carefully controlled that any wine not meeting every standard is legally not Burgundy. It is no wonder that nothing offends Burgundians more than those bottles labeled California Burgundy, Chilean Burgundy, and South African Burgundy. Unlike Bordeaux wines (most of which are produced on single large estates under one ownership), about sixty percent of all Burgundy is purchased in barrel by shippers (or *négociants*) from any number of growers. It is then blended to achieve a certain quality and character and sold under labels as the wine not of a specific grower but of a specific district. Until twenty-five years ago, most Burgundy was produced in this manner, but today forty percent is estate-bottled by even the smallest growers, all of whom hope to reap greater profits through direct sales.

Buyers all over the world engage themselves in heated arguments as to which is the best system. Some insist that nobody maintains consistent standards like an honest, reliable shipper (many of whom are growers themselves); others refuse to accept any wine that is not made and bottled by the vineyard proprietor. In the long run, of course, it all boils down to the producer's integrity and art, no matter who he might be, and the only way a smart buyer can be assured of the quality he's seeking is by learning to decipher the language on the label.

In the effort to simplify what is probably the most complex system of wine labeling in existence, I can only point out the basic essentials, referring those who care to pursue the intricate details to either Alexis Lichine's definitive *Guide* or Hugh Johnson's *The World Atlas of Wine*. First, under the Appellations d'Origine Contrôlée decrees, any wine that qualifies as Burgundy must spell out on the label its eligible boundaries—for example, the region, "Bourgogne"; the district, "Côte de Nuits"; the commune, "Vosne-Romanée"; and the vineyard, "La Tâche." Labels must further specify the legal commune designation—for example, "Appellation Vosne-Romanée Contrôlée." Second, if a wine is produced and bottled by the grower, the label should bear his name or indicate estate bottling; if produced by a shipper, his name as *"négociant"* should appear on the label.

As for the Burgundy vintages, suffice it to say that today the possibility of finding—not to mention paying for—a bottle of something like a '29 Richebourg, a '45 Musigny, or any other old red from a great year in the Côte d'Or is about as remote as stumbling across a 1789 Madeira—unless, of course, you happen to make friends with a grower willing to share his dusty treasures. Since the production of the finest Burgundy has always been so small, even a '61 Clos de la Roche or '69 Grands-Echézeaux is now rare and costly. Wines with this type of breeding can never be widely available and, therefore, can never be inexpensive. The world's very finest restaurants usually have a few prize bottles from the fifties or sixties stashed away for special guests or occasions, but even in the three-star citadels of France and at such nobly-stocked New York havens as The Four Seasons, Le Cirque, and Windows on the World, the wine cards rarely list any red Burgundies dating before the early seventies.

When choosing a recent vintage, be wary of generalized ratings. Remember that it often takes years to judge the ultimate development of the reds and the fickleness of the whites. Those little vintage charts might give the '73 whites a fairly high rank, but what they don't point out is that since the wines were lacking in acidity, many have already begun to fade. They say 1976 was the best year in Burgundy since 1969, but who knows when the time will be just right to open an incredibly expensive red or whether a splendid Bâtard-Montrachet will already be over the edge by 1980? Just recently I had the august opportunity to drink a '38 Bonnes-Mares, hardly a great red according to the experts. The wine was round, full, virile, and mature, one of the most remarkable bottles I've ever encountered. When it comes to the wines from the Côte d'Or—especially those during the past decade—I find myself disregarding dates and simply drinking in accordance with my instincts and bank account.

Although even the less prestigious wines produced south of the Côte d'Or are hardly the bargains they once were, it's nevertheless in the Chalonnais, Mâconnais, and Beaujolais that you can find delicious Burgundies at affordable prices—as well as some fascinating countryside, wonderful people, and good sturdy food. Most tourists make the mistake of zipping southward from Beaune on the A-6 autoroute, whereas I enjoy nothing more than cutting off N-74 at Chagny to D-981, meandering down the back-country roads through sheep and goats grazing on rolling hills, and stopping to taste and discuss wine at Rully, Mercurey, Givry, Viré, Azé, Pouilly, and other small villages west of Chalon and Mâcon. This is picnic territory at its best, a quiet, almost bucolic region that seems to beckon for crusty bread, cheese, cured ham, and bottles of fresh, crisp white Montagny or light, smooth Rully. Of course, the best-known labels from the Mâconnais are the officially controlled Pouilly-Fuissé and Saint-Véran. Both are superb white wines, but, owing to their ever-increasing popularity, they are almost as overpriced as the Meursaults and Pulignys in the Côte de Beaune. Equally interesting but so far less exposed are the Mâcons and Mâcon-Villages, simple whites that are reasonable in cost and ideal accompaniments to the many local chicken and crayfish dishes.

The Beaujolais, more than any other district, symbolizes all that is so splendid about Burgundy: lush green hills and valleys; tiny roads twisting from vineyard to vineyard; farmhouses made of saffron-colored bricks; men playing *boule* in the village squares; growers eager to sit down on a barrel and share their wine and conversation; and family-run restaurants with flowered terraces, large platters of coq au vin and *andouillettes,* and gallons of fresh, fragrant wine to be consumed young and with abandon.

Following the Route du Beaujolais, you can't miss the colorful signs pointing directions to Chénas, Fleurie, Brouilly, Morgon, and the other wine-producing hamlets. Once you arrive in town, you'll spot the various *caveaux de dégustation* where, for a couple of francs, you can taste the local wines. The nine classified growths in Beaujolais are Saint-Amour, Juliénas, Chénas, Moulin-à-Vent, Fleurie, Chiroubles, Morgon, Brouilly (the most distinguished of which is Château de la Chaize), and Côtes de Brouilly, all of which can be sampled with ham, goat cheese, and omelets at the popular Maison des Beaujolais south of Mâcon along N-6. Produced in greater quantities is Beaujolais-Villages, hardly a complex wine but still one with the unmistakably youthful, fruity charm and aroma associated with the famous growths. The vast majority of all Beaujolais is well-made and respectable, but always beware of so-called bargain bottles, many of which are fraudulent blends. Beware also of all the annual hype surrounding the Nouveau Beaujolais should you be in the area in November. As every wine enthusiast knows, this new wine is always shipped every year by air express to the far corners of the globe, where it is imbibed ceremoniously as if it were Musigny. Nouveau Beaujolais can indeed be a delightful wine (the '81 vintage, for instance, is proving exceptional), but more often than not—whether in France, New York, London, or wherever—I'll opt any day for a reliable Beaujolais-Villages over a chancy new wine right from the barrel.

"Noble," "balanced," "extraordinary," "harmonious," "virile," "petulant"—these are but a fraction of the expressions that the wonderful wines of Burgundy have inspired for centuries. That the wine even exists has always seemed astonishing given the fact that it is produced only on a few favored hillsides in an overall unfavorable climate, that it is made from grapes that yield very little to the acre, and that it defies our most sophisticated scientific knowledge. But for many of us who revere fine wines, Burgundy remains in a class by itself, a testimony to man's ability to adhere to nature's demands while artfully transforming a grape into a liquid miracle.

## POSTSCRIPT

Since this essay was first published, many of my beloved wines of Burgundy have proved to be as quixotic as ever. The '76 reds mentioned in the piece (especially those from the Côte de Beaune) have indeed developed as rich, long-lived wines that should still be drinking well in 1990, but the full-bodied '76 whites that seemed to have such longevity reached their peak in the early eighties. Likewise, I was convinced that the best '80 reds from the Côte de Nuits, although a late, wet vintage, would hold up a good decade, but recent tastings suggest that every bottle should be consumed now. The vintage that seems to have deceived everyone was '82: fat, delicate whites of low acidity that have already faded, and round, well-balanced reds that showed brilliantly when they hit the market but have lost much of their luster. The tannic, potent '83 reds everybody was worried about, on the other hand, have come through as the greatest Burgundies since

1978, and these days I'll spend virtually any amount for a splendid '83 Puligny-Montrachet or Meursault. The Burgundies to watch now are the '85 reds—ripe, concentrated, complex wines that should really begin to open up in the next few years.

# THE GLORY OF
# DESSERT WINES

*1985*

O f the important bottles resting in my modest wine cellar, the ones that I treasure almost as much as the vintage Burgundies, clarets, and Cabernets are a few old beauties intended to be consumed as dessert wines after a very special meal. There are two precious bottles of '67 Château d'Yquem now worth about a hundred bucks apiece; a rich, complex malmsey Madeira produced by Cossart in 1916; a few bottles of Warre's '45 vintage Port; a '76 Wehlener Sonnenuhr Z. B. Prun Trockenbeerenauslese that's no longer available on the market; two luscious 5-*puttonos* Tokaji Aszús from Hungary; a number of deep-brown Oloroso Sherries; and a few bottles from a case of Beaulieu's '72 Late-Harvest Riesling I lugged back east from the Napa Valley well over a decade ago. I have a few other dessert wines, but these superlatives are among my most prized possessions, after-dinner wines to be served with the same pomp and ceremony accorded a slab of foie gras or a full tin of fresh beluga caviar. One of the '67 Yquems I've been guarding so carefully will finally be given air following this year's Christmas dinner, and already I can visualize the astonished expressions of my guests as they take the first sip of that golden nectar, nibble a little creamy Roquefort, and savor once again a privileged gustatory moment.

The fact that dessert wines have never played an important gastronomic role in American culture is most likely due to our long exposure to cheap and sugary domestic wines that bear about as much resemblance to carefully made sweet wines as processed blue cheese does to genuine Gorgonzola. And this is sad, for, as anyone knows who has nursed a glass of vintage Port while spreading ripe Stilton on water biscuits, or savored a superb cake with an old oloroso, or terminated a meal with freshly shelled walnuts and a vintage Sauternes, the right sweet wine can provide nothing less than perfect postprandial fulfillment.

Surely the best-known dessert wine is Port, a veritable aristocrat that has become almost synonymous with English breeding, style, and taste. Produced by British families along the upper Douro River in northern Portugal since 1703, Port is a perfumed, mellow, fortified wine that should never be drunk with anything more obtrusive than a wedge of ripe Stilton, nuts, or perhaps a tart apple. Although much of Port's distinctive flavor derives from the soil and climate in which the grapes are grown, what the British have perfected over the centuries is the technique of introducing a gentle sweetness in the wine by adding just enough alcohol to kill the yeast before fermentation is complete, thus retaining a certain amount of the grapes' natural sugar. The very finest Port is vintage Port, a deep-colored, rich, velvety wine made only from grapes of a certain vintage (and amounting to only about five percent of a shipper's annual production) and held a couple of years in wood before being allowed to age at least ten to fifteen years in the bottle. (Because of the crust it throws while aging, old vintage Port must be decanted.) The next-best type, tawny, is a judicious blend of wines from various vineyards and vintages that is aged several years in wood and allowed to take on the brownish tinge from which its name derives. Ruby, the youngest of nonvintage ports, is given just enough time in casks to achieve the consistent character associated with its shipper, to be bottled early, and to be marketed for immediate drinking. For a person tasting a well-made tawny or ruby for the first time, the wine can be an exciting new experience, but once you've decanted an old, crusted '45 Warre, '48 Graham, '54 Hunt's, or '63 Cockburn, you'll understand fully the British passion for the vintage produce, and you'll no doubt agree with Dr. Samuel Johnson that "claret is the liquor for boys; Port for men."

While Port is pitifully neglected in the United States, sweet Spanish Sherry is simply misunderstood. Often, alas, identified with the overly sugared, insipid domestic product, authentic Oloroso (or "brown Sherry") is one of the world's most delectable dessert wines, especially in the medium-sweet or cream variety. Like all genuine Sherry made in and around Jerez de la Frontera, Oloroso begins its natural development in barrels as an unblended, dry wine that must undergo numerous rackings for clarification as it develops. (In racking, the wine is drained from its barrel into a new, sterile one, leaving the lees, or sediment, behind.) Only when the cellar master notices that the wine in certain barrels displays both a slightly darker color than the rest and a higher level of glycerine does he blend the aged wine with a sweet wine to form an oloroso. The process is complex, time-consuming, and costly, but the result is a subtle wine that is dark, not too sugary, and full of rich, nutty flavor. "A marvelous searching wine," as Shakespeare once put it, "and it perfumes the blood e'er one can say 'What's this?' "

"Gentlemen, this is as soft as rainwater," Thomas Jefferson pronounced while making a toast with a glass of Madeira. Ironically, this beautiful but rarely savored wine was one of the most fashionable in England and America during the eighteenth and nineteenth centuries, consumed not only after a meal but also quite often with cold meats, fish, and poultry. Unfortunately, after Prohibition Madeira never regained its lofty status with Americans, most of whom began to regard it primarily as a cooking wine. Made on the eponymous Portuguese island by a lengthy heating method (*estufagem*) that gives the fortified wine its distinctive smoky odor and toasty flavor, Madeira is known for its longevity and marketed only after it has aged at least twenty or thirty years in wood. The blended wine is produced in four types: the dry *sercial;* the soft, clean *verdelho;* the full, darker, sweet *bual;* and the rich, full-bodied, ambrosial *malmsey.* A prized old *malmsey* is hard to come by, but since Madeira has not been in public favor for half a century, it's not unusual to find, at relatively modest cost, any number of nineteenth-century *buals,* as well as plenty of *buals* from the great vintages of 1926, '20, '10, and 1900.

Almost as neglected as Madeira in this country is Marsala, the dark, aromatic Sicilian dessert wine that has the appealing flavor of burnt sugar and that most of us identify as a key ingredient in the Italian cream dessert called *zabaglione.* Developed and introduced into England in the eighteenth century by John Woodhouse, Marsala, like its Portuguese cousin, enjoyed great popularity as a dessert wine until twentieth-century producers began flavoring it with everything from bananas to coffee to broccoli. In recent years, however, the wine, under strict government control, has undergone a return to proper vinification, resulting in a pure product that can hold its own with the finest Sherries and Madeiras. By law, the basic grade of Marsala, *"fine,"* must be aged in wood at least five months before it is bottled. *"Superiore,"* the second-best grade and the most popular one in England, is aged at least two years in barrels, with a minimum of additives. And the highest grade, *"vergine"*—which, like Sherry, is achieved by blending younger wines with older vintages—must undergo a minimum aging in the barrel of five years and can contain no added musts (new wines) for flavor. A *fine* Marsala is much too dry to be served as a dessert wine, but there's hardly any confection that can't be enhanced by a semi-sweet *superiore* such as Rallo's Riserva des Nonno, Pellegrino's SOM, or the venerable Garibaldi Dolci. On the other hand, a luxurious, full-bodied, nutty old *vergine,* such as Florio's or Pellegrino's Vecchia Riserva, should never be served with anything more complicated than a well-aged, crumbly piece of Parmesan or some walnuts. Because of the small demand, the finest *superiores* and *vergines* are still relatively difficult to find outside major metropolitan areas, but, once you've located a bottle, the rewards will prove amazing.

One Italian dessert wine that is still relatively unknown in the United States except to patrons of the very finest Italian restaurants is Vin Santo, a soft, semisweet, amber wine produced throughout Italy and prized particularly by Tuscans. Made from local grapes that are partially dried on wires to concentrate the natural sugar and then are crushed in the winter, the young wine is generally blended with some old wine, barreled, and allowed to age anywhere from three to twenty years. Since Vin Santo's basic sweetness is masked and balanced by its austere, elevated alcoholic content, it is a wine capable of standing up to many sweet desserts that can virtually destroy a delicate Port, Oloroso, or even Sauternes.

Although there are connoisseurs for whom a postprandial glass of vintage Port, Sherry, or Madeira represents the ultimate in gustatory satisfaction, there are also those who insist that nothing equals the taste sensation of an unfortified, elegant French Sauternes, German Trockenbeerenauslese (TBA for short), Hungarian Tokay, or California Late-Harvest Riesling— all produced by a completely natural process called botrytisation. Depending on local climate and whims of nature, some grapes are attacked by an ugly, pearl-gray mold called *Botrytis cinerea* (often referred to as "the noble rot"), which causes a condition that dehydrates the fruit and increases sugar concentration to as much as forty percent. The result is a golden, rich, intensely sweet wine that should be consumed only in small amounts and with nothing more complicated than cheese, fresh fruit, or nuts. Because the overripe, botrytised grapes must be hand-picked, and because one bottle made from the concentrated juice demands many more grapes than does a regular bottle of wine, the cost can be formidable.

The most famous and sought-after botrytised French wine is Château d'Yquem, a golden, highly perfumed, unctuous Sauternes, a single bottle of which often requires the fruit from two entire vines. This is a wine once poured by the czars, and from only the finest decanters. Owned today by Count Alexandre de Lur-Saluces, Château d'Yquem still distributes no more than 66,000 bottles of its nectar per year, making this probably the rarest wine produced in the entire region around Bordeaux and surely one of the most expensive (a case of '59 Yquem reaped a cool $1,650 at auction not long ago). I make no pretense about my love for Yquem, but I also bemoan the fact that so few people are acquainted with the other lovely and much-less-expensive sweet wines produced in the commune of Sauternes. One of the most seductive, for example, is Château Suduiraut, a honeyed, complex beauty that many equate with Yquem and that can be bought for as little as $15 to $20 a bottle (compared with $60 to $75 for an Yquem). Less costly are such labels as Château Filhot, Château d'Arche, and Château Lamothe, all elegant Sauternes, all available in serious wineshops. Equally unknown are the luscious sweet wines produced in Sauternes's adjoining commune called Barsac. I've known snobs who like to dismiss Barsacs as "the poor man's Sauternes," but on more than one occasion I've found Château Nairac, Château Caillou, and especially Château Coutet to display the same virtues as a fine Sauternes. Because of the small demand up till now, Barsacs are still difficult to find outside the finest restaurants, but from what I've been told by merchants, the availability of the wines is increasing as more and more interested consumers learn about their quality and value.

Just as precious (and expensive) as a great Château d'Yquem is a florid, delicate German Beerenauslese (BA) or Trockenbeerenauslese. Produced mainly from botrytised Riesling grapes in the cool, northernmost Rhine and Mosel valleys, Spätlese, Auslese, Beerenauslese, and Trockenbeerenauslese are, in ascending order, some of the sweetest and most respected of dessert wines. The first two, whose names indicate simply some degree of special grape selection at time of harvest, are intensely fruity wines that go well with simple cakes and cheeses. Nectar-sweet BAs and TBAs, both of which are made only in the very best years and in very small quantities, are so rare, stately, extraordinary, and costly that very few bottles exist on the market at any given time. To sip a '71 Beerenauslese by Otto Dünweg is a privilege; to sip a Trockenbeerenauslese such as H. Braun's '76 Niersteiner Auflangen is divine.

Of Hungarian Tokay, Voltaire wrote: "This wine invigorates every fiber of the brain and brings forth an enchanting sparkle of wit and good cheer from the depths of the soul." Once guarded by Cossacks for the table of Catherine the Great, this most concentrated of all sweet wines seems to capture more than any other the romance of the grape, surpassing, in the eyes of some, even the many legends surrounding the great Champagnes of France, Madeira, Château d'Yquem, and Germany's Trockenbeerenauslesen. Produced since the seventeenth century in the foothills of the Carpathian Mountains close to the Russian border, Tokay has long been revered as a wine not only with sublime flavor but also with remarkable curative powers (it was claimed, for example, to have promoted the rapid recovery of King George IV of England from a dangerous surgical operation). Technically, the main difference between this noble, soft wine and other botrytised wines is that the late-harvest, mold-afflicted (*aszú*) grapes are placed into buckets (*puttonos*), crushed, and their juice added to the general run of wine, resulting in combinations that produce several styles of Tokay. Depending on the quality of the overall vintage, anywhere from one to six *puttonos* are added, the maximum number yielding the richer, more concentrated wine. Thus, the label on every bottle of Tokay states 1 *puttono*, 2 *puttonos*, 3 *puttonos*, and so forth. A 1-putt Tokay (to use the abbreviated term) is slightly sweet, whereas a 5-putt, made with at least half botrytised grapes, is like nectar. Some connoisseurs enjoy a glass of 3-putt Tokay with a dessert such as lemon soufflé, but since even the finest 5-putt '76 Tokaji Aszú costs less than $25 for a full bottle, why not savor the more complex wine with apple strudel, apple crêpes, or a thin apple tart?

There are a few California sweet wines that can already compete convincingly with certain French Sauternes and German botrytised Rieslings. Still resting in my cellar, for instance, are four dusty masterpieces I sampled when I first visited the famous California vineyards: a '69 Wente Brothers Riesling Auslese, the first natural botrytised wine ever produced in California; a '72 Beaulieu Riesling that should be magnificent today; a revered '73 Riesling Auslese by Wente; and Freemark Abbey's exquisite '73 Edelwein. The occasion will have to be special indeed before I remove the cork from one of these prizes. If you're lucky, you may still find a half bottle of Freemark Abbey's '78 Edelwein selling for less than $20, but today the finest available sweet wines from California are the Late-Harvest Johannisberg Rieslings of Château St. Jean and Joseph Phelps—intensely fruity, honeyed, beautiful wines that you can be proud to serve at the end of any great meal.

The world of sweet wines can be mysterious and confusing, but once you're exposed to one or two distinguished bottles, you'll know what you've been missing. Not a month goes by that I'm not introduced to still another new dessert wine, the latest being the slightly effervescent, fruity, rich, full-bodied Muscat de Beaumes-de-Venise imported from the Côtes-du-Rhône district in southern France and stocked in our best wineshops. Perhaps next month it will be a suave new oloroso, a rare old Madeira, or a perfected *eiswein* from New York State. And the month after that I may learn that a few sweet Monbazillacs from the Dordogne in southwestern France have finally surfaced here. In any case, there can be no doubt that these very special wines are destined to add an entirely new and sweet character to very special celebrations.

# UNDERSTANDING THE WHITE
# FRUIT BRANDIES

*1982*

The dinner at Rendez-Vous de Chasse in Colmar had been glorious, just the type of sophisticated fare you might expect in a first-rate Alsatian restaurant: slabs of fresh foie gras consumed with vintage Gewürztraminer, small cups of silky frogs'-leg soup, local trout stuffed with vegetables and truffles and baked in wine, creamy natural farmhouse Münster served with sliced ripe apricots, a few beer fritters, and a bottle of excellent Riesling. Yes, the food and wines were exemplary, but, for once, we had not cared about ordering a dozen different dishes to taste, we had not asked the captain a thousand questions, and we had not lingered over dessert because of our eager anticipation to sample what we'd been told was one of the finest collections of white fruit brandies in Alsace—meaning the world.

"*Vous voulez une belle eau-de-vie?*" the captain finally asked, pouring the strong coffee.

"*Oui, je crois,*" I nodded, glancing at my companions just casually enough so as not to betray our primary reason for dining here. "And could you tell us which flavors you have, *monsieur?*"

"*Ah, monsieur,* we have pear and raspberry and purple plum and apricot and white currant and peach and mountain cranberry and huckleberry and . . ."

On and on he went, listing almost every fruit imaginable, plus a few we had never even heard of. When our excitement became evident and we began designating all the different brandies that simply had to be opened, the smiling captain made the sensible suggestion that we settle up the dinner bill, retire to a small salon near the entrance, and let the waiter bring in the various bottles along with more coffee. Quite obviously we were not the first hedonists to dine at Rendez-Vous de Chasse with ulterior motives, nor were we the first foreigners to be utterly stunned by the revelation of drinking these crisp, clear, potent brandies (referred to in France as *alcools blancs* or *eaux-de-vie*) on their own home territory.

One by one we tasted: Kirsch (cherry), Poire (pear), Mirabelle (yellow plum), Quetsch (purple plum), Pêche (peach), Fraise (strawberry)—all served well chilled in small stemmed glasses. Slowly, the entire atmosphere of the miniature room was transformed synesthetically into an exotic orchard by the vast symphony of aromas, and even if we were breaking every rule in the sacred gustatory order of things, the experience was not only sensually overwhelming but virtually indescribable. All four of us, of course, had had occasional opportunity in the past to sip an imported Poire or Kirsch, but not till that fragrant evening in Colmar did we get the full impact of just how unique and varied these postprandial distillates are and just how beautifully they serve as the necessary coda to a well-orchestrated meal.

That most Americans remain unaware of the distinctive fruit brandies of Alsace, Switzerland, and the Black Forest region of Germany is most probably due to the fact that until fairly recently there simply were not that many available in this country. It's also true that when it comes to digestives, we often seem to be a nation hopelessly addicted either to standard brandy or to all those overly sweet mixed drinks and fruit-*flavored* cordials that do about as much good for the digestion as my otherwise beloved Bourbon Manhattans. Don't get me wrong: nobody on earth appreciates a great Cognac, Calvados, Armagnac or slivovitz more than I, and there are indeed occasions when nothing tastes better than a well-concocted Stinger or Black Russian. But the time has come, it seems to me, to familiarize ourselves as much as possible with all the wonderful colorless fruit brandies presently being shelved in liquor stores across the country.

Although there are clear brandies made in Germany, Switzerland, Austria, Hungary, and Italy, the finest and widest variety come from Alsace. Alsatians have been producing their *eaux-de-vie* (waters of life) since the Middle Ages. This enterprise, inspired by the extraordinary variety of wild fruits and berries found on the slopes of the Vosges Mountains, was developed at family stills set up—often for medicinal purposes—on farms and vineyards. Records show that by the sixteenth century these spirits were being shipped in huge quantities from Strasbourg and Colmar to Germany, Holland, and Great Britain. So renowned were they in the seventeenth century that none other than the valet of Louis XIV once reported that he "often prevented the king from getting a stomach ache, as a consequence of his robust appetite, by suggesting that he drink, in small doses, the fruit alcohols that Alsatians make so well." The famous nineteenth-century German poet Heinrich Heine usually devoted his stanzas to love, but on at least one occasion he was enraptured enough by these beguiling brandies to write: "Give me another glass / Of that Alsatian Kirsch / Of that clean water from the slopes / Which inebriates the body / And gladdens the soul." Today the distillation of these same *eaux-de-vie* is still conducted as small family businesses, limited primarily to grape growers who supply the world with such glorious Alsatian wines as Riesling, Sylvaner, and Gewürztraminer. Visit the vineyards at Ammerschwihr, Mittelwihr, Ribeauvillé, and Éguisheim, and you'll just as likely be given the chance to sample a producer's clear brandy as his wine—both in the familiar tall, slender Alsatian bottle.

A genuine fruit brandy, unlike flavored cordials, gins, and vodkas, is made exclusively from the fruit whose name it bears, meaning that up to sixty pounds of raspberries or cherries are needed to produce a single quart of Framboise or Kirsch. The actual process is relatively simple. First, the ripe fruit is crushed and allowed to ferment, then the mash is distilled. All distillates, including such spirits as Cognac, Scotch, and Bourbon, are crystal clear when they come from the still, but, unlike the brandy and whiskeys, which acquire color and smoothness from being aged in barrels, the *eaux-de-vie* are either placed directly into glass demijohns, fiberglass containers, or sometimes pottery, or given a short period in wood for special flavor before being shifted to neutral containers to prevent their taking on color. The containers are loosely stoppered, and over a period of months, the brandy loses its rough edge and develops finesse through oxidation. It is usually bottled with a high alcohol content—86 to 90 proof and often higher. As is true with any Bourbon, Armagnac, or slivovitz, the difference between great fruit brandies and poor ones lies not only in the quality of ingredients but, indeed, in the distiller's art. A well-made *eau-de-vie* has an intense, well-defined fruit bouquet, as well as a distinct natural fruit taste. Mediocre examples are thin and languid as a result of either minimum fruit content or careless distillation. And the worst are produced from fruit that is low-grade or simply overripe. In any case, once you've savored a truly distinguished fruit brandy, you'll easily be able to pinpoint a dull one.

So far, the only fruit brandies that are generally available in better wine and spirit shops throughout this country are Pear, Raspberry, Kirsch (which is never referred to as Cherry), and Yellow Plum. But in Europe you can find *eaux-de-vie* made from prunes, blueberries, currants, apples, peaches, huckleberries, cranberries, quince, rose hips, and blackberries. Some producers also pride themselves on their ability to make brandy out of gentian root, holly, acacia flowers, shadbush, sorb, juniper berries— almost anything, in fact, that grows and contains sugar. One of the most memorable examples in Alsace is a white alcohol made from the macerated hulls of Gewürztraminer grapes. I've not yet had the chance to taste the *eau-de-vie de Cognac* which I understand is now available in western France, but once, in the Loire Valley, I was served a salubrious, clear digestive made from Muscat grapes. Europeans do indeed take their white brandies very seriously, both as a superlative gustatory climax to a meal, and as a means to what the French traditionally refer to as "making the Alsatian hole," or pleasantly stimulating digestion.

Europeans also faithfully proclaim the ability of these brandies to assuage all sorts of ailments. "Elderberry and blackberry *eaux-de-vie* are useful in aiding digestion," writes one particularly colorful enthusiast. "Huckleberry boasts of two almost miraculous properties: it can cure certain intestinal pain while reestablishing the internal flora of the intestine; and it is said to improve eyesight—particularly night vision, giving those who drink it the eyes of a cat. Dogrose is said to be a stimulant to the heart." Be that as it may, there is no doubt that the delicate power of these brandies does wonders for warming the soul.

Although no genuine fruit brandy is inexpensive, prices vary radically from label to label. It's highly unlikely, for example, to find a decent bottle of Poire William (equivalent to our Bartlett pear) for under twenty-five dollars, and the very finest can run as high as fifty. The most spectacular Poires are those containing a whole pear in the bottle, and producers who execute this feat in the traditional way literally tie the bottles around tiny pear buds in the trees, allow the pear to grow inside the bottle, then fill the bottles with pear brandy. No doubt these Poires have a certain fascination and aesthetic appeal, but since more and more pears are now being inserted in bottles with fused-on bottoms, it's wise to check carefully before spending an extra ten bucks on pear brandy that is not necessarily any better simply because it is dramatically bottled. A delicate Framboise, considered by many to be the most intriguing of all fruit brandies, can easily run about forty dollars for such labels as Massenez and Danflou, and a premium Swiss Kirsch like Dettling could hardly be purchased for less than thirty dollars. The Mirabelles and Fraises average about twenty-five dollars a bottle, the Quetsch a little less, while a bottle of Zwack's Barack Palinka (distilled from apricots) should cost no more than about twenty dollars.

Although you can generally count on any well-made *eau-de-vie* being at least as expensive as respectable Cognac or Armagnac, don't forget that a bottle of one of these powerful, high-proof, clear brandies can last a long time after being opened since so little is consumed on any given occasion. Personally, I try to keep at least three flavors always in stock, not only because people with a passion for, say, Poire may have an equal dislike for Framboise, but also because nothing is nicer than offering guests an interesting selection of *eaux-de-vie*.

As to the correct way to serve white alcohols, epicures do have their differences of opinion. Should the brandy be poured into snifters and, like

Cognac, warmed with the hand? Or should it be served cold in stemmed glasses so that the already pronounced bouquet is not further intensified? Should the bottle be kept in the freezer to deaden the alcoholic bite, or does pouring the brandy at room temperature into well-frosted glasses suffice to remove the edge and, at the same time, safeguard the spirit's delicate nose? Should an exceptional Mirabelle be sipped strictly by itself, or is it permissible to serve coffee and, perhaps, a few accompanying petits fours?

I, for one, am dead against applying the same snifter principles to *eaux-de-vie* as to Cognac, but I'm equally against virtually destroying half their character by storing these fragrant beauties at arctic temperatures. Ideally, I submit, any fruit brandy demonstrates its worth best by being chilled quickly on ice and served in very cold stemmed glasses, thus releasing a smooth but distinctive bouquet and flavor when the barely cool brandy comes in contact with the frosted glass. I can't imagine interrupting the ambrosial aroma and taste of a great Mirabelle or Framboise by nibbling at the same time on even the most innocent of confections. But a good cup of fresh black coffee, I find, not only enhances the alcohol but also contributes a great deal to the overall digestive principle.

"Distilled alcohol," wrote that esteemed French philosopher of gastronomy Brillat-Savarin, "is the monarch of liquids and carries palatal exaltation to the highest degree. All its diverse preparations have opened up new sources of ecstasy." For most Americans, at least one of these sources has remained undiscovered far too long. Certainly, men and women of good taste will continue to find pleasure and harmony in a beautiful Cognac, a fifty-year-old Armagnac, a velvety Port, or a racy liqueur, but the next time a restaurant captain asks ever so quietly, ever so politely, *"Un petit digestif?"* those with adventure in the blood will think again.